FACING THE FUTURE

AMERICAN INDIAN STUDIES SERIES

SERIES EDITOR
Gordon Henry

EDITORIAL BOARD
Kimberly Blaeser
Joseph Bruchac
Heid Erdrich
Matthew Fletcher
P. Jane Hafen
Winona LaDuke
Patrick Lebeau
John Petoskey
Michael D. Wilson

Shedding Skins: Four Sioux Poets
Edited by Adrian C. Louis | 978-0-87013-823-2

Writing Home: Indigenous Narratives of Resistance
Michael D. Wilson | 978-0-87013-818-8

National Monuments
Heid E. Erdrich | 978-0-87013-848-5

The Indian Who Bombed Berlin and Other Stories
Ralph Salisbury | 978-0-87013-847-8

Facing the Future: The Indian Child Welfare Act at 30
Edited by Matthew L. M. Fletcher, Wenona T. Singel, and Kathryn E. Fort | 978-0-87013-860-7

FACING THE FUTURE

THE INDIAN CHILD WELFARE ACT AT 30

Edited by Matthew L. M. Fletcher, Wenona T. Singel, and Kathryn E. Fort

Michigan State University Press | East Lansing

Copyright © 2009 by Michigan State University

☻ The paper used in this publication meets the minimum requirements of ANSI/NISO Z39.48-1992 (R 1997) (Permanence of Paper).

Michigan State University Press
East Lansing, Michigan 48823-5245

Printed and bound in the United States of America.

15 14 13 12 11 10 09   1 2 3 4 5 6 7 8 9 10

LIBRARY OF CONGRESS CATALOGING-IN-PUBLICATION DATA
Facing the future : the Indian Child Welfare Act at 30 / edited by Matthew L. M. Fletcher, Wenona T. Singel, and Kathryn E. Fort.
p. cm. — (American Indian study series)
Includes bibliographical references.
ISBN 978-0-87013-860-7 (pbk. : alk. paper) 1. United States. Indian Child Welfare Act of 1978. 2. Indian children—Legal status, laws, etc.—United States. I. Fletcher, Matthew L. M. II. Singel, Wenona T. III. Fort, Kathryn E.
KF8210.C45F33 2009
346.7301'7808997—dc22
2009006390

Cover design by Erin Kirk New
Book design by Charlie Sharp, Sharp Des!gns, Lansing, Michigan

Cover art is "The Children are the Future" ©2009 by Kelly Church and is used with permission of the artist. For more information on the artwork of Kelly Church visit *www.backlash.org*.

g green Michigan State University Press is a member of the Green
press Press Initiative and is committed to developing and
INITIATIVE
encouraging ecologically responsible publishing practices. For more information about the Green Press Initiative and the use of recycled paper in book publishing, please visit *www.greenpressinitiative.org*.

Visit Michigan State University Press on the World Wide Web at
www.msupress.msu.edu

Contents

vii   FOREWORD
        Michael D. Petoskey

xi   ACKNOWLEDGMENTS

xiii   INTRODUCTION: Indian Experience and Randall Kennedy's Mythology
        Matthew L. M. Fletcher and Wenona T. Singel

3   Working on the Front Lines: The Role of Social Work in Response to the Indian Child Welfare Act of 1978
        Suzanne L. Cross, Angelique G. Day, and Emily C. Proctor

13   The Indian Child Welfare Act of 1978 and Its Impact on Tribal Sovereignty and Governance
        Terry L. Cross and Robert J. Miller

28   ICWA and the Commerce Clause
        Matthew L. M. Fletcher

50   Reparations, Self-Determination, and the Seventh Generation
        Lorie M. Graham

111   A Practitioner's View from Thirty Years on the Cutting Edge of the Indian Child Welfare Act
Mary Jo B. Hunter

127   Differing Concepts of "Permanency": The Adoption and Safe Families Act and the Indian Child Welfare Act
B. J. Jones

148   The Disconcerting Vicissitudes of State Judicial Power: Determining If Good Cause Exists to Deny Transfer in ICWA Cases
Allie Greenleaf Maldonado

164   Keeping It in the Family: The Legal and Social Evolution of ICWA in State and Tribal Jurisprudence
Lorinda Mall

221   Holding Back the Tide: The Existing Indian Family Doctrine and Its Continued Denial of the Right to Culture for Indigenous Children
Aliza G. Organick

235   A Decade of Lessons Learned: Advocacy, Education, and Practice
LeAnne E. Silvey

245   Where Have All the Children Gone? When Will They Ever Learn?
Maylinn Smith

270   In Defense of ICWA: The Constitution, Public Policy, and Pragmatism
Carol L. Tebben

293   CONTRIBUTORS

Foreword

Michael D. Petoskey

For the dreams of the children . . .

Human life is sacred, as is all life. New, helpless life comes into this world and is dependent on our care. What will we do to ensure that each new human being is given the opportunity to reach his or her full potential? Each child deserves love and nurturing. It is our obligation as parents, family, and community to ensure that each is loved and nurtured. The Creator would have it be so.

For us as Indians, much is at stake, because it is about nurturing community and culture, while honoring our traditions. After all, we are fond of saying: "The children are our future." In Michigan, most of the tribes number around four thousand members, or less. Thus, the task is not as challenging as solving the world's problems, or those of the United States of America, or those of the State of Michigan. Given that context, we are a finite community with relatively few families in number. The task before us is manageable. We must be able to rise above our human frailties and the dysfunction that is the result of outsider oppression.

Lest anyone prematurely jump to the wrong conclusion, we should recognize that most Indian families, by far, are doing well as families, and their children are

---

These are the thoughts of a Grand Traverse Band of Ottawa and Chippewa Indians tribal member and longtime tribal judge who has served in several Michigan tribal communities. A significant portion of his career's work has been devoted to the planning, implementation, and development of child protection systems in those communities

loved and nurtured. It seems to always be, as in other societies, that a few bring (create) most of the challenges (problems) to the rest of us.

Indian Child Welfare and Tribal Child Protection

Indian Child Welfare Act cases in state courts are very important to us for all the reasons mentioned above. They involve significant, meaningful rights. These kinds of cases are so important, in fact, that their existence has been the impetus for many tribes in the State of Michigan and elsewhere to embark upon the process of developing their own judicial and child protection systems. For example, the Pokagon Band of Potawatomi Indians and the Little River Band of Ottawa Indians both desired to establish their tribal courts upon federal reaffirmation in 1994 so that they could begin to immediately transfer their Indian Child Welfare Act cases from state courts into their respective tribal courts. The numerous reasons behind the urgency and priority is beyond the scope of this preface, but suffice it to say that self-government and self-determination are motivating factors.

Child protection cases are the most time consuming and resource intensive of any of the myriad kinds of cases handled in our courts. The tribes mentioned above were advised to put a plan together to develop both the legal and service infrastructures that would be necessary to provide for the assertion of tribal sovereignty, while also providing for the needs of the children and parents who were involved. The legal infrastructure principally means the adoption of a well thought out child protection code. Without it, what standards would apply? How would the proposed court handle the matter? What would it do? Moreover, how should the court do it? On the services and resources side, these cases can take on a life of their own as service providers work to rehabilitate and support parents through mitigation of the circumstances that gave rise to the charges of abuse and/or neglect against them. In addition, almost all of the children, who become wards of the court because of these kinds of actions, need specialized services because of the abuse and/or neglect.

The Wisdom of Collaboration

Many now understand that courts alone cannot solve community problems. We have long understood that raising children is a community responsibility. In the development of its child protection system, the Pokagon Band of Potawatomi Indians wisely identified the various components of the system and brought the various stakeholders to the table to plan and implement its system. The Tribal Chairman, Tribal Operations Officer, Director of Pokagon Social Services, Indian Child Welfare caseworker, Captain of Pokagon Law Enforcement, General Counsel,

Court Administrator, and Chief Judge all committed to a collaborative process to plan and develop both the legal and services infrastructure necessary to provide for child protection cases. In particular, the development of a draft child protection code for legislative consideration by the Tribal Council took place over several meetings to address the concerns and questions of each of the stakeholders. The result has been called "one of the very best tribal child protection codes" by staff at the National Indian Child Welfare Association. It is so because of the thought, discussion across the table, and collaboration over time that went into its production.

Tribal Court Advantages

As a forum within the community itself, a tribal court is better situated to exercise authority in tribal child protection matters for many different reasons.

First and foremost, tribal courts are familiar with the childrearing practices of the community. These kinds of cases are about childrearing responsibilities. Additionally, the tribal court is part of the community and is grounded in its culture and traditions. It is positioned to use community values and norms to encourage and support change.

Secondly, tribal courts are familiar with the services that are available to mitigate the circumstances that gave rise to the charges of abuse and/or neglect, as well as the services that are available to provide for the special needs of children who have been abused and/or neglected. Tribal courts are well positioned to ensure that the services ordered are tailored to meet the needs of the unique individual human beings who are involved. Also, tribal courts can easily ensure that service efforts are active and reasonable. Cookie-cutter programs and services need not apply, and rote actions and responses are not acceptable. Parents and service providers must be engaged.

Thirdly, tribal courts do not have overwhelming caseloads, for the most part, and can devote whatever time is necessary for successful resolution of the case, as well as whatever is necessary for each and every hearing.

Fourthly, tribal members are more responsive to the community forum than they are to the courts of the dominant society. American Indians have long suffered at the hands of the law. It has been used to suppress and dominate. Therefore, it is not surprising that most Indians have a negative view of the law and of courts. In fact, many have a "Robin Hood" mentality, rooting for the underdog and operating on the fringes. Day-to-day and week-to-week survival is the priority. Sometimes it is the only priority. This history and these perceptions carry over to tribal government institutions as well, but tribal court judges are uniquely positioned to look people in the eye, speak from the heart, and change these perceptions as they relate to our own institutions. After all, these are our own standards (law), not those of outsiders.

Fifthly, most tribal judges are rooted in a problem-solving, consensus-oriented, peacemaking, healing and wellness philosophy. It is ingrained in our temperament, at the foundation of our relationship to the parties before the bench, and in the process used as the "case" proceeds. For example, it is my practice to have an in-chambers conference with all of the attorneys representing all the parties prior to each and every hearing to develop the common ground, share information, and problem-solve. Together we take whatever time is needed before formally proceeding.

Enjoy the rest to follow. *Miigwetch!*

Acknowledgments

Many people, most especially the contributors, have made this project a wonderful experience. This book grew out of the Third Annual Indigenous Law Conference hosted by the Indigenous Law and Policy Center at the Michigan State University College of Law, March 16 and 17, 2007. We thank the two people most responsible for the logistics of hosting a major Indian law conference, Indigenous Law and Policy Center staff attorney Kathryn E. Fort and program coordinator Ashley Harding. Their work in making the conference happen, which for several weeks of the year requires them to handle the comings and goings of over twenty presenters and around one hundred conference participants, is perhaps the most amazing aspect of this project. We cannot thank them enough.

In addition to the hard work of the contributors to this volume in writing their chapters, we must thank Hannah Nokomis Bobee and Alicia Ivory for spending the summer of 2007 editing the notes and the formatting of the chapters to suit the requirements of the Press.

We wish to thank our families for their support during the life of this project: Loretta and Jim Singel; June and Richard Fletcher; Pete Singel; Zeke, Katie, Nolan, Benjamin, and Laura Fletcher; and Ross, David, and Thomson Fort.

This collection and the remarkable work contained within is dedicated to Matthew and Wenona's sons, Owen Waabmigizi Singel-Fletcher and Emmett Waasamowin Singel-Fletcher, the most beautiful Indian children in the world.

Introduction

Indian Experience and Randall Kennedy's Mythology

Matthew L. M. Fletcher and Wenona T. Singel

Randall Kennedy offered a stinging indictment of the Indian Child Welfare Act in the final chapter of his 2003 book *Interracial Intimacies: Sex, Marriage, Identity, and Adoption*.[1] The eleven other chapters in his book offer no discussion whatsoever of American Indian law and policy, making the final and twelfth chapter appear a little out of place. But as Martha Minow's work implies, the reason for the special chapter is the special character of American Indian law—Indians are different, an exemption, requiring a separate argument.[2] The relevant portion of Professor Kennedy's work offers a rejection of racial matching of children to prospective parents in the context of adoption. In short, he argues that there is no reason to match African American children to African American parents, Latino/a children to Latino/a parents, and so on. The same should be true, Kennedy argues, for American Indian children, but there is the inconvenient Indian Child Welfare Act to consider; hence, the separate chapter.

Kennedy's main argument is this: American Indian children are no different legally than African American children when it comes to adoption or foster-home placement. Or, put another way, *American Indians are not different at all and there should be no separate law applying to American Indians*. Kennedy's thesis has a sort of superficial appeal. If African American children are no different than Latino/a children or Asian children or white children, then how can American Indian children be different?[3] Kennedy argues that ICWA requires officials to reach for a kind of "racialist communalism"—a "dubious" result in his mind,[4] but one very consistent with the "measured separatism" that American Indian law and policy has always sought.5 Kennedy labels Indian tribes child-stealing bigots by asserting that ICWA foments a kind of "racialist opportunism," with tribes using the statute as a "snare... [to] capture children with no previously established tribal association."6

This is no different on a fundamental level from arguing that there really should not be an American Indian law. ICWA, like most of modern federal Indian law, was designed to prevent the extinction of unique tribal cultures and to prevent the forced assimilation of Indian peoples into the greater American polity.7 Kennedy argues:

> Asserted fears of cultural "extinction," however, are overblown—a rhetorical boogeyman. What is called "extinction" is actually the transformation of cultures through interaction with others—a benefit (and bane) that is virtually unavoidable in the absence of strong (and decidedly unpleasant) efforts to distance groups from the assimilative forces of the modern world. I see little virtue in burdening the living, particularly youngsters who have no choice in the matter, for the sake of preserving—freezing—group identities as they are presently constituted.8

And this is no different than the argument made by the assimilationists of the nineteenth and early twentieth centuries, arguing that Indian people can only survive by destroying themselves. Kennedy argues that "the modern world"—as opposed to what we can presume he means primitive (even savage) Indian cultures—is simply better than what Indian people have now. It is a very complex obfuscation of an old ethnocentric argument about the relative qualities of two "cultures"—Indian versus non-Indian. Kennedy makes clear in the opening portions of his chapter what he thinks of Indian cultures and Indian communities by reciting statistics about the poverty, unemployment, and social catastrophes ongoing in Indian Country.9 In Kennedy's eyes, Indians have had the benefit of a separate law, a striving toward "measured separatism," and look what good it has all done—none at all. Again, this is similar to the ethnocentric motivations of the old-style assimilationists—"Kill the Indian to Save the Man."10 The United States tried assimilation to disastrous consequences, and Indian people have been fighting it ever since. And, if federal policy changes again in the future in a manner to Kennedy's liking, Indian people will continue to fight it. Perhaps in earlier times, the notion that Western culture was superior held sway with many Indian people, but with the advent of unending war against terrorism, global warming, and other environmental disasters, and an increasing belligerence of the American public toward minorities and criminals, many Indian people who might have been on the fence are no longer so sure about the benefits of assimilation.

Kennedy seems to be saying that "measured separatism" is a mistake that harms

Indian people more than it helps. In this view, fighting assimilation is futile because the invasiveness of "the modern world" cannot be denied. Moreover, Kennedy asserts, if Indian cultures "freeze," they will die.[11] That a separate Indian law and policy is then a detriment to Indian people (and especially Indian children) and is undesirable is implied by Kennedy's thesis.[12]

The chapters of this book provide the very best responses to Professor Kennedy—and these responses are grounded in experience, not theory unmoored to the reality of the application of the Indian Child Welfare Act. For the Act is the remarkable culmination of a centuries-long history of abuses by non-Indians, generations upon generations of culture, Indian knowledge and experience, and language destroyed.

Professor Suzanne L. Cross—along with her co-authors Angelique G. Day and Emily C. Proctor—begins the book with a report from the trenches. The field of social work is where the hardest and most important work involving Indian children takes place. The role of the tribal social worker is barely acknowledged by critics of the Act, including Professor Kennedy, although their frontline actions shape much of the core of the Act's meaning.

Terry L. Cross and Professor Robert J. Miller demonstrate the significance of the Act on the continuing development of tribal governments. In many ways, Congress demonstrated confidence in and reliance upon Indian tribes and their courts when it conferred exclusive and concurrent jurisdiction over the adjudication of Indian children to tribal courts. This second chapter places the Act in a greater context of tribal sovereignty.

Professor Matthew L. M. Fletcher's chapter is an attempt to place the Act in the greater context of American constitutional law. There are few American statutes so heavily reliant on race and ethnicity as the Act; but given the history of the American Constitution—partly intended to remove all tribal relations from the discretion of the states—the Act is consistent with the original public meaning of the Constitution.

Professor Lorie M. Graham's contribution offers a theory as to the greater meaning of the Act in the context of the history of tribal-American relations. Much of the history of Indian affairs in America involves property dispossession, assimilation, and cultural destruction. As opposed to the pan-American Indian notion of looking seven generations ahead when making important public policy decisions, the Bureau of Indian Affairs has rarely looked forward at all—until the Indian Child Welfare Act.

Professor Mary Jo B. Hunter offers an excellent on-the-ground history of the Act from the perspective of an Indian lawyer—and now a law school clinician—who has practiced Indian family law during the entire thirty-year history of the statute.

Judge and professor B. J. Jones, perhaps the leading scholar and practitioner of the Indian Child Welfare Act, contributes his research into a developing legal quandary involving the Act—the Act's interpretation in light of the Adoption and

Safe Families Act, which often undermines the effective judicial implementation of the Indian Child Welfare Act, leading to tragic consequences.

Allie Greenleaf Maldonado offers a look at emerging fractures in the implementation of the Act in state courts, focusing on Michigan.

Lorinda Mall contributes an empirical study of how the interpretation of the Act has evolved in state and tribal courts, focusing on Arizona.

Professor Aliza Organick writes about a critical question in the viability of the Act and whether state courts will write exceptions into the statute as a matter of common law, such as the Existing Indian Family "doctrine," focusing on where it all began—Kansas.

Continuing the interdisciplinary character of this collection, Professor Le Anne E. Silvey's chapter offers a retrospective of the issues related to the pedagogy of the Act from the perspective of a family ecologist. Her experiences at the Michigan Indian Child Welfare Agency, forming the basis of this chapter, are invaluable.

Professor Maylinn Smith provides a practical guide to representing the interests of individual Indian parents and families. She writes from the perspective of a law school clinician.

Professor Carol L. Tebben looks at the constitutionality of the Act in the context of its broader public policy. She argues that the policy of the statute should be a critical and perhaps dispositive measure of the viability of the Act under the Constitution.

NOTES

1. RANDALL KENNEDY, INTERRACIAL INTIMACIES: SEX, MARRIAGE, IDENTITY, AND ADOPTION 480–518 (Pantheon Books 2003).
2. MARTHA MINOW, NOT ONLY FOR MYSELF: IDENTITY, POLITICS & THE LAW 75 (The New Press 1997).
3. Professor Kennedy goes on to argue that there are three serious problems with ICWA. First, congressional fact-finding leading up to the enactment of the statute that the Indian child welfare crisis was caused by race discrimination was incorrect. Second, congressional fact-finding about the impact of placing Indian children in non-Indian homes was incorrect. And third, state court judges make bad decisions in ICWA cases in order to avoid ICWA's effects. Randall Kennedy, *supra* note 1, at 488.
4. Randall Kennedy, *supra* note 1, at 488.
5. CHARLES F. WILKINSON, AMERICAN INDIANS, TIME, AND THE LAW: NATIVE SOCIETIES IN A MODERN CONSTITUTIONAL DEMOCRACY 14–19 (Yale University Press 1987).
6. Randall Kennedy, *supra* note 1, at 517–18.
7. *Mississippi Band of Choctaw Indians v. Holyfield*, 490 U.S. 30 (1989); Establishing Standards for the Placement of Indian Children in Foster or Adoptive Homes, to Prevent the Breakup of

Indian Families, and for Other Purposes, H.R. Rep. 95-1386, at 9 (July 24, 1978).
8. Randall Kennedy, *supra* note 1, at 513.
9. Randall Kennedy, *supra* note 1, at 481–82.
10. *Official Report of the Nineteenth Annual Conference of Charities and Correction* (1892), 46–59. Reprinted in Richard H. Pratt, *The Advantages of Mingling Indians with Whites*, in AMERICANIZING THE AMERICAN INDIANS: WRITINGS BY THE "FRIENDS OF THE INDIAN," 1880–1900, at 260–71 (Harvard University Press 1973).
11. American Indian law scholars and other writers long have been fighting the perception that tribal people simply want to return to the "good old days" of living in tipis and wigwams, that ancient Indian cultures are immutable and perfect as they are, and that Indian people simply cannot learn anything new. *See* SHERMAN ALEXIE, FLIGHT (Grove/Atlantic 2007); LOUISE ERDRICH, FOUR SOULS (HarperCollins 2004); KRISTEN A. CARPENTER, *Contextualizing the Losses of Allotment through Literature*, 82 NORTH DAKOTA LAW REVIEW 605-26 (2006); MATTHEW L. M. FLETCHER, *Looking to the East: The Stories of Modern Indian People and the Development of Tribal Law*, 5 SEATTLE JOURNAL OF SOCIAL JUSTICE 1-26 (2006); ANGELA R. RILEY, *Good (Native) Governance*, 107 COLUMBIA LAW REVIEW 1049-1125 (2007); WENONA T. SINGEL, *Cultural Sovereignty and Transplanted Law: Tensions in Indigenous Self-Rule*, 15 KANSAS JOURNAL OF LAW & PUBLIC POLICY 357-67 (Winter 2006).
12. Kennedy drops several hints about an underlying argument that perhaps is even more fundamental than the benefits and inevitability of assimilation. He notes that while Indian people were "[o]ften cruelly stereotyped as 'savages,' Indians have also been romanticized as emblems of independence, free-spiritedness, and martial glory (*in contrast to the widespread association of blacks with dependence, servility and cowardice*)." Moreover, Kennedy claims, "Native Americans as a group have also been credited with positive traits *often denied to the Negro*, including intelligence, bravery, nobility, and capacity for improvement." Perhaps Kennedy's argument favoring the assimilation of Indian people is a function of a lasting, racialist jealousy of American Indians. Randall Kennedy, *supra* note 1, at 482–83 (emphasis added, footnote omitted).

FACING THE FUTURE

Working on the Front Lines

The Role of Social Work in Response to the Indian Child Welfare Act of 1978

Suzanne L. Cross, Angelique G. Day, and Emily C. Proctor

The social-work role, attitudes, patterns of response, and timeliness are vital to compliance with the Indian Child Welfare Act (ICWA).[1] This requires professional social workers to be knowledgeable about ICWA, the doctrines in place designed to circumvent the process, and cultural competency to make appropriate decisions that have life-altering and lifelong impact on American Indian children, their families, and ultimately, tribal communities. In addition to the need and support for an excellent ICWA training program for all agency administrators and social workers, a mechanism is required to ensure that the information gained from training will be supported and implemented for the benefit of all U.S. tribal nations.

Social Work Education

Although ICWA was passed thirty years ago, many social workers and most social-work students are unfamiliar with, and sometimes unwilling to comply with, this law. The lack of knowledge of the Act begins in the classroom with textbooks devoting only a short paragraph or two to the topic. The students are expected to read, understand, and digest information that is vital to the lives of American Indians, without classroom discussion or case analysis. All schools of social work should be required to have at least one unit (class period) dedicated to ICWA: its rationale, implementation process, case analysis, and consequences of noncompliance. Instead, it is often viewed as an optional topic for focus and discussion.

In addition to the need for more in-depth study and inclusion of the Act in the curriculum, there is a need to address some resistance from faculty members and field supervisors. Several do not agree with the premise that American Indian children benefit by being raised only by tribal people. These are the very professionals who need to be advocating, teaching, and supporting ICWA, not making statements such as "I don't agree with ICWA; as long as the children have a loving family, it does not matter who raises them." Clearly this reflects their personal point of view. All social workers have a right to their own value systems; however, the National Association of Social Work (NASW) professional code of ethics requires suspension of personal value systems to meet the needs of clients. These faculty members and field supervisors are not only failing to be in compliance with their professional code of ethics, they are also in noncompliance with a federal law. It is extremely unfortunate that their attitudes quickly filter down to the students.

Students both tribal and non-tribal, from a number of non Michigan social-work programs, have shared that while in class, they had wanted to discuss ICWA, and that the professors indicated that ICWA must be a state law and does not apply to their studies. Also, students in field placements both in and out of state have indicated that when they attempt to follow ICWA, they often hear comments such as "That takes too much time, and the children are probably not Indian anyway." At this point, the students feel they have no recourse and need to follow the guidance of their professors or field supervisors to be able to receive an acceptable grade. Thus, they are provided with little motivation to learn the importance of compliance with ICWA, while sacrificing opportunities to assist Indian families. Contrarily, there have been some students who were willing and independent enough to demand to do what is right by following the guidelines of ICWA, regardless of the possible repercussions.

Conversely to those professors who resist teaching about ICWA, there are those who do want to provide lectures with case analysis in the classroom; but they are sometimes met with disinterest from a few students. These students may quietly disengage from the discussion of the topic, while others may state their disagreement with the premise of ICWA. These students are obviously frustrated, which creates a challenge to motivate them to learn about the Act. Professors may find that it will take time and skill to change minds in regard to the legitimacy of ICWA, the importance of the role of the social workers, and the legal obligation for compliance. Although when a breakthrough occurs, many of these students become allies, and as professional social workers insist on the implementation of ICWA.

Sometimes the breakthroughs occur outside of the classroom, in tribal communities where students can experience the impact of ICWA on families. For example, a qualitative study was conducted, entitled *American Indian Grandparents Parenting Their Grandchildren in Michigan*, which included students as research assistants.[2] These students interviewed thirty-one individual grandparents and facilitated twenty-seven focus groups within the state. The students learned that of the thirty-one individual grandparents interviewed, only seven grandparents found ICWA to be helpful, fifteen found it was not helpful, and nine were not aware of the Act. These statistics are certainly small in number, but made an enormous impact on the twelve undergraduate students and four graduate students who were involved in the study. They had the opportunity to hear many of the grandparents' situations; two are provided to demonstrate the learning process. The first situation was that of a loving couple who had provided care for their grandson since birth, and then experienced the child's removal from their care when he was two-and-a-half years of age. The second situation was of a healthy, employed grandfather, who worked for his tribal nation and resided on the reservation, having to wait nine months to be able to obtain custody of his fourteen-year-old grandson, who was placed in a nearby town with a non-Indian family. These situations are only two examples of the family disruptions that are evidence of noncompliance with ICWA. As a result of the students' involvement in this research project, they gained invaluable knowledge of, and witness to, the devastating impact of noncompliance. Therefore, it is a wise investment to include undergraduate and graduate students in research projects, especially when the focus is on ICWA.

It is understandable that all students cannot have this experience, but faculty members need to be creative in the development of learning opportunities for students to increase their education and awareness of ICWA. The reward for time spent on student inclusion is that professional social workers are prepared to be advocates of ICWA and willing to share their commitment, knowledge and experience.

Judicially Created Exceptions to ICWA

There are several terms, developed to allow the circumventing of the Indian Child Welfare Act, that have proven to be pivotal in child welfare cases involving American Indian children. Several terms have become a part of the definition of what constitutes an Indian family and the meaning of culture.[3] It appears that many of these terms have resulted from the frustration at the amount of time that is required to follow ICWA and work with tribal nations.

There are variations to the doctrine that have been utilized by courts which include the "Indian Family Exception" doctrine, the "Indian Family" doctrine or the "Existing Indian Family" doctrine.[4] These doctrines have a major impact on the outcome of cases, and more importantly, the lives of Indian children and tribal nations. The Existing Indian Family doctrine and variations have been applied in several states, including California, Indiana, Kansas, Kentucky, Louisiana, Michigan, Oklahoma, and Washington.[5]

As social workers, both tribal and non-tribal, it is a professional responsibility to be knowledgeable about ICWA, the variations of the doctrine, its accompanying terminologies, and the resulting impact on the lives of tribal children. Also, as advocates, it is important to share with community members the importance of ICWA, the circumventions, and the resulting loss of children. This information is vital in providing families with an awareness of what others have experienced, and it may help to prepare them to seek legal representation in a timely manner. Unfortunately, many Indian families remain unaware of ICWA until they arrive in court and find that it is "too late to fight or make changes," as expressed by many grandparents.[6]

Tribal Social Worker Point of View

Tribal social work is a challenge, especially for recent graduates entering the field of child welfare with a desire to work for their own tribal nation. When hired, they are expected to be prepared to take on any case that is assigned to them, to know where to begin and what to do as soon as they are part of the social services team. The learning curve is extremely steep because social workers, especially tribal social workers, are in high demand. Upon reflection, social workers may view this as one of the best experiences they have had; however, making the adjustment at the time can be difficult.

Another aspect of tribal social work is the number of roles the worker is asked to fulfill. One may not only be the child protective services worker, but also the foster care worker. The dual role puts the worker in a delicate situation: being part of the child removal process, giving testimony in court with regard to the parents progress in meeting the goals of the service plan, and then being in the role of assisting them in working toward getting back their children, whom the worker has just helped to remove.

As a tribal social worker, it is important to work collaboratively to provide services and, if at all possible, to conduct the investigations with the local department of human services.[7] This may be difficult in some situations, but if the social workers are able to have an open and honest relationship, they can assist each other and present several different strategies to one another, until the best service plan for a particular family is agreed upon.

When the social workers are able to visit family homes together, a level of comfort is established by the tribal family members being aware of the tribal member's (tribal social worker's) presence and witness to what is happening during the investigation. The tribal social worker is also able to share with the non-tribal social worker some of the cultural issues that may occur and cause uneasiness for the tribal members. It is also beneficial for the families to have both social workers involved in the case from the beginning of the investigation, to the action plan, and all court appearances, as necessary.[8]

As a tribal social worker, there is value in attending state court as well as tribal court hearings. Differences can be observed and may help prepare the tribal social worker by providing an understanding of how the two systems operate differently. Such differences include the pace, type of questions that are asked, time allowed for testimony, and expectations of the courts (state and tribal).

On a personal level, the role of tribal social worker can be extremely challenging. It is difficult to be a member of the tribal community and participate in cultural events, knowing that you have just removed someone's children and they are also in attendance at the event. Also, in a close tribal community, the worker is viewed as a member of a particular family and someone's son or daughter, sister or brother, etc.—not only as a professional. This may lead to complications in the professional-client relationship when the worker's family members are asked to put forth requests for favors and leniency to the social worker. In addition, the worker's family members may experience resentment or be challenged as a result of a decision the social worker has made in regard to close friends, extended family members, or coworkers. This not only puts the tribal social worker in a difficult position, but also his or her family.

Non-tribal Social Worker/Non-tribal Agency

Federal and state standards within child protective services policies include the requirement of the State Department to contact the tribe once abuse or neglect has been substantiated within an American Indian family. It may be more advantageous to contact the tribe once the referral is received and the family's tribal affiliation is identified. During the thirty-day investigation process, it is helpful to make contact with Indian outreach workers and the tribal social services workers to gain an understanding of the best culturally competent service options that are available to the family. It is important for non-tribal social workers to become familiar with services available to the tribal members provided by each tribe, due to substantial differences in resources. When non-tribal social workers are able to embrace a partnership with tribal professionals, services to families are always enhanced, and families are better served by this collaboration.

In Michigan, child welfare policies mandate that child protective services (CPS) investigations be completed within a thirty-day time frame from the time the initial referral is made to the office. This bureaucratic time frame is firmly adhered to, even when large caseloads are a reality, allowing little time for non-tribal social workers to engage with families and build rapport. Policies also mandate that the first interview be completed with either the victim or the alleged perpetrator of the child abuse and neglect within twenty-four to seventy-two hours of receipt of the referral, depending on the immediacy of the allegations presented in the referral. This time frame does not appear to allow for the non-tribal social worker to follow the NASW Code of Ethics in compliance with the social-work value of cultural competence.[9] Non-tribal social workers—and especially those who work for non-tribal agencies—should expect that it will take time before they are trusted and accepted by the American Indian people with whom they work.[10]

Allegations of improper supervision and physical neglect are the two most frequently substantiated forms of neglect in American Indian communities. Allegations of improper supervision of children are often substantiated because many non-tribal social workers are often unaware of, or discredit, the important role of extended family and tribal communities in the care of children, because they are unfamiliar with the traditional rearing of children, which is a tribal and clan responsibility.[11] Non-tribal social workers must understand that it is not unusual for families to gather as a group to help resolve problems that at first glance appear to be specific to an individual "nuclear" family.[12]

A positive strategy for a referral for physical neglect is to build trust in working with American Indian families by first providing assistance in the process of resolving tangible problems. These include financial-support programs, food and housing assistance, and training and employment referrals. Assisting the client to meet these immediate needs helps to build rapport by the clients becoming aware of the value of the relationship with the non-tribal social worker.

For a non-tribal social worker, it is difficult to investigate any referral; however, one of the most difficult is a referral to investigate an American Indian family that is parenting a child identified as allegedly being sexually abused. When conducting an investigation, it is advisable to begin by collecting less invasive information to put the family member at ease. Time can be spent in discussion of the clients' tribal affiliation, tribal activities, and the family's level of involvement with their tribe. The conversation can then begin to focus on the allegations in the referral.

The non-tribal social worker needs to be aware of the setting in which social services are provided to American Indian families.[13] A non-tribal social worker affiliated with a non-tribal governmental agency that is not held in positive regard by many American Indians in a particular community may find it more advantageous to conduct home visits. This means not requiring office visits, even if it means that the social worker needs to drop off paperwork to be completed by the clients. However, agency supervisors may discourage this type of service to American Indian families because it requires an additional time commitment and may appear to be showing favoritism to one particular population.

Often, American Indian clients are appreciative in receiving assistance from programs available to them that are developed through their own tribal nation—such as housing, utility, and food assistance resources. However, to meet the needs of some clients and families, services offered by both tribal and non-tribal agencies may need to be considered. Also, the non-tribal social worker needs to be aware of the varied number of services offered by each tribe. Some tribal-nation social and human services are quite comprehensive, while others are limited, based on the tribal nation's resources. Also, some tribal agencies offer services to only tribal members, while other tribal agencies may offer services to members of different tribes.

It is important to provide American Indian families with all of the options from both tribal and non-tribal agencies and allow the families to choose the resources they want to access and that best fit their needs. Some families may find referrals to culturally competent services much more accessible, and as a result, these services may be more successful in meeting their needs. Non-tribal social workers need to be mindful of the fact that the more choices available to American Indian clients, the better the opportunities for success.

Reflections from a Foster Parent: Suzanne Cross

As a tribal member, former clinical social worker, social-work educator, supporter of ICWA, and one who cares about the welfare of children, I thought it important to step up to the plate and model what I believed in by providing a foster home for children with my husband. We had also thought at the time that if the possibility arose, we would consider adoption.

We obtained our foster care license in Arizona, which was a great experience with enthusiastic social workers and support from a former foster care parent. At the time there was a Fost/Adopt program, which allowed families to become certified for foster care and adoption with the completion of the same training period.

Our first experience was wonderful, and we were able to assist with two male children for a short time. We then moved to Michigan and received approval to be foster parents in a short time because we had received the previous training in Arizona. Our experience in Michigan was challenging and problematic. In preparation for foster care, one task we had completed was a form with a checklist where we could check off the types of difficulties children had that we felt we could not work well with, such as bed-wetting, being withdrawn, acting out, starting fires, etc. My husband and I felt uncomfortable disqualifying any child. But we felt that a child with a history of starting fires would be a real concern for us. So, we indicated that we would not be willing to have a child live with us who had previously started fires. Within the first day, the two children who were placed in our home indicated to us that they both had started fires, as had their mother. We felt that either we were not heard, or the children were not adequately interviewed to ascertain their history of starting fires.

When these two young boys were placed in our home, the social worker brought them to our home along with two laundry baskets of clothes, which, as we would find out later, were too small for the children. The day they were dropped off at our home, we were told to take them to a medical appointment within two days to document their injuries (facial burn, bruises, and pit-bull dog bite). The social worker was fairly new and was obviously suffering from a cold. Therefore, she was in a hurry to leave our home. (Her total stay in our home was approximately seven minutes.) I felt that the children, my husband, and I could have benefited from more of the social worker's time to become acclimated to the new situation.

We followed the directions and took the children to a medical facility to document their injuries for an upcoming court date, which was in two days. We had a difficult time at the medical facility because no Medicaid cards had been given to us when the children were brought to our home. Needless to say, it was a frustrating day working with the human services office. Because the children were from one county and because they were identified as "Indian," they were brought to our home in a different county. After four hours, the situation was resolved by a conversation with a supervisor at the local county office who indicated, "You do not have the right to seek medical treatment for these children." So, I responded by stating, "If I don't have the right to seek medical treatment for these children who were placed in my home two days ago, then you'd better send a social worker over here to pick them up." We then received approval for medical services within twenty minutes.

There were three additional causes of frustration while being a foster parent. First, no dentist in our area was willing to take Medicaid for payment despite my explanation that I had a seven-year-old child who had been sent home from school with dental pain. Secondly, I had a child who had been extremely disappointed a number of times after traveling two-and-a half-hours one way for visitation with his mother, and finding that she was not at the agency for the visit because she forgot to get permission from her parole officer to be off her tether for the visit. The third example was the lack of receipt of payment for the child's care months after the child left our home; this was only obtained by contacting our state representative's office, which did result in the check being delivered overnight. Fortunately, my husband and I were both gainfully employed and were able to provide for the child (the other child had been placed in a facility due to his anger issues). This particular experience gave me pause for thought, and I wondered what would have happened if we had not had an adequate income. Perhaps we would have been cited for inadequate care!

Recommendations

From their varied experiences, the authors would like to share recommendations that may improve education about the implementation of, and compliance with, ICWA, as well as improvements in the delivery of child welfare services.

- Require presentations to university social-work departmental deans and directors on the importance of ICWA, and encourage ICWA training to be held

during faculty and in-service meetings. This would highlight the importance of ICWA from the administration to the faculty, and filter down to all students.
- Require child welfare experts who are invited as presenters at the schools of social work or social-work programs to include ICWA issues in their presentations—especially those that promote a focus on cultural aspects.
- Require all field supervisors to obtain ICWA training to ensure that students will be encouraged and supervised in practice to comply with the law.
- Promote a Fost/Adopt type of program nationwide to allow persons who want to be considered for foster and adoptive parenthood to qualify for both with one set of training sessions that incorporate all the requirements for both. This would be most beneficial; in situations where the rights of the biological parents are terminated, the child's life would be less disrupted if the foster parents already providing care adopted him/her.
- Develop and promote a nationwide foster-parent training program to encourage and support American Indian families that are willing to provide care for Indian children.
- During a placement, the social workers should be required to spend at least one hour with the children and foster parents to acclimate them to this significant life event. The social workers need to provide the foster parents with adequate directions and necessary documents to care for the children placed in their homes.
- Develop tribal and non-tribal agency partnerships to conduct investigations and removals, develop service plans, provide court testimonies, and collaborate on reunification plans or termination proceedings.
- Educate non-tribal social workers about the tribal services that may be offered for tribal members. Many are unaware of the existence of these services, even though the tribal nation may be nearby. If there is no contact made with the tribe, culturally relevant services may go unutilized. Also, it is important for the non-tribal social workers to know that tribal resources differ from tribe to tribe due to resources and eligibility requirements. Therefore, the non-tribal social worker needs to interact with each tribal nation to become aware of services offered to members.
- In-depth training should be provided for tribal and non-tribal social workers to testify in court. Training would provide the tools necessary to assist in the most serious decisions involving child removal, reunification, termination of parental rights, and adoption. If the social worker, tribal or non-tribal, is not prepared, a great disservice to the tribal nation, family, and child is likely to occur.
- Social workers need to assess the degree to which families utilize extended family care providers. Allegations of improper supervision may be substantiated because the social workers are unaware of, or discredit the important role of, extended family in the care of American Indian children.

- In particular, the non-tribal social workers need to be aware of the cultural differences of American Indian clients. They need to understand that American Indians not only assess them individually but also collectively as to their expertise and commitment before relationships are developed.[14]

NOTES

1. Indian Child Welfare Act, 1978 (P.L. 95-6078) 25 U.S.C. 1901 et. seq. (2001), 1–25; 25 U.S.C. §§ 1901 et seq.
2. S. L. CROSS, AMERICAN INDIAN GRANDPARENTS PARENTING THEIR GRANDCHILDREN IN MICHIGAN: A QUALITATIVE STUDY REPORT 2005 (Michigan State University School of Social Work 2005).
3. S. CROSS, *Indian Family Exception Doctrine: Still Losing Children despite the Indian Child Welfare Act*, 85 JOURNAL OF CHILD WELFARE (4): 671–90.
4. S. L. PEVAR, THE RIGHTS OF INDIANS AND TRIBES 344–47 (3d ed., New York University Press 2004).
5. *See generally Crystal R. v. Superior Court*, 59 Cal. App. 4th 703, 69 Cal. Rptr. 2d 414 (1997); *In re S.C.*, 833 P.2d 1249, 1252–56 (Okla. 1992); *In re Adoption of Crews*, 118 Wash.2d 561, 825 P.2d 305, 308–12 (Wash. 1992); *Hampton v. J.A.L.*, 658 S0.2d 331 (La. App. 2 Cir., 1995); *In re Adoption of T.R.M.*, 525 N.E.2d 298, 303 (Ind. 1988); *In re Adoption of Baby Boy L.*, 231 Kan. 199, 643 P.2d 168, 175 (Kan. 1982).
6. S. L. Cross, *supra* note 2.
7. U.S. Department of Health & Human Services/Administration for Children and Families Child Care Bureau, *Tribes and States Working Together: A Guide to Tribal-State Child Care Coordination*, PSC Contract No. 233-03-0021, April 2005.
8. J. W. GREEN, CULTURAL AWARENESS IN THE HUMAN SERVICES (3d ed., Allyn & Bacon 1999).
9. NASW, *Standards for Cultural Competence in Social Work Practice* (NASW 2001).
10. H. N. Weaver and White, *The Native American Family Circle: Roots of Resiliency*, 2 JOURNAL OF FAMILY SOCIAL WORK (1): 67–79 (1997).
11. E. D. Edwards and M. E. Edwards, *Social Work Practice with American Indian and Alaskan Natives*, SOCIAL WORK: A PROFESSION OF MANY FACES (A. T. Morales and B. W. Sheafor, eds., Allyn & Bacon 1998).
12. T. L. Cross, *Drawing on Cultural Traditions in Indian Child Welfare Practice*, 67 SOCIAL CASEWORK (5): 283–89 (1986); Edwards and Edwards, *supra* note 11.
13. Weaver and White, *supra* note 10.
14. *Id.*; E. D. Edwards and M. E. Edwards, *American Indians: Working with Individuals and Groups*, 1980 SOCIAL CASEWORK 498–506.

The Indian Child Welfare Act of 1978 and Its Impact on Tribal Sovereignty and Governance

Terry L. Cross and Robert J. Miller

Sovereignty and Child Welfare Policy Decisions

Sovereignty, simply stated, is the right of a political entity to govern its own affairs. American Indian tribes are recognized as having inherent sovereignty as political units that predate the existence of the United States. For tribal nations, like states, this sovereignty is shaped and limited by federal law and exercised through the structures of governance. One area clearly retained by tribes is the right to govern the relationships between the tribe and its citizens, the relationships among tribal members, and between tribal members and others they relate to domestically or in business interactions. This area, known as civil regulatory jurisdiction, includes determination of citizenship, child custody matters, and child protection and dependency, among many other considerations. However, it is one thing to have inherent powers of self-governance, and quite another thing to exercise those rights. Exercising sovereignty requires first and foremost the will to do so. It also requires a policy-level decision to assert the inherent powers. Sovereignty is exercised only when the infrastructure and resources are applied to make that intention real through the structures of governance.[1]

Throughout history, tribes have exercised their sovereignty in different ways at different times. They have exercised jurisdiction over a variety of matters, choosing items over which it is feasible or beneficial to assume governance. Also over time, federal laws and policies have limited or affirmed tribal sovereignty in several areas. Few federal laws have affirmed tribal sovereignty in the same way the Indian Child Welfare Act of 1978 (ICWA) has done. In essence, the Act does two very important things. Firstly, it sets up criteria for states to follow when taking an Indian child into state custody, requiring the states to recognize tribal sovereignty in several ways. Secondly, it sets up a framework for tribes to exercise their sovereignty over child welfare matters. Each of these major areas of ICWA offer, and in fact often require, that tribes make intentional policy-level decisions regarding matters of sovereignty. The premise of this chapter is that ICWA not only enhances tribal sovereignty through its language, but that it has also fostered and facilitated the development of the governance infrastructure necessary for tribes to exercise sovereignty well beyond the bounds of child welfare. The remainder of this chapter describes the nature of these policy-level decisions and their relationship to sovereignty. Finally, the implications for the future of tribal governance are discussed.[2]

ICWA and Tribal Citizenship

It has been well established that only tribes can determine the citizenship of their members. On the face of it, this right seems straightforward and simple. From time immemorial, tribes have used custom and law to determine membership. These rules are as varied as the tribes themselves. The federal government, during the allotment era, intruded on this right by introducing the notion of blood quantum and enrollment. Enrollment carries with it the recognition by the federal government of an individual Indian's citizenship in a particular tribe for the purposes of determining eligibility for certain services, rights, and resources. However, enrollment and membership, while parallel, are not necessarily the same. The framers of ICWA intentionally used the term "member" instead of "enrolled" for this reason. In addition, the real-life experience of many Indian families would make the intent and implementation of ICWA impossible. For example, some children may be 100 percent Indian by blood, yet not enrolled in a tribe due to their being from so many tribes that they do not meet the formal enrollment qualifications of any one tribe. Another child may be full-blood, yet have parents of the wrong gender to enroll them in their particular tribes. Still others may not be enrolled due to residency requirements. Siblings in the same families may have differing status, and parents may have enrollment in different tribes than their own children.[3]

The practical solution for this real-life problem was to leave the language open and to allow tribes to determine membership for the purposes of ICWA. The first sovereign action stimulated by ICWA is a policy-level determination regarding membership. Some tribes have elected to adhere strictly to their enrollment, others have extended their jurisdiction through tribal ordinances to include non-enrolled members, and still others have chosen to decide the matter on a case-by-case basis. Whatever the mechanism, the choice is a policy-level decision exercising sovereign power.

Order of Placement Preference

The placement preferences are among the rules that states are to follow under ICWA. The Act lays out criteria for both foster care and adoption, but in both cases, defers to tribes the right to establish different criteria for their citizens. Preferences established under tribal law shall be the criteria for the states to follow with regard to that tribe's children, if they are different from those stated in ICWA. While this is a minor provision of ICWA that few tribes have exercised, it does extend tribal sovereignty into the realm of state court proceedings and clearly establishes the right of a tribe to regulate how its members are treated in some civil actions by another jurisdiction.[4]

Here again, a policy-level decision to exercise the authority of regulating foster placements, even beyond the bounds of tribal jurisdiction, is required. Some tribes choose to enact or to not enact such rules as a matter of intentional policy; others have yet to engage in the policy-level decision, and rely on the power and authority of ICWA in this matter.

Full Faith and Credit

Perhaps the most far-reaching and sovereignty-affirming provision under ICWA is the requirement that states recognize the acts and decisions of tribal courts as equal to their own. The full faith and credit provision solidly anchors the sovereign authority of tribal courts as the legal equals to state courts. To take full advantage of this provision, a tribe must first establish the governance structures necessary to have and operate a court, including authorizing documents, policies and procedures, and the appropriate laws and codes. ICWA further goes on to facilitate the establishment of such courts.[5]

Those tribes that did not have court systems prior to the passage of ICWA were presented with the major policy-level decision as to whether to exercise their sovereign authority over child welfare matters. In doing so, they have had to determine which matters to govern, and to what extent to assert jurisdiction both on and near tribal lands as well as off-reservation. Even many tribes with existing court systems had to decide whether to exercise their rights, and if so, to gear up for implementation.

ICWA further recognizes a tribe's sovereign authority in the eligibility provisions, declaring that a state has no jurisdiction in cases where a tribe has already established jurisdiction and taken custody. Many of these affirmations of tribal sovereign authority are unique in federal law and represent a major statement of federal policy supporting tribal governments in general.[6]

Sovereignty and Tribal Family and Juvenile Courts

ICWA addresses the establishment of tribal courts and affirms that a tribal court, established for the purposes of ICWA, is what the tribe says it is. In other words, the nature of the tribal court is up to the tribal government and can be based on custom and tradition, or on whatever model a tribe deems appropriate. While most tribes that have developed courts have elected to develop them based on the existing mainstream models, several have chosen alternatives that are more culturally based. ICWA stimulated the development of tribal courts across Indian Country. While many tribes chose not to develop courts, they did so in the context of a policy-level decision to determine whether to exercise their sovereign authority to do so. In reality, these decisions have more often been made based on the availability of resources to effectively carry out the responsibilities of operating a tribal court. However, resources notwithstanding, the evolution of tribal courts was positively impacted by ICWA, and tribes that have developed the infrastructure to operate effective court systems have also strengthened their governance capacity in other civil regulatory matters, such as domestic disputes, adult protection, divorce, and custody disputes between parents.

Tribal Codes

While ICWA does not specifically address the development of tribal codes involving children, it assumes that a tribal code is the governance mechanism by which a tribe establishes and implements its jurisdiction over all aspects of child well-being. This includes child protection, dependency, custody, permanency, adoption, status offenses, ICWA interventions, placement preferences, etc. In addition to the implications that tribes will enact codes specific to child welfare, it also implies that tribal codes will govern the licensing of foster care providers and residential facilities. This authority would extend to licensing professionals to work in tribal service areas. Many tribes now exercise their sovereign right to license foster homes, and that right is now recognized in federal regulations beyond ICWA. Under the Adoption and Safe Families Act (ASFA), "foster family home" is defined as a foster home that is licensed by the state. The regulations also recognize that, for purposes of Title IV-E eligibility, the term "foster family home" includes homes located on or near Indian reservations that are licensed by a tribal licensing or approval authority. The commentary to the regulations explicitly recognizes the right of tribes to operate "a system for licensing or otherwise regulating Indian foster and adoptive homes" on or near the reservation. The decision to license foster homes is another example of a policy-level decision in part presented to tribes by ICWA.[7]

Soon after the passage of ICWA, many tribes made the decision to enact child welfare-related codes. Early in that process, it was usual practice for attorneys to draft the tribal code based on the law of the state in which the tribe was located. While this was the convenient and expedient course, it represented only a partial expression of sovereignty. Over the nearly thirty years of development and evolution of tribal child welfare services, many tribal codes have been revised to be more reflective of tribal values, beliefs, and standards. This is evident in the tribal definitions of child abuse and neglect that are unique to a specific tribe.[8]

Nowhere is the departure of tribal law from state law more stark and necessary than in the area of adoption. While state laws require the termination of rights of the biological parents, tribal codes are increasingly being changed to conform to tribal customs allowing adoption without termination. This may very well be one of the most important legal developments in tribal law, representing an exercise of sovereign authority to base law on tribal custom rather than mainstream standards. Tribes reaching this level of lawmaking have made an intentional decision to base their interventions on their own tribal teachings and customs. Where state laws base their right to intervene in the internal affairs of families on the concept of *parens patriae*, or the state as guardian of its citizens, tribal laws are increasingly based on traditional teachings (e.g., "Children are sacred, and we have an obligation to our creator to protect them"). While these legal conceptions have always held the possibility for development, ICWA created an environment in which the evolution of tribal law and governance could readily move toward greater and greater expressions of sovereignty.[9]

Tribal-State Agreements

ICWA authorizes intergovernmental agreements between tribes and states for purposes of implementing the Act. This direct recognition of tribes and states as equal partners in the implementation of child welfare for tribal children has enabled agreements ranging from local protocol agreements to statewide agreements involving multiple tribes. Typically, agreements have ranged from funding agreements to clarification of jurisdictional boundaries. More recent legislation in child welfare now requires state court improvement projects to consult with tribal courts. Historically, tribes often shunned relating to states due to their trust relationship with the federal government; but ICWA has opened an opportunity to enter into a new dialogue on an equal government-to-government footing.[10]

The Problem of Public Law 280

Perhaps one of the greatest historic and current threats to tribal sovereignty is Public Law 280. This law was enacted by Congress in 1953 as part of the termination era of federal Indian policy, when Congress actually sought to terminate or end the federal political relationship with the Indian nations. The Act provided for state criminal jurisdiction over reservations in five, and later six, specifically named states, and also for a limited form of state civil jurisdiction. While legal scholars argue that P.L. 280 did nothing to diminish tribal civil-regulatory jurisdiction, in practice at least two states, California and Alaska, operate as if tribes have no jurisdiction over child welfare, even on their own lands. These two states alone are home to more than half of all of the federally recognized tribes in the United States, greatly influencing the number of tribes that have been able to fully assert their jurisdiction.[11]

ICWA includes a provision for tribes to end state jurisdiction by setting up a process of "retrocession" from P.L. 280. While this provision was intended to strengthen tribal sovereignty, some have suggested that it may have actually weakened the position of tribes by at least implying that state courts share jurisdiction for child welfare on nonexempt reservations in P.L. 280 states. Whether this is true or not is a matter of conjecture, but the question of P.L. 280 continues to inhibit many tribes from asserting full jurisdiction.[12]

Submission to Federal Rules: The Power of the Purse Strings

Not all aspects of sovereignty are positive. The federal government of the United States often implements national policy via the power of the purse strings. Under the division-of-powers provisions of the U.S. Constitution, things like child welfare are within the exclusive jurisdiction of states and tribes under their sovereign powers. Yet the federal government has evolved to include a process to ensure uniform child welfare policies among the states. To accomplish this, the federal government provides a substantial share of funding to support state services, but sets policy for states to follow if they want access to the funds. Since funding of child welfare at the state level would be difficult without federal assistance, states are locked into the regulations. Tribes are increasingly gaining access to these same programs and are usually subject to the same regulations as the states. While tribal sovereignty legally is maintained in this relationship, voluntary submission to federal regulation and oversight by taking certain funds is a policy-level decision that tribes enter into with intent, often agreeing in some measure to compromise the extent of their authority for the welfare of their members.[13]

Case-Level Decisions

Each ICWA case provides a tribe an opportunity to exercise its sovereignty through the governance structures of the tribe. First, the tribe must determine membership/citizenship. As discussed earlier, this decision will depend on many factors, some of which are matters of policy and some of which are the circumstances of the child and family. Once membership is determined, a decision regarding intervention in a state court case must be made. To intervene means that the tribe becomes a party in the state court proceedings, and is able to offer testimony and to give input in the planning for the child. It is rare in federal law for one jurisdiction (tribal) to be able to intervene in the court proceedings of another (state) as a full party. (Federal courts invite states as full parties into federal cases when state laws are at issue in a federal case.) This process represents an extension of a tribe's authority throughout the nation for the express purpose of protecting individual children. Finally, the tribe's right under ICWA to request transfer of jurisdiction from the state court to the tribal court is a further affirmation of sovereign tribal authority over its dependent members. Every decision in this series of choices made possible by ICWA is an exercise of legitimate tribal authority, requiring both effective governance infrastructure and informed policy-level decisions.[14]

Implications for the Future of Tribal Governance

The Nations Building model, developed by Stephen Cornell, Joseph Kalt, and the Harvard Project on American Indian Economic Development, has identified several cornerstones that are needed for successful tribal economic development. One of the cornerstones is a safe business environment, characterized by reliable business codes, courts, and assurance that business activities will be isolated from undue political interference. This principle can be applied equally to the field of child welfare. In those tribal communities where families and outside jurisdictions trust the fairness of the systems that respond to child maltreatment and custody issues, child welfare services remain relatively stable. When elected tribal officials insert themselves into the child welfare decisions due to family relationships or political influence, trust in tribal institutions is eroded. True self-government requires systems of checks and balances that allow elected officials to hold child welfare managers and staff accountable without attempting to micromanage complex social problems.[15]

There are several emerging trends that point to a positive evolution in tribal governance as it relates to child welfare. First, as described above, several tribes are writing codes that conform to their traditional teachings, as in the case of customary adoptions. Several tribes are reinventing child welfare services with service integration models that blur the lines of services that have historically been performed in isolation from one another in mainstream society. When tribes elect to develop "systems of care" models, or to develop collaborative service designs blending drug courts, child welfare, and substance abuse treatment, they are showing innovations in governance. Another emerging trend is the certification of tribal workers. The National Indian Child Welfare Association (NICWA) now offers a certification program nationwide. Certification of staff helps tribes to ensure competency in a relatively complex and critical service area. Tribes are beginning to require certification as a way to raise the standard of child welfare services. Such innovations are the hallmarks of self-determination and strong governance.[16]

Another implication for the future of tribal governance is the expanding role of youth and families in the determination of the services delivered to them. Citizen participation is central to successful self-government. In child welfare, citizen participation takes many forms. In some communities, advocates and local advocacy organizations evaluate political candidates' positions on children's issues. Others have families and elders guiding services from the position of advisors who serve on committees. When community members volunteer to become foster or adoptive parents, they are becoming part of, and helping to shape, the system. In some communities, tribal governments are increasingly supporting the development of nongovernmental services by locally incorporated and controlled charitable organizations. Finally, some communities are creating multidisciplinary teams, commissions, or governing boards to oversee child welfare as a way to isolate difficult case decisions from political influences. Each of these strategies increases the accountability of the service providers and further helps to strengthen the tribal program.[17]

As in other areas, resources, or the lack thereof, greatly influence the degree to which tribal governments choose to express sovereignty in child welfare matters. Advocates on a national level have expanded the resources available to tribes, and continuing efforts are likely to dramatically increase available resources in the near future. In addition, many tribes now have resources from their own enterprises to support a comprehensive continuum of child and family services. As more and more resources become available, tribes will be increasingly faced with high-level policy choices regarding the degree to which they express their sovereignty. As tribes make the choice to be self-governing, the structure of governance will need to keep pace with the roles and responsibilities assumed.[18]

Self-Determination and Self-Governance

There are several illuminating examples that prove our point that the tribal exercise of governmental powers over child welfare issues is worthwhile, not only to serve the absolutely crucial need to help tribal children, but also because this effort has a very valuable secondary effect by also helping Indian nations. It is self-evident that tribes help themselves when they carry out their *parens patriae* duty to protect their most vulnerable citizens, tribal children, and help prepare them to be future adult citizens and tribal leaders. It is equally obvious that tribal nations benefit themselves by ensuring that their future citizens are raised in a healthy, safe, and educated environment. But tribes also help themselves in another way when they take on child welfare responsibilities and develop the administrative and judicial resources to address these issues. It is clear that when tribes develop these capabilities, they grow and mature as governments, and they exponentially increase their capacity to govern their citizens, to use their sovereignty, and to exercise jurisdiction over their territories and all persons found there.

Tribal programs such as child welfare departments help tribes to develop their governance abilities and to train tribal employees and tribal citizens in management skills. For example, debating and drafting tribal codes and establishing departments and courts to handle such issues further increases the abilities of tribal governments and expands the scope of their sovereignty and authority. The thirty-year history of the Indian Self-Determination and Education Assistance Act clearly proves this point.

In 1970, President Nixon gave the name "self-determination" to a new era of federal Indian policy when he issued a landmark statement that the United States should allow the tribal nations and individual Indians a far greater voice in determining federal Indian affairs. The principal legislative initiative of this era is the Indian Self-Determination and Education Assistance Act of 1975 (ISDEAA). This act instituted a fundamental philosophical change in the administration of Indian affairs. The act gave tribes and Indians a broader voice in their own lives, in setting federal Indian policies, and in creating and operating federal Indian programs. The act also allows tribes to contract with the federal government for the delivery of federal services. In this situation, tribes contract with the United States to take over the operation of social and economic federal programs that are administered for the benefit of Indians and tribes. Tribal governments can redesign the programs within certain limitations, and if they can run the program more efficiently than the federal government, the tribe then can use this efficiency to provide even more services than the federal program would have done otherwise. They can also receive the federal funding in one lump payment, for example, and can keep the interest on these funds and provide even more services to their citizens under the contract. While tribal programs continue to be federally funded, the programs are planned and administered by the tribes themselves. Thus, federal "domination" of Indian affairs is supposed to end.[19]

Not surprisingly, the Bureau of Indian Affairs (BIA) and the Indian Health Service (IHS) resisted tribes contracting out federal programs, employees, and funding. Congress and tribal leaders counteracted the federal bureaucracy and have finally succeeded, to a significant extent, in placing many of the federal programs and dollars designated for Indians and tribes into tribal hands. For many years, tribal nations have had to fight, lobby, and litigate over several issues of funding and responsibilities under the act. They have succeeded at the Supreme Court level, for example, in prying away from the federal agencies the funding needed to operate these contracted programs.[20]

Congress obviously has considered the self-determination idea a success. It has amended and strengthened the ISDEAA several times and severely chastised the BIA for dragging its heels in drafting regulations to implement the act and congressional intent to end the federal domination of Indian affairs. In 1994, for example, Congress enacted the Tribal Self-Governance Act to expand the idea of tribes running federal programs, and even to allow self-governance tribes to consolidate and manage all the programs administered by the BIA. The Self-Governance Act also allows tribes to contract out the programs of other Department of Interior agencies that have some "special geographical, historical, or cultural significance" to a tribe. Only a few tribes have so far been able to pry programs away from non-BIA or non-IHS federal agencies, but even this limited success is a precursor to future opportunities for tribal governments and congressional intent in this arena.[21]

Congress has also delegated federal responsibilities to tribes in such areas as alcohol regulation, environmental control, and protection of historic and cultural items in Indian Country. The Clean Water Act and the Clean Air Act, among other environmental laws, expressly grant tribes authority to be treated as states to exercise the authority to set the environmental standards for their reservations, which the federal government will then enforce. Even the protection of religious and cultural issues and the pursuit of the cleanest environment possible are proper objectives for tribal governments to strive for under these federal statutes. So far, only a few tribes have utilized the opportunities available to take more control of their reservations and to control all persons found therein, so there is yet much room for tribes to exercise and develop their governance abilities in these specific areas.[22]

Plainly, when Indian nations exercise these kinds of governmental powers, it increases and improves tribal capabilities and the extent of tribal governance. Not only do tribal governments benefit when they improve their abilities, but empirical studies have shown that reservation residents, Indian and non-Indian, receive benefits from the improvement of tribal governance and the increased efficiencies that tribal operations can bring to federal programs. One study by the Harvard Project on American Indian Economic Development graphically demonstrates the ability of tribes to improve on the work of the federal government. This is a natural and logical result that one would expect, because tribal employees and tribal citizens are inherently more concerned about the quality of life on their reservation than federal employees who operate the same programs but might not have the same dedication and concern as tribal citizens. In addition, one would expect tribal employees to work harder and smarter to make federal programs beneficially impact their reservations. The Harvard Project studied forty-nine tribes that had assumed all or part of the BIA forestry program for their reservations. The study showed that tribes that managed their own forests improved on the BIA performance in every way. The cash return to the tribes was higher under tribal management than under the BIA, and overall forest health was improved. It is really not surprising that the people who live on the reservation, work for the tribal government, and who are often tribal citizens have the knowledge, motivation, and interest to care for tribal assets better than outsiders.[23]

The benefit to tribes themselves from building capable departments and agencies is well demonstrated by another Harvard study. This study of eighty-nine tribes showed that reservations where the tribal governments had developed impartial court systems that were perceived to be fair and free of political influence had 5 percent better employment rates than reservations where the court system was not perceived as fair and impartial. What better proof is needed that when tribes improve and increase their operations and abilities, they improve conditions on their reservations and can then govern their reservations more effectively as fully operating governments?[24]

Consequently, it is obvious that if tribes carry out their *parens patriae* responsibilities to protect their youngest and most vulnerable citizens, it creates a win/win situation. These actions protect tribal interests in their children, protect and develop future tribal citizens and leaders, help develop tribal governance abilities, and protect tribal sovereignty and jurisdictional control of their reservations. Thus, it is clear that tribal nations need to determine their futures for themselves and to protect their children and citizens. They can do this even better by exercising self-governance in all matters possible, especially by using the tools ICWA provides to develop tribal programs to protect their children and, at the same time, to increase their sovereign authority and capacity.

Conclusion

Few people understand or recognize the unique and complex political position that American Indian children are in. They are citizens of two nations, and by virtue of this status, many of them are currently inadequately protected from child abuse and neglect. Child protection is a matter of civil law—a matter that societies and governments have declared sovereign authority over; a matter that tribal governments have authority over, if they choose to exercise it.

Historically, tribes exercised this sovereignty in full. We had customs and traditions for regulating civil matters such as child protection and custody. Tribal elders acted as judges. Traditional leaders governed as stewards and protectors of family well-being. Our clan and kinship systems functioned as social service providers. Then the capacities and resources that allowed the full exercise of tribal sovereignty were diminished by forced dependence, destruction of traditional governing structures, and displacement of natural helping traditions.[25]

Tribal sovereignty and responsibility to be the stewards for the safety of our children, however, were never diminished. The concept of tribal sovereignty is based in international law, the United States Constitution, treaty law, and numerous federal laws and policies. Whether or not a government can fulfill all its obligations to its citizens, sovereign governments are responsible for the safety and well-being of those citizens. Tribes, like states, have sovereign authority over, and responsibility for, the protection of children. Whether funds are available or not, child protection is, and always has been, within the authority of tribal governments and, indeed, is a moral obligation if not an outright responsibility.

As early as the 1960s, the federal government recognized the need for uniform national policies to address child abuse and neglect, and began creating funding strategies to back up the policies. Unfortunately, in the development of these policies and their funding mechanisms, Indian children were forgotten. Tribal governments were overlooked or not considered viable service providers. For example, the Child Welfare and Adoption Assistance Act of 1980, which created Title IV-E of the Social Security Act, failed to include language authorizing Indian tribes to operate the program. Federally, the BIA dramatically failed to fill the gap. The states also failed in their attempts to provide meaningful services.[26]

Many things have changed. In the last thirty years, tribes have reasserted themselves and have begun exercising the sovereignty that they always had but could not always implement. But some tribes, even today, have yet to recognize this important aspect of sovereignty—caring for and protecting their children; carrying out their *parens patriae* duty.

Many tribes recognized these facts and led the charge to enact ICWA in 1978. Beginning with that Act, tribes began in earnest to reclaim their responsibility for the protection of tribal children. Today, almost every tribe in the nation provides some form of child welfare services to their children. However, the funding strategies of earlier decades are still in place and continue to prohibit tribes from exercising full authority in child protection because of the lack of access to resources. Tribal court development has been inhibited by Public Law 280, which gave states concurrent jurisdiction over child welfare matters involving tribal children, combined with a critical lack of funding for tribal courts. Tribal courts have been an essential element of exercising sovereignty in child protection. Still, in other places, tribal leaders have been reluctant to exercise their sovereignty due to the potential political consequences, or for fear that tribal infrastructure will not be equal to the task.[27]

In too many places, our children are literally dying from the failure of the federal government to empower tribal responses to child protection issues. If we are to become healthy nations, then every tribal government needs to reclaim the stewardship roles of our past leaders, assert its authority over child maltreatment, and exercise its sovereignty over child protection. Tribal leaders who stand up for children are to be commended. Those who walk the halls of Congress seeking resources for child protection are unsung heroes. Those leaders who are willing to take the political heat in their communities for hard decisions that protect children should have all of our support. There is no aspect of sovereignty more important than protecting the well-being of children. We can do something about abused and neglected children in our communities, but we must have the courage to confront our own fears, and we must recognize and support our tribal leaders who take a stand on this difficult but important issue and confront abuse as an expression of tribal sovereignty.

NOTES

1. BLACK'S LAW DICTIONARY 1252 (5th ed. 1979); *United States v. Wheeler*, 435 U.S. 313 (1978); *Santa Clara Pueblo v. Martinez*, 436 U.S. 48 (1978); *Montana v. United States*, 450 U.S. 544 (1981); *Miss. Band of Choctaw Indians v. Holyfield*, 490 U.S. 30 (1989); Stephen Cornell, *Sovereignty, Prosperity and Policy in Indian Country Today*, 5 COMMUNITY REINVESTMENT 5–7, 9–13 (1997).
2. ROBERT J. MILLER, NATIVE AMERICA, DISCOVERED AND CONQUERED: THOMAS JEFFERSON, LEWIS & CLARK, AND MANIFEST DESTINY 163–72 (Praeger Publishers 2006); Robert J. Miller, *Economic Development in Indian Country: Will Capitalism or Socialism Succeed?*, 80 OR. L. REV. 757, 780–98 (2002); Robert J. Miller, *American Indian Influence on the United States Constitution and Its Framers*, 18 AM. INDIAN L. REV. 133, 141–46 (1993); Indian Child Welfare Act of 1978, 25 U.S.C. §§ 1901–63.
3. *Santa Clara Pueblo v. Martinez*, 436 U.S. 48 (1978).
4. 25 U.S.C. § 1915 (2000).
5. 25 U.S.C. § 1911(d) (2000).
6. 25 U.S.C. § 1911(a) (2000).
7. 42 U.S.C. § 672(c)(1) (2000); 45 C.F.R. § 1355.20(a)(2) (2007); 65 Fed. Reg. 4034 (2000).
8. NATIONAL INDIAN CHILD WELFARE ASSOCIATION, DEVELOPING A MODEL TRIBAL CHILD ABUSE AND NEGLECT PROGRAM: DATA APPLICATION: FINAL REPORT (2006); KATHLEEN A. EARLE AND AMANDA CROSS, CHILD ABUSE AND NEGLECT AMONG AMERICAN INDIAN/ALASKA NATIVE CHILDREN: AN ANALYSIS OF EXISTING DATA (National Indian Child Welfare Association 2001); TERRY L. CROSS AND DAVID SIMMONS, DEVELOPMENT AND IMPLEMENTATION OF TRIBAL FOSTER CARE STANDARDS (National Indian Child Welfare Association 2000); KATHLEEN A. EARLE, CHILD ABUSE AND NEGLECT: AN EXAMINATION OF AMERICAN INDIAN DATA (National Indian Child Welfare Association 2000) (all documents on file with the authors).
9. TERRY L. CROSS ET AL., DEVELOPING CULTURALLY BASED TRIBAL ADOPTION LAWS AND CUSTOMARY ADOPTION CODES (National Indian Child Welfare Association 2003); *In re LE, minor Child*, CC-99-502 (Family Court of Fort Belknap Indian Cmty. of Mont., Feb. 11, 2000); White Earth Band of Ojibwe Judicial Code tit. 4a (customary adoption code) (all documents on file with the authors); BLACK'S LAW DICTIONARY 1003 (5th ed. 1979).

10. Minn. Dep't of Human Serv., *Minn. Tribal/State Agreement* (Feb. 2007); State of Wash. Dep't Social Servs., *Agreement Regarding Child Custody Services and Proceedings*; EDDIE F. BROWN ET AL., TRIBAL/STATE TITLE IV-E INTERGOVERNMENTAL AGREEMENTS: FACILITATING TRIBAL ACCESS TO FEDERAL RESOURCES (National Indian Child Welfare Association 2000); (all documents on file with the authors) http://www.acf.dhhs.gov/programs/cb/laws_policies/policy/pi/pi00index.htm#2006.
11. 18 U.S.C. § 1162(a) (2000); 28 U.S.C. § 1360(a) (2000).
12. Doe v. Mann, 415 F.3d 1038 (9th Cir. 2005), *cert. denied*, 126 S.Ct. 1909 (2006).
13. U.S. CONST. amend. IX & X.
14. 25 U.S.C. § 1911(b)–(c) (2000).
15. Stephen Cornell and Joseph P. Kalt, *Reloading the Dice: Improving the Chances for Economic Development on American Indian Reservations*, in WHAT CAN TRIBES DO? STRATEGIES AND INSTITUTIONS IN AMERICAN INDIAN ECONOMIC DEVELOPMENT 36–37 (Stephen Cornell and Joseph P. Kalt, eds., University of California 1992); Robert J. Miller, *Economic Development in Indian Country: Will Capitalism or Socialism Succeed?*, 80 OR. L. REV. 757, 842–55 (2002).
16. National Indian Child Welfare Association certification program, *available at* (last visited June 22, 2007).
17. *See, e.g.*, Tribal CASA (Court Appointed Special Advocate) programs, *available at* http://www.casanet.org/program-services/tribal/start-casa.htm (last visited June 22, 2007).
18. In the fall of 2006, the reauthorization of the Promoting Safe and Stable Families Act, 42 U.S.C. 629 (2003), increased tribal funding for family preservation and support services from a 1% allocation to 3%, representing an annual increase of approximately 10–15 million dollars for tribal programs. *See* http://www.nicwa.org/policy/index.
19. Indian Self-Determination and Education Assistance Act of 1975, 25 U.S.C. §§ 450–450n; *Message from the President of the United States Transmitting Recommendations for Indian Policy*, H.R. Doc. No. 91-363, 91st Cong., 2d Sess. (July 8, 1970); Michael P. Gross, *Indian Self-Determination and Tribal Sovereignty: An Analysis of Recent Federal Indian Policy*, 56 TEX. L. REV. 1157 (1978).
20. *Cherokee Nation of Okla. v. Leavitt*, 543 U.S. 631 (2005).
21. 25 U.S.C. §§ 458-aa–458-hh (2003); Tadd M. Johnson and James Hamilton, *Self-Governance for Indian Tribes: From Paternalism to Empowerment*, 27 CONN. L. REV. 1251 (1995).
22. 18 U.S.C. § 1161 (2000) (tribes control the use of alcohol in Indian country); Robert J. Miller and Maril Hazlett, *The "Drunken Indian"—Myth Distilled into Reality through Federal Indian Alcohol Policy*, 28 ARIZ. ST. L.J. 223, 233–35, 262–63 (1996) (tribes were delegated authority over alcohol in Indian country); 33 U.S.C. § 1377 (2000) (tribes authorized to assume responsibility for water quality); 42 U.S.C. § 7601(d) (2000) (tribes authorized to assume responsibility for air quality); *Ariz. Public Service Co. v. EPA*, 211 F.3d 1280 (D.C. Cir. 2000) (upholding EPA granting authority to tribe to set air quality standards on reservation that impacted non-Indians); *City of Albuquerque v. Browner*, 97 F.3d 415 (10th Cir. 1996), *cert. denied*, 522 U.S. 965 (1997) (Pueblo of Isleta could set water standards for farming and religious uses that impacted upstream city); *Nance v. EPA*, 645 F.2d 701 (9th Cir.), *cert. denied*, 454 U.S. 1081 (1981) (Northern Cheyenne Tribe could designate

reservation air shed as Class I even if it impacted off-reservation non-Indians and neighboring tribe); *see* http://www.nathpo.org/ (as of November 2006 only sixty-six tribes have been delegated federal powers by the National Park Service to operate tribal historic preservation offices and to protect historic and cultural sites on Indian lands) (last visited June 22, 2007).

23. Stephen Cornell and Joseph P. Kalt, *Reloading the Dice: Improving the Chances for Economic Development on American Indian Reservations*, in WHAT CAN TRIBES DO? STRATEGIES AND INSTITUTIONS IN AMERICAN INDIAN ECONOMIC DEVELOPMENT 15, 182–83, 199–200 (Stephen Cornell and Joseph P. Kalt, eds., University of California 1992) (tribes taking control of forestry from the BIA led to dramatic improvements in productivity, up to a 40% increase, and with better forest management); David D. Haddock and Robert J. Miller, *Can a Sovereign Protect Investors from Itself? Tribal Institutions to Spur Reservation Investment*, 8 J. SMALL & EMERGING BUS. L. 173 (2004).

24. WHAT CAN TRIBES DO?, *supra* note 23, at 28–30; Robert J. Miller, *Economic Development in Indian Country: Will Capitalism or Socialism Succeed?*, 80 OR. L. REV. 757, 842–48 (2002) (stating that the role of tribal governments in developing reservation economies and economic development is crucial).

25. KARL N. LLEWELLYN AND E. ADAMSON HOEBEL, THE CHEYENNE WAY: CONFLICT AND CASE LAW IN PRIMITIVE JURISPRUDENCE (University of Oklahoma Press 1941); CHARLES F. WILKINSON, AMERICAN INDIANS, TIME AND THE LAW (Yale University Press 1987); Tom Tso, *The Process of Decision Making in Tribal Courts*, 31 ARIZ. L. REV. 225, 227–30 (1989) (explaining Navajo peacemaker courts, and elders serving as judges).

26. Terry L. Cross et al., *Child Abuse and Neglect in Indian Country: Policy Issues*, 81 FAMILIES IN SOCIETY (1): 49–58 (2000).

27. *See, e.g., Statement of the National Indian Child Welfare Association for the House Ways and Means Income Security and Family Support Subcommittee Hearing Regarding Challenges Facing the Child Welfare System* (May 15, 2007); *Testimony of the National Indian Child Welfare Association as Represented by Connie Bear King before the Senate Finance Committee Regarding Keeping America's Promise: Health Care and Child Welfare for Native Americans* (March 22, 2007); *Written Testimony of Arlene Templer, MSW, ACSW, CSC Tribal Social Services Division Manager of the Department of Human Resources Development (DHRD), Confederated Salish and Kootenai Tribes (CSKT) of the Flathead Nation before the Senate Committee on Finance Hearing on "Fostering Permanence: Progress Achieved and Challenges Ahead for America's Child Welfare System"* (April 25, 2006); DELORES SUBIA BIGFOOT ET AL., IMPACTS OF CHILD MALTREATMENT IN INDIAN COUNTRY: PRESERVING THE SEVENTH GENERATION THROUGH POLICIES, PROGRAMS AND FUNDING STREAMS (National Indian Child Welfare Association 2006); JODY BECKER-GREEN ET AL., THE TULALIP TRIBES STARTING EARLY STARTING SMART PROGRAM EXPERIENCE: USING THE RELATIONAL WORLDVIEW MODEL TO DEVELOP A PROJECT BLUEPRINT (National Indian Child Welfare Association 2006) (all documents on file with the authors).

ICWA and the Commerce Clause

Matthew L. M. Fletcher

Despite the fact that the Indian Child Welfare Act[1] (ICWA or Act) is a monumental piece of legislation—it affects every Indian child born in the United States *and* it serves as one of the most stinging rebukes of states' rights by Congress in the twentieth century—the Supreme Court has decided only one case involving the Act. That case, *Mississippi Band of Choctaw Indians v. Holyfield*,[2] did not address any challenges to the constitutionality of the Act. But in the years since *Holyfield*, a few state courts and a few commentators have expressed doubts as to the constitutionality of the Act under the Indian Commerce Clause and the Tenth Amendment.[3]

This chapter will address only one of several potential constitutional challenges to the Act—those relating to the Indian Commerce Clause and the Tenth Amendment. The questions of equal protection and substantive due process have been addressed elsewhere in the scholarship,[4] but no one has addressed in detail the question of the Commerce Clause and states' rights.

For our purposes, we interpret Article I, section 8, clause 3 of the U.S Constitution, which reads, "Congress shall have Power . . . To regulate commerce with foreign nations, and among the several states, and with the Indian tribes."[5] From this language derives the Indian Commerce Clause. This chapter will attempt to determine whether Congress had authority to enact the Indian Child Welfare Act. This inquiry is limited, however, to determining whether the Indian Commerce Clause alone authorizes Congress to enact ICWA. Since Congress offered additional (albeit vague) sources of authority,[6] the analysis conducted and the conclusion reached in this chapter is not the entire story. Nevertheless, even a narrow and strict originalist reading of the Indian Commerce Clause must compel the interpretation that Congress had authority under the Clause to enact ICWA.

An Originalist Perspective of "Commerce" with Indian Tribes

The predominant mode of modern constitutional interpretation likely is "originalism."[7] Originalists hold that the only legitimate interpretation of ambiguity in the Constitution is through discerning the original meaning of the Constitution to the Framers and/or ratifiers of the time period around the Constitutional Convention of 1787 and the ultimate ratification of the Constitution in 1789.[8] Originalism is the product of conservative scholars and judges intent on wiping away the work of the Warren Court and its notion of a "living constitution."[9] Originalists tend to be textualists as well, meaning that they would follow the plain meaning of the provisions of the Constitution first and above all other possible interpretations.

Originalism can be for everybody, which could be its most serious fault. One of the major problems with originalism is the almost impossible task of discerning the original meaning or intent of the Constitution, opening the door to a plethora of competing interpretations.[10] Consider the question of the Second Amendment, about which federal courts have marshaled significant and persuasive historical evidence that supports two separate and competing interpretations of the right to bear arms.[11] Not all federal and state court judges label themselves as "originalists," but an increasing minority of judges (and two or more Supreme Court justices) attempt to follow its tenets. As a matter of clarity and an attempt to appeal to conservative judges and scholars, this chapter will attempt to provide an originalist perspective of the Indian Commerce Clause, as well as the Tenth Amendment's relation to Indian affairs.

There are at least two schools of thought on originalism. The first critical school elevates "original meaning" or "original understanding" to the most critical and legitimate form of meaning.[12] The original meaning of the terms and phrases of the Constitution includes the understanding of the average reader of the Constitution around the time of the ratification or shortly thereafter. Of course, the average reader did not tend to write down their interpretation of the Constitution, so the proponents of the original meaning look to secondary sources, such as the interpretation of the Constitution given by the First Congress, or the early statements of the Framers. Of particular note are the Federalist Papers, authored by James Madison, Alexander Hamilton, and John Jay for the purpose of convincing the New York constitutional convention to ratify the Constitution.[13] Often, the proponents of the original meaning look to the dictionaries of the day to discern the public meaning of constitutional provisions.[14]

A second major school of originalism moves "original intent" to the forefront.

The original intent of the Framers includes the purposes that the Constitution was intended to serve.[15] The evidence used to discern the original intent of the Constitution includes the statements and notes of the Framers during the Constitutional Convention, and the debates surrounding each state's decision on whether to ratify the Constitution. The Federalist Papers also serve as a primary source of authority for the proponents of original intent, and in general any of the statements of any of the Framers could be used to discern the intent of the Framers. The general principles governing the use of historical evidence tend to be looser here than for the discovery of original meaning, but both groups tend to use the same kinds of evidence to suit their purposes.

Despite the emphasis on historical evidence, all interpreters of the Constitution must begin with the plain language of the document. Article I, section 8, clause 3 reads, "Congress shall have Power... To regulate commerce with foreign nations, and among the several states, and with the Indian tribes." Congress stated that it would primarily rely on this language for authority to enact the Indian Child Welfare Act, but it was not doing so because of the language alone. Almost one hundred years of Supreme Court precedent strongly supported Congress's view of its authority under the Indian Commerce Clause, with the Court holding on numerous occasions that congressional authority under the Clause was "plenary." The Court's jurisprudence in the area as of 1978 had almost entirely been "hands-off," with the Court often holding that the question of whether congressional authority under the Indian Commerce Clause was sufficient was a non-justiciable political question. In short, the Court had never struck down an Act of Congress in Indian affairs, even those that appeared to transgress the boundaries of "commerce."

The one exception, which could barely be called an exception, was *United States v. Kagama*,[16] where the Court upheld congressional authority to extend federal criminal law and federal court jurisdiction into Indian Country under the Major Crimes Act.[17] The Court held that the Indian Commerce Clause could not be held to be the sole source of authority for Congress's action,[18] but that sufficient structural, statutory, and political sources of authority existed instead.[19]

It suffices to state for now that as of 1978, the great weight of legal authority would hold that congressional power under the Indian Commerce Clause was broad, plenary, exclusive of state authority, and subject only to a rational-basis test for constitutionality.[20] In other words, Congress would have believed and understood that its authority under the Indian Commerce Clause was sufficient to enact ICWA. This incredibly broad power has since come under scrutiny by legal scholars and even a few judges, most notably Justice Thomas. These challenges will be discussed in the final portion of this chapter.

Once the plain language of the constitutional provision has been deemed ambiguous, then the interpreter may look to interpretative tools. As "Indian Commerce" is undefined by the Constitution—as in fact almost all provisions in the Constitution remain—it is appropriate to begin interpretation of the Clause. There are many potential roads to follow at this point. One of the great flaws of (or opportunities afforded by) the Constitution is the lack of an interpretive guide, meaning that there are no interpretative rules to follow. As Yale law professor Jed Rubenfeld wrote:

> In constitutional law ... there are no such overarching interpretive precepts or protocols. There are no official interpretive rules at all. In any given case raising an undecided constitutional question, nothing in any current constitutional law stops a judge from relying on original intent, if the judge wishes. But nothing stops a judge from ignoring original intent, if a judge wishes. Or suppose a plaintiff comes to court asserting an unwritten constitutional right. Under current case law, judges are fully authorized to dismiss the right because the Constitution says nothing about it. Another admissible option, however, is to uphold the right on nontextual grounds. Evolving American values? Judges can consult them or have nothing to do with them.[21]

We will discuss two interpretive modes, with an emphasis on originalism. The first, another favorite of conservative scholars and judges and that we can dispense with quickly, is textualism. A textualist reading of the Constitution would allow the interpreter the chance to interpret the plain language of the provision as it relates to the other provisions in the Constitution,[22] or (perhaps to some extent) the overall structure of the Constitution.[23]

A textualist reading of the Indian Commerce Clause does not answer the question of whether the Indian Commerce Clause authorizes the Act. However, a textualist reading could lead an interpreter into a significant trap that would tend to obliterate the original meaning and intent of the Indian Commerce Clause. It would work this way. First, a textualist would note that the Indian Commerce Clause is part of a strange trichotomy in the Constitution—sometimes known as the Three Commerce Clauses. Article I, section 8, clause 3 of the Constitution reads: "The Congress shall have Power.... To regulate Commerce with foreign Nations, and among the several States, and with the Indian Tribes ..." The three clauses are the Interstate Commerce Clause, the Foreign Nations Commerce Clause, and the Indian Commerce Clause. A textualist would interpret the three clauses, because they are so linked together, in the same way.[24] As such, a textualist would use the same definition of "commerce" for all three clauses. Therein rests the trap. Two influential originalist legal scholars appear to have fallen into this trap.[25] Decades ago, Professor Albert Abel offered compelling historical evidence that the Indian Commerce Clause should not be interpreted in light of the Interstate or Foreign Nations commerce clauses.[26]

Professor Abel offered historical evidence that tends to show that the original intent of the Framers in drafting the Indian Commerce Clause was completely separate from the other two commerce clauses. First, Professor Abel asserted that "the Indian trade was almost exclusively an *internal* trade."[27] He offered this assertion as a possible argument refuting the notion that Congress's Interstate Commerce Clause authority can never reach inside domestic, intrastate commerce, but rejected it himself because, he stated, "The Indian trade was a special subject with a definite content, which had been within the jurisdiction of congress under the articles of confederation, although with certain ambiguous qualifications omitted from the constitutional provision. *It was thus derived from a totally different branch ... than did the control over foreign and interstate commerce.*"[28] Professor Abel demonstrated that the Interstate and Foreign Nations Commerce Clause had been debated and approved long before James Madison implored the Convention to incorporate an Indian affairs clause into the Constitution:[29]

> The provision for regulation of commerce with foreign nations and among the several states had been published by the committee of detail two weeks, and definitely approved by the convention two days, before the subject of the Indian trade was introduced on the floor of the convention. It was not until several days later that the latter reported out of committee, still encumbered with some of the qualifications attached to it in the articles; and less than two weeks before the close of the convention that it was finally incorporated with the rest of the commerce clause and approved in the form with which we are familiar. By this time, the larger part of the discussion in the federal convention relative to commercial regulations was over, and in that which did take place later there is no language relating even remotely to Indian trade.[30]

Professor Abel, after listing the evidence, concluded, "Whatever regulation of commerce might mean in connection with transactions with the Indians, it was so distinct and specialized a subject as to afford no basis for argument as to the meaning of the rest of the clause."[31] Originalist scholars do not mention these records whatsoever in their discussion of the Indian Commerce Clause. It would appear that a textualist reading of the Indian Commerce Clause in conjunction with the other two commerce clauses likely is implausible. The Framers original intent was to distinguish them.

Moreover, the Framers intended that Congress's authority over Indian Commerce extend beyond mere "commerce." As Professor Robert Stern argued, the Framers intended the Constitution to serve as a "fix" on the problem of the Articles of Confederation, which had allowed the states to muddy the waters of federal Indian affairs policy.[32] Stern asserted that "the whole spirit of the proceedings indicates that ... the draughtsmen meant commerce to have a broad meaning with relation to the Indians ...."[33] In fact, Stern acknowledged that "[t]he exigencies of the time may have called for a more complete system of regulating affairs with the Indians than of controlling commerce among the states . . . ."[34]

But what of the original meaning of the Indian Commerce Clause? The original meaning of the Indian Commerce Clause squares with the original intent of the Framers. Professor Akhil Amar has argued that the First Congress answered the question when it adopted the first Trade and Intercourse Act.[35] The act, in the words of the leading treatise on federal Indian law, "contain[s] the fundamental elements of federal Indian policy: Federal regulation of trade with the Indians, prohibition of purchases of Indian lands except by governmental agents in official proceedings, and punishment of non-Indians committing crimes and trespasses against the Indians."[36] Professor Amar wrote, "It also bears note that none of the leading clausebound advocates of a narrow economic reading of 'commerce' has come to grips with the basic inadequacy of their reading as applied to Indian tribes, or has squarely confronted the originalist implications of the Indian Intercourse Act of 1790, in which the First Congress plainly regulated noneconomic intercourse with Indian tribes."[37] The criminal-law provision of the 1790 Act goes well beyond a narrow definition of "commerce" and represented the First Congress's understanding of the Indian Commerce Clause. As Professor Jerry Mashaw wrote: "From the political perspective of the late eighteenth century, commerce with the Indian tribes may have seemed less like regulating interstate commerce than like some combination of the exercise of the war and foreign affairs powers."[38]

In sum, from either the perspective of original meaning or original intent, the Indian Commerce Clause should be interpreted broadly to include subject matters beyond the narrow meaning (whatever it may be) of "commerce." The question, then, is whether Congress's Indian Commerce Clause authority extends into the realm of social legislation and regulation of family affairs as provided for in the Indian Child Welfare Act.

Purposes and Scope of the Act: Limiting the States in their Constitutional Arena

The Indian Child Welfare Act operates in a unique area in the realm of federalism. All areas of family law, including child custody, child endangerment, and adoption, are within the realm of state law.[39] There is nothing in the Constitution that authorizes Congress to legislate in the area of family law. Because the U.S. Constitution is an enumerated-powers constitution, as opposed to a plenary-powers constitution, whatever is not listed in the enumerated powers in Article I, for example, is reserved to the states by definition. In sum, the People did not delegate the powers to legislate in the field of family law to Congress. Of course, the Tenth Amendment, as we will see in the next section, explicitly reserves all nondelegated powers to the states or the People.

The Act, however, explicitly infringes on state authority to legislate and implement family law as it relates to Indian children. In fact, that was its very purpose. Congress took testimony from innumerable sources and concluded that with Indian children, the states had failed miserably and tragically. In *Mississippi Band of Choctaw Indians v. Holyfield*,[40] Justice Brennan's opinion for the Court reiterated many of the findings of fact that compelled Congress to intervene.[41] The House Report accompanying the Act relied on findings that "approximately 25–35 percent of all Indian children are separated from their families and placed in foster homes, adoptive homes, or institutions."[42] Extrapolating Minnesota statistics to the nation, Congress found that about 90 percent of the placements were in non-Indian homes.[43] Congress found "shocking" the disparity in placement rates for Indians and non-Indians: Indians were placed five times more often than non-Indians in Minnesota; thirteen times more often in Montana; sixteen times in South Dakota (foster care); and ten times more often in Washington (foster care).[44] Congress concluded: "It is clear that the Indian child welfare crisis is of massive proportions and that Indian families face vastly greater risks of involuntary separation than are typical of our society as a whole."[45]

Congress also found that state judges and child welfare agencies contributed to the wholesale removal of Indian children from Indian Country, using inappropriate methods.[46] Congress found that "many social workers, ignorant of Indian cultural values and social norms, make decisions that are wholly inappropriate in the context of Indian family life and that are wholly inappropriate in the context of Indian family life and so they frequently discover neglect or abandonment where none exists."[47] Moreover:

> An Indian child may have scores of, perhaps more than a hundred, relatives who are counted as close, responsible members of the family. Many social workers, untutored in the ways of Indian family life or assuming them to be socially irresponsible, consider leaving the child with persons outside the nuclear family as grounds for terminating parental rights.[48]

State agencies, Congress found, also engaged in systematic race discrimination. Congress found that "[o]ne of the grounds most frequently advanced for taking Indian children from their parents is the abuse of alcohol. However, this standard is applied unequally. In areas where rates of problem drinking among Indians and non-Indians are the same, it is rarely applied to non-Indian parents."[49] Moreover, Congress found, "Discriminatory standards have made it virtually impossible for most Indian couples to qualify as foster or adoptive parents, since they are based on middle-class values."[50] Finally, Congress found, "The decision to take Indian children from their natural homes is, in most cases, carried out without due process of law.

For example, it is rare for either Indian children or their parents to be represented by counsel or have the supporting testimony of expert witnesses."[51]

The impact on Indian children, of course, was devastating. The *Holyfield* Court quoted one social psychiatrist: "[Indian children] were finding that society was putting on them an identity which they didn't possess and taking from them an identity that they did possess."[52] On the impact of the removal of Indian children from Indian Country on Indian tribes, the Court quoted the tribal chief of the Mississippi Band of Choctaw Indians, Calvin Isaac: "Culturally, the chances of Indian survival are significantly reduced if our children, the only real means for the transmission of the tribal heritage, are to be raised in non-Indian homes and denied exposure to the ways of their People."[53] The Act's primary sponsor, House Representative Morris Udall, stated: "Indian tribes and Indian people are being drained of their children and, as a result, their future as a tribe and a people is being placed in jeopardy."[54]

Congress's ultimate conclusion, reached after years of hearings and testimony, is remarkable for its damnation of state courts and agencies: "[T]he States, exercising their recognized jurisdiction over Indian child custody proceedings through administrative and judicial bodies, have often failed to recognize the essential tribal relations of Indian people and the cultural and social standards prevailing in Indian communities."[55] Congress could have removed state jurisdiction over Indian children, but given that many Indian tribes in 1978 were unprepared to handle the influx of cases, Congress instead opted

> to protect the best interests of Indian children and to promote the stability and security of Indian tribes and families by establishing minimum federal standards for the placement of such children in foster or adoptive homes or institutions which will reflect the unique values of Indian culture and by providing for assistance to Indian tribes and organizations in the operation of child and family service programs.[56]

The Act established a "dual jurisdiction scheme," whereby the tribal courts would have exclusive jurisdiction to adjudicate Indian children domiciled in Indian Country, and presumptive jurisdiction to adjudicate Indian children domiciled outside of Indian Country.[57]

The Department of Justice argued that the Act, as applied to Indian children living far off the reservation, could violate the Tenth Amendment:[58]

> As we understood [25 U.S.C. § 1915], it would, for example, impose those detailed procedures on a New York State court sitting in Manhattan where that court was adjudicating the custody of an Indian child and even though the procedure otherwise applicable in this State court proceeding were constitutionally

sufficient. While we think that Congress might impose such requirements on State courts exercising jurisdiction over reservation Indians pursuant to Public Law 83-280, we are not convinced that Congress' power to control the incidents of such litigation involving nonreservation Indian children and parents pursuant to the Indian commerce clause is sufficient to override the significant State interest in regulating the procedure to be followed by its courts in exercising State jurisdiction over what is a traditionally State matter. It seems to us that the Federal interest in the off-reservation context is so attenuated that the 10th Amendment and general principles of federalism preclude the wholesale invasion of State power contemplated by [25 U.S.C. § 1915].[59]

Of course, Congress attempted to rectify the alleged constitutional infirmity by relying upon more than just the Indian Commerce Clause,[60] but the Department of Justice's Tenth Amendment concerns require additional contemplation.

The Strange Case of Indian Tribes and the Tenth Amendment

The Tenth Amendment has served as both a weak or nonexistent restriction on Congress's authority under the Commerce Clause and also a relatively powerful one, depending on the era. From the last decades of the nineteenth century until 1937, the Supreme Court often relied upon the Tenth Amendment to limit congressional power to regulate commerce.[61] The strongest statement of states' rights during that period came in *The Child Labor Case* (*Hammer v. Dagenhart*),[62] where the Court struck down a federal statute banning the shipment of goods made by children working more than eight hours a day or six days a week. The Court noted that if it upheld federal authority to regulate child labor, "all freedom of commerce will be at an end, and the power of the States over local matters may be eliminated, and thus our system of government be practically destroyed."[63] But in *United States v. Darby*,[64] the Court noted that the Tenth Amendment's limitation on Congress's power under the Commerce Clause was a "truism."[65] From 1937 until 1995, the Court had not struck down a single federal statute regulating commerce, even that which on the surface appeared to be completely internal commerce[66] or involved subject matters often considered to be matters of exclusively state control.[67] The Court adopted a permissive rule whereby the Court would not inquire into congressional authority under the Commerce Clause so long as there was a rational basis to link the congressional action to commerce.[68]

In 1995, the Court struck down aspects of a federal gun-control act criminalizing the possession of guns near public schools.[69] In 2000, the Court struck down a federal statute imposing criminal penalties on individuals who committed violence motivated by the gender of the victim.[70] While the Court in both of these cases referenced the Tenth Amendment's reservation of state power to regulate family affairs,[71] neither relied on a Tenth Amendment bar. The Court articulated a new rule: "[T]he proper test requires an analysis of whether the regulated activity 'substantially affects' interstate commerce."[72]

In addition, the Court in recent decades has resurrected the Tenth Amendment from its status as "truism." In *Gregory v. Ashcroft*,[73] the Court noted that the Tenth Amendment, alongside the Guarantee Clause, authorizes the states "to determine the qualifications of their most important government officials"[74]—in that case, state judges, which had the effect of barring the application of the federal Age Discrimination in Employment Act of 1967 to those judges.[75] The next term, in *New York v. United States*,[76] the Court struck down a federal statute offering incentives to states to adopt a rigorous regulating scheme relating to low-level radioactive waste.[77]

New York offered a spin on the *Darby* Court's labeling of the Tenth Amendment as a truism that turned a "tautology" into a relatively powerful limit on congressional authority, one that only the Court could constitutionally identify. First, the Court agreed with the *Darby* Court.[78] Next, the Court noted that the Tenth Amendment does serve as a "limit" that "restrains the power of Congress."[79] Of course, Justice O'Connor's majority opinion implicitly reserved to the Supreme Court the authority to determine whether the federal government exceeded the limits of the Tenth Amendment.[80] The *New York* Court adopted an "anti-commandeering" rule as the standard for when Congress has violated the Tenth Amendment: "Congress may not simply 'commandee[r]' the legislative processes of the States by directly compelling them to enact and enforce a federal regulatory program."[81] The Court added, in an attempt at clarification, that "[w]hile Congress has substantial powers to govern the Nation directly, including in areas of intimate concern to the States, the Constitution has never been understood to confer upon Congress the ability to govern according to Congress' instructions."[82] The Court concluded, "We have always understood that even where Congress has authority under the Constitution to pass laws requiring or prohibiting certain acts, it lacks the power directly to compel the States to require or prohibit those acts."[83]

The question, then, under the Court's Tenth Amendment jurisprudence after *New York*, might be whether the Indian Child Welfare Act could be said either to commandeer the regulatory mechanisms of the states or to require the states to adopt a particular regulatory mechanism. It is debatable, perhaps, whether a jurisdictional scheme and minimum federal standards relating to the placement of Indian children amount to a "commandeering" of state regulatory mechanisms, but that statement of the law is incomplete without a reminder that the Tenth Amendment and congressional authority under the Indian Commerce Clause simply do not match up.

The Tenth Amendment would reserve the powers and authorities of the states, absent a particular provision in the Constitution granting that power to the federal government. In many areas, such as commerce or taxation, the federal government and the states retain a concurrent power, subject to the Supremacy Clause.[84] But what about situations where the Constitution reserves *no* powers and authorities to the states? There are at least two such areas, and they are somewhat related: foreign affairs and Indian affairs. It is well settled that no foreign affairs powers are reserved to the states under the Constitution.[85]

It is equally well settled that no Indian affairs powers are reserved to the states. As James Madison lamented in Federalist No. 42:

> The regulation of commerce with the Indian tribes is very properly unfettered from two limitations in the articles of Confederation, which render the provision obscure and contradictory. The power is there restrained to Indians, not members of any of the States, and is not to violate or infringe the legislative right of any State within its own limits. What description of Indians are to be deemed members of a State, is not yet settled, and has been a question of frequent perplexity and contention in the federal councils. And how the trade with Indians, thoughnot members of a State, yet residing within its legislative jurisdiction, can be regulated by an external authority, without so far intruding on the internal rights of legislation, is absolutely incomprehensible. This is not the only case in which the articles of Confederation have inconsiderately endeavored to accomplish impossibilities; to reconcile a partial sovereignty in the Union, with complete sovereignty in the States; to subvert a mathematical axiom, by taking away a part, and letting the whole remain.[86]

One of the flaws of the Articles of Confederation identified by Madison was the problem of the proviso in Article IX, clause 4 relating to Indian tribes. The whole clause read: "The United States in Congress assembled shall also have the sole and exclusive right and power of ... regulating the trade and managing all affairs with the Indians, not members of any of the States, *provided that the legislative right of any State within its own limits be not infringed or violated* . . . ."[87] The proviso to the grant of authority to Congress to deal in Indian affairs exclusively undermined the purpose of the exclusive grant, rendering the entire provision "incomprehensible" to Madison.[88] As implied earlier, the solution proposed by Madison during the 1787 Constitutional Convention was to eliminate the states from the question of Indian affairs in the entirety.[89] The Supreme Court's decisions in the field of the Tenth Amendment and Indian affairs are uniform: The states have no authority (except that expressly granted by Congress) in Indian affairs.[90]

Regardless of whether one views congressional authority under the Commerce Clause as sufficient to enact the Indian Child Welfare Act, the Tenth Amendment poses no bar whatsoever on congressional authority under the Act. As the Court stated decisively in *Seminole Tribe of Florida v. Florida*, "[T]he States . . . have been divested of virtually all authority over Indian commerce and Indian tribes."[91] In short, in this unique area of federal law, the Supreme Court cannot use its power to interpret the Tenth Amendment to restrict any action of Congress under the Indian Commerce Clause.[92]

Nevertheless, some California appellate courts followed the suggestion of the 1978 Department of Justice letter and applied the Tenth Amendment to hold that ICWA was unconstitutional as applied to certain off-reservation Indian children.[93] These courts held, as the Justice letter suggested, that Congress's interest (and by logical extension, the tribe's interest) in Indian children domiciled far from their tribe's lands does not outweigh the state's interest in adjudicating the children.[94] But the federal or tribal "interest" in Indian children, regardless of where they are domiciled, is irrelevant in the original understanding of the Indian Commerce Clause.[95] Congress—and only Congress—has the authority to determine who is an Indian or not for purposes of national legislation on Indian affairs.[96] Since the Tenth Amendment reserves nothing to the states and, more importantly, *grants* nothing to the states,[97] its presence in the Commerce Clause equation is eliminated. In fact, several courts have rejected Tenth Amendment challenges to ICWA.[98] But they have done so with little or no analysis of the original understanding of the Indian Commerce Clause and its relationship to the Tenth Amendment.

The Constitutionality of ICWA under the Original Public Meaning of the Indian Commerce Clause

With the Tenth Amendment out of the picture, the question of determining whether Congress's authority under the Indian Commerce Clause is sufficient to enact the Indian Child Welfare Act becomes a much simpler task. Under the Interstate Commerce Clause, the test applied by the Supreme Court—with the Tenth Amendment's reservation of states' rights built in—is "whether the regulated activity 'substantially affects' interstate commerce."[99] But since that test assumed that states' rights have a role to play in the equation, it should not be applicable in the analysis of whether ICWA is constitutional under the Indian Commerce Clause.

The general test that the Supreme Court adopted and applied as to whether an act of Congress was authorized by the Indian Commerce Clause is the so-called "rational basis test."[100] According to the Court, so long as the statute is rationally related to the "fulfillment of Congress' unique obligation toward the Indians . . ."[101] the exercise of congressional authority is authorized by the Constitution. If we were to tweak this test to conform to the original public meaning of the Indian Commerce Clause, we would have to take into consideration, for example, how the First Congress understood the extent of congressional power under the Indian Commerce Clause.

The First Congress enacted the Trade and Intercourse Act of 1790, extending federal criminal law and jurisdiction into Indian Country as applied to non-Indian and Indian crimes, which in turn implicitly defined "Indian Commerce" to include not only economic intercourse, but also social interactions between Indians and non-Indians. As explained above, the original understanding of "Commerce" under the Interstate and Foreign Commerce clauses differs substantially from "Indian Commerce." The question then is whether Congress could have rationally believed that the removal and placement of Indian children is a question of "Indian Commerce."

This restatement of the test is not so dissimilar from the Interstate and Foreign Commerce Clause test that the Supreme Court adopted and applied from 1937 to 1995. The Court "defer[red] to what is often a merely implicit congressional judgment that its regulation addresses a subject substantially affecting interstate commerce 'if there is any rational basis for such a finding.'"[102] According to Justice Souter's dissent in *Lopez*, the Court deferred to Congress because "it reflects our respect for the institutional competence of the Congress on a subject expressly assigned to it by the Constitution and our appreciation of the legitimacy that comes from Congress's political accountability in dealing with matters open to a wide range of possible choices."[103] Of course, Justice Souter's formulation of past Commerce Clause doctrine appeared in a dissent to a case that apparently wiped away much of that deference.[104]

But the Indian Commerce Clause is different. Given that the Framers intended, and the First Congress understood, that the states should have no role whatsoever (absent congressional consent) in the field of Indian affairs, Supreme Court deference to the actions of Congress under the Indian Commerce Clause should be at its "zenith."[105] And Supreme Court deference from long before the time of *Kagama* until the advent of the Rehnquist Court was all but absolute, with the Court often refusing to question the exercise of congressional (and delegated executive branch) Indian affairs powers, labeling its exercise a non-justiciable political question.[106] It would be a monumental misreading of history for a judge to disregard the difference between the Indian Commerce Clause and the rest of the Commerce Clause. There is no serious doubt that the First Congress would have viewed ICWA as applied on or near reservation land as well within the purview of Indian Commerce.

But the more difficult question is whether the original public meaning of the Indian Commerce Clause supports the application of ICWA to Indian children with a nominal tie to Indian Country. This was the exact concern posed by the Department of Justice in 1978 and by the California appellate court in 2001.[107] The argument goes like this: ICWA applies to an Indian child domiciled far from Indian Country who is eligible for membership in an Indian tribe, but who perhaps has never lived in or even visited his reservation.[108] The state or the child's advocate argues that the definition of "Indian child" is overinclusive, meaning that it includes within its grasp children who are not really Indians. These children should be adjudicated in state courts as would other non-Indian children. ICWA amounts to an intrusion into Tenth Amendment-reserved states' rights.[109] Of course, this exact theory was advanced by the State of Mississippi in *United States v. John*—and the Court rejected the claim.[110] There, the State "suggest[ed] that since 1830 the Choctaws residing in Mississippi have become fully assimilated into the political and social life of the State, and that the Federal Government long ago abandoned its supervisory authority over these Indians."[111] Moreover, an understanding of the original relationship between the Indian Commerce Clause and the Tenth Amendment undermines this argument.

There is a different way to view this claim from an originalist perspective. Consider that the Constitution assumes at least two classes or categories of Indians— "Indians not taxed"[112] and, presumably, "Indians taxed."[113] Indians not taxed were excluded from the population count for purposes of representation, but neither class could vote, regardless.[114] The claim that some Indians have "assimilated" and are therefore under state jurisdiction (reserved by the Tenth Amendment) ignores the fact that Congress has *exclusive* authority as of the ratification to determine who is an Indian (Not Taxed) and who is not (Taxed).[115] Consider, for example, the Stockbridge-Munsee Community in Wisconsin.[116] The tribe agreed in 1735 to settle in a small community in western Massachusetts, a praying town.[117] Around 1831, the tribe agreed to remove west to Wisconsin.[118] In 1843, Congress disestablished the tribe and subjected its members to state jurisdiction.[119] A mere three years later, Congress repealed the 1843 act and restored the tribe's status as an Indian tribe, presumably restoring their "Indians Not Taxed" status.[120] State courts and state officers are simply not authorized to make their own determination about who is an Indian and who is not, especially when the program or policy the states are interpreting is not their own.[121]

Conclusion

Although Congress hedged its bet when it listed more than the Indian Commerce Clause alone as its stated sources of constitutional authority to enact the Indian Child Welfare Act, there was ample authority in the Clause. The Indian Commerce Clause is to be interpreted differently from the Interstate and Foreign Commerce clauses. Both the original intent of the Framers and the original public meaning of the Indian Commerce Clause compel this result. A resort to the Tenth Amendment reservation of non-enumerated rights does nothing to reduce congressional authority under the Indian Commerce Clause, because all historical evidence points to an inescapable conclusion: the original intent and meaning of the Indian Commerce Clause was to make Congressional authority plenary and *exclusive* as to the states.

NOTES

1. Pub. L. 95-608, 92 Stat. 3069 (1978), *codified as amended at* 25 U.S.C. § 1901 et seq.
2. *Miss. Band of Choctaw Indians v. Holyfield*, 490 U.S. 30 (1989).
3. *E.g.*, *In re Bridget R.*, 41 Cal. App. 4th 1483, 1510-11 (1996). *Cf. Agua Caliente Band of Cahuilla Indians v. Superior Court*, 148 P.3d 1126, 1136-38 (Cal. 2006) (applying the Tenth Amendment in conjunction with the Guarantee Clause to find a waiver of tribal sovereign immunity).
4. *E.g.*, Carole E. Goldberg, *Descent into Race*, 49 UCLA L. REV. 1373 (2002); Cheyañna L. Jaffke, *The "Existing Indian Family" Exception to the Indian Child Welfare Act: The States' Attempt to Slaughter Tribal Interests in Indian Children*, 66 LA. L. REV. 733, 755-57 (2006); Christine Metteer, *The Existing Indian Family Exception: An Impediment to the Trust Responsibility to Preserve Tribal Existence and Culture as Manifested in the Indian Child Welfare Act*, 30 LOY. L.A. L. REV. 647, 672-87 (1997). For a view that ICWA violates the due-process and equal-protection clauses, *see* Christine D. Bakeis, *The Indian Child Welfare Act of 1978: Violating Personal Rights for the Sake of the Tribe*, 10 NOTRE DAME J. L. ETHICS & PUB. POL'Y 543 (1996).
5. U.S. CONST. art. I, § 8, cl. 3.
6. *See* 25 U.S.C. § 1901(1) (relying upon the Indian Commerce Clause "and other constitutional authority" for the plenary power of Congress in Indian Affairs); 25 U.S.C. § 1901(2) ("Congress, through statutes, treaties, and the general course of dealing with Indian tribes, has assumed the responsibility for the protection and preservation of Indian tribes and their resources . . . .").
7. *See* Morton J. Horowitz, *Foreword—The Constitution of Change: Legal Fundamentality without Fundamentalism*, 107 HARV. L. REV. 30, 44 (1993).
8. *See generally* RAOUL BERGER, GOVERNMENT BY JUDICIARY (Harvard University Press 1977); ROBERT BORK, THE TEMPTING OF AMERICA: THE POLITICAL SEDUCTION OF THE LAW (The Free Press 1990). *Contra* Mitchell N. Berman, *Originalism is Bunk*, 84 N.Y.U. L. REV. 1 (2009) (questioning whether originalism is "true").
9. *See* JAN CRAWFORD GREENBURG, SUPREME CONFLICT: THE INSIDE STORY OF THE STRUGGLE FOR CONTROL OF THE UNITED STATES SUPREME COURT 38-39, 179, 213-15 (Penguin 2007); CASS R. SUNSTEIN, RADICALS IN ROBES: WHY EXTREME RIGHT-WING COURTS ARE WRONG FOR AMERICA 36-37 (Basic Books 2005); Robert H. Bork, *Neutral Principles and Some First Amendment Problems*, in MODERN CONSTITUTIONAL THEORY: A READER 92-100 (John H. Garvey, T. Alexander Aleinikoff & Daniel A. Farber, eds., 5th ed., Thomson/West 2004). *Cf.* ANTONIN SCALIA, *Response*, in A MATTER OF INTERPRETATION: FEDERAL COURTS AND THE LAW 137, 139 (Princeton University Press 1997) (asserting that originalism should be used to prevent the judicial creation of "novel" constitutional rights).
10. *See* STEPHEN BREYER, ACTIVE LIBERTY: INTERPRETING OUR DEMOCRATIC CONSTITUTION 117 (Knopf 2006).
11. *See* Erwin Chemerinsky, *A Well-Regulated Right to Bear Arms*, WASH. POST, March 14, 2007, at A15 ("Each side of the debate marshals impressive historical arguments about what 'militia' and 'keep and bear arms' meant in the late 18th century. In the past few years, two other federal courts

of appeals exhaustively reviewed this history, and one determined that the Framers intended the individual rights approach, while the other read history as supporting the collective rights approach."). *See generally District of Columbia v. Heller*, 128 S. Ct. 2783 (2008).

12. *E.g.*, RANDY E. BARNETT, RESTORING THE LOST CONSTITUTION 100–09 (Princeton University Press 2004).

13. *See* Gregory E. Maggs, *A Concise Guide to the Federalist Papers as a Source of the Original Meaning of the United States Constitution*, 87 B.U. L. REV. 801 (2007).

14. *E.g., United States v. Lopez*, 514 U.S. 549, 585–86 (1995) (Thomas, J., concurring) (quoting several dictionaries contemporaneous to the ratification of the Constitution as evidence of the original meaning of "commerce").

15. *See* H. Jefferson Powell, *The Original Understanding of Original Intent*, 98 HARV. L. REV. 885 (1985). Professor Powell's paper is a landmark critique of originalism. *See* Mary L. Dudziak, *Remembering Powell on the Original Understanding of Original Intent*, in LEGAL HISTORY BLOG, *available at* http://legalhistoryblog.blogspot.com/2007/03/remembering-powell-on-original.html.

16. *United States v. Kagama*, 118 U.S. 375 (1886).

17. *Kagama*, 118 U.S. at 385.

18. *Kagama*, 118 U.S. at 378–79.

19. *Kagama*, 118 U.S. at 379–80.

20. *See generally* Robert Laurence, *The Indian Commerce Clause*, 23 ARIZ. L. REV. 203 223–26 (1981).

21. JED RUBENFELD, REVOLUTION BY JUDICIARY 5 (Harvard University Press 2006).

22. *See* Antonin Scalia, *Common-Law Courts in a Civil-Law System: The Role of the United States Federal Courts in Interpreting the Constitution and Laws*, in A MATTER OF INTERPRETATION, *supra* note 9, at 3, 23–25.

23. *See generally* CHARLES BLACK, STRUCTURE AND RELATIONSHIPS IN CONSTITUTIONAL LAW (Louisiana State University 1969) Akhil Reed Amar, *Intratextualism*, 112 HARV. L. REV. 747 (1999).

24. This is a canon of construction known as *ejusdem generis*—"of the same sort." Scalia, *supra* note 9, at 26.

25. *See* Randy Barnett, *The Original Meaning of the Commerce Clause*, 68 U. CHI. L. REV. 101, 146 (2001); Saikrishna Prakash, *Against Tribal Fungibility*, 89 CORNELL L. REV. 1069, 1087–90 (2004); *see also* Saikrishna Prakash, *Our Three Commerce Clauses and the Presumption of Intrasentence Uniformity*, 55 ARK. L. REV. 1149, 1167 (2003) ("One might expect that the Indian commerce subpart would be read in a similar manner as its counterparts."); *id.* at 1168 (noting that the Court's Indian Commerce Clause jurisprudence has only been established by "judicial fiat"). *Cf. United States v. Lara*, 541 U.S. 193, 215, 224 (2004) (Thomas, J., concurring in the judgment) (citing *United States v. Morrison*, 529 U.S. 598 (2000); *United States v. Lopez*, 514 U S. 549 (1995); *id.* at 584–93 (Thomas, J., concurring)).

26. *See* Albert S. Abel, *The Commerce Clause in the Constitutional Convention and in Contemporary Comment*, 25 MINN. L. REV. 432, 467–68 (1941); *see also Cotton Petroleum Corp. v. N.M.*, 490 U.S. 163, 192 (1989) (noting in dicta that "the Interstate Commerce and Indian Commerce Clauses have very different applications").

27. Abel, *supra* note 26, at 467.
28. Abel, *supra* note 26, at 467 (citing ARTICLES OF CONFEDERATION art. IX(4)) (emphasis added). The "qualification" referred to by Professor Abel is the notorious proviso in the Indian Affairs Clause reserving some state authority that so infuriated James Madison. *See* THE FEDERALIST NO. 42 (James Madison) (Clinton Rossiter, ed., 1961) (referring to the proviso as "absolutely incomprehensible"); 1 RECORDS OF THE FEDERAL CONVENTION OF 1787, at 316 (Madison) (Max Farrand, ed., Yale University Press 1966) ("By the federal articles, transactions with the Indians appertain to Congs. Yet in several instances, the States have entered into treaties & wars with them.").
29. *See* 2 RECORDS OF THE FEDERAL CONVENTION OF 1787, at 324 (Madison) (Max Farrand, ed., Yale University Press 1966).
30. Abel, *supra* note 26, at 467–68 (citing 2 RECORDS, *supra* note 29, at 321).
31. Abel, *supra* note 26, at 468.
32. *See* Robert L. Stern, *That Commerce Which Concerns More States Than One*, 47 HARV. L. REV. 1335, 1342 (1934).
33. Stern, *supra* note 32, at 1342.
34. Stern, *supra* note 32, at 1342 n. 27.
35. Act of July 22, 1790, 1 STAT. 137 (1789–1799), *codified as amended at* 25 U.S.C. § 177 (hereinafter Trade and Intercourse Act of 1790).
36. COHEN'S HANDBOOK OF FEDERAL INDIAN LAW § 1.03[2], at 37 (Nell Jessup Newton et al. eds., LexisNexis 2005) (citing FRANCIS PAUL PRUCHA, THE GREAT FATHER: THE UNITED STATES GOVERNMENT AND THE AMERICAN INDIANS 30 (University of Nebraska 1984)).
37. Akhil Reed Amar, *America's Constitution and the Yale School of Interpretation*, 115 YALE L.J. 1997, 2004 n. 25 (2006); *see also* Akhil Reed Amar, AMERICA'S CONSTITUTION: A BIOGRAPHY 108 n. (Random House 2005) ("It also bears notice that the First Congress enacted a statute regulating noneconomic interactions and altercations—'intercourse'—with Indians. . . . Section 5 of this act dealt with crimes—whether economic or not—committed by Americans on Indian lands.") (citing Trade and Intercourse Act of 1790).
38. Jerry L. Mashaw, *Recovering American Administrative Law, 1787–1801*, 115 YALE L.J. 1256, 1300 (2006).
39. *See Egelhoff v. Egelhoff ex rel. Breiner*, 532 U.S. 141, 151 (2001) (citing *Hisquierdo v. Hisquierdo*, 439 U.S. 572, 581 (1979)). *See generally United States v. Morrison*, 529 U.S. 598, 615–16 (2000); *Boggs v. Boggs*, 520 U.S. 833, 861 (1997) (Breyer, J., dissenting); *United States v. Lopez*, 514 U.S. 549, 564 (1995).
40. *Miss. Band of Choctaw Indians v. Holyfield*, 490 U.S. 30 (1989); Jay S. Bybee, *The Tenth Amendment among the Shadows: On Reading the Constitution in Plato's Cave*, 23 HARV. J. L. & PUB. POL'Y 551, 564 (2000) (citing *Lopez*, 514 U.S. at 564).
41. *Holyfield*, 490 U.S. at 33–36.
42. Establishing Standards for the Placement of Indian Children in Foster or Adoptive Homes, to Prevent the Breakup of Indian Families, and for Other Purposes, H.R. Rep. No. 95-1386, at 9

(July 24, 1978); *see also Holyfield*, 490 U.S. at 32–33 (citing *Indian Child Welfare Program, Hearings before the Subcommittee on Indian Affairs of the Senate Committee on Interior and Insular Affairs*, 93rd Cong., 2d Sess. at 15 (1974) (hereinafter 1974 Hearings) (Statement of William Byler)).

43. H.R. Rep. No. 95-1386, at 9; *see also Holyfield*, 490 U.S. at 33 (citing 1974 Hearings, *supra* note 42, at 75–83).
44. H.R. Rep. No. 95-1386, at 9.
45. H.R. Rep. No. 95-1386, at 9.
46. *See* 25 U.S.C. § 1901(4) ("[A]n alarmingly high percentage of Indian families are broken up by the removal, often unwarranted, of their children from them by nontribal public and private agencies and that an alarmingly high percentage of such children are placed in non-Indian foster and adoptive homes and institutions ....").
47. H.R. Rep. No. 95-1386, at 10.
48. H.R. Rep. No. 95-1386, at 10.
49. H.R. Rep. No. 95-1386, at 10.
50. H.R. Rep. No. 95-1386, at 11.
51. H.R. Rep. No. 95-1386, at 11.
52. *Holyfield*, 490 U.S. at 33 n. 1 (quoting 1974 Hearings, *supra* note 42, at 46 (Statement of Dr. Joseph Westermeyer, University of Minnesota social psychiatrist)).
53. *Holyfield*, 490 U.S. at 34 (quoting *Hearings on S. 1214 before the Subcommittee on Indian Affairs and Public Lands of the House Committee on Interior and Insular Affairs*, 95th Cong., 2d Sess. 193 (1978) (Statement of Calvin Isaac, tribal chief of the Mississippi Band of Choctaw Indians and representative of the National Tribal Chairmen's Association)).
54. 124 CONG. REC. 38102 (1978), *quoted in Holyfield*, 490 U.S. at 34 n. 3; *see also* 25 U.S.C. § 1901(3) ("[T]here is no resource that is more vital to the continued existence and integrity of Indian tribes than their children ....").
55. 25 U.S.C. § 1901(5).
56. H.R. Rep. No. 95-1368, at 8.
57. 25 U.S.C. § 1911.
58. *See* H.R. Rep. No. 95-1368, at 38, 40 (reprinting Letter from Patricia M. Wald, Assistant Attorney General, United States Dept. of Justice, to Hon. Morris K. Udall, Chairman, Committee on Interior and Insular Affairs, House of Representatives (May 23, 1978) (hereinafter Wald Letter). Ms. Wald served as a judge on the D.C. Circuit from 1979 to 1991.
59. H.R. Rep. No. 95-1368, at 40 (citing H. L. A. Hart, *The Relations between State and Federal Law*, 54 COLUM. L. REV. 489, 508 (1954)).
60. *See* 25 U.S.C. §§ 1901(1)-(2).
61. *See* ERWIN CHEMERINSKY, CONSTITUTIONAL LAW: PRINCIPLES AND POLICIES § 3.3.3, at 253 (3d ed., Aspen Publishers 2006).
62. *Hammer v. Dagenhart*, 247 U.S. 251 (1918).
63. *Hammer*, 247 U.S. at 276.
64. 312 U.S. 100 (1941).

65. *United States v. Darby*, 312 U.S. 100, 124 (1941) ("The amendment states but a truism that all is retained which has not been surrendered."); *see also* 3 JOSEPH STORY, COMMENTARIES ON THE CONSTITUTION OF THE UNITED STATES 752 (Hilliard, Gray 1833) ("Th[e Tenth Amendment] is a mere affirmation of what, upon any just reasoning, is a necessary rule of interpreting the constitution. Being an instrument of limited and enumerated powers, it follows irresistibly, that what is not conferred, is withheld, and belongs to the state authorities."), *quoted in New York v. United States*, 505 U.S. 144, 156 (1992).
66. *E.g., Katzenbaugh v. McClung*, 379 U.S. 294 (1964); *Wickard v. Filburn*, 317 U.S. 111 (1942); *United States v. Fainblatt*, 306 U.S. 601 (1939).
67. *E.g., NLRB v. Jones & Laughlin Steel Corp.*, 301 U.S. 1 (1937).
68. *See Hodel v. Indiana*, 452 U.S. 314, 323–24 (1981); Chemerinsky, *supra* note 61, § 3.3.4 at 259–63.
69. *United States v. Lopez*, 514 U.S. 549 (1995).
70. *United States v. Morrison*, 529 U.S. 598 (2000).
71. *See Morrison*, 529 U.S. at 615–16; *Lopez*, 514 U.S. at 564.
72. *Lopez*, 514 U.S. at 559; Chemerinsky, *supra* note 61, § 3.3.5 at 264–69.
73. *Gregory v. Ashcroft*, 501 U.S. 452 (1991).
74. *Gregory*, 501 U.S. at 463.
75. *See Gregory*, 501 U.S. at 470. The Court did not strike down the statute, but instead held on narrower grounds that the language of the statute was ambiguous as to its application to state judges, allowing the Court to read the statute narrowly to avoid the constitutional complications. *See id.*
76. *New York v. United States*, 505 U.S. 144 (1992).
77. *See New York*, 505 U.S. at 151–54, 188.
78. *New York*, 505 U.S. at 156 (quoting *United States v. Darby*, 312 U.S. 100, 124 (1941)); *see also id.* at 156–57 ("The Tenth Amendment ... is essentially a tautology.").
79. *New York*, 505 U.S. at 156; *see also id.* at 157 ("[T]he Tenth Amendment confirms that the power of the Federal Government is subject to limits that may, in a given instance, reserve power to the States.").
80. *See New York*, 505 U.S. at 157 ("The Tenth Amendment thus directs *us* to determine ... whether an incident of state sovereignty is protected by a limitation on an Article I power.") (emphasis added).
81. *New York*, 505 U.S. at 161 (bracket in original) (quoting *Hodel v. Virginia Surface Mining & Reclamation Ass'n, Inc.*, 452 U.S. 264, 288 (1981)).
82. *New York*, 505 U.S. at 162 (citing *Coyle v. Smith*, 221 U.S. 559, 565 (1911)).
83. *New York*, 505 U.S. at 166 (citing *FERC v. Mississippi*, 456 U.S. 742, 762–66 (1982); *Hodel v. Virginia Surface Mining & Reclamation Ass'n, Inc.*, 452 U.S. 264, 288–89 (1981); *Lane County v. Oregon*, 7 Wall. 71, 76 (1869)).
84. *See generally Gibbons v. Ogden*, 22 U.S. 1 (1824).
85. *See generally* LOUIS HENKIN, FOREIGN AFFAIRS AND THE US CONSTITUTION 83–148 (2d ed., Transnational 1996).

86. FEDERALIST No. 42, at 269 (James Madison) (Clinton Rossiter, ed., 1961).
87. ARTICLES OF CONFEDERATION art. IX, cl. 4 (emphasis added).
88. FEDERALIST No. 42, at 269 (James Madison) (Clinton Rossiter, ed., 1961).
89. *See Worcester v. Georgia*, 31 U.S. 515, 559 (1832) ("The ambiguous phrases which follow the grant of power to the United States, were so construed by the states of North Carolina and Georgia as to annul the power itself. The discontents and confusion resulting from these conflicting claims, produced representations to congress, which were referred to a committee, who made their report in 1787. The report does not assent to the construction of the two states, but recommends an accommodation, by liberal cessions of territory, or by an admission, on their part, of the powers claimed by congress. The correct exposition of this article is rendered unnecessary by the adoption of our existing constitution. That instrument confers on congress the powers of war and peace; of making treaties, and of regulating commerce with foreign nations, and among the several states, and with the Indian tribes. These powers comprehend all that is required for the regulation of our intercourse with the Indians. They are not limited by any restrictions on their free actions. The shackles imposed on this power, in the confederation, are discarded."). *See generally* Robert N. Clinton, *The Dormant Indian Commerce Clause*, 27 CONN. L. REV. 1055, 1098–1164 (1994).
90. *See Seminole Tribe of Florida v. Florida*, 517 U.S. 44, 62 (1996); *Oneida County, N.Y. v. Oneida Indian Nation of N.Y.*, 470 U.S. 226, 234 (1985). *Cf. United States v. Forty-Three Gallons of Whiskey*, 93 U.S. 188, 194 (1876) (holding that congressional authority under the Indian Commerce Clause is exclusive).
91. *Seminole Tribe*, 517 U.S. at 62.
92. Of course, the California Supreme Court has interpreted the Tenth Amendment in conjunction with the Guarantee Clause to hold that tribal sovereign immunity is no defense where a tribe refuses to comply with a state campaign-contribution law. *See Agua Caliente Band of Cahuilla Indians v. Superior Court*, 148 P.3d 1126, 1135–39 (Cal. 2006). ICWA could not be construed in any way as implicating the Guarantee Clause. *Cf. Gregory v. Ashcroft*, 501 U.S. 452 (1991).
93. *See In re Santos Y.*, 112 Cal. Rptr. 2d 692, 731 (Cal. App. 2001); *In re Bridget R.*, 49 Cal. Rptr. 2d 507 (1996). The California legislature attempted to overrule *Bridget R.*, *see* CAL. WELF. & INST. CODE § 360.6, but the *Santos Y.* Court reached the same result regardless *see Santos Y.*, 112 Cal. Rptr. 2d at 722.
94. *See Santos Y.*, 112 Cal Rptr. 2d at 731.
95. *Cf. United States v. John*, 437 U.S. 634, 652–53 (1978) (holding that the exercise of state jurisdiction over "assimilat[ed]" Indians does not deprive the federal government of authority under the Indian Commerce Clause).
96. *See Miami Nation of Indians of Indiana, Inc. v. United States Dept. of Interior*, 255 F.3d 342, 346–47 (7th Cir. 2001) (Posner, J.), *cert. denied*, 534 U.S. 1129 (2002); STEPHEN L. PEVAR, THE RIGHTS OF INDIANS AND TRIBES 18 (3rd ed., NYU Press 2002).
97. *Agua Caliente Band of Cauhilla Indians v. Superior Court*, 148 P.3d 1126, 1143 (Cal. 2006) (Moreno, J., dissenting) (citing *Carcieri v. Norton*, 290 F. Supp. 2d 167, 189 (D. R.I. 2003); *City of Roseville v.*

Norton, 219 F. Supp. 2d 130, 153–54 (D. D.C. 2002)).
98. *E.g., In re Bird Head*, 331 N.W.2d 785, 792–93 (Neb. 1983) (Colwell, D.J., dissenting) (raising Tenth Amendment claim in dissent); *In re A.B.*, 663 N.W.2d 625, 636–37 (N.D. 2003), *cert. denied sub nom., Hoots ex rel. A.B. v. K.B.*, 541 U.S. 972 (2004); *In re Guardianship of D.L.L. & C.L.L.*, 291 N.W.2d 278, 280–81 (S.D. 1980). *See generally* COHEN'S HANDBOOK OF FEDERAL INDIAN LAW, *supra* note 36, § 11.06, at 849–50.
99. *United States v. Lopez*, 514 U.S. 549, 559 (1995).
100. *See Del. Tribal Bus. Comm. v. Weeks*, 430 U.S. 73, 85 (1977). *Cf. Morton v. Mancari*, 417 U.S. 535, 555 (1974) (applying rational-basis scrutiny to an Indian preference in employment regulation because the regulation was based on a political, rather than racial, classification).
101. *Weeks*, 430 U.S. at 85 (quoting *Mancari*, 417 U.S. at 555).
102. *United States v. Lopez*, 514 U.S. 549, 603 (Souter, J., dissenting) (quoting *Hodel v. Virginia Surface Mining & Reclamation Ass'n, Inc.*, 452 U.S. 264, 276 (1981)); *Heart of Atlanta Motel, Inc. v. United States*, 379 U.S. 241, 262 (1964); *Katzenbaugh v. McClung*, 379 U.S. 294, 303–04 (1964).
103. *Lopez*, 514 U.S. at 604 (Souter, J., dissenting) (citing *FCC v. Beach Communications, Inc.*, 508 U.S. 307, 313–16 (1993)).
104. *Cf.* MARK TUSHNET, THE NEW CONSTITUTIONAL ORDER 93–94 (Princeton University Press 2003) (arguing that the Court will defer less to Congress where it acts beyond its explicit enumerated powers).
105. *Cf. Hamdan v. Rumsfeld*, 126 S. Ct. 2749, 2825 (2006) (Thomas, J., dissenting) (arguing that the Court's deference to the President during wartime is at its "zenith").
106. *E.g., Tee-Hit-Ton Indians v. United States*, 348 U.S. 272, 281 (1955); *Tiger v. Western Investment Co.*, 221 U.S. 286, 315 (1911); *United States v. Kagama*, 118 U.S. 375, 383 (1886); *United States v. Holliday*, 70 U.S. 407, 419 (1865).
107. *See In re Santos Y.*, 112 Cal. Rptr. 2d 692, 731 (Cal. App. 2001); Wald Letter, *supra* note 58.
108. 25 U.S.C. § 1903(4) (defining "Indian child").
109. Variants of this argument are the equal-protection and due-process claims whereby the California courts held that the only reason children in this category are subjected to ICWA's restriction of state jurisdiction and different standards is race, necessitating, in the court's view, strict scrutiny analysis. *See* COHEN'S HANDBOOK OF FEDERAL INDIAN LAW, *supra* note 36, § 11.06, at 851–52.
110. *United States v. John*, 437 U.S. 634, 652–53 (1978).
111. *John*, 437 U.S. at 652.
112. U.S. CONST. art. I, § 2, cl. 3.
113. *See Elk v. Wilkins*, 112 U.S. 94, 112 (1884) (Harlan, J., dissenting) ("At the adoption of the constitution there were, in many of the states, Indians, not members of any tribe, who constituted a part of the people for whose benefit the state governments were established. This is apparent from that clause of article 1, § 3, which requires, in the apportionment of representatives and direct taxes among the several states 'according to their respective numbers,' the exclusion of 'Indians not taxed.' This implies that there were, at that time, in the United States, Indians who were

taxed; that is, were subject to taxation by the laws of the state of which they were residents. Indians not taxed were those who held tribal relations, and therefore were not subject to the authority of any state, and were subject only to the authority of the United States, under the power conferred upon congress in reference to Indian tribes in this country.")

114. *See, e.g.*, Ann Marie Plane and Gregory Button, *The Massachusetts Indian Enfranchisement Act: Ethnic Contest in Historical Context, 1849–1869*, 40 ETHNOHISTORY 587 (1993); Orlan J. Svingen, *Jim Crow, Indian Style*, 11 AM. INDIAN Q. 275 (1987). *Cf. Elk*, 112 U.S. at 109 (holding that an Indian could not become a citizen without an Act of Congress or a treaty right expressly stating so); *Scott v. Sanford*, 60 U.S. 393, 404 (1853) ("[The Indian race], it is true, formed no part of the colonial communities, and never amalgamated with them in social connections or in government. But although they were uncivilized, they were yet a free and independent people, associated together in nations or tribes, and governed by their own laws.").

115. *E.g.*, Caleb Cushing, Relation of Indians to Citizenship, 7 Op. Atty. Gen. 746, 750 (1856) (citing statutes and treaties making certain Indians American citizens, including the Stockbridge Indians).

116. *See Wisconsin v. Stockbridge-Munsee Community*, 366 F. Supp. 2d 698 (W.D. Wis. 2004), *aff'd*, 554 F.3d 657 (7th Cir. 2009).

117. *See Stockbridge-Mursee Community*, 366 F. Supp. 2d at 703.

118. *See Stockbridge-Mursee Community*, 366 F. Supp. 2d at 703–04.

119. *See Stockbridge-Munsee Community*, 366 F. Supp. 2d at 704; Act of March 3, 1843 § 7, 5 STAT. 645, 647 (1843).

120. *See Stockbridge-Mursee Community*, 366 F. Supp. 2d at 704; Act of August 6, 1846, 9 STAT. 55 (1846) (restoring the Stockbridge Indians "to their ancient form of government, with all powers, rights, and privileges, held by them under their customs and usages, as fully and completely as though the [1843] act had never been passed").

121. *Cf.* Pevar, *supra* note 96, at 18.

Reparations, Self-Determination, and the Seventh Generation

Lorie M. Graham

1. Seven Generations

> In each deliberation, we must consider the impact of our decisions on the next seven generations.
> —Great Law of the Haudenosaunee[1]

> [T]he grandmothers and grandfathers . . . thought about us as they lived, confirmed in their belief of a continuing life.
> —Simon Ortiz, poet and writer[2]

Indigenous teachings on law and family help define our responsibility toward future generations—how the decisions that we make today can impact the well-being of each generation to come. This message is particularly relevant in this time of climate change, warfare, and lack of respect for basic human rights. So too is it an important message as we reflect upon the thirtieth anniversary of the Indian Child Welfare Act of 1978 (ICWA) and look forward to the future, as the title of the book suggests we do. We are just over one generation removed from this landmark legislation—legislation that I will argue in this paper constitutes partial reparations for human rights violations committed against Native peoples and their children. According to the Haudenosaunee's Great Law of Peace, we have six more generations to consider before we can truly understand the full impact of this law.[3]

However, before looking forward, let us take a moment to look back. The long history of injustices against indigenous peoples of the Americas is well documented.[4]

For purposes of the Indian Child Welfare Act, the relevant historical point would be what one scholar has referred to as the "Native American holocaust of the nineteenth century."[5] It was during this time that the U.S. government officially embraced policies of forced assimilation aimed at the breakup of the American Indian family. As early as 1867 the U.S. Commissioner of Indian Affairs was advocating for the forcible removal of Indian children from their tribal nations as "the only successful way to deal with the 'Indian problem.'"[6] The consequences of these earlier policies are still being felt today by the seventh generation of young children. And these policies were merely the beginning of what would amount to over one hundred years of U.S. policies aimed at separating the Indian child from his family and nation.[7]

In more recent times, the federal government has embraced a policy of self-determination for Native American nations, and has made some attempts to redress the myriad of wrongs committed against them.[8] The Indian Child Welfare Act of 1978 (ICWA)[9] is part of that effort. In this essay, I explore whether ICWA achieves a genuine measure of reparations for some of these wrongs. Working directly with Native American nations and organizations, Congress passed ICWA in response to the massive displacement of Native American children to non-Indian adoptive homes, foster care, and educational institutions by federal, state, and private child welfare authorities. This paper will explore the relevance of this law within the context of emerging international human rights precepts. While ICWA fails to provide complete relief under these principles, it is nevertheless an innovative approach to addressing past wrongs and deterring future ones.

Why is it important that we consider this legislation within the context of international human rights law? First, ICWA clearly has its detractors, from scholars, to judges, to legislators.[10] Every few years, legislation to amend ICWA is introduced in Congress. While some of these amendments seek to clarify ambiguities in the law, others—such as the codification of the "Existing Indian Family doctrine"[11]—would eliminate important safeguards designed to prevent the repetition of human rights abuses against indigenous children and their families.[12] Current domestic case law may not adequately respond to these challenges.[13] Thus, a clear understanding of what the rights of indigenous peoples are under international law, and how ICWA furthers these rights, is a necessary prerequisite to any changes in the law. Secondly, reparations claims are gaining momentum in other areas. For instance, there is a growing movement among Native Hawaiians to redress the illegal overthrow of Hawaiian rule and the loss of Native Hawaiian lands,[14] and a similar movement among African Americans as a means of remedying centuries of slavery and Jim Crow laws.[15] More globally, countries like Australia and Canada are grappling with their own comparable legacies of forcible removal of indigenous children.[16] The successes and failures of ICWA may well serve as important guideposts for these claims. Finally, from the perspective of international law and policy, United

Nations member states are currently considering an important UN document that will further clarify the rights of indigenous peoples throughout the world, particularly as it relates to the question of self-determination.[17] Laws such as ICWA demonstrate how these international human rights precepts might be realized through domestic action.

Part 2 of this paper provides the factual foundation for reparation claims, while part 3 discusses some of the relevant human rights principles that are implicated by these claims. Part 4 discusses reparation principles under international law. Part 5 connects these principles to the Indian Child Welfare Act.

2. The Policy of Removal and Its Ongoing Effects

> A great general had said that the only good Indian is a dead Indian . . . I agreed with the sentiment, but only in this: that all the Indian there is in the race should be dead. Kill the Indian in him and save the man.
> —Captain R. H. Pratt, superintendent of the Carlisle Indian Boarding School, 1880s[18]

> The Indian culture is foreign to me, and I don't think it is valid.
> —Adoption attorney, 1987[19]

Elsewhere I have written about the forcible removal of American Indian children from colonial missionary times to the 1970s.[20] Many others have written about the removal process as well.[21] What follows then is a brief summary of that process and its ongoing effects.

It has been said that children are the most "logical targets of a policy designed to erase one culture and replace it with another," since they are the most "vulnerable to change and least able to resist it."[22] The chiefs of the Iroquois Confederacy were keenly aware of this when they declined an offer in 1774 from the English to "educate" their children:

> You, who are wise, must know that different Nations have different Conceptions of things; and you will not therefore take it amiss, if our Ideas of this kind of Education happen not to be the same with yours. We have had some Experience of it; Several of our young people were formerly brought up at the colleges of the Northern Provinces; . . . but, when they came back to us . . . [they] were neither fit for Hunters, Warriors, not Counsellors. . . . We are however, not the less oblig'd by your kind Offer, tho' we decline accepting it; and, to show our grateful Sense of it, if the Gentlemen of Virginia will Send a Dozen of their sons, we will take great care of their Education, instruct them in all we know, and make Men of them.[23]

Yet starting with colonial missionaries, education became one of the most pernicious means of separating indigenous children from their families and communities.[24] While these colonial missions met with mixed results, they would set the tone for emerging U.S. policies. The United States has a constitutionally based political relationship with Native American nations.[25] Yet early federal Indian policy vacillated between respect for tribal autonomy and support for complete assimilation. By the late nineteenth century, supporters of forced assimilation began advocating for the complete destruction of indigenous cultures. A primary example of this policy was the federal boarding school system, in which Native American children were taken from their homes and placed in federal and church-run institutions around the country. Once there, they were denied the right to speak their language, practice their religion, or partake in any cultural practices.[26] Parental and familial visitations were also restricted. The sufferings of these children were not limited to cultural dislocation. Many faced other types of abuses as well.[27]

When the boarding school system failed to produce a complete metamorphosis in the cultural identities of indigenous children, new forms of forced assimilation were contrived. Those who continued to be ideologically and politically tied to notions of assimilation believed that the answer to the dilemma lay in earlier, longer, and perhaps even permanent removal of American Indian children from their families and communities. If complete assimilation were to be realized, the cohesiveness of the Indian family would need to be destroyed. One example would be the boarding school "outing" system, in which "students [were to] spend a period of one or more years of their school life away from the school in selected white families, under the supervision of the school ... , thus gaining experience in practical self-support and an induction into civilized family life not otherwise attainable."[28] This system of placing American Indian children with Anglo families served as a precursor to the twentieth-century massive displacement of American Indian children to non-Indian adoptive homes, foster care, and institutions.

By the 1920s, the dual system of assimilation by education and massive allotment of land[29] had taken its toll on Native American nations and their families. John Collier, one of the leading reformers of the Progressive Movement, who later became commissioner of Indian Affairs, maintained that "the administration of Indian affairs was a national disgrace—A policy designed to rob Indians of their property, destroy their culture and eventually exterminate them."[30] American Indian children, in particular, were feeling the effects of forced assimilation. A 1928 governmental report on the state of Native American affairs highlighted, among other things, the "dreary existence" of American Indian children living in boarding

> [t]he philosophy underlying the establishment of Indian boarding schools, that the way to "civilize" the Indian is to take Indian children, even very young

children, as completely as possible away from their home and family life, is at variance with modern views of education and social work, which regard the home and family as essential social institutions from which it is generally undesirable to uproot children.[31]

The report also documented the dire socioeconomic conditions of Indian reservations and criticized federal Indian policy for failing to support American Indian self-sufficiency. This laid the groundwork for a shift in federal Indian policy toward one of "self-government" for Native American nations. However, this policy, known as "Indian Reorganization," was short-lived, as the federal pendulum quickly began to swing back toward assimilationist thinking.[32] At the end of World War II, there were calls to "release" American Indians from their tribal cultures and excessive land base, and "assimilate" them into the mainstream culture.[33] Those who had opposed Commissioner John Collier's Indian reforms of the 1930s rallied behind this ideology and pushed for significant changes in federal policy. By 1953 Congress had officially adopted a new policy of rapid and coercive assimilation through "termination."[34] The assimilation practices of this era were aimed at every facet of Indian life—from the land base, to the community structure, to the individual child. Congress began passing a number of laws aimed at ending or limiting the historic relationship between certain tribes and the federal government.[35] Federal health and social welfare programs were cut, and state legislatures and courts were given jurisdiction over certain tribes and their members. This meant that state and local entities were obtaining control over "matters basic to Indian cultural integrity such as education, adoption, and land use."[36] Not surprisingly, Indian education once again became the focus of federal attention. A 1944 congressional report condemned the use of community schools and encouraged a return to off-reservation boarding schools, where the children could "progress" much quicker in the "white man's way of life."[37] As a complement to such schools, the Bureau of Indian Affairs implemented a "Relocation Program" designed to remove American Indians from tribal reservations to urban areas for purposes of work. Most of those who were relocated to the cities under this program endured tremendous poverty as well as cultural isolation. Acoma Pueblo poet Simon Ortiz described his own childhood experiences with termination:

> It was an era which bespoke the intent of U.S. public policy that Indians were no longer to be Indians. Naturally, I did not perceive this in any analytical or purposeful sense; rather, I felt an unspoken anxiety and resentment against unseen forces that determined our destiny to be un-Indian, embarrassed and uncomfortable with our grandparents' customs and strictly held values.... I felt loneliness, alienation, and isolation imposed upon me by the separation of my family, home, and community. There was an unspoken vow: we were caught

in a system inexorably, and we had to learn that system well in order to fight back. Without the motive of a fight-back we would not be able to survive as the people our heritage had lovingly bequeathed us.38

By the 1950s, Congress and the Bureau of Indian Affairs (BIA) were primarily interested in transferring responsibility for Indian education and social welfare programs from the federal government to the states, ignoring the longstanding hostilities between tribes and states of the union. At the urging of the BIA and other federal agencies, states also entered the field of Indian child welfare services. Treaty-guaranteed funds for Indian child welfare services were being distributed to state welfare agencies rather than to tribal governments, and the BIA began referring more on-reservation Indian child welfare cases to states. By the early 1970s, state agencies and state courts were handling most of the Indian child welfare cases. Also, at the urging of the federal government, private institutions took up the cause of assimilating American Indian children into mainstream America. For instance, the Child Welfare League of America established an Indian Adoption Project aimed at placing American Indian children in non-Indian homes, where project supporters claimed the children would receive better care.39 In addition, religious groups continued to be actively involved in the placement of American Indian children outside of the tribal community.40 All of these institutions—schools, child welfare agencies, and courts—were ill equipped, and in some cases unwilling, to address the unique cultural interests and social needs of American Indian families.

In part 5 we will look at the American Indian resurgence of the late 1960s and '70s, which led to the passage of the Indian Child Welfare Act. Leading up to the passage of that law, the Association of American Indian Affairs (AAIA) and other agencies undertook the arduous task of assessing the extent of the Indian child welfare crisis, including the number of American Indian children being removed from their homes, as well as the major causes and effects of this dislocation.41 Conservative estimates indicated that one-third of all American Indian children were being separated from their families and placed in foster care, adoptive homes, or educational institutions.42 Federal boarding schools, mission schools, private training schools, and BIA dormitory programs all contributed to this massive displacement.43 Missing from these statistics were the generations of Native Americans who were previously disconnected from their families as a result of BIA "relocation" programs, federal "outing" programs, and mission-run "educational" placement programs. Additionally, no study could completely capture the effects of years of national paternalism and attempted assimilation on the psyches of Native Americans who were taught, in the words of one former student, that "being American Indian meant that you were something less than a complete being, a 'savage' or a 'pagan.'"44

The AAIA studies and legislative hearings revealed how deeply ingrained the assimilative attitudes of the past had become in our society. The cultural values and social norms of Native American families—particularly indigenous child-rearing practices—were viewed institutionally as the antithesis of a modern-day "civilized" society. Indeed, in a number of the child welfare cases examined, American Indian communities were shocked to learn that the families they regarded as "excellent care-givers" had been judged "unfit" by caseworkers.[45] This disparity in viewpoint was the result of general disdain for American Indian family life. Sen. James Abourezk (D.-S.D.) remarked in 1977 that "[p]ublic and private welfare agencies seem to have operated on the premise that most Indian children would really be better off growing up non-Indians."[46] The legislative history of ICWA mirrored this position, noting, for instance, that many "[s]ocial workers, untutored in the ways of Indian family life or assuming them to be socially irresponsible, considered leaving the child with persons outside the nuclear family as neglect and thus as grounds for terminating parental right."[47] Yet in many indigenous communities, extended family members play an important role in child rearing. For instance, in the Blackfoot community, it is not uncommon for a grandparent to raise one of their grandchildren. This is how cultural knowledge is passed from community to child and from generation to generation.[48]

Cultural bias and stereotypes were also evident in cases involving substance abuse. Studies revealed that in areas where rates of problem drinking among Indians and non-Indians were the same, the Indian family was more likely to have their children removed from the home. Moreover, American Indian families were less likely than non-Indian families with substance-abuse problems to receive supportive services as an alternative to removal of their children.[49] Caseworkers and teachers also ignored the disciplinary practices of Indian families, alleging that American Indian children lacked close parental supervision and strong discipline. Alternative indigenous forms of discipline to physical punishment, including teasing, ostracism, peer pressure, and storytelling, were seen as too permissive. Yet, as the legislative history of ICWA notes, "[w]hat is labeled as 'permissiveness' may often, in fact, simply be a different but effective way of disciplining children."[50] Removal was thus seen as a tool for separating American Indian children from their "inferior" culture and heritage.[51] Additionally, in instances where it was necessary to remove a child from the home, extended family members were often disqualified as foster or adoptive parents for reasons that had nothing to do with their ability to care for the child.[52]

American Indian children and their families were not faring much better in state courts. The House Committee on Interior and Insular Affairs agreed with advocates of ICWA that "the abusive actions of social service agencies would be largely nullified if more judges were themselves knowledgeable about Indian life and required a sharper definition of child abuse and neglect."[53] The "best interest of the child" standard was, and in some cases still is, being narrowly interpreted by state courts without recognition of, or appreciation for, the cultural and familial values of Native American nations. Parents were often not properly notified of court dates and rarely had legal representation or the supporting testimony of expert witnesses on Indian child-rearing practices available to them.[54]

Moreover, extended family members and tribes were rarely, if ever, consulted about the children's welfare. And there was no avenue available for the state courts to be informed of the familial resources available to the children in their own communities. Similarly problematic were the unclear lines of demarcation between state- and tribal court jurisdiction over Indian child custody proceedings.[55]

A number of economic factors were also identified as contributing to the crisis. For instance, in "voluntary" waiver of parental rights cases, there was evidence that state welfare agencies were conditioning the availability of social services on parents agreeing to the waiver. Other families who became aware of these tactics were less inclined to seek services that could have alleviated some of the social conditions ultimately cited as grounds for removal by those same agencies. Another major economic factor contributing to the crisis was an increase in demand for American Indian children in the private non-Indian adoption market, which led to an increase in abuses against Indian children and their families.[56]

Studies demonstrate the devastating effects of these policies and practices on Native American children, their families, and their communities. Children of removal experienced long-term emotional, social, and psychological problems, evidenced in part by a suicide rate twice that of the reservation population and four times that of the general population.[57] The evidence also suggested that Native American children were more likely to face significant social problems in adolescence and adulthood as a result of the displacement.[58] Not surprisingly, the effects have been intergenerational. For instance, children that were raised in boarding schools or other educational institutions knew very little of life in a "family," and as parents themselves had no cultural patterns to follow in rearing their own children.[59] In addition, they were being educated in systems that devalued their Native cultures, resulting in further alienation from community and loss of self-esteem. High dropout rates and low employment were the norm for many of these students. The large number of American children raised in foster care similarly perpetuated the destruction of the American Indian family. "Stricken by a 'constant sense of not knowing where they will be or how long they'll be there,'" these children found it difficult in adulthood to establish permanent roots.[60] Additionally, because society frowned upon their cultures, many American Indians sought to deny their own heritages. This denial caused further distress, often leading to some form of substance abuse. AAIA-related studies indicated that removal of a child also "effectively destroyed the family as an intact unit . . . exacerbat[ing] the problems of alcoholism, unemployment, and emotional duress among parents."[61] The constant threat of losing one's child created a sense of hopelessness and powerlessness that made it difficult for the adults to function well as parents. Many feared emotional attachment because of the inevitable loss. One psychologist noted that American Indian parents had become so conditioned to the removal process that they would often place their own children in boarding schools as a matter of course. Others would place the children with social service agencies and hospitals rather than entrusting them to the care of extended family members, showing the effectiveness of governmental policies designed to erase indigenous familial and cultural ways.[62]

Individuals and families were not the only ones victimized by the removal process. A complex symbiotic relationship exists between Native American children and their tribes—what the late professor Vine Deloria refers to as "a multi-generational complex of people and clan and kinship responsibilities that extend to past as well as future generations."[63] Since many of the economic, cultural, and social structures of American Indian communities are built around these kinship networks, the destruction of the family unit contributed substantially to the dire socioeconomic conditions existing on some reservations today. Current social and economic indicators, such as infant mortality, disease, employment, literacy, alcoholism, and suicide among Native Americans, starkly demonstrate the multigenerational effects of these governmental policies.[64] Moreover, the fact that about 20 percent of all American Indian children are still being placed outside their families and tribes suggests that even more needs to be done to repair and strengthen the familial and social networks of Indian communities.[65] As one tribal leader notes, this is a matter of survival: "culturally, the chances of Indian survival are significantly reduced if our children . . . are . . . denied exposure to the ways of their People."[66]

3. Human Rights

> If we do not understand each other, if we do not know the culture or the history of each other, it is difficult to see the value and dignity of each other's societies.
> —Chief Justice Yazzie, Navajo Nation Supreme Court, 1993[67]

Scholars from various disciplines have referred to the treatment of Native peoples in the United States and elsewhere as "ethnic cleansing,"[68] "cultural genocide,"[69] "ethnocide,"[70] and "racism."[71] Each of these terms suggests a grave violation of fundamental human rights. Building on the evidence offered in part 2, this part explores some of the human rights violations that arise out of forcible removal policies. However, neither this section nor the previous one begins to capture the scope and breadth of the historical and ongoing wrongs committed against indigenous children, their families, and their communities. I leave it to others to provide you with a fuller account of these realities.[72] We will see in part 4 that international reparations claims often focus on gross violations of human rights. Two of the violations explored in this part, genocide and systematic discrimination, are "inherently 'gross' violations of human rights."[73] Single or isolated violations of the other two human rights, cultural identity and self-determination, may not be inherently "gross" under customary human rights law, but nevertheless may be deemed "'gross' *ipso facto*" if there is state policy demonstrating a consistent pattern of violations of these fundamental rights.[74]

SELF-DETERMINATION

The first human rights precept to be explored is the right of self-determination. The focus of this section is on contemporary understandings of this precept and, in particular, its application to indigenous peoples. As Professor James Anaya suggests, "self-determination is a foundational principle of international law that bears particularly upon the status and rights of . . . Native . . . people . . . in light of their history and contemporary conditions."[75]

Numerous scholars have written on the origins and content of the right of self-determination.[76] National courts and human rights bodies have similarly expressed their views on the meaning and scope of this right.[77] The term itself is often linked to Wilsonian ideals of democracy and freedom, but its historical origins extend beyond Western political thought.[78] Following World War II, "self-determination of peoples" became a part of international conventional law, most notably in the UN Charter.[79] In the 1960s, it served as a springboard for the process of decolonization and became an integral part of the international human rights movement. Under article 1 of the International Covenant on Civil and Political Rights and the International Covenant on Economic, Social and Cultural Rights, "all peoples have the right to self-determination," including the right to "freely determine their political status," to "freely pursue their economic, social, and cultural development," and to "freely dispose of their natural wealth and resources."[80] Today, self-determination is an accepted principle of customary international law.[81]

Current debates on the principle of self-determination often focus on two questions: who are the "peoples" entitled to this legal right, and how far does that right extend? These issues have been explored in earlier works on indigenous self-determination.[82] For purposes of this paper, neither issue need delay us for too long. First, domestic and international bodies have defined the term "peoples" to include subnational groups that are part of a larger territorial sovereign unit.[83] When one considers the common factors that make up these subnational groups—such as common racial, ethnic, linguistic, religious, or cultural history; some claim to territory or land; and a shared sense of political, economic, social, and cultural goals—indigenous groups of the Americas easily meet these criteria.[84] Another major controversy is the meaning of "self-determination" itself. While some have sought to equate this term with secession and independent statehood,[85] its meaning under contemporary international law extends well beyond this statist framework. For instance, the two major human rights covenants link self-determination to notions of cultural survival, nondiscrimination, economic development, political freedoms, and other basic human rights.[86] This suggests, as argued by Professor Anaya, that "self-determination is not separate from other human rights norms; rather [it] is a configurative principle or framework complemented by the more specific human rights norms that in their totality enjoin the governing institutional order."[87]

In the past several decades, indigenous peoples from around the world have garnered international support for their right to live and develop as distinct communities.[88] Their efforts have brought about significant changes in both conventional and customary international law. One example is ILO Convention No. 169, which recognizes "the aspiration of [indigenous] peoples to exercise control over their own institutions, ways of life, and economic development and to maintain and develop their identities, languages and religions within the framework of the States in which they live."[89] Even more far-reaching in terms of collective rights is the Draft Declaration on the Rights of Indigenous Peoples, which is currently before the General Assembly.[90] The Declaration specifies important freedoms, conditions, and rights necessary for indigenous peoples to be fully in control of their own destinies. Two provisions directly address the right of self-determination: Article 3 of the Declaration mirrors the language found in the two major human rights covenants regarding "the right of self-determination," and article 31 states that "indigenous peoples, as a specific form of exercising their right to self-determination, have the right to autonomy or self-government, in matters relating to their internal and local affairs . . . ." However, equally important are the remaining parts of the Declaration that make up the constituent parts of indigenous self-determination. Part 1 of the Draft Declaration affirms the right to nondiscrimination and full participation in the life of the state. Part 2 addresses collective rights to live as distinct peoples, including protection against genocide and ethnocide. Part 3 protects the cultural, spiritual, and linguistic identities of indigenous peoples. Part 4 addresses the right to education, labor, and communications. Parts 5 and 6 focus on development and socioeconomic rights. And part 7 deals mainly with political rights, including the right to determine citizenship and maintain institutional structures. Admittedly, there has been some controversy surrounding the final adoption of this declaration, particularly in the use of the word "self-determination." While these objections are addressed in more detail elsewhere, most center on a fundamental misunderstanding of what indigenous self-determination embodies under current and emerging principles of international law. In its fullest sense, it embodies the right of indigenous peoples to live and develop as culturally distinct groups, in control of their own destinies, and under conditions of equality. A similar set of "core precepts" can be found in a host of other UN and regional documents that, according to Professor Anaya, are now "widely accepted and, to that extent, ... indicative of customary law."[91] Many of these instruments address basic human rights. Yet it is the collective nature of indigenous rights that is crucial to their survival as peoples.[92] As one UN working group observed, "the harsh lessons of past history showed that recognition of individual rights alone would not suffice to uphold and guarantee the continued dignity and distinctiveness of indigenous societies and cultures."[93] And while some nation-states oppose international recognition of collective self-determination for indigenous peoples as contrary to liberal theories of constitutionalism, Professor Rebecca Tsosie offers a different formula, one in which "the concept of self-determination ... bridge[s] the gap between the individualistic focus of liberalism and the group focus of tribalism."[94] While indigenous groups are not looking to dismantle nation-states, they do insist on the right to control their own lands, resources, and decision making institutions, and to maintain their own distinct cultures. Existing and emerging international norms on the rights of indigenous peoples, including self-determination, set the foundation for new political relationships that strengthen existing "political alliances" without engaging "the historical cycle of conquest, oppression, and domination."[95]

From a reparations perspective, the right of indigenous self-determination has a dual function, which aligns with Professor Anaya's approach to distinguishing between the principle's substantive elements and its remedial prescriptions. Substantive self-determination includes the right to participate in "the creation of or change in institutions of government," as well as the right to "make meaningful choices in matters touching upon all spheres of life on a continuous basis."[96] "The substance of the norm," however, "must be distinguished from the remedial prescriptions that may follow from a violation of the norm, such as those developed to undo colonization."[97] Thus, for instance, certain actions on the part of a state, such as the removal of indigenous children for purposes of eradicating a culture or people, can constitute a violation of the substantive aspects of self-determination including the right to live and develop as culturally distinct groups. However, an appropriate remedy for this and other related human rights violations might also focus on maintaining or improving various core aspects of self-determination, such as social welfare and development, cultural integrity, and self-government.[98] Specific state policies might include provisions similar to those found in the Indian Child Welfare Act, such as the right of indigenous nations to adjudicate or be involved in future removal cases, as well as the right to seek funds for their own culturally relevant child welfare programs. Similarly, rehabilitative steps may be necessary to undo the intergenerational cultural and psychological harms caused by the removal policy. The relevant provisions of ICWA that incorporate these international precepts of indigenous self-determination are explored in part 5 of this paper.[99]

GENOCIDE AND ETHNIC CLEANSING

The term *genocide* was coined in 1943 by Raphel Lemkin and first appeared in print in his 1944 book *Axis Rule in Occupied Europe: Laws of Occupation—Analysis of Government—Proposals for Redress*. The use of this term in conjunction with the treatment of indigenous peoples and their children, while perhaps controversial, is consistent with Lemkin's definition of "genocide":

> New conceptions require new terms. By "genocide" we mean the destruction of a nation or of an ethnic group. This new word . . . is made from the ancient Greek word *genos* (race, tribe) and the Latin *cide* (killing), thus corresponding in its formation to such words as tyrannicide, homicide, infanticide, etc. Generally speaking, genocide does not necessarily mean the immediate destruction of a nation. . . . It is intended rather to signify a coordinated plan of different actions aiming at the destruction of essential foundations of the life of national groups, with the aim of annihilating the groups themselves. The objectives of such a plan would be disintegration of the political and social institutions, of culture, language, national feelings, religion, and the economic existence of national groups, and the destruction of the personal security, liberty, health, dignity, and even the lives of the individuals belonging to such groups. Genocide is directed against the national group as an entity, and the actions involved are directed against individuals, not in their individual capacity, but as members of the national group.[100]

According to Lemkin, acts of "ethnocide," which has been described as "the destruction of a culture without the killing of its bearers," can also constitute genocide.[101]

In 1946, the United Nations General Assembly condemned genocide as a "crime under international law," in that it denies "the right of existence to entire human groups."[102] Around the same time, the United Nations Charter and the Universal Declaration of Human Rights provided for the universal promotion and protection of human rights and fundamental freedoms. Shortly thereafter, the 1948 Convention on the Prevention and Punishment of Genocide was unanimously adopted by the General Assembly.[103] Article 2 of the Convention defines genocide as "any of the following acts committed with intent to destroy, in whole or in part, a national, ethnical, racial or religious group, as such: (a) Killing members of the group; (b) Causing serious bodily or mental harm to members of the group; (c) Deliberately inflicting on the group conditions of life calculated to bring about its physical destruction in whole or in part; (d) Imposing measures intended to prevent births within the group; (e) *Forcibly transferring children of the group to another group.*"[104] Despite some open questions on scope,[105] this definition is an accepted part of international law.

The Restatement (Third) of the Foreign Relations Law of the United States notes that this "definition is generally accepted for purposes of customary law" and is thus "part of the law of the United States to be applied as such by State as well as federal courts."[106] Article 6 of the Draft Declaration on the Rights of Indigenous Peoples similarly recognizes "the collective right" of indigenous peoples "to live in freedom, peace and security as distinct peoples and to full guarantees against genocide . . . , including removal of indigenous children from their families and communities under any pretext."[107] According to the International Court of Justice (ICJ), individuals are not the only ones that can be found guilty of genocide; a state that commits or is complicit in the commission of genocide may also be in violation of the Genocide Convention.[108]

Ethnic cleansing is a related, yet arguably broader human rights violation. It includes "the elimination of an unwanted group from society" either by genocide or forced migration.[109] The U.S. State Department adopted a similar definition with respect to the Kosovo/Serbia conflict, noting that ethnic cleansing includes "the systematic and forced removal of members of an ethnic group from their communities to change the ethnic composition of a region."[110] Recently, the ICJ "stress[ed] the difference between genocide and 'ethnic cleansing': while 'ethnic cleansing' can be carried out by the displacement of a group of persons from a specific area, genocide is defined by the . . . specific intent to destroy the group or part of it."[111]

The forcible transfer of American Indian children to non-Indian institutions, foster care, and adoptive homes qualifies as genocide so long as there was an intent to destroy the "essential foundations of the life of [a] national group" through the "disintegration of the political and social institutions, of culture, language, national feelings, religion, and the economic existence of [that] group . . . ."[112] Part 2 of this paper demonstrates that the Indian child removal policies of the nineteenth and twentieth centuries were an integral part of a larger governmental effort to eradicate indigenous cultures and communities in the United States.[113] This effort included the federal allotment policy,[114] which was designed to strip indigenous peoples of their communal land base. It was described by one United States president as the "mighty pulverizing force to break up the tribal mass[es] . . . act[ing] directly upon the family and the individual."[115] Taken together, these policies amounted to what one Supreme Court justice has referred to as "systematic ethnocide."[116]

However, some might contend that the "intent" element of genocide cannot be meant with respect to the forcible transfer of Indian children, because some of the objectives of removal were "benign" (to provide education and training), and because it was done with the alleged "best interest of the child" in mind. However, these claims do not withstand close scrutiny. There is no question that forcible transfers of children from one group to another can constitute genocide.[117] In terms of specific intent, part 2 demonstrates that the erasure of Native American cultures and their communities were predominant goals of the forced assimilation and removal policies. Government documents as well as independent studies show that American Indian children were being removed from their families and communities primarily as a means of preventing them from acquiring knowledge of their culture and tradition, thereby eventually destroying that culture.[118] One commissioner of Indian Affairs proclaimed as early as 1923 that U.S. Indian policy was "designed to rob Indians of their property, destroy their culture and eventually exterminate them."[119] Moreover, recent scholarship suggests that the abuse and neglect that indigenous children suffered at the hands of their substitute caregivers were not the result of "unfortunate and unintended consequences of policies directed towards securing the health and well-being . . . of young people."[120] Rather, they were the result of "deliberate racial hygiene strategies" intended to further the official discourse of civilization and assimilation.[121]

Additionally, a policy of forced removal can still be genocide even if it is motivated in part by "good intentions."[122] This issue was explored in depth by the Australian Human Rights and Equal Opportunity Commission, which was charged with the task of investigating the facts and principles relating to the forcible separation of Aboriginal and Torres Strait Islander children.[123] While the removal process may have been somewhat more successful in Australia, the legal findings of the Australian Commission are equally relevant here. It is true that some U.S. programs were aimed at providing indigenous children with an education, skills training, and religious instruction. However, none of these objectives negate the primary goal of these programs, which was to forcibly separate children from their families and indoctrinate them with Anglo values and beliefs at the expense of their own cultural, familial, linguistic, and religious beliefs. As one United Nations official noted prior to the passage of the Genocide Convention, separating children from their families "forc[es] upon the former at an impressionable and receptive age a culture and mentality different from their parents. This process tends to bring about the disappearance of a group as a cultural unit in a relatively short time."[124] Moreover, as was the case in Australia, the "genocidal impact" of state welfare "practices of preferring non-indigenous foster and adoptive families for Indigenous children" was "reasonably foreseeable," which in turn supports a finding of "intent" under the Convention.[125] Nor does the fact that not all American Indian children were forcibly removed negate this finding. As noted by the Australian Human Rights Commission, "it would be erroneous to interpret the [Genocide] Convention as prohibiting only the total and actual destruction of the group. The essence of the crime of genocide is the intention to destroy the group as such and not the extent to which that intention has been achieved."[126] Thus, while a finding of genocide with respect to the forcible removal of Indian children may be politically troublesome, such a finding would be nevertheless legally sound.

Removal of indigenous children from their homes also raises the issue of ethnic cleansing, which includes the "elimination of an unwanted group from society" either by genocide or forced migration, as well as the "systematic and forced removal of members of an ethnic group from their communities."[127] At Indian boarding schools, Native American children were forbidden to speak their language, practice their religion, partake in any cultural practices, or visit with family.[128] The intent of the government, "as articulated by Army Captain Henry Pratt, a key architect of federal Indian education, was to 'kill the Indian so as to save the man within.'"[129] This intent on the part of the United States to "kill" the various Indian cultures is thus akin to cultural genocide or "ethnocide." Moreover, the forced removal of Indian children to foster care and adoptive homes had the same effect as forced migration. As noted by one United Nations official, this type of separation from family and community at an early age can "bring about the disappearance of a group as a cultural unit in a relatively short time."[130]

SYSTEMATIC DISCRIMINATION

The third human rights violation, systematic racial discrimination, has been recognized as contrary to international law at least since the U.N. Charter of 1945, which provides in article 55 that "the United Nations shall promote . . . universal respect for, and observance of, human rights and fundamental freedoms for all without distinction as to race, sex, language or religion."[131] Similarly, the Universal Declaration of Human Rights, an interpretative guide to the Charter, provides that "All human beings are born free and equal in dignity and rights" and are "entitled to equal protection against any discrimination in violation of this Declaration."[132] Even prior to the Charter and Declaration, there were a number of bilateral and multilateral treaties that spoke to the issue of nondiscrimination based on nationality.[133] Other more recent treaties, such as the 1965 International Convention on the Elimination of All Forms of Racial Discrimination, and the International Covenant on Civil and Political Rights, reaffirm the equality rights articulated in the Charter and Declaration.[134] Moreover, racial discrimination is a violation of customary law "when it is practiced systematically as a matter of state policy."[135]

Professor James Anaya, in his book *Indigenous Peoples in International Law*, discusses the importance of the concept of nondiscrimination as it relates to indigenous peoples: "The nondiscrimination norm is acknowledged to have special implications for indigenous groups which, practically as a matter of definition, have been treated adversely on the basis of their immutable or cultural differences."[136] This right of nondiscrimination for indigenous peoples entails, among other things, affirmation of their right to exist as distinct political and cultural communities. This principle has been articulated in specific UN instruments relating to indigenous peoples, such as ILO Convention No. 169 and the UN Draft Declaration on the Rights of Indigenous Peoples, both of which speak to Native peoples' rights to develop indigenous identities and cultures without assimilation.[137] Yet this right is not often honored by states. As recently as 1997, the UN Committee on the Elimination of Racial Discrimination found

> that in many regions of the world indigenous peoples have been, and are still being, discriminated against and deprived of their human rights and fundamental freedoms and in particular that they have lost their land and resources to colonists, commercial companies, and State enterprises. Consequently, the preservation of their culture and their historical identity has been and still is jeopardized.[138]

Scholars of various disciplines have written extensively on issues of "race" and "racism" as they relate to indigenous-state relations. David Stannard's book *American Holocaust* and Robert A. Williams' book *The American Indian in Western Legal Thought: The Discourse of Conquest* offer compelling historical accounts of the linkages between "racist ideology" and Euro-American policies toward the indigenous peoples of the Americas.[139] According to Williams, these attitudes toward indigenous populations can be traced back to medieval times, when the rhetoric of inferiority and difference were used to relegate non-Christian peoples to the status of "infidels."[140] The legal and political rationalization that supported the Crusades to the Holy Land served as the core foundation for the exercise of control over the indigenous populations of the New World in later centuries.[141] A 1989 United Nations report echoed these findings that "racial discrimination against indigenous peoples is the outcome of a long historical process of conquest, penetration, and marginalization, accompanied by attitudes of superiority and by a projection of what is indigenous as 'primitive' and 'inferior.'"[142]

Here in the United States, starting with the advent of federally funded boarding and mission schools, indigenous children and their families were subjected to laws and practices that discriminated against them. These laws and practices are explored fully in part 2 of this paper.[143] They suggest that unlike other children, American Indian children were forced to endure a system of education that sought to strip them of their identity, language, culture, and community and familial life. The inequity of such a system has been acknowledged in U.S. governmental reports, one of which found that the process of removing Indian children from their homes and families was "at variance with modern views of education and social work, which regard the home and family as essential social institutions from which it is generally undesirable to uproot children."[144] Yet even after the advent of boarding schools, indigenous families continued to be systematically discriminated against through inappropriate and unequal application of child welfare laws. As earlier demonstrated, cultural bias and

Western notions of what constitutes an appropriate family underscored many of the decisions to separate a child from an Indian home or community.[145] For instance, some Indian children were being removed from the custody of their family on the sole grounds that "an Indian reservation is an unsuitable environment for a child and that the pre-adoptive parents were financially able to provide a home and a way of life superior to the one furnished by the natural mother."[146] Cultural bias was evident in other cases, from termination of parental rights for leaving a child with extended family members for long periods of time, to removal on the basis of weak disciplinary practices on the part of the parent.[147] Moreover, American Indian families were less likely than non-Indian families to receive supportive social services as an alternative to removal.[148] Additionally, the "best interest of the child" standard, utilized in most child custody proceedings, has been, and still is being, used by some courts as a tool of removal, based in part on cultural stereotypes of what it means to be part of a Native American nation or community.[149]

As with the issue of genocidal intent, providing indigenous children with skills and training, or believing that one is acting in the "best interest of the child" do not undermine a claim of discrimination. First, evidence suggests that the policy of removal was part and parcel of a larger policy of "deliberate racial hygiene."[150] Second, international law covers both intentional acts as well as those that have the effect of discriminating based on unequal enjoyment of human rights. For instance, the International Convention on the Elimination of All Forms of Racial Discrimination defines "racial discrimination" as including "any distinction, exclusion, restriction or preference based on race, colour, descent or national or ethnic origin which has the *purpose or effect* of nullifying or impairing the recognition, enjoyment or exercise, on an equal footing, of human rights and fundamental freedoms in the political, economic, social, cultural or any other field of public life."[151]

CULTURAL IDENTITY

There are also important linkages between the right to nondiscrimination and the right to "cultural integrity" or identity. Professor Anaya maintains that

> The nondiscrimination norm, viewed in light of broader self-determination values, goes beyond ensuring for indigenous *individuals*.. the same access to ... social welfare programs. It also upholds the right of indigenous *groups* to maintain and freely develop their cultural identities in coexistence with other sectors of humanity.[152]

These protections are articulated in various treaty regimes, such as the U.N. Convention against Racial Discrimination, which has been interpreted by the Committee on the

Elimination of Racial Discrimination (CERD) to include a right of recognition and respect for the distinct cultures and identities of indigenous peoples.[153] Article 27 of the International Covenant on Civil and Political Rights (ICCPR) similarly provides for the right of persons belonging to "ethnic, linguistic or religious minorities . . . , in community with other members of their group, to enjoy their own culture, to profess and practice their own religion [and] to use their own language."[154] This provision has been the basis of a number of favorable decisions supporting indigenous peoples' rights. For instance, in the 1977 case of *Lovelace v. Canada*, the UN Human Rights Committee found that Sandra Lovelace was being denied "the right . . . to access her native culture and language in community with the other members of her group" by a Canadian law that denied the Indian status of all Indian women who married non-Indians.[155] Similar claims could be made with respect to Native children who are forcibly removed from their communities and denied the right to "access [their] native culture and language" in community with other members of their group, in violation of the cultural integrity norm embodied in article 27 of the ICCPR.

Indeed, a child's right to be raised and nurtured in her family and community of origin has been increasingly recognized in international children's rights discourse. For instance, the Hague Inter-country Adoption Convention addresses, among other things, the "world-wide phenomenon involving migration of children . . . from one society and culture to another very different environment."[156] Additionally, article 8 of the Convention on the Rights of the Child recognizes "the right of the child to preserve his or her identity, including nationality, name, and family relations."[157] There are also specific provisions that address the unique needs of indigenous children in terms of language, education, and cultural identity. Although both of these conventions have been widely ratified, this issue of protecting a child's community or "identity of origin" is not without controversy. Professor Barbara Bennett Woodhouse states that the "very notion of preserving children's cultural or ethnic identity seems to conflict with liberal conceptions of parents' and children's individual rights, ideals of color-blind equality . . . ."[158] She notes, however, that missing from this debate of individual versus group identity "is a coherent schema for articulating children's rights to preservation of their identity."[159] As we will see in parts 4 and 5, the Indian Child Welfare Act seeks to protect a child's "identity of origin." Yet it does so in a way that is consistent with generally accepted international norms that seek to protect, when possible, "the child's . . . family and community of origin from disruption," thereby ensuring two essential aspects of reparations—restitution and rehabilitation.[160]

DUTIES OF THE UNITED STATES

One additional question is the United States' legal duty to remedy these human rights violations. In 1978 when the Indian Child Welfare Act became law, the United

States had a clear legal duty to remedy past and ongoing human rights violations against Indian children, their families, and their communities. As we will see in part 4, international law provides for a right of reparations for serious violations of human rights and fundamental freedoms.[161] Moreover, as a member of the United Nations, the United States assumed as early as the 1940s general human rights obligations enunciated in such instruments as the UN Charter and Universal Declaration of Human Rights. By the 1960s, the two major human rights instruments—the International Covenant on Civil and Political Rights, and the International Covenant on Economic, Cultural and Social Rights—were part of international conventional law. Moreover, in the case of genocide and the prohibition against systematic racial discrimination in the manner experienced by indigenous peoples, such rights are recognized as binding on all member states under principles of customary international law.[162] Once a custom is widely accepted as a norm of international law, it binds all governments not expressly and persistently objecting to its development as such.[163] Moreover, as earlier discussed, "consistent patterns of gross violations of internationally recognized human rights" also give rise to customary law. While certain fundamental human rights when "committed singly or sporadically" may not be violations of customary law, "they become violations . . . if the state is guilty of a 'consistent pattern of gross violations' as state policy."[164] In terms of the forcible removal policy, which lasted more than a century in different forms and includes the ongoing intergenerational harms discussed in part 2, it would be difficult to argue against a finding of "consistent patterns of gross violations." Thus, even though the United States did not take action on many of the major human rights treaties cited above—such as the Genocide Convention, the Convention on the Elimination of all Forms of Racial Discrimination and the Covenant on Civil and Political Rights—until after ICWA became law in 1978, this does not preclude us from considering U.S. policies and practices within the context of the standards set in these treaties. Many of the provisions of these treaties have long been an accepted part of customary law. Moreover, as discussed in part 2, the harms resulting from these policies are still being felt by indigenous peoples and their families. Thus the United States has an affirmative duty to remedy these wrongs and their ongoing effects. It is also worth repeating that the forcible removal of Indian children to educational institutions and foster homes in the manner experienced by Indian children were, as early as the 1920s, contrary to prevailing norms of domestic family law, education, and social work—all of which regarded the home and family as the essential social institution.[165]

Moreover, as previously discussed, the principle of self-determination encompasses a duty on the part of states to take remedial measures for violations of a group's substantive right to self-determination. Self-determination is a part of international customary law and, as argued by some, may even be a preemptory norm much like the prohibition against genocide and systematic racial discrimination.[166]

To the extent that indigenous nations in the United States are still being denied effective means to address or participate in matters affecting their children, the substantive aspects of self-determination are not being fulfilled and therefore require an adequate remedy. Additionally, the United States has a duty to ensure that past violations are remedied through programs that effectuate the norms that make up self-determination, which is in part what ICWA is intended to do.[167]

4. Reparations

> [S]ociety cannot simply block out a chapter of its history; it cannot deny the facts of the past.
> —Jose Zalaquett, member of the Chilean National Commission on Truth and Conciliation[168]

> Repair is at the very heart of justice.
> —Professor Elizabeth V. Spelman[169]

Reparation for human rights violations triggers a host of critical questions.[170] Some of those questions are relevant to the issue of ICWA as reparations, such as: When are they warranted? How is it possible to judge certain wrongs by contemporary standards? What constitutes an appropriate remedy or response? And how does one identify the victim class?

Professor Mari Matsuda has suggested that reparations requires "the formal acknowledgment of historical wrong, the recognition of continuing injury, and the commitment to redress, looking always to the victims for guidance."[171] Others equate reparations with the act of "atonement" for the commission of some injustice. For the victims of injustice, the delivery of some form of apology may be an important first step in the process of obtaining justice and healing wounds.[172] Still others consider monetary compensation to the individual as the most important aspect of reparations.[173] In many of these cases, the primary focus is placed on redress for a wrong done. However, beyond this normative goal of reparation, the "making of amends for a wrong,"[174] so too is there a holistic goal: to "restore" or "repair" damaged relationships.[175] This concept of restoration or repair is at the center of many indigenous legal systems. For instance, Justice Raymond Austin has described the goals of the Navajo justice system as not only providing individual restitution to a person for an injury caused, but also repairing familial relationships and regaining harmony within the community.[176] Repairing and rebuilding relationships is also an essential component of the restorative justice movement. As Professor Elizabeth Spelman explains, restorative justice "is not only about fixing the flaws and making up for the imperfections in existing institutions, it's about putting the repair of victims, offenders, and the communities of which they are a part at the center of justice."[177] So too should reparations be viewed with these dual aims in mind: to redress wrongs as well as repair or rebuild relationships. By considering international norms on reparations, as well as some regional and domestic examples, we can see how these dual aims may translate into law and policy.

INTERNATIONAL PRINCIPLES AND GUIDELINES

Reparations claimed a place within the international legal system following World War II and the emergence of international human rights norms and procedures.[178] Today, many international human rights instruments recognize a general right to redress for victims of violations of international human rights law. For instance, article 8 of the Universal Declaration of Human Rights states that "Everyone has the right to an effective remedy by the component national tribunals for acts violating the fundamental rights granted him by constitution or by law."[179] The International Covenant on Civil and Political Rights provides that each state party is to ensure an "effective remedy" for violations of rights and freedoms under the ICCPR.[180] The International Convention on the Elimination of All Forms of Racial Discrimination speaks directly to the issue of reparations in article 6, articulating a right to "just and adequate reparation or satisfaction for any damage suffered as a result of [racial] discrimination."[181] Regional instruments, such as the European Convention of Human Rights, the American Convention on Human Rights, and the African Charter on Human and Peoples' Rights, similarly incorporate notions of "just satisfaction" for breach of a state's human rights obligation.[182] An important corollary to the right of redress is a state's affirmative duty to ensure victims' rights to those remedies. In particular, states have an obligation to provide "reparation to victims for acts or omissions which can be attributed to the State and constitute gross violations of international human rights law or serious violations of international humanitarian law."[183] States also have a general duty to ensure procedures and processes that allow for effective, appropriate, and prompt reparations.[184] Domestic law may also provide a basis for a claim of reparations, particularly where a victim is denied rights equally enjoyed by other members of the state. For instance, in a national inquiry on the separation of Aboriginal children from their families and communities, an Australian human rights commission concluded that the century-long practice of forced removal of indigenous children violated fundamental common-law rights in addition to international human rights principles.[185] Later in this paper, I will consider specific international instruments, regional decisions, and state practices that support indigenous claims to reparations for past and continuing wrongs. As part 3 demonstrates, there are important developments in international law relating to the survival of indigenous peoples that are tied to the recognition and protection of communal rights, which are in turn linked to the right of self-determination.

In 2005, the General Assembly adopted a resolution on "the Basic Principles and Guidelines on the Rights to a Remedy and Reparation for Victims of Gross Violations of International Human Rights Law and Serious Violations of International Humanitarian Law".[186] This resolution was the culmination of several UN studies[187] that had sought to clarify the right to reparations and potential processes for achieving that right. The studies adopt a broad definition of reparations, emphasizing the need to "render justice by removing or redressing the consequences of the wrongful acts and by preventing and deterring violations."[188] The contents of any redress plan would in turn be shaped by the gravity of the violation at issue, the resulting damages, and the needs and wishes of the victims.[189] "[F]ull and effective reparation" would mean pursuing various forms of redress, such as restitution, rehabilitation, compensation, and satisfaction and guarantees of non-repetition.[190] Restitution is designed to restore the victim to pre-violation status whenever possible and includes such things as restoration of liberty, identity, family life, citizenship, property, and employment.[191] Compensation is described as providing for "economically assessable damages" for such things as physical and mental harm, lost opportunities, material damages, harm to one's reputation or dignity, legal costs, and moral damages.[192] Rehabilitation includes offering special types of care for victims to help in the healing process, including medical and psychological care as well as legal and social services.[193] Non-repetition is addressed, among other things, through cessation of continuing human rights abuses; public disclosure of past acts; public acknowledgement and apology for those abuses; official declaration restoring the dignity, reputation, and legal rights of a victim or victim's family; judicial or administrative actions to ensure against future abuses (including mechanisms to monitor and prevent social conflicts); and the promotion of human rights education and training.[194]

While any human rights violation gives rise to the right of redress under international law, the primary focus of the UN studies is on "gross violations of human rights and fundamental freedoms."[195] Commonly identified violations include those explored in part 3 of this paper: genocide, systematic discrimination, and forcible transfer of a population or group. Others include slavery, arbitrary execution, torture, cruel or inhuman treatment, enforced disappearance, and prolonged detention.[196] So too does a state commit a gross violation of human rights if it, as a matter of state policy, "practices, encourages or condones ... a consistent pattern of ... violations of internationally recognized human rights," which includes any human right that is "fundamental and intrinsic to human dignity."[197] As earlier demonstrated, both the right to a cultural identity and the right to self-determination constitute rights that are fundamental to the basic survival and dignity of indigenous peoples.

On the issue of identification of the victim class, international law recognizes the right of reparations for individuals, groups, and communities. For instance, paragraph 1 of the UN Declaration of Basic Principles of Justice for Victims of Crime and Abuse of Power defines "victims" as "persons who, individually or collectively, have suffered harm, including physical or mental injury, emotional suffering, economic loss or substantial impairment of their fundamental rights." Additionally, the UN studies on reparations note that "both individuals and collectivities are often victimized as a result of gross violations of human rights."[198] Where indigenous peoples are concerned, the "individual and collective aspects of victimized persons and groups are in many instances closely related."[199] This concern is particularly compelling in the context of removal, where familial and cultural dislocation affects not only the child, but the child's family and community as well. The UN resolution on reparations acknowledges as much in noting that "contemporary forms of victimization, while essentially directed against persons, may nevertheless also be directed against groups of persons who are targeted collectively."[200] It thus defines victims as "persons who individually or collectively suffered harm."[201]

Finally there is the question of the appropriateness of evaluating past wrongs in light of current-day standards, and the fairness of having those who were not directly responsible for the wrongs pay the costs of reparations. The General Assembly resolution, while not directly addressing these questions, notes that statutes of limitations that might otherwise bar a claim to reparations do not apply to gross violations that constitute a crime under international law.[202] As for other types of human rights violations, the resolution states that domestic laws should not be "unduly restrictive" in this regard.[203] A recent report from the nongovernmental organization Human Rights Watch deals more directly with the issue of the outer

> [T]here are practical limits to how long, or through how many generations ... claims should survive. Because human history is filled with wrongs, many of which amount to severe human rights abuse, significant practical problems arise once a certain time has elapsed in building a theory of reparations on claims of descendancy alone.... For these practical reasons, when addressing relatively old wrongs, we would not base claims of reparations on the past abuse itself but on its contemporary effects. That is we would focus on people who can reasonably claim that today they suffer the effects of past human rights violations through continuing economic or social deprivation.... This approach concentrates on those people who continue to be victimized by past wrongs and seeks to end their victimization ... [thereby] redressing the contemporary impact of past wrongs.... [204]

In cases of injury that do not arise solely out of contemporary injustices, Human Rights Watch suggests that the appropriate focus might be on rectifying or addressing contemporary economic and social rights.[205] As we will see in the next section, several states have developed reparation plans with such a model in mind.

Professor Matsuda echoes many of the sentiments of Human Rights Watch, noting that "the outer limit [of reparation claims] should be the ability to identify a victim class that continues to suffer a stigmatized position enhanced or promoted by the wrongful act in question."[206] For instance, in the case of reparations for Native Hawaiians, Professor Matsuda emphasizes the "continuing group damage engendered by past wrongs" as a basis for maintaining a right to reparations. Evidence of this "stigmatized position" or "continuing group damage" is demonstrated, among other things, by statistical data that suggests that indigenous Hawaiians "are on the bottom of every . . . indicator of social survival: . . . lower birth rates, higher infant mortality . . . , higher rates of disease, illiteracy, imprisonment, alcoholism, suicide and homelessness." Professor James Anaya takes this argument one step further, arguing that there are ongoing substantive violations of Native Hawaiian peoples' right to self-determination, thereby giving rise to remedial measures on the part of the United States.[207] In the case of removal of Indian children, objections based on time have little force, for many of the reasons identified by Human Rights Watch and scholars such as Matsuda and Anaya.[208] While the federal government no longer forces American Indian children to attend boarding schools or supports the removal of Indian children by state welfare agencies, some of the practices and violations addressed by ICWA are ongoing.[209] Moreover, ICWA is necessary both because American Indian children and their families remain in a "stigmatized position" and because it provides some guarantees against repetition of abuse, in part by recognizing an Indian nation's right to self-determination where child welfare matters are concerned. This issue is explored more fully in part 5.

REGIONAL AND DOMESTIC EXAMPLES

The international norms discussed above are finding their way into state practice, which in turn is influencing international jurisprudence. This section explores some of those practices. The following examples are a mere sampling of the many plans currently being considered or implemented by state and regional bodies. They were chosen in part because they offer some helpful insight on the question of ICWA as partial reparations.

The best-known national example of reparations is Germany's redress program for the egregious crimes committed against the victims of the Holocaust. In 1949, the Republic of Germany began working on a series of reparations laws designed to compensate individuals for persecution and injury done by the Nazi regime.[210] In later years, these laws were supplemented to greatly expand the class of victims entitled to compensation.[211] More recently, the focus has been on redress for victims of forced and slave labor.[212] In many cases, redress has come in the form of monetary compensation. Recent estimates indicate that Germany has made payments to victims of the Holocaust in excess of $80 billion dollars.[213] In terms of nonmonetary relief, some have suggested that Germany's official apology was perhaps the "most important . . . event that took place."[214] Others have highlighted the nonmonetary remedies that were not included, such as a forum to allow survivors to tell their stories, as well as attempts at rebuilding communities.[215]

A different reparations claim arising out of World War II involves the United States and its redress plan for Japanese Americans incarcerated in internment camps. In 1942, the United States government passed Executive Order 9066, whereby citizens and residents of Arizona, California, Oregon, Washington, and the territories of Alaska and Hawaii were removed or excluded based on their Japanese ancestry.[216] The alleged justification behind the order was that Japanese nationals or Japanese Americans were likely to act as espionage agents for the Empire of Japan during World War II, a justification that has long since been discredited. In 1948, the U.S. Congress adopted the Japanese-American Evacuation Claims Act, which authorized the settlement of property-loss claims resulting from the internment.[217] In 1988, the U.S. government passed other laws relating to internment, which included, among other things, an official apology for the actions of the government, a public-education fund to educate the public about the internment of Japanese Americans, and compensation to other victims of the war.[218] The U.S. reparations plan to remedy these wrongs incorporated the more commonly known elements of reparations—a national apology, and individual payments to surviving victims. However, it also included some elements of restitution, such as a review of any position, status, or entitlement lost as a result of the government's discriminatory actions, as well as the review of any criminal conviction arising out of those actions. It also called for the United States to discourage the occurrence of similar injustices in the future and to make credible and sincere declaration of concerns over violations of human rights committed by other nations.

While the primary focus of World War II reparations was compensatory, the concept of reparation as embodied in the UN studies extends well beyond monetary relief. The potential breadth of any reparation plan is perhaps most evident in South Africa's response to Apartheid. Members of South Africa's Truth and Reconciliation Commission (TRC) were charged with reviewing past policies of the Apartheid regime and recommending reparation for the victims of such policies. The recommendations proposed by the commission included both restorative and redress measures, incorporating international norms of restitution, rehabilitation, assurances of non-repetition, and compensation.[219] While individual monetary relief was a component of the plan, the major focus was on healing, reconciliation, and capacity building. The commission stressed the importance of developing a comprehensive reparations plan that would improve the quality of life for victims of gross human rights violations and their dependents.[220] These goals were to be realized through a series of proposals that included interim reparations, individual reparation grants, symbolic reparations, community rehabilitation, and institutional and government reform.[221] The proposals offered redress to both the individual and the group by targeting individual needs as well as broader socioeconomic conditions. Yet this emphasis on social and economic rights has raised some questions regarding the appropriate role of development in the reparations process. For instance, while many acknowledge that "individual reparations are undermined if they do not take place in a context of wider programs for social justice and national rehabilitation," some critics warned against governments "conflat[ing] reparations with their development discourse."[222]

Similar issues have arisen in the context of other reparation plans, such as Peru's plan to redress human rights abuses resulting from armed conflict between 1980 and 2000. In November 2000, Peru's Truth and Reconciliation Commission drafted a reparations plan that emphasized six major areas of redress: symbolic reparations, health care, education, restitution of rights, economic reparations, and collective reparations.[223] Many of these programmatic measures were later incorporated into a comprehensive reparations plan that focused on the contemporary effects of past human rights violations.[224] The recommendations were designed to "respond to the collective harms suffered by communities and groups as well as by individual victims and their families," thereby broadly defining the victim class.[225] Thus, a major thrust of the plan was ensuring economic and social rights for individuals as well as groups.[226] From an implementation standpoint, concerns have been raised (similar to the South African situation) over whether the state is seeking "to use development and poverty alleviation programs as a vehicle for reparations."[227] These concerns are well founded, but should not foreclose the possibility of linkages between development and reparations. Development strategies may well be an important part of a state's reparations plan, so long as those strategies are responsive to the harms caused by the violations and not merely used as a pretext to avoid additional state obligations. Indeed, such policies may be an essential part of that plan, when, as in the case of forcible removal of indigenous children, the state's actions were aimed at destroying the social, cultural, and economic well-being of a group.

There are a number of domestic and regional cases involving indigenous peoples that raise similar issues of collective and intergenerational harm. Only a few will be explored here.[228] *The Case of the Mayagna (Sumo) Awas Tingni Community v. Nicaragua*, recently decided by the Inter-American Court of Human Rights, is one of those cases.[229] In 1998, the Inter-American Commission on Human Rights (IACHR) filed an application with the Inter-American Court on Human Rights on behalf of the Awas Tingni Indians against the government of Nicaragua. The original claim before the commission was based on Nicaragua's granting of land concession and logging licenses to foreign companies on lands that the Awas Tingni claimed as ancestral lands. After ruling in its favor, the commission referred the case to the Inter-American Court based on breaches of the American Convention on Human Rights.[230] In 2001, the court ruled that Nicaragua had denied the Awas Tingni certain rights to its ancestral lands and resources. In doing so, the court recognized, among other things, a right to property that encompassed the communal property rights of indigenous peoples.[231] The State of Nicaragua was ordered not only to pay monetary reparations,[232] but also to adopt "measures of a legislative, administrative and whatever other character necessary to create an effective mechanism for official recognition, demarcation and titling of the indigenous communities' properties, in accordance with the customary law, values, usage and custom of these communities."[233] Thus the reparations order made it clear, as do later decisions from the Inter-American system,[234] that "relief" for wrongs committed by states against indigenous populations extend beyond monetary compensation to the protection and promotion of communal rights, such as the right to property.

This is an important development in international law for indigenous peoples generally, including the Native Hawaiians who continue to seek redress for group wrongs. In 1993, the United States officially apologized to Native Hawaiians for its involvement in the "illegal overthrow of the Kingdom of Hawaii" and for "deprivation of the rights of Native Hawaiians to self-determination."[235] However, unlike in the context of Japanese Americans, which involved individual claims and resulted in individual monetary settlements, the U.S. government has not done enough to adequately redress the group wrongs committed against indigenous Hawaiians.[236] These wrongs are both historical (deprivation of the right to self-government followed by illegal confiscation of lands), as well as ongoing (continued suppression of cultural, economic, and political rights).[237] According to Professor Anaya, these wrongs constitute a deprivation of the right to self-determination under international law that the United States has a duty to remedy. In particular, he proposes a negotiated settlement or similar procedure that addresses what he identifies as the core norms of indigenous self-determination: 'cultural integrity, land and resources, social welfare and development, and self-government."[238] As we have already seen, this principle of self-determination is a defining aspect of reparations for indigenous peoples and thus needs to be considered in the drafting of any plan to redress historical and contemporary wrongs.

Canada has faced similar challenges with respect to its treatment of First Nations peoples, most recently relating to the state's one-hundred-year policy of compulsory residential boarding schools for indigenous children. In 1990, First Nations leaders called on the Canadian government and church leaders to acknowledge and remedy the cultural, physical, emotional, and sexual abuses committed against Native children at these institutions.[239] Canada responded by convening a Royal Commission on Aboriginal Peoples, which was charged with, among other things, receiving testimony from victims and their families. While the commission recommended a public inquiry into Canada's residential school system, it was not until 2005, following a series of lawsuits that placed a number of church-run institutions on the verge of bankruptcy, that Canada agreed in principle to a $2 billion settlement plan.[240] Among other things, the plan takes into consideration First Nations' concerns over the intergenerational harm caused by these abuses, addressing wrongs committed against individual boarding school victims as well as the victims' grandchildren, "[who] are survivors as well; for they too, have suffered ... the effects of the residential school legacy."[241] Moreover, similar to South Africa and Peru, Canada's plan focuses on the process of "healing, reconciliation, and ... renewal" of the group.[242] Thus, in addition to monetary compensation to surviving students,[243] the plan establishes a Truth and Reconciliation Commission charged with documenting and publicizing the history of forced separation. Additionally, it provides significant funds to the Aboriginal Healing Foundation to promote intercultural healing.[244] Of course Canada was not alone in its policy of removal. Australia is still grappling with how best to redress policies that resulted in the forcible removal of thousands of Aboriginal and Torres Strait Islander children.[245] Moreover, as part 2 demonstrates, the United States suffers from a similar stigma. In 2000, the assistant secretary of the Bureau of Indian Affairs (BIA) offered a formal apology for that agency's past involvement in the removal of Native children, noting that the BIA had systematically "committed ... acts against the children entrusted to its boarding schools, brutalizing them emotionally, psychologically, physically, and spiritually."[246] Recently, victims of these removal policies have sought monetary relief through the U.S. courts. While some of these cases have been dismissed on procedural grounds, others are still pending.[247] Thus, the Indian Child Welfare Act is to date the most prominent remedial response by the United States to this removal.

In addition to international norms, this part explores state and regional practices regarding reparations for serious human rights violations. While this discussion is not comprehensive enough to demonstrate established customary law, there are several trends in these practices that are relevant to any discussion of ICWA as reparations: that reparations are not limited to individual monetary relief, that the concept of the victim encompasses both individual human beings as well as collectivities, that reparations can be forward-looking in their application and take the form of economic and social reform (which is especially useful when redressing intergenerational harms). Moreover, incorporating elements of healing and repair helps to ensure key aspects of reparations, such as restitution, rehabilitation, and non-repetition of harm.

5. The Indian Child Welfare Act as Reparations

> Let us put our minds together and see what kind of future we can build for our children.
>
> —Hunkpapa Lakota Leader

HISTORY AND PURPOSE

The 1960s marked the beginning of a cultural and political renaissance for indigenous peoples of the United States. Pro-Indian organizations were protesting years of broken treaties and discriminatory treatment of American Indians by federal and state governments. Others fought the battle for recognition of Indian sovereignty in the courtrooms and on Capitol Hill.[248] By the 1970s, U.S. policy toward its indigenous peoples had moved away from a policy of assimilation by termination toward one of self-determination. President Nixon decreed in 1973 that the "right of self-determination of the Indian will be respected and their participation in planning their own destiny will actively be encouraged."[249] Following this decree, Indian nations embarked on new political alliances with Congress, developing legislation designed to promote tribal sovereignty and reverse where possible the ongoing effects of forced assimilation.[250]

In the 1970s, Congress held a series of hearings on the plight of American Indian children and their families. Complementing these hearings were studies on the number of children being removed from their homes, as well as the major causes and effects of this dislocation. These studies supported what most Native American nations already knew—that indigenous children and their families were facing massive displacement as a result of U.S.-sanctioned assimilative policies and practices.[251] Congressional findings noted that "an alarmingly high percentage of Indian families are broken up by the removal, often unwarranted, of their children . . . by non tribal public and private agencies and that an alarmingly high percentage of such children are placed in non-Indian foster and adoptive homes and institutions."[252] Working closely with Native American nations and organizations, Congress passed the Indian Child Welfare Act of 1978 (ICWA), declaring:

> It is the policy of this Nation to protect the best interests of Indian children and to promote the stability and security of Indian tribes and families by the establishment of minimum Federal standards for the removal of Indian children from their families and the placement of such children in foster or adoptive homes which will reflect the unique values of Indian culture, and by providing for assistance to Indian tribes in the operation of child and family service programs.[253]

The law covers various child care placements, such as termination of parental rights, foster care, and adoption, and applies to all Native American children who are members of a federally recognized Indian nation or at least eligible for membership. It allocates child welfare jurisdiction between tribal courts and state courts and establishes placement preferences with American Indian families and communities when possible. Additionally, it encourages and assists American Indian nations in the development of child welfare programs and family courts.

ICWA was specifically designed to achieve a number of interrelated goals. First, the law seeks to reverse the assimilative policies and practices that led to the massive removal of American Indian children to non-Indian institutions, foster care, and adoptive homes.[254] The law acknowledges that Indian children are not "better off" far from the influence of family and community, and that their "best interests" are in fact inextricably connected to those of their tribe. While no law could dictate a change in the attitudes of social workers, educators, and judges regarding indigenous cultures, it could minimize the effects of those lingering attitudes by setting minimum standards and procedures for the future placement of American Indian children outside the home.

Second, ICWA seeks to recognize and respect the familial traditions and responsibilities of Native American nations. When viewed in the context of indigenous familial values, the law recognizes the importance of the kinship structure and the role of the extended family in the rearing of children. For instance, it provides for foster care and adoptive placement preferences with extended family members or other tribal members, and requires state courts to consider the social and cultural standards of tribes when making placement determinations.[255] It also seeks to protect the rights of Native American children to be raised, whenever feasible, in their families and communities of origin by mandating that families receive culturally appropriate remedial services before a placement occurs.[256] Additionally, the Act was designed to be sufficiently flexible to meet the diverse cultural interests and complex social needs of American Indian children, including those with "competing cultural identities"—an issue addressed more fully below. Evidence of this flexibility can be found in state and tribal court opinions that provide for "open adoptions" and other forms of visitations that ensure a cultural link with the child's indigenous roots.[257]

Third, it seeks to promote Indian self-determination in the area of child welfare. ICWA recognizes the sovereign power of Native American nations to develop their own child welfare systems, and reaffirms tribal court jurisdiction over certain child custody proceedings. Additionally, it ensures that tribes and extended family members will have an opportunity to be heard through notification provisions and the ability to intervene in state court proceedings.[258] These provisions recognize the unique symbiotic relationship that exists between a child and her tribe, including the child's human right to access her native culture and language "in community with the other members of her group," as well as the tribe's right to exist as a distinct political community.

When challenged on constitutional grounds, some courts have held that "the provisions of the ICWA were deemed by Congress to be essential for the protection of Indian culture and to assure the very existence of Indian tribes.... [This protection] is a permissible goal that is rationally tied to the fulfillment of Congress's unique guardianship obligation toward Indians."[259] This holding is consistent with U.S. case law upholding federal statutes designed to promote the sovereignty and well-being of Native American tribes and their members.[260] These statutes are directed toward Native peoples not as members of discrete "racial" groups, but rather as members of quasi-sovereign tribal entities.[261] So long as these statutes are rationally tied to the fulfillment of Congress's trust obligation to Indian nations, they do not violate due-process or equal-protection principles.[262] ICWA would similarly pass constitutional muster even under the U.S. Supreme Court's more stringent strict scrutiny test of *Adarand Construction v. Pena*,[263] since it is narrowly tailored to promote and protect the stability of Native American nations and remedy centuries of gross violations of human rights, including systematic discrimination. The D.C. Circuit Court's holding in *Jacobs v. Barr*[264]—that "Congress... had clear and sufficient reason to compensate interns of Japanese ... descent; and the compensation is substantially related (as well as narrowly tailored) to Congress's compelling interest in redressing a shameful example of national discrimination"—applies equally to Congress's attempt through ICWA to redress government-sanctioned policies of forcible removal of Indian children.

Despite some ambiguities in the law, there is a general consensus among Native American nations that ICWA provides "vital protection to American Indian children, families and tribes."[265] Yet the legislation has its critics, many of whom oppose the law on the grounds of "race matching" or a violation of individual freedoms.[266] This paper is not intended to address these claims directly, but to suggest another view of the law—one that is consistent with international precepts on reparations. As parts 2 and 3 demonstrate, Native American children and their families "have been subjected to a singularly tragic fate" that has resulted in serious human rights violations. The Indian Child Welfare Act is one of a host of responses necessary from the United States to remedy these violations. While I agree with some critics of ICWA that the remedial scope of the law does not address all of the "social ills" afflicting indigenous families, it is still an important piece of the remedial puzzle. There is little doubt that centuries of land dispossession, cultural and political oppression, and discrimination have led to many of the social welfare challenges facing Native American nations today. However, since the official policy of the United States for most of its history has been aimed at the breakup of the Indian family via the removal of its children, it makes sense for the United States to adopt legislation directed at those dominant societal institutions responsible for carrying out that policy. This by no means absolves the United States of its responsibility to redress the other ongoing social effects of its past policies, including poverty and its consequences. The remaining part of this paper analyzes some key aspects of ICWA within the four major elements of reparations—guarantees against repetition, restitution, rehabilitation, and compensation.

GUARANTEES AGAINST REPETITION

As Jose Zalaquett of the Chilean National Commission on Truth and Conciliation notes, "truth" is "an absolute, unrenounceable value" in terms of reparation and prevention. Thus, verification of the facts, public disclosure and acknowledgement of those facts, as well as acceptance of responsibility for the abuses arising out of those facts are all important components of any reparation plan.[267] While the word "apology" does not appear on the face of ICWA,[268] both the legislative history and the statute expressly acknowledge the wrongs committed against Native children and their families, and the role governmental officials played in the crisis. Equally important is the extensive fact-finding that accompanied the passage of ICWA. The legislative history, which incorporates evidence from congressional hearings and task forces, states that "the wholesale separations of Indian children from their families is perhaps the most tragic and destructive aspect of American Indian life today."[269] It highlights a number of factors contributing to the "destruction of the Indian family and community life," including federal boarding school and dormitory programs, abusive practices of state social welfare workers and judges, procedural irregularities in the judicial process, and public as well as private foster care and adoption programs.[270] The congressional-findings section of ICWA acknowledges that "an alarmingly high percentage of Indian families are broken up by the removal, often unwarranted, of their children from them by nontribal public and private agencies." The law further acknowledges the substantial role of state officials in the crisis based on their failure to "recognize the essential tribal relations of Indian people and the cultural and social standards prevailing in Indian communities and families."[271]

Affirmative steps in the form of judicial and administrative action are also important in ensuring against the recurrence of human rights violations. Thus, ICWA goes beyond a formal acknowledgment of responsibility to establish "minimum Federal standards" aimed at preventing the repetition of human rights abuses against Native American children and their families. It employs a number of procedural safeguards that are aimed at protecting the "best interests of Indian children" and promoting "the stability and security of Indian tribes and families."[272] These safeguards include the right to transfer child welfare cases to tribal courts, the right of notice and intervention to the child's community, the right to remedial services designed to prevent the further breakup of Indian families and communities, and written protections against improper termination of parental rights.[273] The law requires the application of "prevailing social and cultural standards" of Indian communities in the placement of children and provides preferences for placement to the child's extended family and community when possible.[274] Equally important in terms of non-repetition of harm is the assistance provided to tribes to develop and operate their own child and family service programs. As a result of the law, tribes, urban Indian organizations, and even states are developing innovative early-intervention and family preservation programs.

While ICWA offers vital protection against unwarranted removal of Indian children, one shortcoming of the law is its lack of accountability for those that seek to circumvent its provisions.[275] More needs to be done to ensure that individuals working with children, including lawyers and judges, are aware of the historical and contemporary underpinnings of the law and the abuses that it seeks to remedy. However, mere knowledge of the law may not be sufficient. For instance, some courts have purposely resisted the application of the law by failing to transfer cases to tribal courts, ignoring the community placement preferences, or creating judicial exceptions. One such example is the judicially created "Existing Indian Family doctrine" (EIF), which excludes from the coverage of the Act any child whose parent does not maintain, in the opinion of the judge, a "significant social, cultural, or political" relationship with their tribe.[276] Elsewhere I have argued that these types of judicial exceptions represent a return to the assimilationist thinking of the past.[277] They also undermine key remedial aspects of the law intended to prevent a repetition of abuses. The lawyers and judges that advocate for these exceptions to the law often focus their concerns on the child's individual right not to be tied to a family or community in which she or her parents have no significant (apparent) ties. This argument is similar to the individual versus group dichotomy discussed earlier with respect to the protection of a child's cultural identity. There are many responses to these claims.[278] For purposes of this paper, I will focus my arguments on the question of prevention of human rights abuses. Perhaps one of the best guarantees against repetition of harm where indigenous peoples are concerned is the recognition and promotion of self-determination norms. Earlier I suggested that the removal policy violated the right of self-determination by, among other things, denying indigenous groups the right to live and develop as culturally distinct peoples. To remedy this and other related human rights violations, the United States Congress has embraced, through ICWA, the right of indigenous nations to be in control of their own destinies where matters of child welfare are concerned. This is evidenced in the law's intent to respect "the unique [familial] values of Indian culture[s]," including the right of Indian nations, as distinct political communities, to determine a child's membership or citizenship. The law similarly incorporates into existing child welfare systems the "cultural and social standards prevailing in

Indian communities and families."[279] Judicially created exceptions, like the Existing Indian Family doctrine, that circumvent indigenous views of "family" open the door once again to abusive practices that devalue Indian culture and Indian sovereignty. The procedural safeguards of ICWA offer the best protection against these types of abuses by ensuring meaningful tribal and familial participation in each step of the removal process. This does not mean that a child will never be removed from his family or community of origin. What it does help to ensure, however, is that the removal is not done for reasons that violate the basic human rights of that child and his community.

RESTITUTION

Restitution focuses on the act of restoring victims to pre-violation status. It includes such things as restoration of liberty, identity, family life, and property. Restoration for the types of human rights violations associated with the process of removal is a complex endeavor, both because the harms caused by such abuses are intergenerational and because they affect individuals as well as collectivities (individual child, child to family, child to community, family, family to community, and community). The harms caused by removal were particularly dire for Native American nations, whose societies are built upon these familial and communal connections. As the late Vine Deloria described it, family denotes a "multigenerational complex of people and clan and kinship responsibilities" that extends to past and future generations.[280] Understanding and respecting the complex symbiotic relationship that exists between child and community is essential to understanding and respecting indigenous familial relations. For instance, one major criticism of ICWA is that it favors the collective rights of the community over the individual rights of the child. Yet, these are actually two sides of the same coin. A child's right to love and nourishment (e.g., cultural, emotional, spiritual, and physical) is the community's responsibility; in turn, these collective "responsibilities are [the child's] individual rights."[281] Thus, to place a child outside his or her kinship community absent culturally relevant safeguards is to deny that child basic individual rights. Moreover, from a collective-rights standpoint, it works to break the cycle of indigenous life.

Given this situation, it would be difficult to comprehend a single piece of legislation that could actually restore the individual child and his community to pre-violation status. ICWA is no exception. As some of the critics of ICWA like to point out, the statute is in some ways a "procedural statute for a substantive problem."[282] To restore Indian nations and their families to pre-violation status would require sacrifices that individual states and individual Americans might be unwilling to make, particularly when it comes to the issue of land and resources.[283] It would also mean that Congress would need to do more in addressing the question of adequate group compensation. Moreover, society as a whole would need to do a better job of accommodating cultural pluralism and cultural rights within existing systems of law and policy. With that said, however, the restorative aspects of ICWA can be compelling when the spirit and language of the law are followed, as is demonstrated by this story involving a child who had been removed from her Navajo family at the age of eighteen months:

> She was placed out with a foster family and was never returned to her biological mother. She had no knowledge of her Indian family, and, while she knew she was Indian, her non-Indian adoptive family forbid her to speak of her Indian heritage and passed it off as something that was not important. Later, after battling depression and anxiety about her lost identity, she developed a substance abuse problem and her own children were placed in substitute care. But this time there was the Indian Child Welfare Act and a social worker that knew how to implement it. Even though the mother was never enrolled in her tribe because of her placement in a non-Indian family and thus her children were never enrolled, the social worker notified the Navajo Nation who willingly enrolled the mother and children. But there is more. The Navajo Nation found the mother's maternal aunt who asked that the children be placed with her while the mother sought treatment for her substance abuse problem. Upon visiting the aunt's home to do a home study, the social worker found pictures of the mother at eighteen months of age still on the wall. The aunt told of the grief of the family who could not find the child whom they had helped raise. They told of not being able to get information to even know where she was or if she was all right. Today the mother has over two years of sobriety and has been reunited with her Navajo family. She has found her identity and her children have found a loving home with their extended family.[284]

To better comprehend how the statute might achieve restitution for the multiple victims affected by removal, let us again consider cases involving Indian children who never lived in what some state court judges refer to as an "existing Indian family or home." ICWA is designed to not only prevent the repetition of harm against indigenous children and their families, but to assist indigenous nations in reconstituting their familial structures. It establishes as a primary restorative goal "the continued existence and integrity of Indian tribes ... [by] protecting Indian children who are members of or are eligible for membership in an Indian tribe."[285] Any child who is considered by the tribe to be a member or citizen, whether they are officially enrolled or not, will gain the benefit of the law, giving tribes the opportunity to reconnect with individuals and families dislocated by years of abusive child welfare practices. Thus, decisions that seek to limit the number of children covered under the statute undermine key remedial aspects of the law.[286] If the statute is to achieve its restorative goals, child welfare workers must take into consideration the effects that almost two centuries of coercive separation and assimilation have had on generations of Indian people. One example of the failure of a court to understand these aspects of the law is the case of *In re Bridget R*,[287] in which an appellate court in California used the parent's alienation from their community as strong evidence against the application of ICWA. Courts should not be using the very abuses that caused so many Indian people to be separated from their homes and communities as a basis for ignoring the restorative aspects of ICWA. This is supported by the legislative history of ICWA and the U.S. Supreme Court decision in *Mississippi Band of Choctaw Indians v. Holyfield*, both of which acknowledge the ongoing effects of the removal policy, and in particular the alienation of some Indian parents from their society and community.[288] To assist in the restoration of these familial relationships, ICWA contains a number of provisions designed to ensure that the parental waiver of rights are voluntary, that parents are made aware of all their options regarding possible placement, and that tribes and extended family members have a voice in the process.

Another criticism of the law is that it does not adequately address contemporary issues of mixed ancestry or "competing cultural identities," such as where a Native American father is not married to a non–Native American custodial mother, but the child is nevertheless considered a member or citizen of the father's tribe or nation. A related criticism is the point mentioned earlier regarding whether under ICWA a child's collective identity trumps its individual identity. While this paper is not aimed at the finer points of the Indian Child Welfare Act and its day-to-day application, these criticisms must be considered within the larger context of ICWA as reparations for serious human rights abuses, particularly as it relates to the question of restitution and repair. On the issue of identity, ICWA does not seek to protect the rights of the group at the expense of the rights of the individual, but rather seeks to protect the identity rights of American Indian children within the context of their own historical and contemporary realities. The law does recognize that it is in the best interest of American Indian children to maintain ties with their extended families and communities whenever feasible. Moreover, it does so in a way that acknowledges the unique self-determining status of Indian nations in this country. In particular, it recognizes the ability of tribes to adjudicate child custody cases involving children residing or domiciled on the reservation, and in all other cases to maintain a right of intervention.[289] In either case, the child may end up being removed from the home and even perhaps permanently placed outside the kinship community. However, ICWA is intended to ensure that this does not happen because of a court or agency's unwillingness to "recognize either the vitality or validity of contemporary American Indian cultures and values."[290] Nor is the law designed to undermine the individual survival needs of a child. Indeed, just the opposite is true. By its very terms, it is designed to strengthen families, prevent improper removals, and ensure that when placement is necessary, a child's indigenous familial options are considered and explored. On the point of competing cultural identities, it is important to remember that ICWA is not a law of absolutes. Professor Barbara Atwood, in her postmodern critique of ICWA, argues that the statute is sufficiently broad to encompass a child's multiple identities as well as his or her individual interest in continuity of placement.[291] In particular, she points to substantive provisions of ICWA that allow, under the appropriate circumstances, for "multidimensional, situated interpretations" on issues of placement.[292] One well-known example of this type of accommodation of multiple interests is *In re Adoption of Halloway*, in which a Navajo tribal court fashioned a remedy that sought to protect the child's cultural identity as well as his right to continuity of care.[293] The court awarded permanent guardianship rights to the non-Navajo family who had had custody of the child for over five years, while at the same time recognizing visitation rights with the child's mother and tribe. There are a number of other cases that have fashioned similar remedies to address the "multiple needs and multiple identities" of Indian children.[294] These cases suggest a reading of the statute that is consistent with international human rights precepts, both in terms of cultural-identity protection and self-determination. If restoration of identity and family life are to be achieved, courts and child welfare agencies must be open to creative solutions under ICWA that further these ends. Such solutions would also be consistent with the principle of indigenous self-determination, which "promotes a political order that is less state-centered and more centered on people living in a world of distinct yet increasingly integrated and overlapping spheres of community and authority."[295] ICWA, when properly followed, can help courts and welfare agencies navigate these overlapping spheres of identity and community.

REHABILITATION AND COMPENSATION

Rehabilitation focuses on steps needed to improve the lives of individual victims, their families, and their communities. Like restitution, it is closely linked to the holistic goals of repair and restoration. ICWA attempts to address some of these goals through its rehabilitative provisions. For instance, it authorizes grants to Indian nations and organizations to assist in the development of family service programs and child welfare laws. The funds support social service programs, such as licensing of Indian foster and adoptive homes, counseling and treatment centers, professional child welfare training, education and training of tribal court judges and staff, and legal representation and advice to Indian families involved in child custody proceedings.[296] Tribes, urban Indian organizations, and states have all relied on these grants to develop family preservation programs and special cross-cultural training programs for judges and child welfare workers.[297] For children remaining in the state system, ICWA requires that no Indian child be placed out by state officials without first being provided "remedial services and rehabilitative programs designed to prevent the further breakup of the Indian family."[298]

The two biggest roadblocks to ensuring rehabilitative success are lack of governmental aid, as well as legislative proposals and court decisions that limit the self-determining rights of Native American nations. Inadequate funding for Indian social services has been identified as a key factor in the continued higher-than-normal removal rates of Native American children.[299] Thus, while ICWA helps to prevent unwarranted removals, it does not do enough to address the ongoing effects of past removal policies. There is little question that assimilative policies of the past are an underlying cause of the dire socioeconomic conditions facing Indian communities today. Reversing the effects of these policies will take both time and money. Experts in the field suggest that a good starting place would be to adequately fund ICWA related programs, both in terms of child protection and family preservation.[300] A much larger issue is the inconsistent commitment on the part of the United States to basic human rights precepts regarding indigenous populations, including the right of self-determination.[301] We have already seen that recognition of this right is crucial to achieving basic justice for indigenous peoples in the form of reparations for past and ongoing human rights violations. Indian nations would like nothing more than to be able to get on with the business of improving the lives of their children and families through their own economic, cultural, and social development. While there are a number of domestic impediments to achieving these ends, many could be overcome by the United States firmly embracing the international human rights precepts embodied in the UN Draft Declaration on the Rights of Indigenous Peoples.

There are no provisions in ICWA providing for direct compensation to the victims of removal or their families. Yet it does envision the granting of funds to Native American nations and organizations for such things as family assistance services, subsidies to Indian foster and adoptive children, treatment and counseling facilities for those affected by removal, and legal representation and advice to Indian families involved in child custody proceedings. Such programs represent a form of collective reparations, affording indigenous communities the opportunity for self-determination in the form of social welfare and development. Thus ICWA is consistent with established and emerging international precepts entitling indigenous peoples to "adequate financial and technical assistance, from States and through international cooperation, to pursue freely their political, economic, social, cultural, and spiritual development."[302] This includes funding and otherwise supporting "special projects"—such as ICWA's family assistance, subsidies, and treatment programs—that are designed to improve the living and health conditions of Native peoples and their children. The establishment and continued financing of these programs are also consistent with country practices that emphasize economic and social reform as a means of redressing collective and intergenerational harms, such as those experienced by indigenous peoples as a result of removal.

However, social welfare and development support, particularly in the limited nature provided under ICWA, does not foreclose additional state obligations. For instance, on the issue of direct compensation, nothing in ICWA precludes the award of damages to individuals or their families. However, neither does it address the various procedural and substantive barriers that claimants might encounter in such suits. It is only recently that some of these claims have been filed in U.S. courts, and several have been dismissed on procedural grounds.[303] Two primary hurdles faced by litigants in the United States and elsewhere include difficulties of proof and statutes of limitations. Moreover, there is also the emotional trauma that accompanies any court battle to remedy harms of the nature at issue in these cases. As one Aboriginal organization noted, "the separation issue is a very private and personal one for the people concerned. The stress and trauma of a court case and the resulting loss of privacy is likely to deter many Aboriginal people from bringing a legal action against the Government."[304] The U.N. reparation studies outline a number of steps that might be taken to address some of these concerns, such as adapting the legal system of states to ensure that the right to reparations is "readily accessible," not applying statutes of limitations "to periods during which no effective remedies exist for human rights violations" or to any claims relating to reparations for gross violations of human rights, making evidence in the possession of the government "readily available" to the victims, and recognizing that "records or other tangible evidence may be limited or unavailable" and that claims may be based primarily on "the testimony of victims, family members, and medical and mental health professionals."[305]

Finally, as is the case with rehabilitation, federal budgetary constraints and cutbacks result in a level of uncertainty that significantly undermines compensatory child welfare and development programs for Indian nations. While all countries need flexibility in terms of prioritizing their limited resources, since ICWA involves partial collective reparations for serious human rights violations, a strong argument can be made that it should not be subject to the same type of prioritizing as other federally funded programs. In any event, there is little question that at present, the funding level for tribal child welfare programs is woefully inadequate.

6. Conclusion

> The danger lies in forgetting. Forgetting, however, will not affect only the dead. Should it triumph, the ashes of yesterday will cover our hopes of tomorrow.
> —Elie Wiesel[306]

The forcible removal of indigenous children from their homes and communities constitutes serious human rights violations. While the United States no longer embraces such policies, their effects are ongoing, profoundly disrupting Indian peoples' sense of well-being, family cohesiveness, and cultural survival. This paper demonstrates that ICWA, while not a perfect law,[307] is an important step toward the United States meeting its international obligations to provide reparations for these harms. The statute does not focus on what we often think of as typical reparations—individual monetary relief. Rather, it encompasses the broader international components of reparations: rehabilitation, restitution, prevention of future harm, and collective compensation. Moreover, its basic premise is consistent with principles of human rights, indigenous peoples' rights, and indigenous views on family and community. In particular, it provides "intergenerational" or "seventh generational" justice in the form of indigenous self-determination. If indigenous peoples around the world are to be made whole, as reparation plans often seek to do, this will only occur when nation states have fully embraced an understanding of self-determination that respects indigenous rights to land and resources; social, cultural, and economic development; and some form of autonomy or self-government. A good starting point would be for the General Assembly to adopt the UN Draft Declaration on the Rights of Indigenous Peoples, which has been in draft form for over ten years. By doing so, UN member states would take a giant step toward addressing the second important component of reparations: repairing and rebuilding relationships. Today we live in a world where no society of people can expect to go it alone. Nor do indigenous peoples seem particularly interested in pursuing such an option. However, indigenous peoples have for far too long suffered the ongoing effects of discrimination, oppression, and forced assimilation. States need to acknowledge their duty to work with indigenous communities to repair the unjust relationships that have arisen from these historical and contemporary phenomena. This includes respecting and supporting the rights of indigenous peoples to live and develop as distinct, self-determining communities. The Indian Child Welfare Act is but a small step in that direction.

NOTES

An earlier version of this paper was published at 21 Harvard Human Rights Journal 47 (2008). The author would like to thank Ellen Beckworth and Bradley Mead for their research assistance. For earlier works by the author on the Indian Child Welfare Act, see Lorie M. Graham, *The Past Never Vanishes: A Contextual Critique of the Existing Indian Family Doctrine*, 23 AM. L. REV. 1 (1999), and Lorie M. Graham, *Reparations and the Indian Child Welfare Act*, 25 L. STUDIES FORUM 619 (2001).

1. *See, e.g.*, WINONA LADUKE, ALL OUR RELATIONS: NATIVE STRUGGLES FOR LAND AND LIFE 197–200 (South End Press 1999); What is the Seventh Generation, at http://sixnations.buffnet.net/Culture/?article=seventh_generation.
2. Simon Ortiz, *The Language We Know*, in GROWING UP NATIVE AMERICAN at 32 (Patricia Riley ed., Harper 1993).
3. *See supra* note 1.
4. *See, e.g.*, DAVID STANNARD, AMERICAN HOLOCAUST (Oxford University Press 1992); M. ANNETTE JAIMES, ED., THE STATE OF NATIVE AMERICA: GENOCIDE, COLONIZATION, AND RESISTANCE (South End Press 1992); and WINONA LADUKE, ALL OUR RELATIONS: NATIVE STRUGGLES FOR LAND AND LIFE (South End Press 1999).
5. Kevin Gover, *"There is Hope": A Few Thoughts on Indian Law*, 24 AM. INDIAN L. REV. 219 (1999/2000).
6. *See* H.R. Rep. No. 104-808, 104th Cong. (1996), *available at* http://www.congress.gov/cgi-bin/cpquery/z?cp104:hr808p1.
7. *See infra* notes 18–65 and accompanying text. *See also* Lorie M. Graham, *The Past Never Vanishes: A Contextual Critique of the Existing Indian Family Doctrine*, 23 AM. INDIAN L. REV. 1, 48 (1999).
8. *See, e.g.*, Indian Self-Determination and Education Assistance Act of 1975, Pub L. No. 93-638, 88 Stat. 2203 (1975).

    Some of these legislative responses have been criticized for not going far enough in terms of repairing the wrongs committed against Native peoples, their lands, and their culture. *See, e.g.*, ROY L. BROOKS ED., WHEN SORRY ISN'T ENOUGH: THE CONTROVERSY OVER APOLOGIES AND REPARATIONS FOR HUMAN INJUSTICE 233 (NYU Press 1999). One example cited is the Indian Claims Commission, a quasi-judicial tribunal established by the federal government in the 1940s to address a myriad of Indian claims against the federal government. The commission's primary focus was on land deprivation, but as Professors Brooks and Newton argue, the ICC redress mechanisms were "unabashedly result-oriented" and therefore flawed from the outset. As Newton points out, "the decision [of the Commission] to equate justice with money . . . was the most serious flaw in the commission's design and implementation." These findings were recently confirmed by the Inter-American Commission on Human Rights in a case involving the Western Shoshone. *See Case of Mary and Carrie Dann v. United States*, Case No. 11.140, Inter-Am. C.H.R. 75/02 (Dec. 27, 2002). Other legislative examples critiqued in the Brooks collection of essays include the 1971 Alaska Native Claims Settlement Act, 43 U.S.C.A. §§ 1601–28 (1971); the Native American Graves Protection and Repatriation Act of 1990, 25 U.S.C.A. §§ 3001–13, 18 U.S.C.A. § 1170 (1990); and the Indian Gaming Regulatory Act of 1988, 25 U.S.C.A. §§ 2701–21.
9. Indian Child Welfare Act of 1978, 25 U.S.C. §1901–63 (2000).
10. *See, e.g.*, RANDALL KENNEDY, INTERRACIAL INTIMACIES: SEX, MARRIAGE, IDENTITY, AND ADOPTION 450–518 (Pantheon 2003); H.R. 3156, 104th Cong. (1996) ("To amend the Indian Child Welfare Act of 1978 to exempt voluntary child custody proceeding from coverage under the act"); H.R. 3275, 104th Cong. (1996) ("To amend the Indian Child Welfare Act to exempt from coverage of the act child custody proceedings involving a child whose parents do not maintain significant social, cultural, or political affiliation with the tribe of which the parents

are members"); *Rye v. Weasel*, 934 S.W. 2d 257 (Ky. 1996) (" . . . it is very clear that Congress did not intend that the ICWA should be applied . . . to children who, although Indian by birth, have not lived for many years in an existing Indian family"); *Hampton v. J.A.L.*, 658 So. 2d 331 (La. Ct. App. 1995) (Court held that ICWA was not intended to apply when the child does not live in an Indian environment and the removal will not cause the breakup of an Indian family).

11. See *infra* notes 274-77 and accompanying text. See also *In re Adoption of Crews*, 833 P. 2d 1249 (Wash. 1992) (court held that the child in question was not part of an existing Indian family because neither she, nor her family, ever lived on the reservation and there were no ties to any Indian tribe or community); *In re Adoption of Baby Boy D.*, 742 P. 2d 1059, 1064 (Okla. 1987) (held ICWA is inapplicable where the child never resided in an Indian family and has a non-Indian mother); *S.A. v. E.J.P.*, 571 So. 2d. 1187, 1189 (Ala. 1990) (court held that since the child was never part of an Indian family, never lived in an Indian home, never experienced the Indian social and cultural world, and was born to a non-Indian mother, the "Existing Indian Family exception" did not apply); *Rye v. Weasel*, 934 S.W. 2d 257, 261-62 (Ky. 1996) (held that the "Existing Indian Family exception" was not judicially created, but in fact, reflected congressional intent).

12. See *infra* notes 265-77 and accompanying text. See also Graham, *supra* note 7.

13. *See, e.g.*, ROBERT A. WILLIAMS, JR., LIKE A LOADED WEAPON: THE REHNQUIST COURT, INDIAN RIGHTS, AND THE LEGAL HISTORY OF RACISM IN AMERICA (University of Minnesota Press 2005).

14. *See, e.g.*, S. James Anaya, *The Native Hawaiian People and International Human Rights Law: Toward a Remedy for Past and Continuing Wrongs*, 28 GA. L. REV. 309, 311-12 (1994). See also R. H. K. Lei Lindsey, *Native Hawaiians, Legal Realities, and Politics as Usual*, 24 HAW. L. REV. 693, n. 96 (2002); Jennifer M. L. Chock, *One Hundred Years of Illegitimacy: International Legal Analysis of the Illegal Overthrow of the Hawaiian Monarchy, Hawai'i's Annexation and Possible Reparations*, 17 HAW. L. REV. 463 (1995).

15. *See, e.g.*, Brooks, *supra* note 8, at 309-90. See also Kyle D. Logue, *The Jurisprudence of Slavery Reparations: Reparations as Redistribution*, 84 B.U. L. REV. 1319, 1393-94 (2004); Edieth Y. Wu, *Reparations to African-Americans: The Only Remedy for the U.S. Government's Failure to Enforce the Thirteenth, Fourteenth, and Fifteenth Amendments*, 3 CONN. PUB. INT. L. J. 403, 404 (2004).

16. *See, e.g.*, BRINGING THEM HOME: REPORT OF THE NATIONAL INQUIRY INTO THE SEPARATION OF ABORIGINAL AND TORRES STRAIT ISLANDER CHILDREN FROM THEIR FAMILIES (Sydney: Human Rights and Equal Opportunity Commission, 1997) [hereinafter BRINGING THEM HOME] (reprinted at http://www.austlii.edu.au/au/special/rsjproject/rsjlibrary/hreoc/stolen/indes. html); *Aleck v. Canada*, [1991] A.C.W.S. (3D) 28 (1991); *A.Q. v. Canada*, [1998] 169 Sask. R. 1; *D.A. v. Canada*, [1998] 173 Sask. R. 312; *H.L. v. Canada*, [2003] S.J. No. 298. See also Canada's Indian Residential School Settlement Agreement of May 8, 2006, *available at* http://www.irsr-rqpi. gc.ca/english/pdf/indian_Residential_Schools_Settlement_Agreement.pdf.

17. Draft United Nations Declaration on the Rights of Indigenous Peoples, UN Doc. E/CN4/1995/2, E/CN.4/SUB.2/1994/56 (Oct. 28, 1994) [hereinafter Draft Declaration].

18. *See* David H. Getches et al., CASES AND MATERIALS ON FEDERAL INDIAN LAW 185 (2004).

19. Thomas B. Rosensteil, WHITES ADOPT NAVAJO: SOVEREIGNTY ON TRIAL IN CUSTODY CASE, L.A. TIMES, Feb. 11, 1987, at A1.
20. *See, e.g.*, Graham, *supra* note 7, at 10–32.
21. *See, e.g.*, CLYDE ELLIS, TO CHANGE THEM FOREVER (University of Oklahoma Press 1996); JOHN REYNER AND JEANNE EDER, A HISTORY OF INDIAN EDUCATION (University of Oklahoma Press 1989); MARGARET CONNELL SZASZ, EDUCATION AND THE AMERICAN INDIAN (University of New Mexico Press 1977); Christine Metteer, *Pigs in Heaven: A Parable of Native American Adoption under the Indian Child Welfare Act*, 28 ARIZ. ST. L.J. 589 (1996).
22. CLYDE ELLIS, TO CHANGE THEM FOREVER 3 (University of Oklahoma Press 1996).
23. *See* BENJAMIN FRANKLIN, TWO TRACTS 28–29 (3d ed. 1794); *see also* THE PAPERS OF BENJAMIN FRANKLIN 481–83 (Leonard W. Labaree et al. ed., 1961).
24. *See, e.g.*, MARGARET CONNELL SZASZ, INDIAN EDUCATION IN THE AMERICAN COLONIES (University of Nebraska Press 1988).
25. Beginning with the Continental Congress, the United States pledged to "secure and preserve the friendship of the Indian nations." FELIX S. COHEN, HANDBOOK OF FEDERAL INDIAN LAW 47 (Bobbs-Merrill 1982). This pledge was further articulated in the U.S. Constitution, which recognizes the power of Congress to regulate commerce with "foreign nations, and among the several States, and with the Indian tribes." U.S. CONST., art. I, § 8(3). Moreover, through numerous treaties, agreements, statutes, and executive orders, millions of acres of tribal land were ceded to the United States in return for promises to protect the sovereign status of Indian nations, as well as to provide various services and benefits. The U.S. Constitution further recognizes "all Treaties made" and all existing and future treaties shall be considered the "supreme Law of the' Land." U.S. CONST. art. VI, cl. 2.
26. *See* PETER FARB, MAN'S RISE TO CIVILIZATION 257–68 (Dutton 1968).
27. *See generally* DAVID WALLACE ADAMS, EDUCATION FOR EXTINCTION (University of Kansas Press 1995); MICHAEL C. COLEMAN, AMERICAN INDIAN CHILDREN AT SCHOOL (University Press of Mississippi 1993); CLYDE ELLIS, TO CHANGE THEM FOREVER (University of Oklahoma Press 1996).
28. *See* Commission of Indian Affairs, Annual Report 430 (1990). Captain Henry Pratt of Carlisle Indian School's ultimate dream was "to scatter the entire population of Indian children across the nation, with some 70,000 families each taking in one Indian child." *See* Adams, *supra* note 27, at 14.
29. Indian General Allotment Act of 1887, 24 Stat. 388 (1887) (The Allotment Act allowed the President to survey the lands of American Indian nations and then divide those lands into individual allotments, effectively destroying a tribe's communal property system).
30. John Collier, *America's Treatment of Her Indians*, 18 CURRENT HIST. 772 (1923).
31. LEWIS MERIAM ED., THE PROBLEM OF INDIAN ADMINISTRATION 403 (Johns Hopkins Press 1928).
32. Wheeler-Howard Act of 1934, 48 Stat. 984 (1934). It was during this "Indian Reorganization" era that the Johnson-O'Malley Act (J-O'M) was passed by Congress, which authorized the

secretary of the interior to contract with states and private institutions "for the education, medical attention, agricultural assistance, and social welfare, including relief of distress, of Indians." Ch. 147, 48 Stat. 96 (amended and codified at 25 U.S.C. §§ 452–54). While the J-O'M and related policies were aimed at improving the dire socioeconomic conditions on reservations, they had other unforeseen consequences. In addition to public schools, the law encouraged the use of private, state, and local social welfare agencies to meet the needs of Native Americans, opening the door for increased conflict between tribes and states over Indian child welfare issues. The caseworkers in these agencies, and the teachers and administrators in the public schools had no basis for evaluating the cultural values and social norms of Native American communities. The cultural misunderstandings that inevitably arose from this lack of knowledge would contribute significantly to the Indian child welfare crisis of the 1970s.

33. *See, e.g.*, O. K. Armstrong, *Set the American Indians Free*, READER'S DIGEST, August 1945, at 47.
34. Indian Termination Act, H.R. Con. Res., 83rd Cong. (1953).
35. *See, e.g.*, Menominee Tribe Termination Act, 68 Stat. 250 (1954); Klamath Indian Termination Act, 68 Stat. 718 (1954); Federal Supervision Termination Act, 68 Stat. 724 (1954).
36. *See* FELIX S. COHEN, *supra* note 25, at 175 (1982).
37. *See* H.R. Rep. No. 2091, 78th Cong. (1944).
38. Simon Ortiz, *The Language We Know*, in PATRICIA RILEY, ED., GROWING UP NATIVE AMERICAN 34 (Morrow 1993).
39. *See, e.g.*, Bruce Davies, *Implementing the Indian Child Welfare Act*, 16 CLEARINGHOUSE REV. 179, 181 (1982).
40. *See generally* Patrice Kunesh-Hartman, *Comment, The Indian Child Welfare Act of 1978: Protecting Essential Tribal Interests*, 60 U. COLO. L. REV. 131, 136 (1988); Joan Smith, *Young Once, Indian Forever*, IMAGE, July 3, 1988, at 9.
41. Some critics of ICWA have taken issue with these studies, in one case referring to them as "junk social science." *See* Randall Kennedy, *Race, Children, and Custody Battles*, in INTERRACIAL INTIMACIES, *supra* note 10, at 499. While a fuller discussion of this claim of "junk science" is beyond the scope of this paper, it ignores completely the parallel stories and experiences of American Indian children and their families. Moreover, such claims fail to consider the larger historical picture that led to the passage of ICWA, including the need to remedy serious human rights violations, in part, by honoring the self-determining status of American Indian nations. *See infra* notes 246–303 and accompanying text. For a more nuanced analysis of the strengths and weaknesses of the law, *see* Barbara Atwood, *Flashpoints under the Indian Child Welfare Act: Toward a New Understanding of State Court Resistance*, 51 EMORY L. J. 587 (2002). *See also* Russell Lawrence Barsh, *The Indian Child Welfare Act of 1978: A Critical Analysis*, 31 HASTINGS L. J. 1287 (1980).
42. *See, e.g*, STEVEN UNGER ED., THE DESTRUCTION OF AMERICAN INDIAN FAMILIES 1, 12 (Association of American Indian Affairs 1977) [hereinafter American Indian Families]; H.R. Rep. No. 95-1386, 11 (1978), as reprinted in 1978 U.S.C.C.A.N. 7530 [hereinafter House Report]. In some individual states the problem was much worse. Minnesota, Montana, South Dakota, and Washington had

American Indian placement rates that were five to nineteen times greater than the non-Indian rates. In the state of Wisconsin, American Indian children were at risk of being separated from their families at a rate 1,600 times greater than non-Indian children. Moreover, many of these children were being completely cut off from their communities and heritages. At least 85 percent of the placements were in non-Indian homes and institutions, and a high proportion of those placements were out-of-state. *See* House Report, at 9.

43. For instance, in 1971, the BIA school census showed that 34,538 American Indian children lived in its institutional facilities rather than at home. House Report, *supra* note 42, at 9. On the Navajo Reservation alone, 20,000 children in grades K–12 were living in boarding schools at the time of the studies. *Id.*

44. Conversations with the author. *"The Past Never Vanishes": A Contextual Critique of the Existing Indian Family Doctrine*, 23 AM. INDIAN L. REV. 1, 25 (1998).

45. *See* House Report, *supra* note 42, at 9; AMERICAN INDIAN FAMILIES *supra* note 42, at 2.

46. Hon. James Abourezk, *The Role of the Federal Government: A Congressional View*, in AMERICAN INDIAN FAMILIES, *supra* note 42, at 12.

47. AMERICAN INDIAN FAMILIES, *supra* note 42, at 3; House Report, *supra* note 42, at 10.

48. *See* BEVERLY HUNGRY WOLF, THE WAYS OF MY GRANDMOTHER 195 (1980).

49. *See* House Report, *supra* note 42, at 10. *See also* AMERICAN INDIAN FAMILIES, *supra* note 42, at 22; Barsh *supra* note 41, at 1295.

50. *See* House Report, *supra* note 42, at 10; Szasz, *supra* note 24, at 21. For example, Santee Sioux author Charles Eastman wrote about his grandmother's stories of the "Hinakaga (owl) who swooped down in the darkness" and carried the naughty child up into the trees. *Id.* Clark Wissler in a study on Native cultures noted in particular that "admonition and mild ridicule" were more predominant forms of discipline than "force or punishment." *Id.*

51. For instance, in one 1977 California case, a child was removed from the custody of her extended family on the sole ground that 'an Indian reservation is an unsuitable environment for a child and that the pre-adoptive parents were financially able to provide a home and a way of life superior to the one furnished by the natural mother." *See* AMERICAN INDIAN FAMILIES, *supra* note 42, at 3.

52. *See, e.g., Indian Child Welfare Program: Hearings before the Subcomm. on Indian Affairs of the Senate Comm. on Interior and Insular Affairs*, 93rd Cong. 70, at 5 (1974) [hereinafter 1974 Hearings].

53. H.R. Rep. No. 95-1386, 11 (1978), as reprinted in 1978 U.S.C.C.A.N. 7530 [hereinafter House Report].

54. In one such case, a child was held in foster care for seven months under a state ex parte emergency removal order before a hearing was scheduled. And even then, the mother was notified of the hearing only by publication, despite the fact that she had continuously lived at the same address from which the child had been removed. *See Decoteau v. District County Court*, 87 S.D. 555, 211 N.W.2d 843 (1977). *See generally* 1974 Hearings, *supra* note 51, at 65–69; House Report, *supra* note 42, at 11.

55. Historically, tribes have clashed with states laying claim to jurisdiction over matters essential

to tribal survival; family matters are no exception. *See, e.g.*, Barbara Ann Atwood, *Fighting over Indian Children: The Uses and Abuses of Jurisdictional Ambiguity*, 36 UCLA L. Rev. 1051 (1989).

56. The Lost Bird Society, an organization charged with helping American Indian children find their families, maintains that before ICWA was passed, thousands of children were illegally taken from their families and put up for adoption.

57. *See* Troy R. Johnson ed., *The Indian Child Welfare Act: Unto the Seventh Generation: Conference Proceedings* (University of California 1993) [hereinafter Conference Proceedings]. *See generally* AMERICAN INDIAN FAMILIES, *supra* note 42, at 8.

58. The American Academy of Child Psychiatry agreed, noting that "There is much clinical evidence to suggest that Native American children placed in off-reservation non-Indian homes are at risk in their later development. Often enough [the children] are cared for by devoted and well-intentioned foster or adoptive parents. Nonetheless, particularly in adolescence, they are subject to ethnic confusion and a pervasive sense of abandonment...." *Indian Child Welfare Act of 1977: Hearing on S. 1214 before the Senate Select Comm. on Indian Affairs*, 95th Cong. 538 (1977) (statement of Drs. Carl Mindell and Alan Gurwitt, American Academy of Child Psychiatry).

59. Graham, *supra* note at 7, 30–32.

60. Barsh, *supra* note 41, at 1291 (quoting 1974 Hearings, *supra* note 51, at 58).

61. Margaret Plantz et. al., *Indian Child Welfare: A Status Report, Final Report of the Survey of Indian Child Welfare and Implementation of the Indian Child Welfare Act of 1980*, ES-1 at 54 (1988).

62. House Report, *supra* note 42, at 12.

63. VINE DELORIA, INDIAN EDUCATION IN AMERICA 22 (Fulcrum Publishing 1991).

64. *See, e.g.*, Jonathon B. Taylor and Joseph P. Kalt, *American Indians on Reservations: A Databook of Socioeconomic Change between the 1990 and 2000 Censuses*, available at http://www.ksg.harvard.edu/hpaied/pubs/documents/americanindiansonreservationsadatabookofsocioeconomic-change.pdf.

65. *See infra* notes 294–303 and accompanying text. *See also* Troy R. Johnson, *Introduction*, THE INDIAN CHILD WELFARE ACT: UNTO THE SEVENTH GENERATION (University of California 1993).

66. 1974 Hearings, *supra* note 51, at 193 (quoting Chief Calvin Isaac of the Mississippi Band of Choctaw Indians). One particularly problematic practice is the application of the "Existing Indian Family doctrine" by state courts to circumvent the provisions of ICWA. *See infra* notes 275–278 and accompanying text for a discussion of how this doctrine undermines key remedial aspects of the law.

67. *See* Lisa Driscoll, *Tribal Courts: New Mexico's Third Judiciary*, 32 N.M. B. BULL., Feb. 18, 1993, at A5.

68. *See, e.g.*, Earl M. Maltz, *Brown and Tee-Hit-Ton*, 29 AM. INDIAN L. REV. 75, 99 (2005); John R. Wonder, *"Merciless Indian Savages" and the Declaration of Independence: Native Americans Translate the Ecunnaunuxulgee Document*, 25 AM. INDIAN L. REV. 65 (2001); Robert Laurence, *Symmetry and Asymmetry in Federal Indian Law*, 42 ARIZ. L. REV. 861, 896–97 (2000). *See also* Kenneth C. Davis, *Amnesia*, N.Y. TIMES, Sept. 3, 1995, at E1.

69. *See, e.g.*, DAVID E. STANNARD, AMERICAN HOLOCAUST: THE CONQUEST OF THE NEW WORLD

(Oxford University Press 1993) (describing the treatment of American Indians in the Americas as "purposeful genocide"); Barbara Ann Atwood, *supra* note 41, at 602 (discussing the treatment of American Indian children at white-run boarding schools as "blatant cultural genocide"); Matthew L. M. Fletcher, *Sawnawgezewag: "The Indian Problem" and the Lost Art of Survival*, 28 AM. INDIAN L. REV. 35, 39–41 (2004) (discussing the "genocide perpetrated on Indian people"); Robert B. Porter, *A Proposal to the Hanodaganyas to Decolonize Federal Indian Control Law*, in SOVEREIGNTY, COLONIALISM, AND THE INDIGENOUS NATIONS 183 (Carolina Academic Press 2005) ("...throughout the 222 years of United States history, every conceivable policy objective has been attempted, ranging from the pursuit of peaceful coexistence—through the Treaty, Reorganization, and Self-Determination policies—to outright genocide—through the Warfare, Removal, Reservation, Allotment, and Termination policies.").

70. *See, e.g.*, Robert A. Williams, Jr., *Frontier of Legal Thought III: Encounters on the Frontiers of International Human Rights Law- Redefining the Terms of Indigenous Peoples' Survival in the World*, 1990 DUKE L. J. 660, 665 (states that indigenous peoples have been pushed to the brink of extinction by policies of ethnocide); John P. Lavelle, *Rescuing Paha Sapa: Achieving Environmental Justice by Restoring the Great Grasslands and Returning the Sacred Black Hills to the Great Sioux Nation*, 5 GREAT PLAINS NAT. RESOURCES J. 40, 80–81 (2001) (describes the treatment of the Sioux tribes as ethnocide); *See also County of Yakima v. Confederated Tribes and Bands of Yakima Indian Nation*, 502 U.S. 251, 276 (1992) (Justice Blackmun, concurring in part and dissenting in part) (describing allotment as a "systematic 'ethnocide,'" quoting H. SHUSTER, THE YAKIMAS: A CRITICAL BIBLIOGRAPHY 70 (Indiana University Press 1982)).

71. *See, e.g.*, DEAN NEU AND RICHARD THERRIEN, ACCOUNTING FOR GENOCIDE: CANADA'S BUREAUCRATIC ASSAULT ON ABORIGINAL PEOPLE (Palgrave 2003) (describing the removal and indoctrination of First Nations children as a "force of racism, applied bureaucratically and rationalized economically at arm's length." Working insidiously as psychological terrorism); ROBERT A. WILLIAMS, JR., LIKE A LOADED WEAPON: THE RHENQUIST COURT, INDIAN RIGHTS, AND THE LEGAL HISTORY OF RACISM IN AMERICA 97–113 (Princeton University Press 2005) (discussing the racist underpinnings of nineteenth and twentieth century Supreme Court precedent); ROBERT A. WILLIAMS, JR., THE AMERICAN INDIAN IN WESTERN LEGAL THOUGHT: THE DISCOURSES OF CONQUEST 316–17 (Oxford University Press 1990) (describing Chief Justice John Marshall's reliance on the European "doctrine of discovery" as an act of implementing "1000 years of European racism and colonialism" on America).

72. *See, e.g.*, Stannard, *supra* note 68. Neu & Therrien, *supra* note 70.

73. RESTATEMENT (THIRD) OF THE FOREIGN RELATIONS LAW OF THE UNITED STATES, § 702 (m) (American Law Institute 1987).

74. According to the RESTATEMENT (THIRD) OF THE FOREIGN RELATIONS LAW OF THE UNITED STATES "all rights proclaimed in the Universal Declaration and protected by the principal International Covenants are internationally recognized human rights, but some rights are fundamental and intrinsic to human dignity. Consistent patterns of violations of such rights as state policy may be deemed 'gross' *ipso facto*." *Id*. This paper contends that both the right

of self-determination and the right of cultural identity are fundamental aspects of indigenous peoples' dignity as peoples.

75. S. James Anaya, *The Native Hawaiian People and International Human Rights Law: Toward a Remedy for Past and Continuing Wrongs*, 28 GA. L. REV. 309, 320 (1994).

76. *See, e.g.*, S. James Anaya, *A Contemporary Definition of the International Norm of Self-Determination*, 3 TRANSNAT'L L. & COMP. PROBS. 131 (1993); ANTONIO CASSESE, SELF-DETERMINATION OF PEOPLES (Cambridge University Press 1995); HURST HANNUM, AUTONOMY, SOVEREIGNTY, AND SELF-DETERMINATION (Penn Press 1990). *See also* Lorie M. Graham, *Resolving Indigenous Claims to Self-Determination*, 10 ILSA J. OF INT'L L. & COMP. L. 385 (2004); *Self-Determination for Indigenous Peoples after Kosovo: Translating Self-Determination "Into Practice" and "Into Peace,"* 6 ILSA J. OF INT'L & COMP. L. 455 (2002).

77. *See, e.g.*, Reference Re Secession of Quebec, [1998] 37 I.L.M. 1340; Hum. Rts. Comm., The Right to Self-Determination of Peoples (art. 1): 13/03/84, CCPR General Comment 12.

78. *See* S. JAMES ANAYA, INDIGENOUS PEOPLES IN INTERNATIONAL LAW 98 (Oxford University Press 2004).

79. U.N. CHARTER art. 1, para. 2.

80. International Covenant on Civil and Political Rights, Dec. 16, 1966, 999 U.N.T.S. 171, 6 I.L.M 368 (1967) (G.A. Res. 2200, 21 GAOR, Supp., 16 U.N. Doc. A/6316 at 52) (entered into force March 23, 1976); International Covenant on Economic Social and Cultural Rights, Dec. 16, 1966, 993 UN.T.S. 3, 6 I.L.M. 360 (1976) (Annex to G.A. Res. 2200, 21 GAOR Supp. 16, U.N. Doc. A/6316 at 490 (entered into force Jan. 3, 1976).

81. *See* Hannum, *supra* note 75, at 14; Anaya, *supra* note 77, at 97.

82. *See* Graham, *supra* note 75, *Resolving Indigenous Claims to Self-Determination*, at 386–98; Graham, *supra* note 75, *Self-Determination for Indigenous Peoples after Kosovo*, at 460–66.

83. *See, e.g.*, Reference Re. Secession of Quebec, 37 I.L.M. 1340, 1373 (1998); Report of the Human Rights Committee, U.N. GAOR, 47th Sess., Supp. No. 40, at 52, U.N. A/47/40 (1992).

84. *See* Graham, *supra* note 75, *Resolving Indigenous Claims to Self-Determination*, at 388–89.

85. *See id.* at 389–90; Graham, *supra* note 75, *Self-Determination for Indigenous Peoples after Kosovo*, at 462.

86. *See supra* note 79 and accompanying text.

87. *See* Anaya, *supra* note 77, at 99. A related concern is that application of the principle of self-determination beyond the colonial context leads to violence and unrest. However, elsewhere I have suggested another scenario—that violence and unrest may be averted or minimized by international processes and institutions that address early on alleged violations of a group's claim of self-determination. *See* Graham, *supra* note 75, *Resolving Claims to Indigenous Self-Determination*.

88. *See, e.g.*, Anaya, *supra* note 77, at 45–58; *See also Programme of Activities for the International decade of the World's Indigenous People* (1995–2004) (para. 4), G.A. Res. 50/157, ¶ 4 Dec. 21, 1995). Introduction *available at* http://www.unhchr.ch/html/menu6/2/fs9.htm.

89. General Conference of the International Labour Organisation, Convention Concerning Indigenous

and Tribal Peoples in Independent Countries (Convention 169), Adopted June 27, 1989, 28 I.L.M. 1382 (entered into force Sept. 5, 1991).
90. Draft United Nations Declaration on the Rights of Indigenous Peoples, U.N. Doc E/CN.4/1995/2, E/CN.4/Sub.2/1994/56 (1995). In 1982, the UN Economic and Social Council and Human Rights Commission authorized the formation of a Working Group on Indigenous Populations. By 1993, a Draft UN Declaration on the Rights of Indigenous Peoples was completed. That same year, the General Assembly proclaimed the International Decade of the World's Indigenous People. These two events were conceptually linked in that adoption of the Declaration by the General Assembly was a major goal of the decade. While the Declaration was not adopted by the end of the decade, it was recently approved by the Human Rights Council and sent to the General Assembly for adoption during the 2006 session. However, at the request of several African countries, consideration of the Declaration was delayed until the next year.
91. Anaya, *supra* note 77, at 70.
92. In other works I have discussed the collective aspects of the declaration and how they might impact final adoption. *See* Graham, *supra* note 75, *Resolving Indigenous Claims to Self-Determination*, at 385.
93. *See* Report of the Working Group on Indigenous Populations in its Sixth Session, U.N. ESCOR CN.4, U.N. Doc. E/CN4/Sub.2/1988/24 at 21, para. 77 (1988).
94. Rebecca Tsosie, *Tribalism, Constitutionalism, and Cultural Pluralism: Where Do Indigenous Peoples Fit within Civil Society?*, 5 U. PA. J. CONST. LAW 357, 376 (2003).
95. *Id.* at 378.
96. Anaya, *supra* note 77, at 81–82.
97. *Id.* at 80.
98. *Id.* at 129–56.
99. *See infra* notes 246–303 and accompanying text.
100. RAPHAEL LEMKIN, AXIS RULE IN OCCUPIED EUROPE, ch. 1C (Carnegie Endowment for International Peace 1944).
101. FRANK CHALK AND KURT JONASSOHN, THE HISTORY AND SOCIOLOGY OF GENOCIDE: ANALYSES AND CASE STUDIES 8–10 (Yale University Press 1990).
102. G.A. Res. 96, U.N. G.A., 1st Sess. (Dec. 11, 1946), *available at* http://www.armenian-genocide.org/Affirmation.227/current_category.6/affirmation_detail.html. *See also* BRINGING THEM HOME, *supra* note 16, part 4.
103. United Nations Convention on the Prevention and Punishment of the Crime of Genocide, Dec. 9, 1948, 1021 U.N.T.S. 78 (entered into force January 12, 1951).
104. United Nations Convention on the Prevention and Punishment of the Crime of Genocide, Dec. 9, 1948, 1021 U.N.T.S. 78 (1948) (emphasis added).
105. *See* Stannard, *supra* note 68, at 280–81.
106. RESTATEMENT (THIRD) OF THE FOREIGN RELATIONS LAW OF THE UNITED STATES § 702 (American Law Institute 1987).
107. Draft United Nations Declaration on the Rights of Indigenous Peoples, art. 6, U.N. Doc. E/

CN.4/1995/2, E/CN.4/Sub2/1994/56 (1994). For a discussion of the draft declaration and the United States' position regarding various provisions *see* Lorie M. Graham, *Resolving Indigenous Claims to Self-Determination*, 10 ILSA J. OF INT'L & COMP. L. 385 (2004); Lorie M. Graham, *Self-Determination for Indigenous Peoples after Kosovo: Translating Self-Determination "Into Peace" and "Into Practice,"* 5 ILSA J. OF INT'L & COMP. L. 455 (2002). *See also* S. JAMES ANAYA, INDIGENOUS PEOPLES IN INTERNATIONAL LAW (Oxford University Press 2004).

108. *See* Application of the Convention on the Prevention and Punishment of the Crime of Genocide, Bos. & Herz.—Serb. & Mon., May 9, 2006, 2006 I.C.J. 38 (May 9, 2006).

109. *See* Karyn Becker, *Genocide and Ethnic Cleansing, available at* http://www.munfw.org/archive/50th/4th1.htm (last visited May 29, 2006).

110. *See* U.S. State Department Report, May 1999, *available at* http://italy.usembassy.gov/pdf/other/kosovo.pdf (last visited May 29, 2006).

111. *See* International Court of Justice Press Release 2007/8, *available at* http://www.icj-cjj.org/icjwww/ipresscom/ipress2007/ipresscom_2007-8_bhy_200702026.htm.

112. RAPHAEL LEMKIN, AXIS RULE IN OCCUPIED EUROPE 79, 147 (H. Ferting 1973)(1944); *see also* BRINGING THEM HOME, *supra* note 16, at part 4.

113. *See supra* notes 18–65 and accompanying text.

114. General Allotment Act of 1887, 24 Stat. 388 (1887).

115. President Theodore Roosevelt, State of the Union Message, 1901, *available at* http://www.humanitiesweb.org/human.php?s=h&p=a&a=i&ID=1683.

116. *See County of Yakima v. Confederated Tribes and Bands of Yakima Indian Nation*, 502 U.S. 251, 276 (1992) (Justice Blackmun, concurring in part and dissenting in part) (describing allotment as "systematic 'ethnocide,'" quoting H. SHUSTER, THE YAKIMAS: A CRITICAL BIBLIOGRAPHY 70 (Indiana University Press 1982)).

117. United Nations Convention on the Prevention and Punishment of the Crime of Genocide, Dec. 9, 1948, 1021 U.N.T.S. 78, art. 2 (1948).

118. *See supra* notes 18–65 and accompanying text.

119. John Collier, *America's Treatment of Her Indians*, 18 CURRENT HIST. 772 (1923).

120. *See* Judith Bessant, *Unintended Consequences or Deliberate Racial Hygiene Strategies: The Question of Child Removal Policies*, in HARD LESSONS 187 (Richard Hil and Gordon Tait, eds., Ashgate Publishing 2004).

121. *Id.* at 187–201.

122. *See* BRINGING THEM HOME, *supra* note 16, part 4 ("The debates at the time of the Genocide Convention establish clearly that an act or policy is still genocide when it is motivated by a number of objectives") (citing LORNA LIPPMANN, GENERATIONS OF RESISTANCE: MABO AND JUSTICE 12–13 (Longman Cheshire 1994)).

123. *See* BRINGING THEM HOME, *supra* note 16, part 4.

124. *Id.* at part 4 (citing United Nations Secretary-General, UN Doc. E/447 1947).

125. *Id.* at part 4 (citing Sarah Pritchard, *"International Law,"* in ABORIGINES AND TORRES STRAIT ISLANDERS, LAWS OF AUSTRALIA (Law Book Co. 1993); L. KUPER, THE PREVENTION OF

GENOCIDE 12–13 (Yale University Press 1985)).
126. Id.
127. See U.S. State Department Report, May 1999, available at http://italy.usembassy.gov/pdf/other/kosovo.pdf (last visited May 25, 2006).
128. See, e.g., Graham supra note 7, at 16; Carole E. Goldberg, Individual Rights and Tribal Revitalization, 35 ARIZ. ST. L. J. 889, 902 (2003).
129. See Raymond Cross, American Indian Education: The Terror of History and the Nation's Debt to the Indian People, 21 U. ARK. LITTLE ROCK L. REV. 941, 944 (1999).
130. See BRINGING THEM HOME, supra note 16, at part 4 (citing United Nations Secretary-General, UN Doc. E/447 1947).
131. See U.N. Charter art. 55, para 1.
132. See Universal Declaration of Human Rights, G.A. Res. 217A, art. 1, para. 7., U.N. G.A.O.R., 3d Sess., U.N. Doc. A/810 (Dec. 12, 1948)
133. See, e.g., The Balkan Pact of 1934, February 9, 1934, 7 MOFA TREATY COLLECTION, 67–68 (1934); The Treaty of Versailles of 1919, June 28, 1919, THE TREATIES OF PEACE 1919–1923 (Carnegie Endowment for International Peace 1924); The Faisal-Weizman Agreement of 1919, January 3, 1919, available at http://www.jewishvirtuallibrary.org/jsource/History/faisaltext.html.
134. See United Nations Convention on the Elimination of All Forms of Racial Discrimination, G.A. Res. 1904, 18th Sess. (Nov. 20, 1963), available at http://www.unhchr.ch/html/menu3/b/9.htm; International Covenant on Civil and Political Rights, Dec. 16, 1966 999 U.N.T.S. 171, 6 I.L.M. 368 (1967), G.A. Res. 2200A, 21st Sess. (Dec. 16, 1966), available at http://www.ohchr.org/english/law/ccpr.htm.
135. See RESTATEMENT (THIRD) OF THE FOREIGN RELATIONS LAW OF THE UNITED STATES, § 702 (American Law Institute 1987).
136. See Anaya, supra note 77, at 130
137. See International Labour Organisation, United Nations Convention Concerning Indigenous and Tribal Peoples in Independent Countries, I.L.O. Res. 169, 76th Sess. (Sept. 5, 1991), available at http://www.unhchr.ch/html/menu3/b/62.htm; and Draft United Nations Declaration on the Rights of Indigenous Peoples, U.N. Doc. E/CN4/1995/2, E/CN.4/SUB.2/1994/56 (Oct. 28, 1994). See also S. James Anaya, International Human Rights and Indigenous Peoples: The Move toward the Multicultural State, 21 ARIZ. J. INT'L & COMP. LAW 13, 23–25 (2004).
138. General Recommendations XXIII: Indigenous Peoples, U.N. Doc. CERD/C/51/misc13/Rev. 4, para. 3 (1997).
139. See Stannard, supra note 68, at 268–81. See also ROBERT WILLIAMS, THE AMERICAN INDIAN IN WESTERN LEGAL THOUGHT: THE DISCOURSE OF CONQUEST (Oxford University Press 1990); ROBERT A. WILLIAMS, JR., LIKE A LOADED WEAPON: THE RHENQUIST COURT, INDIAN RIGHTS, AND THE LEGAL HISTORY OF RACISM IN AMERICA 102 (University of Minnesota Press 2005).
140. See Williams, supra note 70, at 13–57.
141. Id.
142. Report of the United Nations Seminar on the Effects of Racism and Racial Discrimination

on the Social and Economic Relations between Indigenous Peoples and States, U.N. Doc. E/CN4/1989/22, HR/PB/89/5 at 5 (1989). Although in direct contradiction to natural law theory, the processes of colonization, seizure of land, and attempts at outright destruction of indigenous cultures were further supported and advanced through state-centered norms and procedures. *See* S. JAMES ANAYA, INDIGENOUS PEOPLES IN INTERNATIONAL LAW 26–31 (Oxford University Press 1996). It is only in the last century that international law has shifted away from being an "instrument of colonialism" to protecting the rights of individuals and groups, including indigenous peoples. *Id.* However, this rhetoric of conquest and inferiority is still evident in some domestic legal systems, suggesting that the issue of discrimination against indigenous peoples is ongoing. *See, e.g.*, ROBERT A. WILLIAMS, JR., LIKE A LOADED WEAPON: THE RHENQUIST COURT, INDIAN RIGHTS, AND THE LEGAL HISTORY OF RACISM IN AMERICA 172 (University of Minnesota Press 2005). *See also* Lorie M. Graham, *The Racial Discourse of Federal Indian Law*, 42 TULSA L.REV. 103 (2006).

143. *See supra* notes 18–65 and accompanying text.
144. LEWIS MERIAM, ED., THE PROBLEM OF INDIAN EDUCATION 403 (1928).
145. *See supra* notes 44–55 and accompanying text.
146. STEVEN UNGER, ED., THE DESTRUCTION OF AMERICAN INDIAN FAMILIES 1, 3 (Association of American Indian Affairs 1977).
147. *See supra* notes 47–51 and accompanying text.
148. *See supra* note 48 and accompanying text.
149. *See supra* notes 52–54 and accompanying text.
150. *See* Bessant, *supra* note 119, at 187.
151. *See* United Nations Convention on the Elimination of All Forms of Racial Discrimination, G.A. Res. 1904, 18th Sess. (Nov. 20, 1963), *available at* http://www.unhchr.ch/html/menu3/b/9.htm (emphasis added).
152. *See* Anaya, *supra* note 77, at 129.
153. *Id.* at 130.
154. International Covenant on Civil and Political Rights, Dec. 16, 1966, 999 U.N.T.S. 171, 6 I.L.M 368 (1967) (G.A. Res. 2200, 21 GAOR, Supp. 16 U.N. Doc. A/6316 at 52, art. 27 (entered into force March 23, 1976)).
155. Lovelace v. Canada, Communication No. R.6/24, Report of the Human Rights Committee, U.N. GOAR, 36 Sess. Supp. No. 40 at 166, U.N. Doc. A/36/40, Annex 18 (1977); *see also* Anaya, *supra* note 7 at 101.
156. Hague Intercountry Adoption Convention, May 29, 1993 (entered into force May 1, 1995), *available at* http://www.hcch.net/index_en.php?act=conventions.text&cid=69.
157. Convention on the Rights of the Child art. 8, Sept. 2, 1990, 44 U.N. GAOR Supp. (No. 49) at 167, U.N. Doc. A/44/49.
158. Barbara Bennett Woodhouse, *Protecting Children's Rights of Identity across Frontiers of Culture, Political Community, and Time*, in FAMILIES ACROSS FRONTIERS (Nigel V. Lowe, ed., Martinus Nijhoff Press 1996).

159. Barbara Bennett Woodhouse, *'Are You My Mother?": Conceptualizing Children's Identity Rights in Transracial Adoptions*, 2 DUKE J. GENDER L. & POL'Y 107 (1995).
160. *See infra* notes 283–93 and accompanying text.
161. *See infra* notes 177–96 and accompanying text.
162. *See generally* RESTATEMENT (THIRD) OF THE FOREIGN RELATIONS LAW OF THE UNITED STATES, § 702 (American Law Institute 1987); Anaya, *supra* note 7, at 97; THOMAS BUERGENTHAL, INTERNATIONAL HUMAN RIGHTS IN A NUTSHELL 277, 279 (West Pub. Co. 1995); *Oyama v. California*, 332 U.S. 633, 649–50, 679 (1948).
163. *See* FRANK C. NEWMAN AND DAVID WEISSBRODT, INTERNATIONAL HUMAN RIGHTS: LAW, POLICY AND PROCESS 18 (2d ed., Anderson Pub. Co. 1996)(1990).
164. RESTATEMENT (THIRD) OF THE FOREIGN RELATIONS LAW OF THE UNITED STATES, § 702 (American Law Institute 1987)
165. *See* Merriam Report, *supra* note 31. *Cf. Meyer v. Nebraska*, 262 U.S. 390 (1923); *Pierce v. Society of Sisters*, 268 U.S. 510 (1925).
166. *See* Anaya, *supra* note 77, at 97.
167. *See infra* notes 246–303 and accompanying text.
168. Jose Zalaquett, *Balancing Ethical Imperatives and Political Constraints: The Dilemma of New Democracies Confronting Past Human Rights Violations*, 43 HASTINGS L.J. 1425 (1992).
169. *See* Elizabeth V. Spelman, REPAIR: THE IMPULSE TO RESTORE IN A FRAGILE WORLD 51 (Beacon Press 2003).
170. *See generally* Mari J. Matsuda, *Looking to the Bottom: Critical Legal Studies and Reparations*, 22 HARV. C.R.-C.L. L. REV. 323, 373–74 (1987).
171. *Id.* at 397.
172. *See* ELIZABETH V. SPELMAN, REPAIR: THE IMPULSE TO RESTORE IN A FRAGILE WORLD 83 (Beacon Press 2003).
173. For a more extended discussion on financial restitution to address human rights violations *see, e.g.*, LAZER BARKAN, THE GUILT OF NATIONS: RESTITUTION AND NEGOTIATING HISTORICAL INJUSTICES (West Group 2000).
174. BLACK'S LAW DICTIONARY 602 (2d Pocket ed. 2001).
175. MERRIAM-WEBSTER'S COLLEGIATE DICTIONARY 945 (11th ed. 2003).
176. *See* GETCHES ET AL., FEDERAL INDIAN LAW 422 (American Casebook Series 2005).
177. ELIZABETH SPELMAN, REPAIR: THE IMPULSE TO RESTORE IN A FRAGILE WORLD (Beacon Press 2002).
178. *See generally* Christian Tomuschat, *Reparation for Victims of Grave Human Rights Violations*, 10 TUL. J. INT'L & COMP. L. 157 (2002).
179. Universal Declaration of Human Rights, G.A. Res., 217A, art. 8, U.N. GAOR, 3d Sess., U.N. Doc A/80 (Dec. 12, 1948).
180. International Covenant on Civil and Political Rights, Dec. 16, 1966, 999 U.N.T.S. 171, 6 I.L.M 368 (1967) (G.A. Res. 2200, 21 GAOR, Supp. 16 U.N. Doc. A/6316 at 52) (entered into force March 23, 1976).

181. United Nations Convention of the Elimination of All Forms of Discrimination, art. 6, *supra* note 133. Other important conventions offering similar protections for violation of human rights include: article 39, Convention of Rights of the Child, *supra* note 156; article 39, Draft UN Declaration on the Rights of Indigenous Peoples, *supra* note 136; and article 12 of ILO Convention No. 169 Concerning Indigenous and Tribal Peoples in Independent Countries, *supra* note 136.

182. *See, e.g.*, The European Convention of Human Rights and Fundamental Freedom as Amended by Protocol no. 11, Council of Europe, November 4, 1950, art. 13 (entered into force Nov. 1, 1998), *available at* http://wwwechr.coe.int/NR/rdonlyres/D5CC24A7-DC13-4318-B457-5C9014916D7A/0/EnglishAnglais.pdf; The American Convention on Human Rights OTS Treaty Series no. 36, 1144 U.N.T.S. 124, Nov. 22, 1969, art. 63 (entered into force July 18, 1978); The African Charter on Human and Peoples' Rights of October 21, 1986, art. 20–21, OAU Doc. CAB/LEG/67/3 Rev. 5, 21 I.L.M. 58 (1986).

183. *Basic Principles and Guidelines on the Right to a Remedy and Reparation for Victims of Gross Violations of International Human Rights Law and Serious Violations of International Humanitarian Law*, G.A. Res., UNGAOR, 60th Sess., UN Doc. A/Res/60/147 (December 16, 2005) (Basic Principles) at para. 15, *available at* http://www.ohchr.org/english/law/remedy.htm.

184. *Id.* at para. 11.

185. Bringing Them Home, *supra* note 16.

186. *Basic Principles and Guidelines on the Right to a Remedy and Reparation for Victims of Gross Violations of International Human Rights Law and Serious Violations of International Humanitarian Law*, G.A. Res., UNGAOR, 60th Sess., UN Doc. A/Res/60/147 (Dec. 16, 2005) (Basic Principles).

187. *See, e.g.*, Theo van Boven, *Study Concerning the Right to Restitution, Compensation and Rehabilitation for Victims of Gross Violations of Human Rights & Fundamental Freedoms: Final Report* (E/CN.4/SUB.2/1993), reprinted in 59 Law & Contemp. Prob. 283 (1996) [hereinafter van Boven I]; *See also* Theo van Boven, *Revised Set of Basic Principles and Guidelines on the Right to Reparation for Victims of Gross Violations of Human Rights and Humanitarian Law*, E/CN.4/Sub.2/1996/17 (May 24, 1996) [hereinafter van Boven II].

188. *See* van Boven I, *supra* note 186, para. 137(3); *See also* van Boven II, *supra* note 186, para. 7.

189. van Boven I, *supra* note 186, para. 137(4); Basic Principles, *supra* note 182, para. 18.

190. *Id.*

191. *Id.* at para. 19.

192. *Id.* at para. 20.

193. *Id.* at para. 21.

194. *Id.* at para. 22–23.

195. van Boven I, *supra* note 186, para. 137(1); van Boven II, *supra* note 186, para. 8 & 9; Basic Principles, *supra* note 182, Preamble.

196. van Boven I, *supra* note 186, para. 13; *See also* Restatement (Third) of the Foreign Relations Law of the United States, § 702 (American Law Institute 1987).

197. *Id.*

198. Theo van Boven, *Appendices: Appendix C: United Nations: Economic and Social Council: Distribution:*

General: E/CN.4/SUB.2/1993/8, 2 July 1993: Original: English: Commission on Human Rights: Sub-Commission on Prevention of Discrimination and Protection of Minorities: Forty-fifth Session: Item 4 of the Provisional Agenda: Review of Further Developments in Fields with which the Sub-Commission has been concerned Study concerning the right to restitution, compensation and rehabilitation for victims of gross violations of human rights and fundamental freedoms: Final report submitted by Mr. Theo Van Boven, Special Rapporteur, 59 LAW & CONTEMP. PROB. 283, 288 (1996).

199. van Boven I, *supra* note 186, para. 14–17.
200. Basic Principles, *supra* note 182, Preamble.
201. *Id.* at para. 8.
202. Basic Principles, *supra* note 182, at para. 6.
203. *Id.* at para. 7.
204. *See* Human Rights Watch, An Approach to Reparations, *available at* http://hrw.org/english/docs/2001/07/19/global285.htm (last viewed May 29, 2007).
205. *Id.*
206. Matsuda, *supra* note 169, at 385.
207. *See* Anaya, *supra* note 74, at 320.
208. There are two important elements—the ongoing damage suffered by a particular group, and the fact that fraud, misrepresentation, and denial often prevent timely presentation of such claims.
209. *See supra* notes 18–65 and accompanying text.
210. *See, e.g.*, The Supplementary Law for the Compensation of the Victims of National Socialist Persecution (1953), The Federal Law for Reparations for Victims of National Socialist Persecution (1956), The Final Federal Compensation Law. *See also* Barry A. Fisher et al., *What Happens Next?*, 20 WHITTIER L. REV. 91, 106–12 (1998); German Compensation for National Socialist Crimes, *available at* http://ushmm.org/assets/frg.htm (last viewed May 29, 2007).
211. Over the years, the class of victims has been expanded to include immigrants from the Soviet Union, survivors in East Germany, and non-Jews who were unable to file claims under the original laws. *See generally* Robert Hochstein, *Jewish Property Restitution in the Czech Republic*, 19 B.C. INT'L & COMP. L. REV. 423, 432–33 (1996). In 1995, Germany and the United States signed the U.S.-German Nazi Persecution Agreement (the "Princz Agreement") to compensate survivors who were U.S. nationals at the time of the Holocaust. *See* Barry A. Fisher et al., *What Happens Next?*, 20 WHITTIER L. REV. 91, 113 (1998). More recently a number of corporations have agreed to pay compensation to individuals of forced and slave labor. *Id.* at 117.
212. *See* Michael J. Bazyler, *The Holocaust Restitution Movement in Comparative Perspective*, 20 BERKELEY J. INT'L L. 11, 22–32 (2002).
213. *See* Michael J. Bazyler and Amber L. Fitzgerald, *Trading with the Enemy: Holocaust Restitution, the United States Government, and American Industry*, 28 BROOKLYN J. INT'L L. 683, 719 (2003).
214. *See Transcript: The Strategies Used to Achieve Non-Monetary Goals*, 25 FORDHAM INT'L L. J. 177, 196–97 (2001).
215. *Id.*

216. *See* Exec. Order No. 9066, 7 Fed. Reg. 1407 (Feb. 19, 1942).
217. 62 Stat. 1231 (July 2, 1948). The compensation was aimed at loss or damage to real or personal property that was the "reasonable and natural consequence of the evacuation or exclusion of such person by the appropriate military commander from a military area" under EO 9066 and which was not covered by insurance.
218. The Restitution Act, 102 Stat. 903 (August 10, 1988). In 1988, Congress also passed the Civil Liberties Act, Pub. L. No. 100-383, 102 Stat. 903 (1988), calling for the review of criminal convictions of U.S. citizens and residents of Japanese ancestry who were convicted of crimes under EO 9066, and for the restitution of up to $20,000 per person for persons convicted under that order.
219. The plan was "aimed at the granting of reparation to, and the rehabilitation and the restoration of the human and civil dignity of, victims of violations of human rights." *See* The Promotion of National Unity and Reconciliation Act 34 of 1995, *available at* http://www.doj.gov.za/trc/legal/act9534.htm.
220. *See generally* Marianne Geula, *South Africa's Truth and Reconciliation Commission as an Alternative Means of Addressing Transitional Government Conflicts in a Divided Society*, 18 B.U. INT'L L. J. 57, 65 (2000).
221. Interim reparations were intended for those victims who had an urgent need for public services, such as medical attention, psychological counseling, family welfare and other such programs. Individual reparations grants would take the form of monetary relief intended to help cover the cost of daily life for the victims. Symbolic reparations were designed to cover legal and administrative services denied to victims or their families by the Apartheid regime. Proposals began with setting aside certain days for remembrance of victims lost during the regime, and moved into more tangible services provided to the surviving families of victims. Community reparations were proposed as a means of group healing and included such things as the naming of streets or public facilities after victims, the placing of community memorials and monuments, and the holding of public ceremonies to celebrate the lives of the victims. *See* Promotion of National Unity and Reconciliation Act, No. 34 (July 26, 1995) *available at* http://www.doj.gov.za/trc/legal/act9534.htm. *Cf.* Rosemary Nagy, *Postapartheid Justice: Can Cosmopolitanism and Nation-Building Be Reconciled*, 40 LAW & SOC'Y REV. 623, 639–47 (2006).
222. *See* The Reparation Report, issue 7, at 5 (May 2006), *available at* http://www.redress.org/reports/the%20reparation%20report%20vol%207%2028%20final%20june%2006.pdf (last visited May 29, 2007).
223. For a detailed description of Peru's reparation plan, *see* http://www.cverdad.org.pe/ingles/ifinal/conclusiones.php (last visited May 29, 2007). *See also* the Reparation Report, *supra* note 221, at 7.
224. *Id.* at 8.
225. *Id.* at 7.
226. *Id.* at 8.
227. *Id.* at 9.
228. For a more comprehensive look at international, regional, and domestic decisions relating to indigenous peoples rights, *see* S. James Anaya, *supra* note 77.

229. *The Case of the Mayagna (Sumo) Awas Tingni Community v. Nicaragua, Judgment of August 31, 2001*, reprinted in 19 ARIZ. J. INT'L & COMP. LAW 395, 438 (2002).
230. *See* S. James Anaya and Claudio Grossman, *The Case of Awas Tingni v. Nicaragua: A New Step in the International Law of Indigenous Peoples*, 19 ARIZ. J. INT'L & COMP. LAW 1, 2–8 (2002) (describes Awas Tingni's path to the Inter-American Court).
231. Anaya, *supra* note 77, at 145.
232. The court ordered Nicaragua to pay the Awas Tingni $50,000 in damages and indemnify them for $30,000 in legal expenses. The monetary reparations seem to have been less than those actually suffered, due to procedural errors relating to the presentation of actual damages. *See* S. James Anaya and Claudio Grossman, *supra* note 229, at 8.
233. *See Inter-American Court of Human Rights: The Case of the Mayagna (Sumo) Awas Tingni Community v. Nicaragua: Judgment of August 31, 2001*, reprinted in 19 ARIZ. J. INT'L & COMP. LAW 395, 438 (2002).
234. *See, e.g., Case of Mary and Carrie Dann v. United States*, Case No. 11.140, Inter-Am. C. H.R. No. 75/02 (Dec. 27, 2002).
235. Pub. L. No. 103–150, 107 Stat. 1510 (1993).
236. *See* Matsuda, *supra* note 169; Anaya, *supra* note 74. *Cf. Rice v. Cayetano*, 528 U.S. 495 (2000); *Arakaki v. Lingle*, 477 F.3d 1048 (9th Cir. 2007); and *Doe v. Kamehameha Schools*, 470 F.3d 827 (9th Cir. 2006).
237. *See* Anaya, *supra* note 74, at 342.
238. *Id.* at 342.
239. *See generally* Canada's Indian Residential School Settlement Agreement of May 8, 2006, *available at* http://www.irsr-ropi.gc.ca/english/pdf/indian_residential_schools_settlement_agreement.pdf. *See also Aleck v. Canada*, [1991] A.C.W.S. (3d) 28 (1991); *A.Q. v. Canada*, [1998] 169 Sask. R. 1; *D.A. v. Canada*, [1998] 173 Sask. R. 312; and *H.L. v. Canada*, [2003] S.J. No. 298.
240. *See* Agreement in Principle (Nov. 20, 2005), *available at* http://www.irsr-roi.gc.ca/english/pdf/alp_english.pdf.
241. Matt Ross, *Abuse Survivors Finally to Receive Compensation*, in INDIAN COUNTRY TODAY, B1 (Dec. 7, 2005) (quoting Assembly of First Nations Chief Phil Fontaine). *See also* Indian Residential Schools Agreement in Principle FAQs, in CBC NEWS ONLINE (Nov. 25, 2005).
242. Canadian Justice Minister Irwin Cotler noted that "no agreement can erase the memories of generations of pain and suffering . . . , and that is why this agreement goes beyond monetary recognition . . . to provide healing, to provide reconciliation, to provide the capacity for renewal." *See* INDIAN COUNTRY TODAY, *supra* note 240, at B1.
243. Lump-sum payments will be paid to residential school victims in the amount of $10,000, plus $3,000 for every year they attended the residential school. However, these awards do not override pending individual lawsuits.
244. Minister's Message on Canada's Residential Schools Resolution, *available at* http://www.tbs-sct.gc.ca/0607/oirs-bropa/oirs-bropa01_e.asp.
245. *See generally* BRINGING THEM HOME, *supra* note 16. *See also* Antonio Buti, SEPARATED:

ABORIGINAL CHILD SEPARATIONS AND GUARDIANSHIP LAW (Sydney Institute of Criminology 2004).

246. *See* Kevin Gover, *Remarks at the Ceremony Acknowledging the 175th Anniversary of the Establishment of the Bureau of Indian Affairs*, 25 AM. INDIAN L. REV. 161, 162 (2000). Attempts were made to have similarly worded apologies from Congress, but the proposed resolution failed to gain final approval. For instance, Senator Brownback from Kansas introduced a resolution that, among other things, offered an apology for "the forcible removal of Native children from their families to faraway boarding schools where their Native practices and languages were degraded and forbidden." *Available at* http://calwater.ca.gov/tribal/state_and_federal_legislation/historic_resolution_of_apology_5-6-04.pdf (last visited May 29, 2007).

247. *See generally* Boarding School Healing Project, *available at* http://www.boardingschoolhealingproject.org/suits1.htm (last visited May 29, 2007).

248. *See generally* CHARLES E. WILKINSON, AMERICAN INDIANS, TIME, AND THE LAW 82–83 (Yale University Press 1987).

249. President Richard M. Nixon, *Special Message to the Congress on Indian Affairs*, 1970 Pub. Papers 564 (July 8, 1970).

250. *See, e.g.*, Indian Self-Determination and Education Act of 1975, Pub. L. No. 93-638, 88 Stat. 2203 (1975). However, despite its common usage in domestic laws and policies, the United States has taken a different position in international discussions regarding the use of the term "self-determination" with respect to indigenous peoples. *See* Graham, *supra* note 79.

251. *See supra* notes 41–65 and accompanying text.

252. 25 U.S.C. § 1901.

253. 25 U.S.C. § 1902. Congress's power to pass such a law is derived from the special relationship between American Indian tribes, their members, and the U.S. government. 25 U.S.C. § 1901.

254. 25 U.S.C. § 1901 (3), (4), (5).

255. 25 U.S.C. § 1915.

256. 25 U.S.C. § 1912(d).

257. *See* Graham, *supra* note 7, at 49–52; *see also* Atwood, *supra* note 41 at 663–66.

258. 25 U.S.C. §§ 1911, 1912(a), 1931–1934.

259. *See, e.g., In re Armell*, 550 N.E.2d 1060, 1068 (Ill. App. Ct. 1990). *But see In re Bridget R.*, 49 Cal. Rptr. 2d 507 (1996). *See generally* Christine Metteer, *The Existing Indian Family Exception: An Impediment to the Trust Responsibility to Preserve Tribal Existence and Culture as Manifested in the Indian Child Welfare Act*, 30 LOY. L.A. L. REV. 647 (1997).

260. *See, e.g., Morton v. Mancari*, 417 U.S. 535, 554 (1974).

261. *See Id.*

262. *See Id.* at 541–42 (1974). *See generally United States v. Lara*, 541 U.S. 193, 210 (2004) (Held that federal law that allowed tribes to prosecute criminals did not violate double jeopardy, because the law was not a grant of federal power, but merely a return of sovereignty previously held by the tribe.).

263. *Adarand Construction v. Pena*, 115 S.Ct. 2097 (1995). *See also* Metteer, *supra* note 231.

264. *Jacobs v. Barr*, 959 F.2d 313 (D.C. Cir. 1992), *cert. denied*, 506 U.S. 831 (1992).
265. *Amendments to the Indian Child Welfare Act: Hearings before the Senate Committee on Indian Affairs*, 104th Cong., 2d Sess. 303 (1996) [hereinafter 1996 Hearings] (statement of Jack F. Trope, for AAIA); *See also* statement of Ron Allen, president of the National Congress of the American Indian: "The National Congress has never advocated that the Indian Child Welfare Act be amended. Our tribes have taken the position that ICWA works well and, despite some highly publicized cases, continues to work well." *Id.* at 134.
266. *See, e.g.*, Kennedy, *supra* note 41; Christine D. Bakeis, *The Indian Child Welfare Act of 1978: Violating Personal Rights for the Sake of the Tribe*, 10 NOTRE DAME J. L. ETHICS & PUB. POL'Y 543, 557 (1990). *See also* Amicus Curiae Brief for American Academy of Adoption Attorneys, *In re Bridget R.*, 49 Cal. Rptr 2d 507 (Civ. No. B093520)
267. van Boven I, *supra* note 186, para. 137 (11).
268. Recently, the Child Welfare League of America, an agency involved in the removal of Indian children, offered a formal apology to American Indian nations for its involvement in the taking of American Indian children from their homes and families.
269. House Report, *supra* note 52, para. 137 (11).
270. *Id.*
271. 25 U.S.C. § 1901.
272. *See* H.R. Rep. No. 1386, at 8 (1978), reprinted in 1978 U.S.C.C.A.N. 7530.
273. 25 U.S.C. § 1911, 1912, 1913.
274. 25 U.S.C. § 1915.
275. One recent amendment supported by indigenous groups is the imposition of criminal sanctions against any person other than the birth parent who deliberately evades ICWA, as well as provisions mandating attorneys and social welfare agencies to inform American Indian parents of their rights under ICWA.
276. *See* Graham, *supra* note 7, at 34–43.
277. *Id.*
278. *See supra* notes 155–59 and accompanying text; *See also* Graham, *supra* note 7.
279. 25 U.S.C. § 1901(5).
280. VINE DELORIA, INDIAN EDUCATION IN AMERICA 22 (American Indian Science and Engineering Society 1991).
281. *Indian Child Welfare Amendments: Hearings on S. 1976 before the Senate Select Committee on Indian Affairs*, 100th Cong. 97 (1988), at 97 (statement of Evelyn Blanchard).
282. *See* Kennedy, *supra* note 41, at 498.
283. *Cf. City of Sherrill v. Oneida Indian Nation*, 544 U.S. 197 (2005).
284. *Hearings on H.R. 1448 Amendments to the Indian Child Welfare Act before the Subcommittee on Native American and Insular Affairs*, 103rd Cong., 2d Sess. (1995) (reprinted at 1005 WL 283199) [hereinafter cited as 1995 Hearings] (statement of Terry Cross, Executive Director, National Indian Child Welfare Association). *See also* Bruce Davies, *Implementing the Indian Child Welfare Act*, 16 CLEARINGHOUSE REV. 179, 181 (1982).

285. 25 U.S.C. § 1901(3).
286. 25 U.S.C. § 1915.
287. 49 Cal. Rptr. 2d 507 (1996).
288. *See* House Report, *supra* note 52, at 12; *Miss. Band of Choctaw Indians v. Holyfield*, 490 U.S. 50, 51 n. 25 (1989).
289. *See* 25 U.S.C. § 1911.
290. Donna Goldsmith, *Individual vs. Collective Rights: The Indian Child Welfare Act*, 13 HARV. WOMEN'S L. J. 1, 10 (1990).
291. Barbara Atwood, *supra* note 41.
292. *Id.* at 27.
293. *See* Graham, *supra* note 7, at 50. This case does not deal directly with the interpretation of ICWA, but is nevertheless indicative of the types of remedies available to courts under that statute.
294. *See* Atwood, *supra* note 41, at 28.
295. Anaya, *supra* note 77, at 156.
296. 25 U.S.C. § 1913.
297. Other federal statutes address more directly the issues of educational, cultural, and language revitalization. Examples include: Tribally-Controlled School Grants Act of 1988, Indian Education Act of 1988, 25 U.S.C. § 2501 (2002), Tribally Controlled Community College Assistance Act of 1978, Pub. L. No. 95-471, 92 Stat. 1325, Native American Graves Protection and Reparation Act of 1990, 25 U.S.C.A. § 3001-13, 18 U.S.C.A. § 1170, Native American Language Act of 1990, Pub. L. No. 101-477, 104 Stat. 1152 (1990) (codified as amended at 25 U.S.C. §§ 2901-06 (2000), and Indian Child Protection and Family Violence Act of 1990, 25 U.S.C. § 3201 et seq. (2000). An important feature of these laws is the significant role that tribes and Indian organizations played in their development and implementation—a far cry from the days when the BIA and other federal agencies controlled every aspect of Indian life. Although these laws were not part of the original ICWA redress plan, they provide important rehabilitative services to Indian people who continue to suffer the ongoing effects of removal and forced assimilation.
298. 25 U.S.C. § 1912(d).
299. Atwood, *supra* note 41, at 13.
300. *Id.* at 622-23.
301. *See generally* Graham, *supra* note 7.
302. Draft United Nations Declaration, *supra* note 136, art. 38.
303. *See generally* Boarding School Healing Project, *available at* http://www.boardingschoolhealingproject.org/suits1.htm.
304. *See* BRINGING THEM HOME, *supra* note 16, chap. 4.
305. *See* van Boven I, *supra* note 186, para. 137 (12-20).
306. Stannard, *supra* note 68, at xiii.
307. *See, e.g.*, Marcia Yablon, *The Indian Child Welfare Act Amendment of 2003*, 28 FAMILY L. Q. 689 (2004).

A Practitioner's View from Thirty Years on the Cutting Edge of the Indian Child Welfare Act

Mary Jo B. Hunter

When I started my career as an attorney (circa 1982), I spent a lot of time defending people for entrusting their children to the care of their extended family members or to the grandparents of the children. Now, the social scientists, social workers and child protection workers have come to accept and respect the practice that has been a traditional aspect of Native families for generations. Yet, in 1978, Congress had to enact the Indian Child Welfare Act so that such cultural norms were respected prior to removing Indian children or placing the children once they had been removed from their parents.

Like many clinicians, my entry into academia was through the clinical offices of law school. Unlike most clinicians, I am an American Indian/Native American attorney, and unlike many, I did not desire, nor have I ever desired, to become a doctrinal teacher. I believe that my best teaching is providing an avenue for law students to learn practical skills. In addition, my clinical teaching has been a method for me to encourage both Indian and non-Indian law students to understand the body of Indian law, but specifically, to learn and understand the Indian Child Welfare Act of 1978.[1]

In my research, I have not found many reflective articles by Native clinicians.[2] Nor have I read any articles that describe the path of a clinician that intertwines their career with a specific piece of legislation, as is the case with me. My career has been on a parallel path with the Indian Child Welfare Act. ICWA is like a guiding light in my work, and I celebrate its existence. This piece reflects my work and my life, as I start with my initial exposure to ICWA as a law student and continue with my various career opportunities, which seemed to consistently include practicing law in areas where I applied the Indian Child Welfare Act.

In 1979, I had the pleasure of being hired as a law clerk for the Native American Law Project (NALP) of the Los Angeles American Indian Center. At that time, the center was located in central Los Angeles on Washington Boulevard. The attorneys who worked there were a group of talented and motivated people. All of the attorneys were non-Indians, and most of the paralegals and law clerks were Indian.[3] This was the *Bakke* era.[4] So it was a time when those of "us" in law school felt privileged to be there. The main question many of "us" had was whether there would be more American Indian/Native American students admitted to law school. Our lives had led us to having little belief in our own abilities and aptitude and qualifications to be in law school. Thankfully, we were wrong about the long-term impact of *Bakke*.

At the NALP, I was assigned to work with an attorney named Katy Jo Steward. Katy Jo was a dynamo who constantly talked about a recent law that had been passed that was important for Native families. Every other sentence out of her mouth seemed to be about that statute, something called the Indian Child Welfare Act. She was working on a case where she wanted to apply the law. My assignment was to research certain aspects of the law. At that time, this task was relatively simple, as there was not much to research except for reading the law itself and attempting to apply it to the facts of our case. Today, I do not recall the facts of that case or the outcome of Katy Jo's work on that case. As a law clerk, I did not go to court with her. What I do recall, however, is my own fascination with the law and how it came to be. It was truly love at first reading! So, that was the beginning of my love affair with the Indian Child Welfare Act of 1978.

This love of the Indian Child Welfare Act began with my reading the congressional findings found at the beginning of the law.[5] I was especially mindful of § 1901 (3), which stated

> That there is no resource that is more vital to the continued existence and integrity of Indian tribes than their children and that the United States has a direct interest, as trustee, in protecting Indian children who are members of or are eligible for membership in an Indian tribe.

My recollection of reading that portion of the Act was that our Indian children are literally worth their weight in gold for our tribal survival. Reading that passage empowered me as a Native person, as a law student, and as an aspiring lawyer. Perhaps my career was destined from that reading. Our Native children *are* our most important resource.

Like many people of color, many aspects of my career have been quite serendipitous. Perhaps this is due to my reliance on the Creator and leaving the final outcome of job searches, hires, and relocations to my spiritual beliefs. I tend to do as much as I can to seek out new and different opportunities for my legal career. However, in the final analysis, I seek answers from "Mauna," the earth maker, to provide me with proper direction and guidance. Although there have been times when I have initially questioned why a particular possibility did not pan out, I have come to realize that answers to come if I am patient. As I have continued on my career path, I have grown in my spiritual beliefs. As a card-carrying member of the Native American Church,[6] I have come to walking the "Red Road" of sobriety and caring about my fellow Native people as key tenets of my life.[7] These tenets have formed and directed my legal career.

During law school, I did not have many opportunities to return to my home state of Wisconsin. About midway through school, I did have an opportunity to fly home and visit. On that visit, I was advised by my maternal great-uncle, Edmund Lincoln, about the responsibilities of becoming a lawyer. He told me that when I received that degree (referring to my J.D.) that it would be important for me to realize that I had not obtained that piece of paper alone. He went on to say that because of those who had supported and assisted me, that piece of paper did not belong solely to me. That piece of paper belonged to all of us. He indicated my family and friends who were present when he was speaking as well as my Tribe. I have never forgotten those words. Those words have guided me in my career.

I consider my cultural heritage to be one of my many blessings in this life. I am extremely proud of my Ho-Chunk heritage. That pride has sustained me and enabled me to continue in the work that I do on behalf of Native children and families. When I think about what our Native children lose when displaced from their tribal homes, I recall my own "Indian name" and what it means. *Rascatweiga* means "a name that stands out," and it was given to me by Frank Lincoln, my maternal great-grandfather and Bear Clan member. I was told that this name was given to me to assure that I would be recognized when I enter the spirit world or go to heaven. This naming ceremony was done when I was an infant. My family cared about me and my life and my afterlife. Spirituality is and was central to my family life. This is an attribute of one's tribal connections that are lost if the connection to one's tribe is lost. I think of that each time that I am involved with children who are subjects of cases involving the Indian Child Welfare Act. I wonder if they have been named according to their tribal customs.

There are so many aspects of being a member of a tribe that are important to me. As I have joked on many occasions, it is better than being in any club or sorority/fraternity, and I even get a membership card! There is the familial aspect—with so many relatives, due to our extended family relations.[8] Being raised in the familial community of my maternal uncle, I was raised as a member of the Bear Clan. The mores, values, and teachings of the Bear Clan have been taught to me as I was growing up. They remain with me to this day.

My initial exposure to the Indian Child Welfare Act was in 1979. At that time, very few lawyers and judges were aware of the Act. So, it was cutting-edge to simply have knowledge of the Act's history and existence. My law-clerk experience provided me with the unique opportunity to be on the cutting edge by exposing me to the Indian Child Welfare Act. That early exposure enabled me to interview successfully for my first full-time employment after law school.

My first full-time position as an attorney was with the legal services office of Southern Minnesota Regional Legal Services (SMRLS) in Saint Paul, Minnesota. I began working with SMRLS in 1982. My first position was as an attorney based in a nonprofit American Indian organization in Saint Paul. The Saint Paul American Indian Center was housed in a large room with partitioned-off spaces for the staff. However, the attorneys' office needed to be in a more secure area to allow for confidentiality. So, the only area that was sealed was an office that was located in the back through the center's food shelf. To reach our offices, our clients had to walk through shelves of canned foods and dry goods. Nevertheless, that position was my training ground. My supervisor was Janet ("Jan") Werness, and she was an exceptional teacher for a new attorney. She guided my every move, and I learned so much from her for which I remain truly grateful.

Serendipitously, Jan Werness also had an interest in the Indian Child Welfare Act. My initial training involved learning how to interview clients, usually mothers, who had been served with Child in Need of Services or Protection (CHIPS) petitions. The majority of the clients were American Indian, as we were located within the "Indian Center," so we were able to handle many cases involving the Indian Child Welfare Act. Part of the initial interview process at that time was educating our clients about ICWA, as most of them were unaware of the Act and its protections. So, our initial interviews with clients included advising and educating them about the protections of ICWA for them as parents of Native children who qualified under the Act.

Educating our clients about the Act meant explaining when ICWA did or did not apply. Often, it was necessary to advise potential clients that ICWA did not apply to divorces.[9] Rather, ICWA applies only to "foster care placements," "termination of parental rights," "preadoptive placements" or "adoptive placements" as defined by the Act.[10]

After that, our work involved educating the opposing counsel as well as the judges about those same protections under the Act. At the Indian Child Welfare Act's fourth and fifth year of existence (circa 1985 and 1986), the Act was considered to be a reasonably new, and therefore unknown, law. As practitioners, it was our duty to educate and advise others about the Indian Child Welfare Act. Sometimes, this meant that we had to spoon-feed judges the information about the Act. Our briefs were usually of an explanatory nature rather than simply advocacy. Being on the cutting edge of ICWA in the early 1980s meant educating parties and judges about ICWA.

Finally, I decided to fulfill my desire to work in the criminal-defense arena. In the mid '80s, I went to work at the Neighborhood Justice Center (NJC). The NJC is a nonprofit criminal-defense firm in Saint Paul, Minnesota. My hiring at the NJC resulted in an immediate rise in the number of American Indian clients who were served by that agency. One of my most memorable and rewarding cases was one that was referred to me by Jan Werness of SMRLS. Naturally, it was a criminal case that involved arguing the Indian Child Welfare Act. Talk about cutting edge! It was an effort to argue ICWA in an arena that usually does not involve such arguments.

The case that was referred to me by Ms. Werness involved a teenage boy who had been charged with contempt. The contempt charge was a juvenile-delinquency charge that was considered a criminal charge. However, the charge arose from the child running away. His initial citation was for being a runaway, which is considered a status offense, meaning that the charge is by reason of the child's status as a juvenile or minor. Status offenses are cases that are subject to the protection of the Indian Child Welfare Act.[11] Based upon that premise, I took the case and argued successfully that the contempt charge was subject to the Indian Child Welfare Act, since the matter arose from a status offense. Since the charge involved a possible out-of-home placement, the child was entitled to the protections of the Indian Child Welfare Act. The order was in the juvenile court and was not a public order at that time. Therefore, the order was not able to be publicly utilized. However, the argument was an innovative one.

During this period of time, I decided that I wanted to do work in tribal courts. In the mid to late '80s, Minnesota did not have any viable and active tribal courts except for the tribal court on the Red Lake Reservation.[12] At that time, the Red Lake Band of Ojibwe Tribal Court required that those who practiced in their court had to be fluent in Ojibwe. Since I did not speak their language, that was not a possibility for me to gain experience in tribal court practice.

So, I took a position with Nevada Legal Services at their Carson City office. I was hired to work on the cases involving Indian clients. That meant that my practice would include tribal courts all over the northern part of the State of Nevada. I was delighted to have the opportunity to practice in tribal courts. However, I also represented Indian clients who had cases in the state courts. So, I soon began representing clients who were involved with the Indian Child Welfare Act.

One of my most memorable cases actually took place in Las Vegas, Nevada. Although the legal services offices included one in Las Vegas, I was assigned a case there because I was the only attorney who was familiar with the Indian Child Welfare Act. I flew down to Las Vegas from Carson City, Nevada, to represent a couple who had lost their children in a state court action. The family had been traveling through

Las Vegas and had stopped at a casino. The couple made an unwise choice to leave their children in the car while they went into the casino to gamble. The children were initially removed under emergency placement aspects of ICWA.[13] However, as the action proceeded, the couple was unable to have the children returned to them despite their efforts to cooperate with whatever was asked of them. Because the state court had not fulfilled all of their obligations under ICWA, I filed a Motion to Dismiss for failure to abide by the notice requirements of ICWA.[14] In addition, I personally contacted the tribe involved, which was the Standing Rock Sioux Tribe. I spoke with their ICWA specialist, who agreed to fly to Las Vegas to be present at the hearing. She sought to intervene in the case if she was unable to have the matter transferred back to the Standing Rock Sioux Tribal Court. We worked together on behalf of this family to have them reunited. I am proud to say that we were successful in getting the matter transferred back to the jurisdiction of the tribal court so that the children could eventually be returned to their parents. I have no doubt that the parents who had been traveling through Las Vegas regret their poor judgment to this day.

Again, these efforts, which are standard practice now under ICWA, were on the cutting edge of ICWA practice in the late 1980s. It required educating the court with memorandums of law, and being willing to make valid legal arguments that were sometimes ignored by state courts. It required that practitioners go beyond the norms of practice and work with tribal representatives to advocate for Indian families. Today, that effort is a key aspect of meaningful representation on Indian Child Welfare Act cases. Practitioners must contact tribal representatives when they are actively involved in cases. Yet, early on, many tribes did not have representatives, or those tribes that had representatives did not have the financial ability to send them all over the country.

As part of my practice, I was representing parents in many of the cases. Parents were often unaware of the Indian Child Welfare Act as a law that protected their rights as Native parents. Often, the process of educating about the Act included educating my clients. The other part of the education process was educating social workers about the different parenting styles of American Indian parents. It was still common for workers to consider Indian children "abandoned" by their parents, although the parents had left the children with either grandparents or aunts and uncles. I was educating social workers that leaving children with safe and appropriate caretakers was common within the extended family and should not be considered a form of abandonment. Workers who were able to recognize the tribal values in utilizing the extended family were pioneers of ICWA practice in the late 1980s and early 1990s.

I returned to the Midwest in 1989 to work with my own tribe, the Ho-Chunk Nation. However, I was quickly terminated as someone who was considered problematic. Due to my values and education, I was not willing to be controlled by tribal politics and stand idly by as the tribe's resources were used inappropriately. As many of us say who have worked for our own tribal governments, one has not really practiced in the field of Indian law if one has not been fired by a tribe.

As is often the case, one misfortune is sometimes the catalyst for another opportunity. A friend's brother, Joe Young, is an attorney. Joe informed me that a friend of his was leaving his position with the University of North Dakota School of Law, where he was a clinical instructor. Joe suggested that I approach the law school, as they were actively seeking his replacement. I contacted them and I was invited for an interview. After my interview, an offer was made in a relatively short time for me to be the supervising attorney of the Native American Law Project. I moved to North Dakota in the late summer of 1989 to begin my career as a clinician. Although I did not know anyone in Grand Forks, North Dakota, I moved there with my almost two-year-old child. To allow me to get settled, I took along one of my relatives, a teenager, to assist with my child as I settled in for the first two weeks. Personally, I was familiar with the extended family assisting with child care. Since I utilized this tribal practice, I am not surprised to see families who are in the child protection system use the same practice. It is not inherently a bad practice. It requires that the parents use good judgment in determining who the child-care person will be.

My experiences in Grand Forks were many and varied. In many respects, my move to North Dakota was a turning point. One of the turning points was discovering that I derived immense enjoyment from teaching. And what I enjoyed teaching was practical skills. My own law school experience included a clinic course that was based on simulated experiences. My position at UND was teaching practical skills to law students with live clients. Teaching in a live client clinic is not for the faint of heart!

We traveled weekly on a two-hour ride west to the Devil's Lake Sioux Tribe reservation, as it was known at that time. (It has since been renamed the Spirit Lake Sioux Tribe.) The law students and I provided legal services to tribal members. We practiced in the tribal court for the most part. However, we also accepted cases from tribal members that were being heard in state court. Thus, I was once again representing clients in state court on cases involving the Indian Child Welfare Act.

One of the first cases that we had was in state court in Grand Forks, North Dakota. I asserted that the Act had not been adhered to, and I sought a dismissal of the case. The judge quite frankly took me to task for seeking to apply a federal law to an action in his state court proceeding. That was the beginning of my realization that much education was needed, despite the Act having been in effect for ten years. Since the clinic was on hiatus, I was appearing in court without any law students. I was thankful that I was the one to incur the wrath of the state court judge rather than a law student. Although the motion to dismiss the case was denied, the state court judge did agree that the provisions of the Act should be complied with from that point on in the case. Some progress was made with that judge, although he did not fully comply with the provisions of the Act that allow for a dismissal where there is noncompliance.[15] That is not surprising, as judges are not usually willing to dismiss actions involving children, due to a concern with their best interests.

I had been warned by friends and colleagues that practicing law in North Dakota would be different, especially for a Native woman. I found that to be true as I adapted to living in Grand Forks. It was surprising to find that the team name of "Fighting Sioux" was considered to be acceptable. However, I was actually shocked to learn that a local high school's team name was the "Redskins"! Frankly, I was appalled. While I was there, I signed petitions requesting that both names be changed. My understanding is that the high school team's name was changed, but that the University of North Dakota has not respected the wishes of those who are offended by the "Fighting Sioux" name.[16] That was the climate that I was warned about when I moved to North Dakota. Yet I do not regret my move there, as it allowed me to meet other attorneys who shared my passion for representing the underrepresented.

While I was at UND School of Law, I became acquainted with attorneys from Dakota Plains Legal Services in South Dakota. One of these attorneys, B. J. Jones, shared my interest in the Indian Child Welfare Act. We discussed cases and shared war stories and developed a professional respect that I believe continues to exist to this day.

While I was at UND, I began to do trainings on ICWA. I had agreed to teach some classes for the late Kenneth Sayers of the Council Lodge Institute. I had shared with Ken my desire to provide tribal people with information on the Act that would be of benefit to them in state court proceedings. In 1990, I prepared a training manual that included information on the Act, a copy of the Act itself, as well as the BIA Guidelines for State Courts. I included templates of forms such as a Motion to Transfer and a Motion to Intervene in State Court for tribal use. The manual was hastily put together as we prepared to go to Nevada to do the training.[17] For that time, it was definitely a cutting-edge effort. I am proud of that work, although from this point in time it appears dated.

Around that time, B. J. Jones had come up to the UND campus for some event. I showed him the manual and he was quite impressed with it. So, I gave him a copy. To this day, I tease him that he got the idea for his book from my training manual![18] Although I enjoy teasing him, his book has become the primer on the Act for a great many people, both tribal and non-tribal. It is an honor to have had this longstanding professional relationship with B. J. Jones. He has been working on the leading edge of ICWA for many years.

Both B. J. Jones and I were on the appellate panel of judges for the Turtle Mountain Band of Chippewa while I resided in North Dakota. One of our conversations was about the need for tribes and states to be made aware that ICWA was designed for the state courts. It was not a federal law that was applicable to the tribal courts.

This became an aspect of the education that was provided around ICWA. Today, it is common knowledge that the federal law applies to the state courts. However, that information was still not understood by most tribal and non-tribal people even when the Act was ten to fifteen years old.

It was during my tenure at UND School of Law that I began to realize that I needed to make personal changes in my life. Most importantly, I needed to return to the Red Road and change the way that I conducted myself in my own life. Many of the cases that I worked on involved the need for parents to follow a case plan. In the majority of the case plans that the law students and I reviewed, alcohol use was a problem for the parents. It occurred to me that it was hypocritical for me to tell Indian parents to be sober if I was not practicing sobriety myself. So, I began my journey to sobriety. It has been much easier to advise and counsel clients about the need for sobriety when I am living a sober lifestyle. In addition, sobriety has enabled me to return to a fuller life in terms of my spirituality. Spirituality is a cornerstone of Indian culture. Practicing my spirituality has enriched my life and allowed me to withstand the pressures of practice in the area of child custody and the concomitant issues arising from those cases.

It was during this personal change that the Native American Law Project worked with a couple who had five children whom they were in danger of losing due to their alcohol use. We counseled them on the need to be sober to properly parent their children. As was often the case, they challenged me as to whether or not I used alcohol. I explained to them my recent decision to abstain from alcohol and to lead a life on the Red Road. I was quite forthright in how I had come to this decision. It was not clear to me if they took my advice seriously. However, I was leaving UND for a position with Hamline University School of Law, so I was not able to see the completion of the case.

I had been offered a position at Hamline, and I was ready to return to a jurisdiction where there were other attorneys working on cases involving the Indian Child Welfare Act. I had been invited to a working-group meeting of attorneys who were assisting Anita Fineday in preparation for her oral arguments on an important case.[19] While attending the meeting, I realized that it was time to return to Minnesota, as ICWA practitioners there were on the cutting edge of ICWA issues.

I began my position with Hamline University School of Law in November 1993. My new position as clinical instructor involved teaching a Child Advocacy Clinic. No longer would I be teaching law students about representing parents. Rather, we would be representing children and youth in a variety of venues. Since I had been providing services as a guardian *ad litem* at the previous clinic, I was excited about being able to work on behalf of children in a more direct fashion. Frankly, I was ready to change course, as I had become somewhat disillusioned with parents who did not make the obvious changes to retain custody of their children. Needless to say, I may have been experiencing some professional "burnout" when I opted to change my employment and move to Saint Paul, Minnesota.

The position in Saint Paul was important, as it would allow me to be six hours closer in travel time to my elderly parents. In addition, I knew many members of my tribe who lived in the Twin Cities area, as well as many old friends. It was beneficial on both a professional and personal level to move to Minnesota. I was excited about changing my focus of teaching to the area of children and the law. It was an opportunity to build the clinic course in child advocacy from very little. I started my new position in mid-semester, which was a bit daunting. However, my enthusiasm was not dampened by such an odd start date.

Initially, the clinic was strictly about representing children and youth. We represented children in juvenile court in both delinquency and civil cases. Both the Ramsey and Hennepin County public defenders' offices assisted in providing us cases. Eventually, I added cases in which we acted as the guardians *ad litem* to our caseload.

Native people in the Twin Cities had consistently raised the issue that many of the child protection cases that involved ICWA matters were assigned guardians *ad litem* who were not Native American. To address this cultural gap, Judge Robert Blaeser of the Hennepin District Court enlisted a group of American Indian attorneys to be specially trained to work as guardians *ad litem*.[20] Since he was aware that I had worked as a guardian *ad litem* in North Dakota, he invited me to be a part of this group. So, the Child Advocacy Clinic began working on cases where I would be appointed the guardian *ad litem*. The certified student attorneys in the clinic would work on the cases under my supervision to learn how to represent the best interests of children. Interestingly, the law students found that perspective to be more in keeping with their ideals when we had discussions in class about the cases. So, the clinic evolved to the law students being assigned a case or two of straight legal representation of a child or children, along with a case or two where we were the guardians *ad litem* on the child protection case. This dual assignment of roles allowed the law students to compare and discuss the different perspectives of legal representation and how it relates to the best interests of children.

In addition, the law students were able to practically apply the different standards under the Indian Child Welfare Act in the cases involving the Act while learning about the applicable standards in non-ICWA cases. For example, the standard of proof in cases where parental rights are being terminated differs between the two types of cases. In the non-ICWA case, some states such as Minnesota utilize a clear and convincing standard. In ICWA cases, the standard of proof that is required to terminate parental rights is proof beyond a reasonable doubt.[21] Having cases that applied the legal standards and concepts allowed the law students to gain hands-on experience in the application of the Indian Child Welfare Act. As the students become lawyers, it is my hope as a clinician that they will have gained valuable experience about the Indian Child Welfare Act that will benefit Indian children, families, and tribes in the future.

Most recently, the Child Advocacy Clinic has begun representation of a third type. We have been providing legal representation to guardians *ad litem* who are involved in Indian Child Welfare Act cases. Due to our work as guardians *ad litem* on cases involving the Act, the Hennepin County District Court Guardian *ad Litem* Program sought our services as attorneys for their guardians *ad litem* who had contested cases involving the Indian Child Welfare Act. This provides a third avenue of learning for the law students as they represent guardians *ad litem* who are appointed to represent the best interests of children in cases involving the Indian Child Welfare Act. The intersection of the Act with the standard of the best interests of the child allows for a deeper understanding of both.

In addition to the work that has been done on ICWA cases in the clinic, I have been involved in community efforts stemming from the Indian Child Welfare Act. One of the efforts that I have been involved with is the creation of the East Metro ICWA Task Force. The former director of an American Indian shelter for youth spearheaded an effort to have Ramsey County, the county in which Saint Paul is located, to utilize and recognize Native children and youth for better application of the Indian Child Welfare Act at the front end of cases. The initial formation was quite informal, as we were a group of people on a mission. We met with the county attorney after obtaining the support of the chief judge of the district. Our efforts culminated after almost a year in a county agreement that outlined their responsibilities under the Indian Child Welfare Act.[22] The benefit of creating a local agreement is that it allows for communication and dialogue between the grass-roots community and those charged with enforcement of the laws. In addition, the ongoing effort to create practical solutions to apply the Indian Child Welfare Act remains long after the agreement is reached. Today, the East Metro ICWA Task Force continues to meet. The members of the group dialogue on issues involving the Act outside of the judicial arena. It is a viable avenue to address ICWA issues. The task force is another cutting-edge approach to work on ICWA issues.

As part of my individual efforts to remain at the forefront of efforts under the Indian Child Welfare Act, I have made countless presentations to judges, attorneys, social workers, teachers, and almost anyone who will listen, to educate them about the Indian Child Welfare Act. Despite the Act being thirty one years old, education about the Act is still a crucial element. Unfortunately, the Act is sometimes not covered, or only glossed over, in training social workers and judges. Therefore, it remains critical that training and education are continued on the Indian Child Welfare Act.

An area that continues to need to be addressed is the standard of active efforts. The problem of continued lack of use of active efforts continues. There remains a tendency by agencies and courts to use the language of reasonable efforts in these cases. Why is there such a reluctance to apply the correct standard? Is it ignorance? Is it resistance? Why is compliance with this aspect of ICWA an ongoing area where application of the correct standard is slow to occur? Surely, those who are responsible for applying active efforts are intelligent, well-trained professionals who should simply be able to read the various sources in the law that require active efforts.

There are several sources and definitions of active efforts. For example, 25 U.S.C. 1912 (d) requires that "any party seeking to effect a foster care placement of, or termination of parental rights to, an Indian child under State law shall satisfy the court that active efforts have been made to provide remedial services and rehabilitative programs designed to prevent the breakup of the Indian family and that these efforts have proved unsuccessful."

Another source is the Federal Register Guidelines to State Courts, which states:

> Any party petitioning a state court for foster care placement or termination of parental rights to an Indian child must demonstrate to the court that prior to the commencement of the proceeding active efforts have been made to alleviate the need to remove the Indian child from his or her parents or Indian custodians. These efforts shall take into account the prevailing social and cultural conditions and way of life of the Indian child's tribe. They shall also involve and use the available resources of the extended family, the tribe, Indian social service agencies and individual Indian care givers.[23]

Another source requiring the application of the active efforts standard is found in the Minnesota Tribal/State Agreement (1998). It uses the following definition:

> Active Efforts means active, thorough, careful and culturally appropriate efforts by the LSSA to fulfill its obligations under ICWA, MIFPA and the DHS Social Services manual to prevent placement of an Indian child and at the earliest possible time to return the child to the child's family once placement has occurred.[24]

The Minnesota DHS Social Services Manual, XIII-3521, has the same definition as the Tribal State Agreement:

> A Minnesota Case where the father's parental rights were terminated, had a relative available but the children were not placed with the relative. The Court of Appeals reinstated the father's parental rights because the county had not placed the child with the available relative. The Court held that the county must make active efforts to reunite a family and, in an action to terminate

parental rights, the county must prove "beyond a reasonable doubt" that they made active efforts.[25]

Active Efforts in Foster Care Placements: ICWA defines foster care placements as "any action removing an Indian child from its parent or Indian custodian for temporary placement in a foster home or institution or the home of a guardian or conservator where the parent or Indian custodian cannot have the child returned upon demand, but where parental rights have not been terminated."

Active Efforts in Termination of Parental Rights Proceedings: ICWA defines termination of parental rights as "any action resulting in the termination of the parent-child relationship."

Active efforts are not required in voluntary placements. The experts tell us that the Active Efforts standard is not applicable in voluntary placements per ICWA.[26]

Is that the end of the story? Practitioners should continue to argue that where an local social services agency (LSSA) is working with the parents to utilize a voluntary placement prior to an actual filing of a petition, the standard of active efforts should be utilized. ICWA predates the current trends and cost-saving efforts of agencies to "divert" families from actual child-protection petition filings and work with them prior to a petition. But, what happens if the parents do not work well with the "voluntary placements" within those situations. Are the parents truly able to request a return of their children? No, the agency immediately puts into place an emergency protection order and the children are not able to be returned. It is in those types of situations that there is a need for active efforts to have been made with the family while the guise of a voluntary placement proceeds.

Another arena that remains in the forefront is that cultural ramifications under the Indian Child Welfare Act need to be explained to those applying the Act. It is often difficult for the non-Indian to understand the full impact of cultural connections to one's tribe. It is important that those of us who practice in this area continue to educate about that important connection. I consider that to be an important aspect of my life's work, and I attempt to teach the law students who take my class about that as a critical component of practice in the area of Indian Law, and specifically, in the application of the Indian Child Welfare Act.

Practicing in Minnesota has been a pleasure in terms of the efforts made by the State of Minnesota legislature in enacting the Minnesota Indian Family Preservation Act (MIFPA).[27] Having a state statute that further defines the Indian Child Welfare Act is certainly proof of its importance. In addition, tribal leaders and the Minnesota Department of Human Services entered into an agreement that further delineates practice under the Act and MIFPA.[28] The agreement was originally adopted in 1993 and has recently been updated and revised. Thus, Minnesota is on the leading edge of ICWA practice.

The work that I have done throughout my career has been amazingly intertwined with the Indian Child Welfare Act. Surprisingly, I did not make a conscious effort to be an ICWA practitioner. I attribute my path to the Creator's guidance as I have come to walk the Red Road. My journey has been guided by the Creator and directed by the many American Indian children and families that I have worked with over the last thirty years. I continue to receive cards, letters, and telephone calls from past clients who are doing well. In addition, I often see children in the community who give me a special nod or a hug. Those are the most important recognitions! I feel the warmth of my Uncle Edmund's smile as the children acknowledge me, and I know that I am fulfilling my life's mission.

My path has led to working on cases for all children. It has been my pleasure to be involved in developing a model law school curriculum for abused and neglected children with Victor Vieth of the APRI's National Center for Prosecution of Child Abuse.[29] Despite the efforts of many involved with cases concerning children, there are cases of actual abuse and neglect that require prosecution. It is my hope to be involved in some small way in teaching law students practical methods that will enable them to work effectively in that arena. Where the Indian Child Welfare Act is a part of such cases, it is my hope to provide appropriate education on the Act for their use.

It seems that the Indian Child Welfare Act, like the miner's canary, is on the "cutting edge of societal evolution."[30] The phrase seems a better description of the Act than of a radio show. Today, the cutting edge of the Act involves greater understanding and application of the "active efforts" needed to remove Indian children.[31] The use of tribal-state agreements as to the Indian Child Welfare Act is on the rise as more states are utilizing such agreements. And, many states are beginning to create state statutes to inform the application of the Act.[32] Further, Indian communities and practitioners are making efforts to prevent the spread of the use of the Existing Indian Family exception.[33] Therefore, at thirty years, the Indian Child Welfare Act is the basis for many cutting-edge issues.

NOTES

The author kindly thanks Matthew Fletcher and Wenona Singel for allowing me to capitalize on the name of the conference held March 16 and 17, 2007, at the Michigan State University campus.

1. 25 U.S.C. § 1901 et seq.
2. *But see* Christine Zuni Cruz, *Four Questions on Critical Race Praxis: Lessons from Two Young Lives in Indian Country*, 73 FORDHAM L. REV. 2133 (2005).
3. The term "Indian" will be used for this article, as that is the term that I have grown up hearing as

my ethnicity. The term "Indian" refers to indigenous people of North America for the purposes of this article.

4. *Board of Regents of the University of California v. Bakke*, 385 U.S. 589 (1967).
5. 25 U.S.C. § 1901.
6. The Native American Church was the subject of several federal cases. *E.g., Native American Church of North America v. Navajo Tribal Council*, 272 F.2d 131 (10th Cir. 1959); *Native American Church of New York v. United States*, 633 F.2d 205 (2d Cir. 1980).
7. A term for a way of life for many American Indians/Native Americans seeking to live spiritually and in sobriety. According to Terri Jean, the term is "a metaphor for living within the Creator's rules—a life of truth, friendship, respect, spirituality, and humanitarianism." TERRI JEAN, 365 DAYS OF WALKING THE RED ROAD: THE NATIVE AMERICAN PATH TO LEADING A SPIRITUAL LIFE EVERY DAY (Adams Media Corporation 2003).
8. PAUL RADIN, THE WINNEBAGO TRIBE (University of Nebraska Press 1973). THE WINNEBAGO TRIBE originally was published as part of the THIRTY-SEVENTH ANNUAL REPORT OF THE BUREAU OF AMERICAN ETHNOLOGY (Smithsonian Institution 1923).
9. 25 U.S.C. § 1903(1).
10. 25 U.S.C. § 1911(b).
11. 25 U.S.C. § 1903(1).
12. *Cf.* Rachel L. Kraker, Note, *Trumping Tribal Sovereignty One Sex Offender at a Time: How the Minnesota Court of Appeals' Decision in In re Commitment of Beaulieu Disregards the Sovereignty of the Red Lake Band of Chippewa Indians and Sets a Dangerous Precedent for the Disposition of Civil Matters in Indian Country*, 31 HAMLINE L. REV. 273, 285–87 (2008) (noting that Public Law 280 does not apply to the Red Lake Band, which has had a longtime functioning tribal court).
13. 25 U.S.C. § 1922.
14. 25 U.S.C. § 1912(a).
15. 25 U.S.C. § 1914.
16. *See* Kristen A. Carpenter, Sonia Katyal, and Angela R. Riley, *In Defense of Property*, 118 YALE L. J. (forthcoming 2009), manuscript at 55, *available at* http://papers.ssrn.com/s013/papers.cfm?abstract_id=1220665. The North Dakota Board of Education finally approved a schedule for discarding the "Fighting Sioux" nickname. *See* Associated Press, *North Dakota Moves to Change Nickname*, N.Y. TIMES, Oct. 17, 2008.
17. Brooks, Mary Jo, *Practitioners Guide to the Indian Child Welfare Act* (Council Lodge Institute 1990).
18. B. J. JONES, THE INDIAN CHILD WELFARE ACT HANDBOOK (American Bar Association 1995).
19. *See Matter of Custody of S.E.G.*, 521 N.W.2d 357 (Minn. 1994).
20. The Honorable Robert Blaeser is a member of the White Earth Band of Ojibwe. His efforts to utilize American Indian attorneys as guardians *ad litem* on cases involving the Indian Child Welfare Act was an innovative concept. Again, I was involved in cutting-edge efforts under the Act.
21. 25 U.S.C. § 1912(f).
22. Ramsey County Agreement, Susan Gaertner, 1999.

23. Guidelines for State Courts; Indian Child Custody Proceedings § D.2, 44 Fed. Reg. 67584, 67592 (Nov. 28, 1979), D. 2.
24. 25 U.S.C. § 1912(d).
25. *Matter of the Welfare of M.S.S.*, 465 N.W. 2d 412 (MN App. 1991)
26. *See* Jones, *supra* note 18, at 58.
27. MINN. STAT. 260.751 et seq.
28. Minnesota Tribal/State Agreement, revised February 22, 2007.
29. APRI, *Investigation and Prosecution of Child Abuse* (3rd ed., Sage Publications 2004).
30. Lewis Grossberger, *The Rush Hours*, N.Y. TIMES, Dec. 16, 1990 (quoting Rush Limbaugh on describing his radio show).
31. 25 U.S.C. § 1912(d).
32. IOWA CODE ANN. § 232B.1 et seq.
33. *See Native American Rights Fund, A Practical Guide to the Indian Child Welfare Act* 2–4 (2007), *available at* http://doc.narf.org/icwa/index.htm.

Differing Concepts of "Permanency"
The Adoption and Safe Families Act and the Indian Child Welfare Act

B. J. Jones

> I miss you Dad. I miss you mom. I hope you come back and be my best friend. I hope in my heart this dream will come true, cuz without you It's like I'm here with nothing. Not even the air I use to breath with you, love you. Hope you had a good time with me in your life but at least I'll get to see you when I'm older.
> —Native child in South Dakota

The above is from a letter written by a Native child in South Dakota to her parents after a termination of parental rights pursuant to the Adoption and Safe Families Act. This letter was offered by a grandmother of an Indian child to the South Dakota Indian Child Welfare Act Commission in support of her testimony during a listening session on the Rosebud Sioux Indian Reservation on September 17, 2004.

"Permanency" is all the rage in the child protection arena lately. Congress, bolstered by statistics pointing to long stays for children in the foster care systems operated by state and county governments, proclaimed in 1997 that efforts to reunite children with their biological families had sometimes unsuitably extended the foster care lives of these children.[1] One of the goals of Congress by the enactment of the Adoption and Safe Families Act (ASFA) was to narrow the "reasonable efforts" requirement of federal law and to remove the obligation of states to provide "reasonable efforts" in certain circumstances when the requirement conflicted with the safety of a child and the need of the child for a permanent placement outside the parental home. As one court has stated: "ASFA establishes a child protection system that subordinates parental rights to the paramount concern for the health and safety of the child...."[2]

ASFA theoretically accomplishes this objective of achieving "permanency" for children in the foster care system by eliminating the requirement for states and counties to provide "reasonable efforts" to rehabilitate families to make the safe return of their children possible in certain situations. Those situations, called "aggravated circumstances," include certain situations defined by Congress in the federal law,[3] and conditions left to the state legislatures to define. Not surprisingly, state legislatures have enacted a plethora of scenarios that, if found to exist by state courts, relieve their child protection employees of the obligation to work with families to reunite children removed from them because of allegations of abuse and/or neglect.[4]

Indian tribes and families become very nervous when Congress starts tinkering with the child welfare system, and even more disconcerted when states are given broad latitude to manipulate it. Part of this is due to the demographics of the child welfare system in many states today. Indian children continue to be removed from their homes by state governments at disproportionate rates. Indian children are significantly overrepresented in foster care,[5] with an Indian child three times more likely to be placed in foster care or substitute care than any other child in the general population. In some states, that number is as high as sixteen times more likely.[6] What makes these statistics even more alarming is that these disproportionate removal rates subsist even though many Indian tribes have been quite active in providing for their own children who are in need of removal because of abuse and neglect, both on and off Indian reservations.[7]

Any law, therefore, impacting the rights of children in foster care and their families, and the obligations of state and county governments to provide services to those children and families, is going to disparately impact Indian families and Indian tribes in certain states. What should give Indian tribes and families even more pause, however, is the premise underlying the ASFA, and how the accomplishment of that premise potentially conflicts with the Indian Child Welfare Act. The ASFA presupposes that "permanency" is achieved for a child by: 1) rehabilitating the family from which the child was removed, but only if rehabilitation is deemed probable for that family, by gauging the family's probability for change by rigid standards defined by federal and state law; and 2) if the family is deemed incapable of changing, placing the child permanently with another family as soon as possible, thereby lessening the trauma associated with extended foster care stays. States are provided with both negative and positive incentives for achieving these goals in the form of potential fiscal sanctions if children are left in foster care for periods of time in excess of what the federal law sanctions,[8] and positive affirmations in the form of fiscal bonuses for adopting children out of foster care and into other homes.[9]

Indian children should not languish in foster homes any more than other children, and this paper does not advocate that the underlying goals of the ASFA are always antithetical to the goals of Indian tribes to assure safe homes for Indian children that approximate the cultural traditions of the families of those tribes. Indian children who have been exposed to horrific abuse or neglect by the actions of a parent or other custodian should not merely be returned home under the banner of "preserving" familial and cultural ties. However, when Congress and the states promote the location of finding "alternative homes" as expeditiously as possible for children in foster care, and when statistics demonstrate that states have been woefully inadequate in recruiting Indian families as those "alternative homes," the stark possibility of accelerating the removal of Indian children out of Native homes and into non-Indian homes becomes palpable.[10] This possibility, combined with the evident propensity of states to define aggravated circumstances under state law in such ways that compromise the ability of Indian families to receive necessary remedial services to regain their children, is why many Indian tribes are opposed to the application of the punitive provisions of the ASFA to their families.

This modest paper contends that some of the provisions of the Adoption and Safe Families Act are so antithetical to the goals of Congress when it enacted the Indian Child Welfare Act that states should recognize that Congress did not expressly overrule the Indian Child Welfare Act when it enacted the ASFA. State and county child protection agencies should therefore harmonize the ASFA and the Indian Child Welfare Act (ICWA) in such a way that the laudable goals of ICWA, including assuring some permanent cultural affiliation of Indian children, are not overwhelmed by a literal application of the ASFA to Indian children. Finding a "permanent" home for an Indian child without regard to preserving that child's need for her tribal affiliation is not the type of "permanency" for Indian children Congress sought when it enacted ICWA. Indeed, Congress decried the use of a "one size fits all" formula by state agencies and courts for determining what is in the "best interests" of Indian children when it enacted ICWA, because such recipes proved disastrous for Indian families as these prescriptions

> have often failed to recognize the essential tribal relations of Indian people and the culture and social standards prevailing in Indian communities and families. It is the policy of this Nation to protect the best interests of Indian children and to promote the stability and security of Indian tribes and families . . . .[11]

To understand the different paradigms of permanency promoted respectively by ICWA and the ASFA, this paper will examine the history of the treatment of Indian children in the legal system, and how that treatment led to the crisis of displacement facing Indian families and tribes prior to 1978. Taking that history into consideration, the paper contends that the seemingly irreconcilable goals of ICWA and ASFA can be harmonized to achieve the goal of assuring cultural and tribal affiliation while placing Indian children into homes where their future physical, emotional, and cultural security can be assured.

Prior to embarking on an examination of history, however, and in the desire to personalize the dichotomy between the ASFA and ICWA with regard to permanency, I would like to examine the lives of two native children. One child, whom I will not refer to by his real name, but instead will call John, lives on the Lake Traverse Indian Reservation in South Dakota and has been the subject of numerous child custody proceedings before me in the Tribal Court for the Sisseton-Wahpeton Oyate. He represents the epitome of permanency under ICWA. The other child, who unfortunately has been referred to by her name in a Kentucky Supreme Court decision,[12] lives in Kentucky with a non-Indian step-aunt and perhaps epitomizes the goal of permanency under the ASFA. This child will be referred to as Candace.

Recently, one of my clerks at the Sisseton-Wahpeton Oyate Court in South Dakota brought to me a custody petition, along with a consent to custody signed by the parents of a teenage boy named John, in which one of John's aunts was seeking custody of him. I knew John fairly well because he sang frequently in one of the local drum groups that we called upon on occasion to honor the graduates of our Tribal Treatment Court (similar to a drug court) upon their graduation from that program. John was an outstanding singer, was one of the young men in the community who knew how to speak the Dakotah language, and participated in many of the spiritual and cultural ceremonies of the community. I became interested in John's legal file because I recalled signing numerous orders pertaining to the custody of John, most of which were consented to by his parents and family. I asked the clerk to search for all files pertaining to John, and when the clerk brought them to me, to my surprise I discovered that in my over seven years as chief judge for the Oyate, I had signed ten custody orders regarding John, placing custody of him with his mother, father, several grandparents, aunts, uncles, and even his basketball coach on one occasion. My predecessor judges had signed four more orders regarding John. Most of these orders were consented to by his parents, although a couple were the result of contested proceedings.

At first blush, John seemed to lack "permanency" in his life. He went from home to home, laid his head on many a bed at night to rest, and had not developed a significant, and unilateral, psychological bond with his parents or a parental figure. He seemed to have languished in numerous homes throughout his seventeen years of life. He should have therefore manifested the dysfunctions that children who have not resided in a permanent home frequently do, right? He seemed to be the poster child for why the Adoption and Safe Families Act was enacted.

Nothing could be further from the truth. John was emotionally intact, culturally strong, and tribally affiliated. He was a role model to the other youth in the community and had the luxury of calling at least ten elders in the community his "grandparents." He not only knew his extended family, he seemed to have mastered the art of "mooching" off of them.

John's life exemplifies the "essential tribal relations" of Native people that Congress strove to preserve through enactment of ICWA. His "permanency" is his tie to the native community and the cultural practices of that community.

Candace has a different story. She is a full-blood member of the Standing Rock Sioux Tribe who was placed as an infant with her uncle, also a member of the Standing Rock Sioux Tribe. Her uncle gained permanent custody of her through the Standing Rock Sioux Tribal Court. The uncle then married a non-Indian, and the couple moved to Kentucky with Candace to start a new life. After several years together, the uncle and his non-Indian wife separated, and she started divorce proceedings against the uncle, sought to remove Candace's uncle from her home, and also sought the permanent legal custody of Candace, arguing that her home was the only permanent home Candace had known throughout her young life. The tribe sought to intervene in the dispute and argued that the tribal court had exclusive jurisdiction over the proceeding because it had placed the legal custody of the child with the uncle, and the child remained a ward of its court.[13] The wife responded by arguing that although Candace was a member of the Standing Rock Sioux Tribe, she should not be considered Indian for purposes of the Indian Child Welfare Act because she had not lived in an Indian family.

This exception to ICWA, called the "Existing Indian Family" exception,[14] has been recognized by numerous courts as a justification for not applying the Act to certain Indian children, even though they are Indian under the definition adopted by Congress in ICWA. In support of this argument, the wife pointed out that Candace had become rather ensconced in the non-Indian world of Kentucky, did not practice her Native religion, did not speak her Native tongue, and was assimilated into the non-Indian community. The aunt was apparently willing to negate Candace's Native heritage in order to keep her out of the clutches of the tribe and her biological family.

She found a sympathetic audience in the Kentucky Supreme Court, which readily agreed with her that a full-blood Standing Rock Sioux child was not really an Indian. Because of the Kentucky Supreme Court's ruling that Candace was not "Indian" for purposes of ICWA, she was ordered to remain with her stepmother, who apparently was opposed to the tribe having any role to play in her upbringing. Because of the court's ruling, the tribe was not permitted to even intervene in the proceeding involving Candace; it is thus almost impossible for the tribe to track Candace's progress in her current home. However, the anecdotal and sociological information brought to Congress's attention when it enacted ICWA[15] may foreshadow a difficult life for Candace, especially if her stepmother maintains her adversarial relationship with Candace's extended family members and tribe.

The Kentucky Supreme Court obviously was concerned about the need of Candace for permanency when it declared her non-Indian for purposes of ICWA. The court was apparently willing to sacrifice Candace's cultural and tribal identity at the altar of maintaining the type of life she had been living in Kentucky. Candace epitomizes the concept of permanency under the ASFA, because the court went out of its way to stress the need for Candace to remain in the same home she had lived in for several years and even rewrote federal law to preserve that "permanency." Perhaps had the Kentucky Supreme Court been aware of why the Indian Child Welfare Act was enacted, it would not have engaged in such mental gymnastics to defeat Candace's cultural identity.

ICWA vs. ASFA: Why an Indian Child Welfare Act?

Why should special consideration be given to Indian children in the application of the Adoption and Safe Families Act? An examination of why ICWA was enacted perhaps best explains the uniqueness of Indian children in the child welfare system, and why state courts and agencies have a special federal mandate to treat these children differently. This history also explains why the goal of "permanency" for Indian children has been invoked frequently in the past as a justification for removing Indian children from their extended families and tribes.

One of the laws that the United States enacted to preserve the rights of Indian children is the Indian Child Welfare Act (ICWA). On November 8, 1978, Congress passed ICWA in response to the "rising concern ... over the consequences to Indian children, Indian families, and Indian tribes of abusive child welfare practices that resulted in the separation of large numbers of Indian children from their families and tribes through adoption and foster care placement."[16] By limiting states' powers over Indian children, ICWA aims to support Indian families, specifically by maintaining Indian children with Indian caregivers, while honoring a rich cultural tradition and tribal sovereignty.

To understand why the United States enacted the Indian Child Welfare Act for the benefit of Indian children and tribes necessitates an examination of how Indian children and families have been treated by the federal and state governments. By examining this history, the reader will better understand the importance of the law to Indian families and tribes, and why its implementation is so crucial to the survival of Indian families and tribes. This review will hopefully also lay some historical foundation for why Congress did not explicitly apply the ASFA to Indian children when it amended Title IV-E of the Social Security Act in 1997.

NATIVE CHILDREN AND FEDERAL POLICY

American Indian children have been the legal targets of a multiplicity of notions and ideas promoted by policymakers with conflicting agendas regarding their "best interests" and their need for "permanency." In the late 1800s, federal policymakers targeted Indian children as the agents of change in an era when Indian people were perceived as "savages" who needed to be rehabilitated and Christianized in order to survive in an increasingly dominant non-Indian society.[17] Transforming Indian children was perceived as the key to Indian survival in that dominant society, and as a result they were oftentimes removed from their parents and placed in boarding schools where they were denied the right to speak their native languages, practice their spiritual beliefs, or even adhere to their traditional grooming and attire.[18]

Because they were oftentimes the legal guinea pigs for an assortment of notions regarding the future of Indian tribes and their people, a wealth of unique laws and policies flowered simultaneously with their upbringing. Probably never before in this country has there been such a concerted effort to transform a group of people by legally manipulating their children.[19] Contemporary Indian children are the survivors of these policies of cultural degradation. Understanding this history of federal policy toward Indian children is imperative to appreciating why a law such as ICWA exists. Congress, when it enacted ICWA, recognized that Indian tribes should determine the destiny of their children, and has passed several laws designed to protect this tribal prerogative.[20]

Ironically, however, Indian self-determination has not always been kind to Indian children. Tribal self-determination came into vogue in the late 1960s and early 1970s when Congress passed a variety of federal laws that recognized the inherent sovereign rights of Indian nations to determine their own laws and be governed by them. Congress was also turning over federal programs—including social service, education, and health programs impacting Indian children—directly to Indian tribes to permit them to operate them. These laws, especially the ones directly benefiting Indian children, undoubtedly promote the best interests of Indian children by permitting Indian tribes to determine the values important to Indian families without interference. However, Indian tribes, despite the consideration paid to them by federal legislators who recognize their sovereign status, have never been treated by the federal government similarly to the other semisovereign political entities—state governments. At the same time that Congress was promoting Indian self-determination, it was also crafting the "Great Society"—an effort to legislatively provide for the basic needs of all Americans, but especially children, through a system of federal grants to state governments that would be utilized to operate programs to assist children who were deprived of the support of their parents and who needed medical services. Accessing these programs, for Indian children, is just as important as being the beneficiaries of special federal laws designed only for Indian children.[21]

Tribes may have jurisdiction over Indian children, but this jurisdiction does not always mean that tribes can access the necessary funding to provide for their children. This is especially evident in the area of child welfare, where the primary funding source to provide for neglected or abused children—Title IV-E of the Social Security Act—is only available to state governments for those children in state or county custody. This is true despite the acknowledgment in the Indian Child Welfare Act that Indian children placed by Indian tribes should be entitled to all benefits provided under federal and state law.[22]

HISTORY OF THE INDIAN CHILD WELFARE ACT

This historical legacy of the treatment of Indian families laid the foundation for the passage of the Indian Child Welfare Act. By the spring of 1974, the separation of Indian children from their tribes had become a national "crisis of massive proportion." As a result, the Senate Subcommittee on Indian Affairs conducted extensive oversight hearings to address the tribes' concerns about the loss of their children. Those hearings produced overwhelming evidence substantiating the palpable harm inflicted on Indian children, their families, and their tribes by state child welfare practices. One study, for example, revealed that 25 to 35 percent of all Indian children had been separated from their families and placed in adoptive families, foster care, or institutions. Of those placed in foster or adoptive homes, about 85 percent were placed with white families.

As reported by the House:

> Surveys of States with large Indian populations conducted by the Association on American Indian Affairs (AAIA) in 1969 and again in 1974 indicate that approximately 25–35 percent of all Indian children are separated from their families and placed in foster homes, adoptive homes, or institutions.

In addition to the trauma of separation from their families, most Indian children in placement or in institutions have to cope with the problems of adjusting to a social and cultural environment much different than their own. In sixteen states surveyed in 1969, approximately 85 percent of all Indian children in foster care were living in non-Indian homes.

> It is clear then that the Indian child welfare crisis is of massive proportions and that Indian families face vastly greater risks of involuntary separation than are typical of our society as a whole.

Subsequent hearings were held in 1977 and 1978 on the bill that became the Indian Child Welfare Act. At these hearings, there was considerable focus on the destructive effect on tribes as a result of the "massive removal of their children." Mr. Calvin Isaac, tribal chief of the Mississippi Band of Choctaw Indians and representative of the National Tribal Chairmen's Association, spoke on the destructive effect on tribal survival and tribal sovereignty:

> Culturally, the chances of Indian survival are significantly reduced if our children, the only real means for the transmission of the tribal heritage, are to be raised in non-Indian homes and denied exposure to the ways of their People. Furthermore, these practices seriously undercut the tribes' ability to continue as self-governing communities. Probably in no area is it more important that tribal sovereignty be respected than in an area as socially and culturally determinative as family relationships.

This sentiment was echoed in the congressional floor debate on the bill that was to become ICWA. Congressman Udall stated, "Indian tribes and Indian people are being drained of their children and, as a result, their future as a tribe and a people is being placed in jeopardy," while Congressman Lagomarsino pointed out "This bill is directed at conditions which ... threaten ... the future of American Indian tribes."[23]

Indian tribes in South and North Dakota, as well as legislators from South Dakota, were particularly involved in promoting the passage of the Indian Child Welfare Act. From 1969 through 1974, the Association on American Indian Affairs (AAIA), acting at the request of the Devil's Lake Sioux Tribe (now known as the Spirit Lake Tribe) and the Sisseton-Wahpeton Oyate, conducted nationwide studies on the impact of state child welfare practices toward American Indian children. AAIA research indicated that 25–35 percent of all Indian children were placed in either foster homes, adoptive homes, or institutions. The decision to remove these children from their natural families was often a product of state child welfare agents' lack of understanding of American Indian culture and child-rearing practices.[24]

The AAIA study also produced multiple findings that reflected the severity of the problem of Indian children in substitute care. For example, in Minnesota, Indian children were five times more likely to be placed in foster care compared to non-Indian children, while in Montana, Indian children were thirteen times more likely to be placed compared to non-Indian children. In South Dakota, between 1967 and 1974, Indian children made up 40 percent of the state's adoptions, yet Indian children made up only 7 percent of the juvenile population. Also, foster care placements of Indian children were sixteen times those of non-Indian children in South Dakota. Unfortunately, in South Dakota the numbers of Indian children being placed by the State Department of Social Services (DSS) have not decreased that dramatically

(Indian persons represent 8 percent of the population, yet represent over 60 percent of children in DSS custody). In Washington, the adoption rate of Indian children was nineteen times that of non-Indians, while the foster care placement was ten times that of non-Indian children.

A survey of sixteen states in 1969 also revealed that approximately 85 percent of Indian children in foster homes and 90 percent of non-relative Indian adoptees were living with non-Indian families.[25] The results of this survey troubled tribes for a variety of reasons. First, the placement of so many Indian children in non-Indian homes threatened the extinction of the tribes. In short, tribes were losing the most basic necessity for survival—a next generation. Second, the alienation of Indian children from their unique tribal cultures and values resulted in the development of maladaptive behaviors, such as antisocial behavior, depression, and suicide, among alarming numbers of Indian children, as reflected in the 1974 AAIA report.

In 1974 Congress initiated its first hearing on the state of Indian children in substitute care. During testimony before the subcommittee, William Byler, then executive director of the AAIA, commented on the statistical evidence uncovered by the AAIA, stating that the comparatively high rate of outplacement for Indian children was "the most tragic aspect of Indian life today."[26]

The testimony in 1974 also provided the first official acknowledgment by the United States Government that the unwarranted removal of Indian children from their families represented a systematic attempt to destroy native tribes and cultures that resulted in negative outcomes for both tribes and tribal children. In his opening statement, South Dakota Senator James Abourezk, the chairman of the subcommittee, noted that the placement of "Indian children in non-Indian settings" resulted in "their Indian culture, their Indian traditions, and, in general, their entire way of life ... being smothered."[27] Senator Abourezk continued by declaring that this loss "strike[s] at the heart of Indian communities" and had been called "cultural genocide."[28]

Four years later, ICWA was signed into law and is regarded as the most significant piece of legislation affecting American Indian families passed by the United States Congress.[29] The Act states:

> There is no resource that is more vital to the continued existence and integrity of American Indian tribes than their children ... and that an alarmingly high percentage of such children are placed in non-Indian foster and adoptive homes and institutions. The states ... have often failed to recognize the essential tribal relations of Indian people and the culture and social standards prevailing in Indian communities and families. It is the policy of this Nation to protect the best interests of Indian children and to promote the stability and security of Indian tribes and families ....

ICWA establishes minimum federal jurisdictional, procedural, and substantive standards aimed to achieve a dual purpose: (1) to protect Indian children and families; and (2) to stabilize and foster tribal existence. The discussion that follows will provide a broad overview of the Indian Child Welfare Act, and discusses developments in the implementation of the Indian Child Welfare Act since its enactment.

There are both procedural and substantive provisions of the Indian Child Welfare Act. Both are designed to accomplish three primary objectives: (1) to eliminate the need to remove Indian children from their families, both nuclear and extended, because of cultural bias and ignorance; (2) to assure that Indian children who need to be removed for their own protection be placed in foster and adoptive homes that reflect their unique cultures and background; and (3) to encourage tribal court adjudication of child custody proceedings involving Indian children.

ICWA applies to state court "child custody proceedings" involving "Indian children." A child custody proceeding under the Indian Child Welfare Act is defined as a foster care placement, termination of parental rights proceeding, preadoptive placement, or adoptive placement of an Indian child. ICWA does not apply to custody disputes between parents, either as part of a divorce or non-divorce proceeding, nor does it apply to delinquency proceedings involving Indian children who commit acts that would be criminal if committed by an adult. It is important to note that the child custody proceeding need not involve some state action, such as the removal of an Indian child by a state or county child-protection entity, in order for ICWA to apply. ICWA applies to private placements and adoptions as well as those initiated by state and county agencies.

An "Indian child" is defined under the federal law as an unmarried child under eighteen who is a member of a federally recognized Indian tribe, or eligible for membership in a federally recognized tribe, and the natural child of a member of an Indian tribe. Indian tribes, under ICWA, are given the right to determine their own membership, and a state court must defer to a tribal determination of membership. In any child custody proceeding in state court where a party believes, or has reason to believe, that the child involved is an Indian child, there is an affirmative obligation on the part of all parties, and their attorneys, to report such to the court so that notice may be given to the Indian child's tribe. Some courts have carved out an exception to the definition of Indian child, commonly referred to as the "Existing Indian Family exception," and held that the Act should not apply to an otherwise qualified Indian child who has not lived with an Indian family, or who lives with an Indian family with few or no ties to an Indian tribe. The language of the Act does not support such an exception, but these courts have asserted that such an exception is consistent with the legislative history of the Act. Other courts and commentators have strongly criticized this exception, and some state legislatures have taken action to repeal the judicially created exception. The South Dakota Supreme Court seemed to reject this exception in *Matter of Adoption of Baade.*[30]

The procedural requirements of the Indian Child Welfare Act are contained generally at 25 U.S.C. §§ 1911 and 1912. Section 1911 distinguishes between the jurisdiction of state and tribal courts in child custody proceedings involving Indian children. Indian tribal courts are given exclusive jurisdiction over child custody proceedings involving Indian children domiciled on Indian reservations, or who are wards of tribal courts. This rule applies in all states, except states commonly referred to as Public Law 280 states, which were given civil jurisdiction over Indian reservations. In those states, the state courts may exercise concurrent jurisdiction, along with tribal courts, over child custody proceedings involving Indian children. For Indian children domiciled off-reservation, state courts can exercise jurisdiction over child custody proceedings, but the exercise of that jurisdiction is subject to a transfer of jurisdiction to the tribal court of the Indian child's tribe. In general, ICWA favors a transfer of jurisdiction of a child custody proceeding involving an Indian child to a tribal court unless certain findings are made by the state court judge. The parent of an Indian child can always veto a transfer to a tribal court, as can the tribal court decline a transfer of jurisdiction to its court. Many tribes do not transfer jurisdiction over the majority of child custody proceedings involving their children, many times because they lack the financial resources to provide for the children that the state may be able to access.

Notice is a vital component of the Indian Child Welfare Act. The act requires any party to an involuntary child custody proceeding involving an Indian child to give notice to the child's parents, Indian custodian (if one exists), and to the Indian child's tribe of the commencement of the proceeding. Notice is triggered by any suggestion that the child is an Indian child, and any tribe with possible affiliation must be given notice. Most courts have ruled that the failure to give notice under the Act deprives the state court of jurisdiction. In many cases, more than one tribe must be given notice because of differing tribal affiliations among the parents. If a party cannot determine which tribe the child is affiliated with, notice may be given to the Bureau of Indian Affairs, which is then charged with the responsibility to determine tribal affiliation.

Other procedural requirements of ICWA govern the weight of the evidence and type of evidence necessary to sustain an involuntary foster care placement or involuntary termination of parental rights. In order to achieve an involuntary placement of an Indian child outside of his home, the party seeking removal must establish by clear and convincing evidence, supported by the testimony of a qualified expert witness, that the child would suffer severe emotional or physical harm if left in the child's home. The moving party must also establish that active remedial and rehabilitative services were offered to the family in an attempt to avoid removal. To sustain a termination of parental rights, the court must find beyond a reasonable doubt that these requirements are shown. The requirement that a qualified expert witness's testimony support removal or termination is an attempt by Congress to assure that a person with specific knowledge of Indian child-rearing practices testify to the cultural propriety of removal or termination. In general, a qualified expert witness is either a person with specialized knowledge of Indian cultural practices regarding child rearing, or a person with professional knowledge that can aid the court in deciding a child custody matter. The need to demonstrate that active remedial and rehabilitative services are provided to Indian families is similar to the requirement found elsewhere in federal law, except that under ICWA those services have to be provided before removal is effected, as well as afterwards, in an attempt to seek family reunification.

Indian parents and custodians are also entitled to the appointment of counsel in ICWA cases, notwithstanding their need. If a state would otherwise not appoint counsel in a particular matter, but does so because of the mandate of ICWA, that state can apply to the BIA for reimbursement for the expenses of court-appointed counsel.

The Indian Child Welfare Act recognizes that Indian tribes have unique rights that must be preserved in litigation regarding the placement of their children. To protect these rights, the Act gives an Indian tribe the right to intervene at any stage of an ICWA proceeding, and also vests in the tribe the right to request a transfer of the proceeding to a tribal court. Tribes are also given additional time to prepare for litigation after notice is provided, and they also have a fairly unlimited right of discovery in ICWA cases. Lastly, Indian tribes are given an independent right to discover the placement location of their tribal members, and are also given the right to collaterally challenge actions taken by state courts and entities in violation of the Indian Child Welfare Act.

The substantive provisions of ICWA are the placement-preference provisions contained in 25 U.S.C. § 1915. These provisions are designed to assure that Indian children who are removed from their homes be placed in homes that reflect their unique cultures. There are separate placement-preference provisions governing foster care and adoptive placement preferences. Both recognize that Indian tribes should have the right to alter the placement preferences by enacting their own preferences for placement of their children. Absent that, state courts are directed to place Indian children first with their extended families (which in the case of a child of both Indian and non-Indian parents would include the non-Indian family members), second with a home licensed by the tribe, third with a member of the child's tribe, fourth with another Indian family, and as a last resort with a non-Indian family. Despite this mandate of ICWA, many Indian children continue to be placed predominately with non-Indian foster families, primarily due to the failure of some states to recruit sufficient Indian foster families.

The Indian Child Welfare Act has, as one of its primary objectives, eliminating the removal of Indian children from their families and tribes based upon cultural bias or ignorance. Over twenty years after that law's enactment, Indian children have not seen a substantial decrease in the incidence of their removal from their families. In 1996, more than half a million children were in state-run foster care.[31] Indian children are significantly overrepresented in foster care,[32] with an Indian child three times more likely to be placed in foster care or substitute care than any other child in the general population. In some states, that number is as high as sixteen times more likely.[33] Indian children may be in foster care under the legal custody of state or county governments, tribal governments, or under the legal control of the Bureau of Indian Affairs. Although Indian tribes have been able to tap into alternative sources of funding to pay for foster care since the enactment of the Indian Child Welfare Act,[34] Title IV-E of the Social Security Act remains the primary basis for the payment of foster care subsidies for Indian children in substitute care. Unfortunately, despite recent efforts to amend federal law, Indian children remain ineligible for Title IV-E foster care payments unless they are placed by a state court in substitute care, or by a tribal court on a reservation that has a Title IV-E cooperative agreement with the state wherein that tribe is located.[35]

This deficiency inhibits the effective implementation of the Indian Child Welfare Act because Indian tribes are strapped for the resources necessary for them to provide for their children when they are being removed from their families. As a result, many Indian tribes cannot transfer jurisdiction over their children back to their tribal courts, simply because they lack the financial wherewithal to provide foster care subsidies for those children and to provide necessary services for them. Even for children on certain Indian reservations where state courts lack jurisdiction, many Indian tribes, including several in South Dakota, have resorted to requesting state and county assistance in providing child protection services in order to access Title IV-E resources and services for those children.

The biggest obstacle to Indian tribes fully implementing ICWA is their inability to access necessary funding and services. Title IV-E of the Social Security Act is a federal matching-grant program designed to reimburse states for foster care, adoption assistance, and transitional independent-living program payments. The number of children in foster care has increased 65 percent over the past ten years.[36] To address the steadily increasing foster care caseload, Congress recently passed the Adoption and Safe Families Act of 1997.[37] Accessing Title IV-E funds depends, in part, on whether tribes and states comply with the requirements of the ASFA.

HISTORY OF THE ADOPTION AND SAFE FAMILIES ACT

The ASFA was aimed at improving the safety of children and promoting adoption or some other type of permanency for children in long-term foster care. The ASFA mandates the timely placement of children in permanent homes. States are free to adopt more restrictive time restraints, but at a minimum the ASFA requires that any child who has been in foster care for fifteen out of the most recent twenty-two months be reviewed for termination of parental rights and freed for adoption. The ASFA computes the foster care entry based on the date the court finds the child neglected or abused, or sixty days after the child's actual removal from the home, whichever is earlier.

The ASFA contains a requirement that the foster care agency make reasonable efforts to prevent the need for removal of the child, or reasonable efforts to reunify the family. ICWA, on the other hand, mandates that any person or entity seeking the foster care placement of an Indian child demonstrate that active efforts were made to provide remedial and rehabilitative services to the family to prevent the breakup of the family.[38] The burden is on the foster care agency to demonstrate that those active efforts have proven unsuccessful in keeping the family together. The ASFA contains exceptions to the requirement that reasonable efforts be provided in all cases to reunite/rehabilitate a family from whom a child has been removed,[39] and also gives the states the option to adopt other "aggravated circumstances." Thus, ICWA active efforts reunification provisions in some cases may conflict with the termination of reunification efforts mandated by the ASFA.

When Congress enacted the Adoption and Safe Families Act, it was silent on whether all of its provisions should apply to Indian children governed by the Indian Child Welfare Act. Because compliance with the ASFA is a sine qua non to receiving payment for foster care, states have in many situations been forced to choose between complying with the ASFA or ICWA, especially in situations where "aggravated circumstances" under either federal or state law exist, and when the child has been in the foster care system for the number of months where a termination petition is required under the ASFA.

The court systems, both tribal and state, that place Indian children in substitute care are apparently not exempt from the various provisions of the AFSA either. Although there is commentary by the Administration for Children and Families in promulgating regulations to implement the AFSA that recognizes that it does not intend to supersede the various provisions of the Indian Child Welfare Act,[40] the AFSA does not explicitly exempt children governed by ICWA from its coverage.

The South Dakota Supreme Court was recently the first appellate court in the nation to hold that the provisions of the ASFA did not supersede the active efforts requirement of ICWA.[41] Although this decision is very helpful to Indian tribes in South

Dakota concerned about the rising tide of termination of parental rights proceedings in cases governed by ICWA, it does not control the federal government's ultimate position on whether Title IV-E funds will be available to Indian children placed by either state or tribal agencies.

Accessing Title IV-E funds is one of the most critical steps a tribe can take in preserving sparse tribal social services foster care funds. Title IV-E money is of paramount importance to a tribe because the federal government reimburses a large portion of the foster care expenses. This approach allows a tribe to preserve the Bureau of Indian Affairs foster care dollars and tribal monies for those foster care placements that are not eligible for IV-E funding. The tribe will then be able to provide foster care services to more needy Indian children in Indian Country. Further, children who receive IV-E foster care funding are also eligible for medical assistance under Title XIX of the Social Security Act that will pay for the child's various health care needs. Indian children who are not Title IV-E eligible are not automatically eligible for Title XIX benefits and may be forced to rely upon Indian Health Services and its contract health program. Any foster child who was placed by a tribal court and who resided within an Indian Health Service health-delivery area at the time of placement remains eligible for health services through the Indian Health Service, notwithstanding placement off-reservation.

In general, an Indian child residing outside of Indian Country, or an Indian child residing within Indian Country and who is placed in the legal custody of a state or county child protection program, is eligible for Title IV-E funding if at the time of removal, the child's family was eligible for Temporary Assistance for Need Families (TANF), formerly known as Aid to Families with Dependant Children or AFDC, or if the child was eligible for Supplemental Security Income (SSI). Indian children, both those residing outside Indian Country and within Indian Country, are considered citizens of the state in which they are residing for purposes of gaining entitlement to the various programs of the Social Security Act, including Title IV-E. Federal law requires that each state that receives Title IV-E funds must provide child welfare services to all eligible children, including Indian children, who reside in the state.[42] Furthermore, the Administration for Children and Families (ACF), the agency that funds state and some tribal child welfare programs under the various titles of the Social Security Act, expects states to coordinate with tribes for the provision of services and protections to tribal children who are in state or county custody.[43] Failure to confer could result in the termination of benefits under Title IV-B of the Social Security Act.

The problem regarding Indian children domiciled on Indian reservations accessing Title IV-E resources is not that they are ineligible for such services under federal law, but that they can only access those resources through the intercession of state courts or state child protection programs. An Indian child placed in the custody of a tribal child protection program by a tribal court is not, ipso facto, eligible for Title IV-E foster care subsidies, notwithstanding his family's eligibility for TANF prior to his removal. This is because Congress, when it enacted Title IV-E conditioned eligibility for foster care subsidies and other programs under Title IV-E on the child being placed in the custody and control of a state or county government, with no mention of tribal child welfare programs. On Indian reservations, primarily due to the enactment of the Indian Child Welfare Act and the recognition by the courts that Indian tribes retain the inherent rights to apply their own laws to Indian children free of interference from state laws and entities, Indian tribes have the primary responsibility for protecting the welfare of Indian children. Tribes may be reluctant to place their children in state or county custody because of the abuses documented by Congress when it enacted the Indian Child Welfare Act. In addition, state or county child protection programs may balk at honoring tribal court orders placing Indian children in their legal custody because they are bound by certain federal regulations that require the cooperation of the courts that place them. Tribal laws may not mirror these federal requirements, and these agencies may feel that they cannot comply with federal regulations when they are subject to the inconsistent dictates of tribal court orders.

The irony in this apparent congressional oversight in assuring the eligibility of Indian children placed by tribal courts for Title IV-E benefits is that Congress in the Indian Child Welfare Act apparently addressed this issue by assuring tribes that for the purpose of determining eligibility for federal assistance, a tribal foster care license should be the equivalent of a state or county foster care license.[44] Theoretically, therefore, ICWA dictates that an Indian child placed in a tribally licensed home should be eligible for Title IV-E and the corresponding Title XIX medical assistance programs and Title IV-D child-support enforcement programs.

Indian tribes should not have to choose between obtaining necessary funding for the care of their children in foster care and acceding to the punitive provisions of the ASFA. Fortunately, there are alternatives to termination proceedings under the ASFA that are more in line with the goals of ICWA than terminations of parental rights and adoptions. Those include permanent guardianships with extended family members, customary adoptions that are similar to open adoptions where the parental rights are not terminated, and the extension of the period of time that remedial services can be offered to Indian families. In addition, a recent report of the Pew Commission entitled "Fostering the Future: Safety, Permanency and Well-Being for Children in Foster Care"[45] recommends that Indian tribes receive direct funding under Title IV-E of the Social Security Act to give them more leverage to provide for their own children, and to enable them to transfer more of their children out of state and county care. The Administration for Children and Families must also be cognizant of the history behind the Indian Child Welfare Act and not coerce states into some rote compliance with the time periods and strict requirements of the ASFA in cases involving Indian children.

"Permanency" is important for all children, including Native children. It is a malleable concept, however, that has oftentimes been used to justify the removal of Indian children from their families and tribes because of cultural ignorance and bias. Hopefully, the Adoption and Safe Families Act will not join the host of other federal laws that have led to the separation of Indian children from their unique cultural heritages. The excerpt from the letter written by a native child at the beginning of this article points out a crucial aspect of the lives of native children who are removed from their cultures and extended families. During their adolescence, they always come back in search of what they lost. The ASFA does not have to be interpreted in a way that drives a stake between children in need of care and their tribes, and can be interpreted in a manner where both the need for security and tribal affiliation are maintained.

NOTES

1. Adoption and Safe Families Act, Pub. L. No. 105–89, 111 Stat. 2115, (1997) (codified in part at 42 U.S.C. § 671).
2. *In re D.B.*, 670 N.W.2d 67, 2003 SD 113, ¶10.
3. Specifically, 42 U.S.C. § 671(a)(15)(D) mandates that a state need not provide reasonable efforts in the following circumstances: "(D) reasonable efforts of the type described in subparagraph (B) shall not be required to be made with respect to a parent of a child if a court of competent jurisdiction has determined that—the parent has subjected the child to aggravated circumstances (as defined in state law, which definition may include but need not be limited to abandonment, torture, chronic abuse, and sexual abuse); the parent has—committed murder (which would have been an offense under section 1111(a) Title 18, if the offense had occurred in the special maritime or territorial jurisdiction of the United States) of another child of the parent; committed voluntary manslaughter (which would have been an offense under section 1112(a) of Title 18, if the offense had occurred in the special maritime or territorial jurisdiction of the United States) of another child of the parent; aided or abetted, attempted, conspired, or solicited to commit such a murder or such a voluntary manslaughter; or committed a felony assault that results in serious bodily injury to the child or another child of the parent; or the parental rights of the parent to a sibling have been terminated involuntarily."
4. The National Conference of State Legislatures maintains a Web page that reveals the wide diversity of "optional aggravated circumstances" enacted by state legislatures in response to the ASFA at http://www.ncsl.org/statefed/cf/asfasearch.htm. Some states and the District of Columbia merely adopted the federal mandatory aggravated circumstances when they passed ASFA enabling legislation, while a majority of states adopted a variety of other optional

aggravated circumstances that direct state court judges to relieve state child welfare agencies of the obligation to provide reasonable efforts.

5. U.S. DEPARTMENT OF HEALTH AND HUMAN SERVICES, OFFICE OF INSPECTOR GENERAL, OPPORTUNITIES FOR ACF TO IMPROVE CHILD WELFARE SERVICES AND PROTECTIONS FOR NATIVE AMERICAN CHILDREN, August 1994 (OEI-01-93-00110)

6. *Id.*

7. The Indian Child Welfare Act, 25 U.S.C. § 1901 et seq., vests Indian tribal courts with exclusive jurisdiction over Indian children domiciled on Indian reservations who need to be removed due to abuse and neglect, and also gives Indian tribes the right to transfer jurisdiction over their children who are subject to child custody proceedings commenced in state courts back to the tribal courts.

8. Congress conditioned the receipt of foster care maintenance payments from the federal government on compliance with the provisions of the ASFA. *See* 42 U.S.C. § 671. The ASFA requires a state or county child protection program to file a petition to terminate the parental rights, absent compelling circumstances, over a child who has been in the foster care system for fifteen of the previous twenty-two months. 42 U.S.C. § 675(5)(E).

9. Based on a formula a state may be in line for either a $4,000 or $2,000 per adoption bonus for adopting children out of foster care. 42 U.S.C. § 673b.

10. A recent Robert Wood Johnson Foundation report found, for example, that since the enactment of the ASFA, the adoption rate for children of drug- or alcohol-abusing parents has more than doubled. A typical scenario involving the removal of Indian children involves the use of drugs or alcohol.

11. ICWA of 1978, 25 U.S.C. §§ 1901, 1902.

12. *See Rye v. Weasel*, 934 S.W.2d 257 (Ky. 1996).

13. *See* 25 U.S.C. § 1911(a), which declares that an Indian child is a ward of a tribal court, subject to exclusive tribal court jurisdiction, if a tribal court has exercised and continues to exercise jurisdiction over the child in a child custody proceeding.

14. There are numerous variations of the "Existing Indian Family" exception. One of the more pernicious examples is a recent California decision. *In re Santos Y.*, 92 Cal. App. 4th 1274, 112 Cal. Rptr. 2d 692 (2001).

15. According to the AAIA report submitted to Congress in support of the Indian Child Welfare Act, many Indian children who were adopted out to non-Indian families experienced more maladaptive behaviors during their adolescence than other Indian children raised within their extended families and tribes.

16. *See Mississippi Band of Choctaw Indians v. Holyfield*, 490 U.S. 30 (1989).

17. As the founder of one of the first boarding schools, Richard Pratt stated in 1892: "Kill the Indian in him and save the man." Richard Pratt, *A Bid to Redefine Indian Education*, N.Y. TIMES, Nov. 27, 1995.

18. As anthropologist Peter Farb described the boarding school experience: "The children were usually kept at boarding school for eight years during which time they were not permitted to

see their parents, relatives or friends. Anything Indian—dress, language, religious practices, even outlook on life . . . was uncompromisingly prohibited. Ostensibly educated, articulate in the English language, wearing store-bought clothes and with their hair cut short and their emotionalism toned down the boarding school graduates were sent out either to make their way in a white world that did not want them or to return to a reservation to which they were now foreign." PETER FARB, MAN'S RISE TO CIVILIZATION AS SHOWN BY THE INDIANS OF NORTH AMERICA FROM PRIMEVAL TIMES TO THE COMING OF THE INDUSTRIAL STATE, 257–259 (New York, E.P. Dutton & Co., Inc., 1968).

19. One of the best examples of this is the following statement from the commissioner of Indian Affairs: "It is admitted by most people that the adult savage is not susceptible to the influence of civilization, and we must therefore turn to his children, that they might be taught how to abandon the pathway of barbarism and walk with a sure step along the pleasant highway of Christian civilization.... They must be withdrawn, in their tender years, entirely from the camp and taught to eat, to sleep, to dress, to play, to work and to think after the manner of the white man." See Comm'n Ind. Aff. Ann. Rep., H.R. Exec. Doc. No. 1, 50th Cong., 2d Sess., XIX (1888).

20. Examples of these laws include the Indian Child Welfare Act, 25 U.S.C. § 1901 et seq., the Indian Self-Determination and Education Assistance Act of 1975 (Pub. L. 93-638), 25 U.S.C. § 450(a)–(n).

21. As a general proposition, more Indian children domiciled on Indian reservations rely upon programs operated by the states for their subsistence than rely upon tribal programs for their survival. This is largely the result of the legal reality that most of the programs designed to provide for poor children can only be operated by state governments because they are the only legal entities entitled to receive federal dollars to operate such programs. Although this changed somewhat in 1996 with the enactment of the Personal Responsibility and Work Opportunity Reconciliation Act of 1996 (Pub. L. 104–193), which allows tribes to now operate the TANF and child-support enforcement programs, that law fails to appreciate that tribal governments do not have the same resources as states to come up with the necessary fiscal matches to operate those programs.

22. 25 U.S.C. § 1931 (1978).

23. 124 Cong. Rec. H38, 102 (daily ed. Oct. 14, 1978) (statements of Rep. Udall and Rep. Lagomarsino).

24. J. HOLLINGER, ADOPTION LAW AND PRACTICE (New York, Matthew Bender) (Supp. 1992); H.R. REP. NO. 1386 (1978).

25. H.R. REP. NO. 1386 (1978).

26. S. Rep. No. 597, 95th Cong., 1st Sess. 11 (1977).

27. 93rd Cong. 2d Sess. 1, 3 (1974).

28. Id.

29. M. C. Plantz, R. Hubbard, B. J. Barrett, A. Dobrec, *Indian Child Welfare: A Status Report*, CHILDREN TODAY, Jan.–Feb. 1989, at 24–29.

30. *Matter of Adoption of Baade*, 462 N.W.2d 485 (S.D. 1990).

31. CONNA CRAIG AND DEREK HERBERT, STATE OF THE CHILDREN; AN EXAMINATION OF GOVERNMENT-RUN FOSTER CARE (NCPA POLICY REPORT NO. 210) 4 (Aug. 1997).

32. Opportunities for ACF to Improve Child Welfare Services and Protections for Native American Children, Department of Health and Human Services, Office of Inspector General, August 1994.
33. *Id.*
34. Those alternate resources include Title II of the Indian Child Welfare Act, 25 U.S.C. §§ 1931–32, which allows for funding for Indian tribes for the operation of child welfare programs and the application of tribal codes; and Title IV-B of the Social Security Act, 42 U.S.C. § 628, which authorizes direct grants to Indian tribes for the delivery of child welfare services.
35. *See Native Village of Stevens v. Smith*, 770 F.2d 1486 (9th Cir. 1985), *cert. denied*, 475 U.S. 1121 (1986).
36. The State of the Children; An Examination of Government-Run Foster Care, August 1997 NCPA Policy Report Nw. 210, ISBAN #1-56808-07904, by Conna Craig and Derek Herbert, Institute for Children.
37. P.L. 105–89, codified at 42 U.S.C.A. Section 671 et seq. (1998).
38. 25 U.S.C. § 1912(d) provides: "Remedial services and rehabilitative programs; preventive measures—Any party seeking to effect a foster care placement of, or termination of parental rights to, an Indian child under State law shall satisfy the court that active efforts have been made to provide remedial services and rehabilitative programs designed to prevent the breakup of the Indian family and that these efforts have proved unsuccessful."
39. *See* note 5.
40. *See* 65 Fed. Register 4020, January 25, 2000, at 4029, when ACF opined that "Some commenters also requested that we explain how the provisions of the Indian Child Welfare Act work in the context of ICWA. Although we can affirm that States must comply with ICWA and that *nothing in these regulations supersedes ICWA requirements*, we cannot expound on ICWA requirements since they fall outside of our statutory authority." (Emphasis added.)
41. *See Matter of JSB*, 691 N.W.2d 611 (SD 2005).
42. P.L. 96–272; see also Department of Health and Human Services, Office of Inspector General, Opportunities for ACF to Improve Child Welfare Services and Protections for Native American Children, June Gibbs Brown, Inspector General, August 1994.
43. Department of Health and Human Services, Office of Inspector General, Opportunities for ACF to Improve Child Welfare Services and Protections for Native American Children, June Gibbs Brown, Inspector General, August 1994.
44. *See* 25 U.S.C. § 1931(b).
45. Pew Commission Report, May 18, 2004.

The Disconcerting Vicissitudes of State Judicial Power

Determining If Good Cause Exists to Deny Transfer in ICWA Cases

Allie Greenleaf Maldonado

John Wildhorse and His Daughter

John Wildhorse called his daughter over and over again by her Indian name, Waboose, which means rabbit in Odawa; but she didn't turn her head and look at him until he spoke the name given to her by the foster family, Jane. How would the Creator hear his daughter's prayers if she couldn't tell the Creator that it was her, Waboose, praying? John stroked her hair and thought about how much it hurt to have missed her birth. He was in jail for a third drunk-driving offense when she was born, and Waboose's mother was a poly-drug user; the social workers put the girl in foster care the same week she was born. John's Tribal-citizen mother had been at the hospital and gave the girl her Indian name, but the social workers refused to acknowledge his mother's Tribal foster care license and instead placed Waboose with a non-tribal family. John was angry at the social workers, but ultimately he blamed himself for not being there when she was born. He has been sober for over six months now, but he is still at war with himself over having a drink. He works as a janitor and did not get his GED until after he went to jail. He is a large man with dark skin and dark eyes. Sometimes people think he is Mexican—he has even been mistaken for an Arab—but the one thing the dominant culture knows for certain is that he is not one of them. He drank because he was alone. Yet the first time he looked at his daughter, everything changed. Even though his body screams for a drink every second of every day, even though billboards and magazines and television constantly conspire to seduce him, he vows to do whatever it takes to get her back. Otherwise, how will his daughter know her name, and without her name, how will the Creator be able to answer her prayers?[1]

Introduction

Congress enacted The Indian Child Welfare Act (ICWA),[2] in part, as a response to well-documented historical abuses of authority on the part of state agencies and courts.[3] The case above involved a modern-day example of abuse by a Michigan agency that failed to follow ICWA's placement preferences by placing a Little Traverse Bay Bands of Odawa Indians' child in a non-tribal home. Ultimately, a Michigan court honored ICWA in this case by finding that "good cause" did not exist to deny transferring the case to the Tribal court.

In adopting ICWA, Congress intentionally diminished state jurisdiction over Indian children.[4] Yet, as soon as ICWA was signed into law, detractors began crafting arguments designed to nullify the underlying congressional intent in enacting ICWA, particularly the goal of keeping tribal children in tribal communities. For example, some courts have adopted the judicially created "Existing Indian Family Exception" to circumvent ICWA.[5] Other courts have adopted a "best interests of the child" standard that subverts tribal jurisdiction over tribal children.[6] Judicially created mechanisms for avoiding tribal jurisdiction undermine the goals of ICWA. While legislative history and numerous cases from other jurisdictions strongly support adopting the standard of "clear and convincing evidence" in opposing transfer,[7] some courts have ignored ICWA's implied congressional intent and applied a lower standard.[8]

This article attempts to demonstrate that Michigan, as well as the rest of the country, should uniformly adopt the "clear and convincing evidence" standard because it is most closely aligned with the language and purposes of ICWA. In other words, when state courts have to determine whether "good cause" exists to deny transfer of a case involving a tribal child from a state court to a tribal court, the state court should use a "clear and convincing evidence" standard. Michigan should adopt the "clear and convincing evidence" standard because congressional history defies a lower standard; the "clear and convincing evidence" standard respects tribal sovereignty, it offers an honest evaluation for the parties involved, and it prevents bias against tribal courts from entering into the evaluation process.

Background of the Indian Child Welfare Act

Congress enacted ICWA to promote the very survival of tribes.[9] Congressional hearings revealed that an "alarmingly" high number of tribal children were being systematically removed from their tribal homes and placed in non-tribal homes.[10] Before ICWA was enacted, as many as 35 percent of Native American children across the United States were being removed from their homes,[11] and as of 1978, states placed 90 percent of tribal children in non-tribal-citizen homes.[12] Congress enacted ICWA in 1978 to end the systematic removal of tribal children from their tribal communities,[13] and articulated that the primary purpose of ICWA was to stop large numbers of tribal children from being adopted by non-tribal families or placed in non-tribal foster homes and institutions because such placements threaten the well-being and survival of tribal governments.[14]

To achieve the goal of preserving tribal governments, Congress enacted ICWA with a number of provisions vesting tribal governments with tools designed to help protect their future citizens. For example, ICWA affirms exclusive jurisdiction of tribal courts over tribal children domiciled on Indian reservations who must be removed from a custodian's care due to abuse or neglect.[15] ICWA also gives tribes the right to request transfer of jurisdiction over cases involving children who are involved in abuse and neglect child custody proceedings from state courts to tribal courts.[16] ICWA expressly gives tribes the right to petition for invalidation of state court action,[17] the right to alter presumptive placement priorities applicable to state court actions,[18] the right to obtain records,[19] and the authority to enter into agreements with states.[20] Considering the statutory provisions in light of the express legislative history of ICWA[21] confirms an intention by Congress to protect the government-to-citizen relationship between Indian tribes and their children.

The Supreme Court in *Mississippi Band of Choctaw Indians v. Holyfield*

The Supreme Court has addressed ICWA in only one decision, *Mississippi Band of Choctaw Indians v. Holyfield.*[22] In *Holyfield*, the Tribal-citizen mother and Tribal-citizen father of twins were residents and domiciliaries of the Choctaw Reservation in Mississippi.[23] The Tribal mother went off-reservation to give birth in an attempt to avoid Tribal court jurisdiction over the adoption of her twin babies.[24] The Holyfields adopted the twins through a Mississippi state court proceeding that was challenged by the Tribe.[25] On appeal, despite acknowledging numerous failures by the state court to follow ICWA, the Mississippi Supreme Court refused to vacate and set aside the decree of adoption.[26] The court applied state law to find that the children were abandoned and therefore could not maintain the mother's domicile on the reservation.[27] The court also reasoned that because the Tribal-citizen parents went to great lengths to avoid Tribal court jurisdiction, ICWA should not apply.[28]

On appeal, the Supreme Court reversed the Mississippi Supreme Court decision.[29] The Supreme Court held that although ICWA fails to define the term "domicile," Congress did not intend for states to define "domicile" according to state law, because to do so would defeat ICWA's jurisdictional scheme.[30] Therefore, the Supreme Court held that the children were "domiciled" on the reservation for purposes of ICWA giving the Tribal court exclusive jurisdiction.[31] Although the Supreme Court acknowledged that the Tribal parents went to great lengths to avoid ICWA, the Court found this fact to be irrelevant.[32] Since ICWA's dominant mandate protects tribal governments' interests in their future citizens, the wishes of the parents can be subordinated in favor of tribal interests.[33] The Supreme Court's holding in *Holyfield* demonstrates a strong presumption for tribal jurisdiction and tribal sovereignty. The "clear and convincing evidence" standard is a way to enforce the strong presumption for tribal court jurisdiction and tribal sovereignty.

BIA Guidelines

Not only do Congress and the Supreme Court uphold the understanding that ICWA demonstrates a strong presumption for tribal jurisdiction, the Department of the Interior, an arm of the executive branch, has as well. The BIA published Guidelines for State Courts, Indian Child Custody Proceedings which also demand a higher presumption in favor of tribal interests.

The Bureau of Indian Affairs published guidelines to assist states in applying ICWA.[34] The BIA Guidelines do not carry the weight of federal regulations, but many courts have looked to them in determining transfer-of-jurisdiction issues that arise under ICWA.[35]

Section 1911 (b) of ICWA provides that state courts "shall transfer" Indian child welfare proceedings to the jurisdiction of the appropriate tribe in the absence of "good cause" to the contrary. "Good cause" to deny transfer is not defined by ICWA; however, the BIA Guidelines offer instruction for determining good cause.[36] The Guidelines state that a party asserting "good cause" has the burden of demonstrating it.[37] Furthermore, the BIA Guidelines propose a number of considerations that a state court should make before determining whether "good cause" to deny transfer exists:

C.3. DETERMINATION OF GOOD CAUSE TO THE CONTRARY

a. Good cause not to transfer the proceeding exists if the Indian child's tribe does not have a tribal court as defined by the Act to which the case can be transferred.
b. Good cause not to transfer the proceeding may exist if any of the following circumstances exists:
  i. The proceeding was at an advanced stage when the petition to transfer was received and the petitioner did not file the petition promptly after receiving notice of the hearing.
  ii. The Indian child is over twelve years of age and objects to the transfer.
  iii. The evidence necessary to decide the case could not be adequately presented in the tribal court without undue hardship to the parties or the witnesses.

iv. The parents of a child over five years of age are not available and the child has had little or no contact with the child's tribe or members of the child's tribe.
c. Socio-economic conditions and the perceived adequacy of tribal or Bureau of Indian Affairs social services or judicial systems may not be considered in a determination that good cause exists.
d. The burden of establishing good cause to the contrary shall be on the party opposing the transfer.[38]

These detailed guidelines explaining what constitutes "good cause" support a finding that the standard of proof needed to determine if "good cause" exists to deny transfer of a case to a tribal court must be "clear and convincing evidence." If a lesser standard such as "mere discretion" or "preponderance of the evidence" were the standard, then a state court could *at will* circumvent the intent of ICWA and override federal statutory commands and legislative intent.[39] Therefore, after a careful examination of the Guidelines, many courts have held that the standard for determining "good cause" to deny transfer most strongly supported by ICWA's purposes is a finding of "good cause" proven by "clear and convincing evidence."[40]

However, ICWA is interpreted almost exclusively through state courts. Therefore state courts, particularly in Michigan, should adopt a stringent evidentiary standard favoring tribal courts in a case transfer.

Michigan has adopted ICWA's transfer provisions as a Michigan court rule.[41] If a court determines that ICWA applies in a case, the next step is to decide which forum has jurisdiction to hear the proceedings. Section 1911(a) of ICWA affirms the exclusive jurisdiction of tribal courts when the child involved is domiciled on the tribe's reservation.[42] When the child is domiciled outside of the reservation, § 1911(b) creates concurrent but presumptive tribal jurisdiction that requires the state to transfer jurisdiction to the tribe unless "good cause" exists to decline to transfer.[43] The burden of establishing good cause not to transfer rests with the party opposing transfer.[44] Michigan Court Rule 3.980(3) mirrors these transfer provisions of ICWA.

Michigan courts must not allow unfamiliarity and uncertainty regarding tribal courts to factor into decisions regarding transfer. The Supreme Court in *Holyfield* instructs state courts to overcome their distrust of tribal courts: "We must defer to the experience, wisdom, and compassion of the . . . tribal courts to fashion an appropriate remedy in Indian child welfare cases."[45] A Michigan court adopting a "clear and convincing evidence" standard for determining whether "good cause" exists to transfer a case to a tribal court stays connected to the issues relevant under ICWA and is more likely to overcome inherent bias.[46]

At least one Michigan court has acknowledged that Michigan courts must overcome prejudice. The case involved a Tribal child eligible for membership in the Little Traverse Bay Bands of Odawa Indians (LTBB). Immediately after the birth of the child, the State of Michigan removed her from the custody of her non-tribal mother due to the mother's substance-abuse problems. The mother voluntarily terminated her parental rights. The Tribal-citizen father of the child had a history of substance abuse and was incarcerated when the child was born, but he desperately wanted an opportunity to care for his daughter. Although the child's Tribal grandmother immediately made the state aware that she wanted to care for the child, the state placed the child in a non-tribal foster home because the home already cared for the LTBB child's non-tribal siblings. The state moved to terminate the father's parental rights and began efforts for the non-tribal home to adopt the Tribal child. The district court refused to transfer the case to the LTBB Tribal court and then terminated the father's parental rights.

On appeal, the Michigan Court of Appeals overturned the district court's decision to terminate the father's parental rights because the district court failed to apply ICWA. The Court of Appeals remanded the case to the district court for a new hearing on whether "good cause" existed to deny transfer. In a decision that upheld the purposes of ICWA, the district court found that "good cause" did not exist to deny transfer, and therefore ordered the case to be transferred to the LTBB Tribal court. The district court judge, the Honorable William T. Ervin, in a candid decision from the bench, discussed how uncertainty regarding whether the LTBB Tribal court would remove the Tribal child from her current foster care placement had impacted the state's decision making:

> It is somewhat disturbing to the Court [that the Tribe might remove Jane[47] from her current foster home because she] . . . has been placed with the foster parents since, I think she was three days old. . . . But we get to another decision then of good cause as to what I feel is somewhat of a *distrust* of the Tribal Court, saying okay if we transfer this matter to the Tribal Court they will go down and swoop . . . [Jane] out of the home—it's the only home that she has known since she has been born. And one of the reasons that we have the Indian Child Welfare Act is to prevent that type of thing [state bias] from happening. And until you get into a situation like this it really didn't drive it home to me about why the Congress passed the act in the first place. . . . And if you look at the Indian Child Welfare Act and the reasons behind it—it was [enacted] to eliminate prejudice of the white community towards the Native Americans. And although this is not intentional it does bring forward the fact that we are looking at this and saying that [T]ribal court is not going to do a good job with . . . this child. Because we're looking at it from our perspective and that's not what the Indian Child Welfare Act is all about.[48] (Emphasis added.)

Then the judge honored ICWA by transferring the case to the LTBB Tribal court. Using laws unique to LTBB, the Tribal court facilitated an outcome that would not have been possible in state court. The Tribal court allowed Jane's non-tribal foster home to adopt her while simultaneously giving her paternal grandmother joint custody. Accordingly, Jane regularly spends time in her Indian community. Her Tribal half-sister, a champion hoop dancer, has taught Jane how to dance. Jane has her own dance regalia, and she has danced at pow wows. Jane's Tribal grandmother teaches her the Odawa language and Jane recently expressed an interest in learning about traditional medicine. Because of the flexibility of the LTBB Tribal court to craft a solution that specifically fit Jane's needs, she will grow up understanding the delicate and intricate fabric of her Tribal community while preserving her bond to her foster family. Jane as an adult will have an opportunity to make contributions as a citizen of the LTBB because of her significant contact with her Tribe. While Judge Ervin did not specifically state that he was using a "clear and convincing evidence" standard to weigh whether "good cause" existed to deny transfer of the case to LTBB Tribal court, his decision from the bench suggests the standard was used. The judge stated a preference to keep the child with her current foster family. If he wanted to guarantee that result, he could have used the more discretionary standard of "mere discretion" or "a preponderance of the evidence" to prevent transfer of the case. Instead, he found that "good cause" did not exist to deny transfer to Tribal court. He chose to honor the congressional purposes and intent of ICWA by using the higher evidentiary standard of "clear and convincing" evidence, even though he had concerns about the effect that transfer would have on the final placement of the child.

In Michigan, the standard applied to the "good cause" exception under § 1911(b) has not been fully litigated. However, if other Michigan courts also wish to fully honor the congressional intent behind enacting ICWA, they will look to the many well-reasoned opinions applying "clear and convincing evidence" as the standard for determining whether "good cause" exists to deny transfer in an ICWA case.[49] For example, in 2001 the Oklahoma Court of Appeals applied the standard of "clear and convincing evidence" to determine whether "good cause" existed to deny transfer in an ICWA case.[50]

In *In re Adoption of S.W.*,[51] a case of first impression in Oklahoma, the Oklahoma Court of Appeals articulated concern about several of ICWA's mandates and then crafted a ruling to fulfill them. The court offered careful analysis, holding that the party opposing transfer must establish "good cause" according to the "clear and convincing evidence" standard to resist transfer to a tribal court,[52] because the standard proves consistent with the proof applicable to stages of ICWA litigation where the higher standards of "clear and convincing evidence" and "beyond a reasonable doubt" apply.[53] Furthermore, the court held that the use of the "clear and convincing evidence" standard would foster the congressional policy of ICWA favoring jurisdiction of ICWA cases in tribal courts.[54] Finally, the court found "clear and convincing evidence" as the standard necessary to prevent inadvertent incorporation of cultural bias into Indian child welfare proceedings.[55] In this case, Oklahoma proactively supported ICWA's multiple goals of using higher standards in ICWA cases, and preferring tribal court jurisdiction over tribal children.

Courts also utilize the "clear and convincing evidence" standard because it helps preserve tribal culture. The Montana Court of Appeals in *In re M.E.M.*[56] overturned a lower court decision, in part, to help preserve tribal culture. M.E.M. and her mother were citizens of the Standing Rock Sioux Indian Tribe. The Standing Rock Tribal court requested transfer of the adjudication involving the termination of the mother's parental rights.[57] Showing obvious distrust of the Standing Rock Sioux Tribal court, the county welfare department insisted that it would resist transfer unless the Tribal Court gave the county plans for the final outcome of the case.[58] The Tribal Court refused. The district court denied transfer of jurisdiction to the tribal court.[59] The Montana Court of Appeals overturned the district court's termination of the mother's parental rights.[60] The court expressed concern about whether the state could adequately protect the cultural heritage of an Indian child:

> Each individual is an amalgam of the predominant religious, linguistic, ancestral and educational influences existent in his or her surroundings. Indian people, whether residing on a reservation or not, are immersed in an environment which is in most respects antithetical to their traditions. Furthermore, the cultural diversity among Indian tribes is unquestionably profound and often not fully appreciated or adequately protected in our society.[61]

Recognizing the unique ability of the Standing Rock Sioux Tribal court to address the cultural needs of the Tribal child, the Court of Appeals remanded the case back to the district court for a hearing on the issue of jurisdiction, where it directed that the party resisting transfer has by "clear and convincing evidence" the burden of showing "good cause" not to transfer the case to the tribal court.[62]

The legislative history of ICWA characterizes the placement of tribal children in non-tribal settings as "cultural genocide."[63] While many attorneys and state courts focus on ICWA as a mechanism to protect tribal culture, Congress enacted ICWA, in part, to preserve tribal governments by assisting Indian tribes in keeping tribal children in tribal communities.[64]

Before enacting ICWA, Congress took extensive testimony regarding the removal of tribal children from Indian communities.[65] The testimony revealed that the prolific removal of tribal children substantially threatened the existence of tribal governments because tribal children are the future citizens, voters, and leaders of their tribes.⁶⁶ ICWA's principal sponsor, Representative Morris Udall, expressed this sentiment in a statement he made before Congress: "Indian tribes and Indian people are being drained of their children and, as a result, their future as a tribe and a People is being placed in jeopardy."⁶⁷ Thereafter, Congress explicitly found in ICWA's legislative history that "there is no resource that is more vital to the continued existence and integrity of Indian tribes than their children."⁶⁸ Congress understood that continuing to remove mass numbers of tribal children from tribal communities would eventually destroy tribal governments.

Some courts that apply a standard lower than "clear and convincing" evidence to determine whether "good cause" exists to transfer demonstrate bias. The majority of the Supreme Court of Illinois exhibited this kind of decision making in *In Re S.S. v. Iron Bear.*⁶⁹ This case arose from an appeal of the termination of parental rights of Betty Jo Iron Bear, a citizen of the Fort Peck Tribe, and the adoption of her two Tribal-citizen children. Betty Jo lived on the Fort Peck Reservation while her children's non-citizen father retained sole physical custody of them prior to his death.⁷⁰ After the children's father died, his sister filed a petition to terminate Betty Jo's parental rights, claiming that Betty Jo was an unfit parent.⁷¹ She also filed a petition to adopt the children.⁷² Betty Jo moved to transfer the case to Tribal court pursuant to the exclusive jurisdiction provisions in ICWA.⁷³ The circuit court of Kane County denied the motion.⁷⁴ Betty Jo and the Fort Peck Tribe appealed.⁷⁵ The appellate court reversed and remanded the case to the Fort Peck Tribal court, finding that the Tribal court had exclusive jurisdiction of the matter under section 1911 of ICWA.⁷⁶ The majority of the Supreme Court of Illinois overturned the appellate court's ruling, finding that the children maintained the domicile of their dead father, who resided off of the reservation, over the domicile of their living, reservation-domiciled mother.⁷⁷ The holding directly contradicts express language in *Holyfield* disallowing the application of state law to determine domicile. Ultimately, the holding allows the majority to deny the Tribe's right to exclusive jurisdiction anticipated under 25 U.S.C. § 1911(a).

The dissent wrote a stinging rebuttal opinion, arguing that the majority judicially manipulated and misapplied the law. The dissent states:

> Although parts of the majority's recitation of the facts are accurate, the majority improperly supplements the record with matters that are unproven. In so doing, the majority attempts to justify its decision by indulging in unsubstantiated attacks upon the character and morality of Betty Jo, the children's surviving Indian parent. For example, the record does not disclose the cause of Richard's [the father's] death. Nevertheless, the majority states that he died "of a disease he contracted from" Betty Jo. . . . There is nothing in the record to verify the

claim that Richard died from AIDS, or that he contracted the illness from Betty Jo. There is no justifiable reason for the majority to make any reference to the nature or cause of Richard's death. Moreover, the majority fails to explain the relevance of this alleged information with respect to the true issue in the case, which is the Tribe's jurisdiction under ICWA.[78]

The dissent also reveals that the majority's assertion stating that the children have tenuous ties to their Indian community was not supported by the facts in the case. Additionally, the dissent reveals that the majority also selectively omits information from their opinion: "It is also significant, but undisclosed by the majority, that Betty Jo allegedly has had continuing contact with the children, thereby maintaining the children's contact with their Tribal heritage."[79] The dissent reveals that the majority's ruling stems from distrust of tribal courts and ultimately eviscerates the intent of ICWA. The dissent concludes: "The unfortunate effect of the majority's opinion is to revert to and perpetuate the regressive state policies and practices that led Congress to enact ICWA."[80] The dissent exposes the majority's opinion as inappropriately biased, with the intention of yielding a specific result. The majority's unwillingness to place the future of tribal children with the their tribal court exemplifies why ICWA maintains its relevance.

Courts that do not understand the historical role states played in removing Indian children from their homes often use weak standards to undercut ICWA. In 2004, the Supreme Court of South Dakota affirmed an "abuse of discretion" standard (identical to "mere discretion") to review whether a lower court properly denied transfer of an Indian child welfare case to a tribal court.[81] The dissent vehemently objected: "Abuse of discretion is the most relaxed standard and improper considering the intent of Congress and the burden imposed upon those who oppose an ICWA transfer."[82] The dissent reasoned:

> If the presumption is in favor of tribal jurisdiction, then mere discretion to override an ICWA transfer is unacceptable.... It is true that some other courts, like ours, have used the abuse of discretion standard. However, the better reasoned decisions hold that the determination must be supported by clear and convincing evidence of good cause.... Considering the firm congressional intent behind ICWA, the standard most consistent with the act requires clear and convincing evidence of good cause for a state trial court refusal to transfer to tribal court.[83]

Congressional testimony and hearings on ICWA show that the misuse of broad discretion by state courts played a definitive part in the assault on Indian families that led to the reforms started by ICWA.[84] Congress meant for a standard higher than "mere discretion" for refusal to transfer jurisdiction of tribal children to tribal courts, because ICWA intentionally diminished state court discretion in ICWA cases.

The dissent's deeply contemplated logic proved to be persuasive because just one year later, in *People Ex. Rel. T.I.*,[85] the Supreme Court of South Dakota overturned its past approval of the "abuse of discretion" standard in determining whether "good cause" existed to deny transfer of an ICWA case. The court adopted nearly verbatim language from the earlier dissent to justify a holding that "clear and convincing evidence" is the only standard that Congress could have imagined to determine "good cause" to deny transfer.[86] Congress intended for Indian tribes to have jurisdiction over Indian children. Giving states, the same bad actors ICWA was passed to restrain, broad discretion on whether to transfer an ICWA case to tribal court is tantamount to allowing the fox to guard the henhouse.

Using "clear and convincing evidence" provides an honest review of whether "good cause" exists to deny transfer of a case to a tribal court, which was lacking in the earlier-discussed Illinois case *In Re S.S. v. Iron Bear* and the lower court South Dakota case of *In re D.M.* One Kansas State court decision demonstrates this honest review.

In re A.P.[87] was a case of first impression for determining the appropriate standard by which a court could find "good cause" to deny transfer of a case to a tribal court in Kansas. After reviewing congressional intent, the Kansas Court of Appeals concluded that the standard most consistent with ICWA requires "clear and convincing evidence" of good cause for a state trial court to refuse to transfer to a tribal court.[88] When the Kansas Court of Appeals examined the lower court's finding of "good cause" to deny transfer of jurisdiction to the tribal court, the court looked to what the BIA Guidelines suggest constitutes "good cause," and found "good cause" did exist to deny transfer in this case because of the inconvenience of the forum. The Indian child and relevant witnesses all resided in Kansas, while the Oglala Sioux Tribal court is located in Pine Ridge, South Dakota.[89] By using "clear and convincing evidence," the Kansas Court of Appeals fulfilled well-balanced congressional goals of promoting the survival of Indian tribes, while applying a modified doctrine of *forum non conveniens* in appropriate cases to assure that the rights of the Indian child, the Indian parents or custodians, and the rights of the tribe are fully protected.[90] While using a standard of "clear and convincing" evidence does not always guarantee that a case will be transferred to a tribal court, it still best assures a fair outcome.

Conclusion

A survey of state cases, federal intent, and good statutory legal analysis demonstrates the need to uniformly adopt the "clear and convincing evidence" standard. Michigan, which has not yet fully litigated the issue, still possesses an opportunity to honor

ICWA's congressional intent by adopting the "clear and convincing evidence" standard. *Holyfield* plainly states that congressional intent prioritizes uniform application of ICWA over state law.[91] Some courts have worked hard to honor ICWA and the "clear and convincing evidence" standard applied to transfer.[92] Nonetheless, courts are split on the standard for finding "good cause" to not transfer a case to tribal court. However, ICWA was crafted for the benefit of Indian tribes,[93] and the legislative history proves congressional intent to preserve tribal relations with their citizens and future leaders. While applying a "clear and convincing evidence" standard does not guarantee that a tribal court will get jurisdiction of an ICWA case, it requires an honest assessment by the deciding court of what forum Congress intended to have jurisdiction. Not only does congressional testimony support "clear and convincing evidence" as the standard for courts to use, it is properly respectful of tribal sovereignty, and it is in fact the best possible way to evaluate these cases for every party involved. Adopting a standard lower than "clear and convincing evidence" for determining "good cause" to not transfer a case to tribal court plunges tribal children into the disconcerting vicissitudes of state judicial power. Congress enacted ICWA to protect tribal governments and their citizens against state abuses. The only standard that withstands the scrutiny of the legislative history of ICWA for determining whether "good cause" exists to deny transfer is "clear and convincing evidence."

NOTES

1. This account is based on an interview with a party to an Indian Child Welfare proceeding in Michigan state court. Names and telling details have been changed to protect the identity of the parties.
2. 25 U.S.C. §§ 1901–63.
3. *See* 25 U.S.C. § 1901(5) ("The States, exercising their recognized jurisdiction over Indian child custody proceedings through administrative and judicial bodies, have often failed to recognize the essential tribal relations of Indian people and the cultural and social standards prevailing in Indian communities and families.").
4. *See also Miss. Band of Choctaw Indians v. Holyfield*, 490 U.S. 30, 44–45 (1989) ('It is clear from the very text of the ICWA, not to mention its legislative history and the hearings that led to its enactment, that Congress was concerned with the rights of Indian families and Indian communities vis-à-vis state authorities.... Indeed, the congressional findings that are a part of the statute demonstrate that Congress perceived the States and their courts as partly responsible for the problem it intended to correct.").
5. *See generally* Toni Hahn Davis, *The Existing Indian Family Exception to the Indian Child Welfare Act*, 69 N.D. L. Rev. 465 (1993).
6. Amanda B. Westphal, *An Argument in Favor of Abrogating the Use of the Best Interests of the Child*

Standard to Circumvent the Jurisdictional Provisions of the Indian Child Welfare Act in South Dakota, 49 S.D. L. REV. 107 (2003).

7. B. J. JONES, THE INDIAN CHILD WELFARE ACT HANDBOOK: A LEGAL GUIDE TO THE CUSTODY AND ADOPTION OF NATIVE AMERICAN CHILDREN, 39 (American Bar Association 1995).
8. *Id.* at 39–40 (using a Best Interest of the Child standard, for example).
9. In reviewing ICWA, the United States Supreme Court also found that the protection of Indian families is not the only goal. "The act is intended not only to protect the interests of individual Indian children and families but also to protect the interest of the tribes themselves in long-term tribal survival." *In re Elliott*, 554 N.W.2d 32, 34 (Mich. Ct. App. 1996) (citing *Miss. Band of Choctaw Indians v. Holyfield*, 490 U.S. 30 (1989)).
10. *See* 25 U.S.C. § 1901(4); *See also In re Armell*, 50 N.E.2d 1060, 1064 (Ill. App. 1990).
11. H.R. Rep No. 1386, at 9–10, 95th Cong, 2d Sess. (1978), reprinted in 1978 U.S.S.C.A.N. 7530, 7531 [hereinafter House Report].
12. *Id.*
13. Aamot-Snapp, *When Judicial Flexibility Becomes Abuse of Discretion: Eliminating the "Good Cause" Exception in Indian Child Welfare Act Adoptive Placement*, 79 MINN. L. REV. 1167, 1168 (1995).
14. Congress explicitly found that "there is no resource that is more vital to the continued existence and integrity of Indian tribes than their children." 25 U.S.C. § 1901(3). Additionally, testimony before Congress revealed, "These practices [mass removal of Indian children] seriously undercut the tribes' ability to continue as self-governing communities. Probably in no area is it more important that tribal sovereignty be respected that in an area socially and culturally determined as family relationships." *Hearing on S. 1214 before the Subcommittee on Indian Affairs and Public Lands of the House Committee on Interior and Insular Affairs*, 95th Cong., 2d Sess. (1978) [hereinafter, the Hearing].
15. 25 U.S.C. § 1911(a).
16. 25 U.S.C. § 1911(c).
17. 25 U.S.C. § 1914.
18. 25 U.S.C. § 1915(c).
19. 25 U.S.C. § 1915(e).
20. 25 U.S.C. § 1919.
21. *See* the Hearing, at 35 ("The recommendations [to preserve Indian families] are made from the standpoint, as Mr. Byler has stated, of promoting maximum Indian self-determination in solving these problems, and from the standpoint that these problems go to the very heart of the tribal relation and the very survival of Indian tribes.").
22. *Miss. Band of Choctaw Indians v. Holyfield*, 490 US 30 (1989).
23. *Id.*
24. *Id.* at 37.
25. *Id.*
26. *Id.* at 39.
27. *Id.*

28. *Id.* at 40.
29. *Id.* at 54.
30. *Id.* at 51.
31. *Id.* at 53.
32. *Id.* at 51–52 ("The appellees in this case argue strenuously that the twins' mother went to great lengths to give birth off the reservation so that her children could be adopted by the Holyfields. But that was precisely part of Congress' concern. Permitting individual members of the tribe to avoid tribal exclusive jurisdiction by the simple expedient of giving birth off the reservation would, to a large extent, nullify the purpose the ICWA was intended to accomplish.").
33. *Id.* at 49 ("Tribal jurisdiction under § 1911(a) was not meant to be defeated by the actions of individual members of the tribe, for Congress was concerned not solely about the interests of Indian children and families, but also about the impact on the tribes themselves of the 1609 large numbers of Indian children adopted by non-Indians.")
34. Guidelines for State Courts; Indian Child Custody Proceedings, 44 Fed. Reg. 67,584 (1979) [hereinafter BIA Guidelines or Guidelines].
35. *See In re S.E.G.*, 521 N.W. 2d 357, 362 (Minn. 1994).
36. *See* BIA Guidelines.
37. BIA Guidelines at c.4 ("Since Congress has established a policy of preferring tribal control over custody decisions affecting tribal members, the burden of proving that an exception to that policy ought to be made in a particular case rests on the party urging that an exception be made.").
38. BIA Guidelines at 67,590–67,591.
39. In the law-review article *A Minnesota Lawyer's Guide to the Indian Child Welfare Act*, the author explains how the BIA Guidelines weigh the burden of proof: "The BIA Guidelines place the burden of establishing good cause to the contrary on the party opposing transfer by at least clear and convincing evidence, because of the congressional policy advanced in ICWA of making tribal court determinations the preferred course." Peter W. Gorman, *A Minnesota Lawyer's Guide to the Indian Child Welfare Act*, 10 LAW & INEQ. 311, 341 (1992).
40. *See In re S.W. and C.S.*, 41 P.3d 1003, 1013 (Okla. Civ. App. 2002); *In re M.E.M.*, 625 P.2d 1313 (Mont. 1981); *In re J.J.*, 454 N.W.2d 317 (S.D. 1990); *In re M.S.*, 624 N.W.2d 678 (N.D. 2001) ('All evidentiary issues in termination proceedings should be resolved by clear and convincing evidence standard except the ultimate issue of whether continued custody by the parent of Indian custodian would result in serious emotional or physical harm to the child.").
41. M.C.R. 3.980.
42. 25 U.S.C. § 1911(a).
43. 25 U.S.C. §1911(b); *Holyfield*, 490 U.S. at 35; *In re Adoption of S.S. & R.S.*, 167 Ill.2d 250, 264, 657 N.E. 2d 935 (Ill. 1995); *In re Adoption of Halloway*, 732 P.2d 962, 967 (Utah 1986); *In re S.W.*, 41 P.3d 1003, 1008 (Okla. Civ. App. 2001).
44. *See In the Interest of J.L.P.*, 870 P.2d 1252, 1256 (Colo. App. 1994); *In re Armell*, 50 N.E.2d 1060, 1064 (Ill. App. 1990) (*citing* Guidelines, 44 Fed. Reg. 67,591 (1978)).

45. *Holyfield*, 490 U.S. at 54 (quoting *In re Adoption of Halloway*, 732 P.2d 962, 972 (Utah 1986)).
46. For a discussion of judicial subjectivity applied in ICWA proceedings, *see* Robert H. Mnookin, *Child Custody Adjudication: Judicial Functions in the Face of Indeterminacy*, 39 L. & CONTEMP. PROBS. 226 (1975).
47. Although the public record indicates the child's real name, out of respect for her privacy I have changed her name for this article.
48. Tr. of Hr'g at 19–20, *In re Cole*, No. 04-025 NA (Mich. 21st Cir., Jan. 23, 2006).
49. *See In re S.W.*, 41 P.3d 1003, 1013 (Okla. Civ. App. 2002); *In re M.E.M.*, 625 P.2d 1313 (Mont. 1981); *In re J.J.*, 454 N.W.2d 317 (S.D. 1990); *In re M.S.*, 624 N.W.2d 678 (N.D. 2001).
50. *In re S.W.*, 41 P.3d 1003, 1013 (Okla. Civ. App. 2001).
51. *Id.* at 1013.
52. *Id.*
53. *Id.*
54. *Id.*
55. *Id.*
56. *In re M.E.M.*, 635 P.2d 1313 (Mont. 1981).
57. *Id.* at 1314–15.
58. *Id.*
59. *Id.* at 1315.
60. *Id.* at 1317.
61. *Id.* at 1316.
62. *Id.* at 1317.
63. *See The Yavapai-Apache Tribe v. The Honorable Berta Mejia*, 906 S.W.2d 152, 162 (Texas 1995) ("By passing the ICWA, Congress sought to ensure the continued viability of Indian tribes by protecting Indian children from cultural genocide.").
64. *See Miss. Band of Choctaw Indians v. Holyfield*, 490 US 30, 34 (1989) ("Culturally, the chances of Indian survival are significantly reduced if our children, the only real means for the transmission of the tribal heritage, are to be raised in non-Indian homes and denied exposure to the ways of their People. Furthermore, these practices seriously undercut the tribes' ability to continue as self-governing communities.").
65. *Indian Child Welfare Program, Hearings before the Subcommittee on Indian Affairs of the Senate Committee on Interior and Insular Affairs*, 93d Cong., 2d Sess (1974).
66. *See Id.* at 37 ("We are supportive of Indian self-determination in this particular area because parent-child relations go to the very essence of the survival of the tribe."); *See also Id.* at 70 ("When I served those papers [petitioning for due process before terminating an Indian mother's parental rights] we had the following exchange: I gave [the codirector of the county welfare office] the papers. He said why is the tribe so interested in this case? What is the big issue here? I said that the tribe was concerned that if many more of their children were taken, because there's been quite a history of taking these kids from this reservation, that they were afraid that their very survival would be at stake. And, the codirector of this county welfare office

responded to that by shrugging his shoulders and saying, 'So, what?'").
67. 124 Cong. Rec. 38102 (1978).
68. 25 U.S.C. § 1901(3).
69. *In Re S.S. v. Iron Bear*, 657 N.E.2d 935 (Ill. 1995).
70. *Id.* at 938.
71. *Id.*
72. *Id.*
73. *Id.*
74. *Id.* at 939.
75. *Id.* at 937.
76. *Id.* at 938.
77. *Id.* at 940.
78. *Id.* at 946–47.
79. *Id.*
80. *Id.* at 946.
81. *In re D.M.*, 685 N.W.2d 768 (S.D. 2004).
82. *Id.* at 777.
83. *Id.*
84. B. J. Jones, *The Indian Child Welfare Act: In Search of a Federal Forum to Vindicate the Rights of Indian Tribes and Children against the Vagaries of State Courts*, 73 N.D. L. REV. 395, 396 (1997).
85. *People Ex. Rel. T.I.*, 707 N.W. 2d 826 (S.D. 2005).
86. *Id.* at 834 ("If the presumption is in favor of tribal jurisdiction, then mere discretion to override an ICWA transfer is inconsistent with congressional intent.... It is true that some other courts have used the abuse of discretion standard. However, the better reasoned decisions hold that the determination must be supported by clear and convincing evidence of good cause.").
87. 961 P.2d 706 (Kan. App. 1998).
88. *Id.* at 713.
89. The Bureau of Indian Affairs Guidelines for state courts in Indian Child Welfare Act proceedings, which are informative but not binding upon courts, state that good cause may be found not to transfer a case to tribal court if "the evidence necessary to decide the case could not be adequately presented in the tribal court without undue hardship to the parties and witnesses." 44 Fed. Reg. 67, 591 (1979).
90. H.R. Rep. No. 1386, 95th Cong., 2d Sess. (1978), *reprinted in* 1978 U.S.C.C.A.N. 7530, at 21.
91. *Holyfield*, 490 U.S. at 43–47.
92. *See In Re A.P.*, 961 P.2d 706 (Kan. App. 1988); *In Re J.L.P.*, 870 P.2d 1252 (Colo. 1994); *In Re M.E.M.*, 635 P.2d 1313 (Mont. 1981); *In re S.W.*, 41 P.3d 1003 (Okla. Civ. App. 2002); *In re T.I.*, 707 N.W.2d 826 (S.D. 2005); *In re G.S.*, 59 P.3d 1063 (Mont. 2002).
93. Congress intended "good cause" under § 1911(b) to benefit the Indian litigant. *See* H.R. Rep. No. 1386 at 7544.

Keeping It in the Family
The Legal and Social Evolution of ICWA in State and Tribal Jurisprudence

Lorinda Mall

Rose, a Navajo woman, was adopted in the early 1960s by a white couple.[1] She grew up in San Francisco, and by her late twenties she was fighting a losing battle with drug addiction. As a child she never quite fit in, and these struggles climaxed when she was put into a drug-addiction program and her children were taken away by Social Services. Because the Indian Child Welfare Act[2] (ICWA) was passed in 1978, the social worker assigned to her case discovered Navajo relatives with whom to place the children. ICWA mandates that social workers determine whether a child is Indian, and if so, follow heightened placement procedures to remove the child. When the social worker went to visit these newfound Navajo relatives, she was surprised to see pictures of Rose as a child still hanging on the walls.[3] In Rose's day, there were no family preservation programs geared towards the special needs of Indian people. Now, more than forty years after Rose's adoption, we finally have legislation in place that recognizes this strong connection Indian people have with their families, so hopefully there will be no more stories like Rose's story.

Before ICWA was enacted, Rose's story was a common occurrence. Indian children were being taken from their homes at alarming rates.[4] A survey of sixteen states in 1969 revealed that approximately 85 percent of Indian children in foster homes and 90 percent of non-relative Indian adoptees were living with non-Indian families.[5] Based on a report by the Association on American Indian Affairs, the director of that institution stated during congressional hearings that "In Minnesota, one in every eight Indian children under 18 years of age is living in an adoptive home."[6] He went on to state that in "Montana, the ratio of Indian foster care placement is at least 13 times greater. In South Dakota, 40 percent of all adoptions made by the State Department of Public Welfare . . . are of Indian children, yet Indians make up only 7 percent of the juvenile population. . . . In Wisconsin, the risk run by Indian children of being separated from their parents is nearly 1,600 percent greater than it is for non-Indian children."[7] Senator Abourezk (S.D.) stated that the placement of "Indian children in non-Indian settings" resulted in "their Indian culture, their Indian traditions, and, in general, their entire way of life . . . being smothered."[8] He went on to say that this treatment "strike[s] at the heart of Indian communities" and has been called "cultural genocide."[9]

ICWA was enacted to counteract these devastating practices. While today there is still some evidence of high rates of adoption out of the tribe, because there is legislation that sets out a procedure for state social services to follow, the rates are arguably not as high as they would be without such legislation. This, however, does not mean that we should be satisfied with the results and not strive to improve the situation. The damage done to Indian children who were taken from their homes and placed with well-meaning white families can still be seen today, as Rose's story suggests.

The purpose of ICWA and tribal courts is ultimately to maintain the survival of the tribe though retention of its members, especially by protecting Indian children. According to ICWA, it is per se in an Indian child's best interest to remain with his or her family and/or tribe.[10] It has been nearly thirty years since the passage of ICWA, and we are still unclear about exactly how successful this legislation has been.[11] For many, the wanting data can be explained by the lack of accountability in the implementation of the Act.[12] No agency is charged with oversight of ICWA implementation, and no provision was incorporated to provide penalties for noncompliance.[13] Without knowing how ICWA is being implemented by states, it is difficult to draw conclusions about its usefulness and thus justify its continued existence.

What is lost in this framework is what tribes are doing to implement child welfare on the reservation and in urban areas. Without understanding the tribal perspective on ICWA and child welfare in general, we will not have an accurate picture of ICWA implementation and Indian child welfare nationwide. This study has focused on Arizona because of the large Indian land base, and South Dakota because of its high Indian population. By obtaining a more complete picture of the state of ICWA implementation and Indian child welfare, we can best determine how to allocate scarce tribal resources in educating state actors.[14]

A comparison of early ICWA jurisprudence with current interpretations can facilitate the discussion of whether one goal of ICWA, Indian family preservation, is being met, and if not, where we should go from here. This paper will focus mostly on state court cases, for several reasons. First, a great number of ICWA cases start in state court, and as the urban Indian population increases, this number will only continue to grow. Second, many tribes have a policy of allowing state courts to handle ICWA cases and only ask for transfer of an ICWA case if they are not satisfied with how the state court is handling the issue.[15] Third, many tribal courts are not courts of record, and thus do not publish decisions for the vast majority of their cases. Thus, tribal court cases are often difficult to obtain. However, I have been able to obtain some tribal court cases and have interviewed several tribal attorneys that handle ICWA cases, in order to flesh out the tribal perspective on this topic.

In the years following the enactment of ICWA, Arizona state courts were dealing with issues relating to domicile and timing of notice to the tribe as required under the Act. The more recent Arizona cases grapple with issues revolving around concurrent jurisdiction, which ICWA provides for when the child is domiciled off the reservation, such as when transfer of jurisdiction to tribal court is proper. This indicates that Arizona courts have dealt with issues surrounding exclusive tribal jurisdiction in ICWA and are now moving on to the more complicated issues surrounding concurrent jurisdiction, such as transfer of jurisdiction to tribal court, which is often assumed to be outcome-determinative.[16]

Unlike Arizona, South Dakota courts dealt with a great variety of ICWA issues fairly soon after the Act's enactment and now seem to be revisiting the issues. Similarly, South Dakota courts have struggled with what constitutes good cause not to transfer to tribal courts. In addition, South Dakota continues to be plagued with notice issues while simultaneously pushing the envelope and ruling on the interplay between ICWA and the ASFA.

To alleviate both Arizona's and South Dakota's problem areas, states and tribes need to work together to better understand each other's positions. For example, although state social services often complain that tribes do not verify enrollment eligibility quickly enough for them to prepare their cases, this is often due to a lack of tribal funding.[17] To alleviate these tensions, the federal government should provide Title IV-E funding, the primary basis for subsidizing foster care payment for Indian children, directly to the tribes and also allow for separate appropriations to fund culturally appropriate family preservation services.[18] In addition, tribal courts should be strengthened so that they can handle receiving all these ICWA cases. Due to the tribe's lack of resources, tribes often do not ask for transfer to tribal court unless the state is handling the case extremely poorly.[19] Lastly, the state and tribes need to focus on culturally appropriate family preservation methods for optimal reunification rates.[20]

This paper suggests that successful tribal family preservation involves culturally appropriate placement, the use of culturally appropriate family preservation services, and the willingness of the state to work with tribes to incorporate culturally appropriate methods of family preservation in their programs. Culturally appropriate placement includes the state transferring cases to a tribal court when appropriate, and having a policy of placement with family or tribal members, including a good relationship with the tribe in order to be able to locate appropriate placements. Culturally appropriate services must be based on a philosophy of family reunification and not a deficit-based model, as is utilized by most state social services.[21] States, in turn, must back up decisions on maintaining jurisdiction or transferring jurisdiction to tribal court by including tribes in the entirety of the process. In addition, tribes must help in this process by having culturally appropriate services available for Indian children and families, or by being willing to consult with state social services to develop such programs. Thus, the tribe is the key factor in both state and tribal practices for successful ICWA implementation.

In this article, I will first discuss the purpose and controversy surrounding ICWA. Then I will compare important Arizona state court decisions regarding ICWA in the years following its passage with current cases. Following the decision of the Arizona cases will be a note on the evolution of South Dakota's ICWA case law. The next section will incorporate a discussion of tribal court ICWA cases, including the importance of tribal courts, how tribal culture influences the courts, and the implementation of would-be ICWA cases by these courts. Lastly, I will discuss some policies and programs that states, tribes, and social service programs should consider when dealing with Indian children, in order to provide these children and their families with the most appropriate services.

Purpose of ICWA

The purpose of ICWA is twofold: to prevent the wholesale removal of Indian children from their homes, and to promote the stability of tribes.[22] ICWA recognizes, in the Congressional Findings, that there is "no resource more valuable to a culture than its children."[23] As such, Indian children should be given every opportunity to grow up in the cultures into which they were born. ICWA also sets out the basic premise that the best interest of an Indian child runs parallel to the best interests of the tribe.[24] Every child has a right to know its culture, and the best way to ensure this is to set out placement preferences that favor placing Indian children in Indian homes. Likewise, tribes have a great interest in keeping their children in their jurisdiction so that they can become knowledgeable tribal members. ICWA strives to accomplish this by transferring child welfare proceedings to tribal court and mandating a preferred placement schedule.

ICWA provides an Indian tribe with exclusive jurisdiction over any child custody proceeding involving an Indian child who resides or is domiciled on the reservation.[25] The Act further requires that a state court transfer a child custody proceeding to tribal court if the Indian child is not domiciled on the reservation, unless the court finds that there is good cause to refuse to transfer such a case.[26] In a case where the Indian child is not domiciled on the reservation, the parents have an absolute right to veto a transfer to tribal court from state court.[27] In addition, a tribe may decline such a transfer.[28] If an ICWA case remains in state court, the tribe has the right to intervene at any point in the proceeding.[29] ICWA also provides that every state and every Indian tribe must give full faith and credit to the judicial proceedings of any Indian tribe with regard to Indian child custody proceedings.[30] One of the benefits of ICWA is the utilization of tribal courts as a resource to empower tribes to take over the implementation of child welfare services formerly provided by the state.

ICWA provides that in any involuntary proceeding in state court involving an Indian child, notice must be provided to the parents and the child's tribe.[31] Before an Indian child may be placed in foster care, or parental rights terminated, active efforts to provide remedial services and rehabilitative programs must be proved unsuccessful.[32] No foster care placement may be ordered absent a determination, supported by clear and convincing evidence, that continued custody of the child by the Indian parent will "likely result in serious emotional or physical damage to the child."[33] Similarly, no termination of parental rights may be ordered absent a determination, supported by evidence beyond a reasonable doubt, that continued custody of the child by the Indian parent will likely result in serious emotional or physical damage.[34]

ICWA sets out guidelines for a voluntary termination of parental rights by an Indian parent as well. In any case where an Indian parent voluntarily consents to foster care or termination of parental rights, consent shall be valid only if it is executed in writing, and recorded before a judge in a court of competent jurisdiction where the consequences were fully explained and fully understood by the Indian parent.[35] In any voluntary proceeding, the consent of the parent may be withdrawn for any reason at any time in the foster care placement, or at any time prior to the entry of a final decree of termination or adoption.[36] In a similar vein, whenever an adoption falls through, an Indian parent may petition for return of custody, and the court shall grant the petition unless there is a showing that return of custody is not in the child's best interest.[37] Furthermore, under ICWA, if there is a showing that a child was removed or placed in violation of ICWA, the placement or termination of parental rights may be invalidated.[38]

ICWA therefore sets out placement preferences that the state must follow when placing a child in foster care or adoptive homes. In adoption cases, absent good cause to the contrary, a preference shall be given to placement with 1) a member of the child's extended family; 2) other members of the child's tribe; or 3) other Indian families.[39] In foster care placements, absent good cause to the contrary, an Indian child should be placed with 1) a member of the Indian child's extended family; 2) a foster home licensed by the Indian child's tribe; 3) an Indian foster home licensed by a non-Indian licensing authority; or 4) an institution for children approved by an Indian tribe.[40] The Act also provides that a tribe may set out a different order of preference that the state must also follow.⁴¹ Lastly, ICWA sets up several programs whereby tribes can obtain grants to improve their tribal courts, create a system for licensing foster homes, and educate members as both tribal court personnel and social service workers.⁴² However, to date, no appropriations have ever been authorized by Congress.

The Controversy

Much of the academic discussion about ICWA revolves around the perceived racism of requiring an Indian child to be adopted first by Indian parents. Some scholars hold that the requirement that Indian children be placed in Indian homes is a race-based requirement that should fail under the Equal Protection Clause of the U.S. Constitution. The most notable scholar championing this position is Professor Randall Kennedy of Harvard Law School. Kennedy's book *Interracial Intimacies: Sex, Marriage, Identity, and Adoption* largely explores his belief that the policy of racial matching in adoption in general is ill-advised; however he does devote an entire chapter to ICWA.⁴³

According to Kennedy's viewpoint, "race would not be allowed to play any part in the selection of adoptive families, unless there was some compelling justification" determined on a case-by-case basis.⁴⁴ Before we can delve into an analysis of state and tribal implementation of ICWA in any meaningful way, we must debunk the idea that ICWA is a race-based statute that works to the detriment of Indian children. As Kennedy provides the strongest argument against ICWA's tribal preference, a comprehensive appraisal of Kennedy's chapter on ICWA will be beneficial.

Kennedy asserts three arguments as to why there needs to be an ICWA amendment. First, he questions Congress's finding that there was a child-care crisis in Indian Country.⁴⁵ Second, he asserts that Dr. Joseph Westermeyer one of the experts who testified at a congressional hearing, was practicing "junk science," and therefore the Act was based on faulty data.⁴⁶ Third, he argues that ICWA invites bad decisions by judges because the racial-matching policy is so disturbing to some judges that they have liberally interpreted clauses such as "good cause" when deciding whether to transfer an ICWA case to tribal court.⁴⁷

Professor Kennedy finds fault with the process of ICWA enactment Specifically, he disputes the conclusiveness of there being an Indian child-care crisis as determined by congressional hearings.⁴⁸ He points to one of the witnesses recalling her experience of being taken as a child because she was playing in the mud and her feet were dirty.⁴⁹ Kennedy rightly notes that this witness could have been basing her story upon lore that her family told her in order to hide the "ugly realities" of their circumstances.⁵⁰ He ultimately faults Congress for not allowing the witnesses the opportunity to develop their testimony properly so as to be factually persuasive.⁵¹

Kennedy also faults Congress with enacting what he feels basically amounts to a Band-Aid policy. He notes that Congress largely blames state agencies for being racist in unnecessarily taking Indian children from their families.[52] By framing the issues in such a way, Congress made the required "fix" easy—simply limit the state's ability to be racist by limiting their power to make decisions for Indian children.[53] However, as Kennedy wisely points out, much of the problems with Indian children being removed at disproportionate rates may also be due to extreme poverty, drugs, and violence that occur all too often on many reservations.[54] The task of "fixing" these problems, being much more daunting, may not have appealed to many politicians.[55] Kennedy, therefore, agrees with Chief Judge B. J. Jones in his assertion that in the end, ICWA was a "procedural statute for a substantive problem."[56]

Kennedy takes issue with the assumption that an Indian home is better equipped to handle the needs of Indian children.[57] Dr. Westermeyer, one of the expert witnesses at an ICWA hearing, claimed that Indian children growing up in white homes were "ill prepared to occupy their rightful place in American society, and that lack of preparedness in turn rendered them vulnerable to psychiatric and social difficulties."[58] He called this the "apple syndrome."[59] Kennedy correctly notes that Dr. Westermeyer's study not only had no control group, but the small, geographically limited, and nonrandom sample is not up to muster using the scientific method.[60]

While persuasive on some fronts, Kennedy's argument ultimately fails to convince that an ICWA amendment is necessary. First, the political process does not envision that the experts invited to testify at hearings are the basis of proposed legislation. Bills are drafted and often introduced long in advance of picking appropriate witnesses to testify at hearings. Thus, while Kennedy may be right to question the findings of Congress that fault the state agencies for their racism without consideration of the socioeconomic conditions of many tribal members, it is not accurate to state that Dr. Westermeyer's testimony or studies were the basis of ICWA. In fact, the issue of Indian child welfare was subject to congressional hearings as early as 1974.[61] In addition, a version of ICWA was drafted and introduced in 1977, which is one congressional year prior to its enactment.[62] Although that bill did not pass out of committee, the following year it was reintroduced, largely unchanged, as S. 1214 and passed out of the Senate Select Committee on Indian Affairs on November 3, 1977.[63] The House marked up S. 1214 and adopted an amendment in the nature of a substitute, which was subsequently introduced by Representative Udall as H.R. 12533 on June 21, 1978, as a clean bill.[64] However, ultimately the original S. 1214, with several floor amendments, passed the full House and was signed by the President.[65] All three of these bills were remarkably similar, and thus the gravamen of all three bills was drafted prior to the 1977–78 hearings that Kennedy takes issue with.

Second, international law requires that we consider culture when finding homes for children. The Hague Convention on Inter-country Adoption states that in "foster placement, kafalah of Islamic law, adoption or if necessary placement in suitable institutions for the care of children . . . due regard shall be paid to the desirability of continuity in a child's upbringing and to the child's ethnic, religious, cultural and linguistic background."[66] In 1993, the United States adopted the Hague Convention, including this article. Plainly, this means that in addition to a moral obligation, the United States now has an international obligation to ensure that a child in need of a home be placed in one that is sensitive to the child's ethnic, religious, cultural, and linguistic background before they are placed in a home that is devoid of these similarities.

Kennedy's second argument is that there may be other co-occurring reasons why Indian children are taken from their homes at disproportionate levels. He cites the high rates of poverty and alcoholism on the reservation as possible reasons why Indian children have been taken away by state social services at such high rates.[67] Unfortunately, he does not extend this argument to allow for other confounding reasons why an Indian parent would choose not to disclose their Indian heritage. In *In re Bridget R.*, a California court held that unless the Existing Indian Family exception was applied, ICWA would be unconstitutional.[68] This case involved a family who, acting under the advice of an attorney, concealed their Indian heritage in order to facilitate the adoption of their twins, because they felt they could not adequately provide for them. Kennedy calls *In re Bridget R* an example of a parent taking on a fictive (Indian) identity for litigation purposes only.[69] He conveniently forgets the fact that it was an unethical attorney who suggested that the father not disclose his Indian heritage.[70] The father decided to disclose his Indian heritage and challenge the adoption when he was going through a divorce and was largely without access to his children.[71]

Kennedy also mirrors the court's assertion that the father had no ties to his heritage; however, there is reason to question this blind repetition.[72] First, parents commonly assume the responsibility of enrolling their children in the tribe, so the fact the father did not self-enroll, but rather his mother enrolled him, is not proof the father was denying his Indian identity.[73] Second, although he did not inform his Indian family that he and his wife were planning to put the twins up for adoption, he did maintain ties with them, and as soon as his marriage began to fall apart he went to them for support and guidance.[74] Third, his wife also claimed Indian heritage, and intertribal marriages are common.[75] Fourth, the couple lived in a suburb of Los Angeles, Whittier, that is locally known to have a high proportion of Indian inhabitants.[76]

Kennedy frequently states that he feels it is unfair to burden or impose a culture upon children, who have no choice in the matter.[77] Instead he proposes to never look at race or culture when placing children in foster or adoptive homes. He goes on to state that ICWA's placement hierarchy promotes the "freezing" of the tribal culture instead of allowing for cultural evolution.[78] While I may agree that a child has little choice in whether he/she grows up partaking in an Indian culture or a white American culture, under Kennedy's solution the child would still have no choice. Thus, whether they are placed in an Indian home or the home of a randomly chosen couple, the child is still in the same choiceless position. To apply Kennedy's solution would likely result in an overreliance on economic factors in determining child placement because absent cultural connection, many Indian homes would pale in comparison to middle-class white American homes.

Kennedy asserts that Indians marrying non-Indians carries a greater assimilative "threat" than non-Indians adopting Indian children.[79] This is not true, for several reasons. First, an interracial couple still has one parent who is Indian and can pass down a culture's traditions. Second, Indian people are highly aware of the issues involved in marrying someone of a different tribe or a non-Indian. Many Indians think not only about the cultural complexities of raising a so-called mixed-blood child, but also about whether or not their children will be eligible for enrollment in their tribe. However, ultimately people will marry whom they love, a stance that Kennedy himself touts.[80] Who one marries is something that Indian people have some degree of control over. If, in fact, the reason that Indian children are taken from their homes at disproportionate rates is because of cultural bias on the part of state social workers, Indian people have little or no control over their children being taken away. So, clearly the threat of assimilation through intermarriage is not as dangerous as adoption out. Thus, this is exactly the type of situation that Congress should step into and protect Indian tribes and culture.

Kennedy does make an excellent point when he notes that ICWA has invited many judges to find ways around the law.[81] Judges have taken liberties in determining "good cause" to deviate from the placement preferences mandated by ICWA.[82] He notes that although the BIA has developed guidelines for determining what is "good cause," these are merely guidelines and have been given varying degrees of deference by courts because they have not gone through the stringent publication and comment periods as compared to most regulations.[83] Here Kennedy points to some state judges' creation of the Existing Indian Family doctrine, which effectively refuses to apply ICWA to an Indian child who does not come from an "existing Indian family," as an example of this judicial advocacy.[84] The most obvious problem with this doctrine is that the judge is probably a white middle-class man who may not be in the best position to determine what is an Indian family.[85] In the same sense, Kennedy may not be in the best position to determine whether the father in *In re Bridget R.* was really using a fictive identity solely for the purpose of litigation.

Underlying Kennedy's argument is the assumption that permanence in the form of legal adoption is a better option than long-term foster care or kinship/guardian care.[86] The fact that he does not consider kinship/guardian care as an option is unfortunate.[87] As Margaret F. Brinig points out in her article "The Child's Best Interests," in many cases kinship/guardian care offers an alternative that is the least likely to upset the child's placement, since they already know their new caretaker.[88] In fact, many tribes have a tradition of other kin caring for children of what Western society would consider a nuclear family. Thus, this may be a more culturally appropriate option for Indians. For example, in Navajo society it is culturally appropriate, expected, and common for a maternal grandmother to raise the oldest grandchild to ensure that they will not be lonely.[89]

Lastly, Kennedy states that ICWA reaches beyond *Morton v. Mancari*'s proposition that favoring tribal members is constitutional because it is a political favoring and not a racial favoring.[90] Kennedy states that in the placement hierarchies established in ICWA, namely, that an Indian child should first be placed with family members (kinship bias), then with other members of the child's tribe (political bias), and then with other Indian families, is a racial configuration because the last preference is completely based upon race.[91] However, the Act defines "Indian" as a member of a federally recognized tribe or Alaska corporation, making it a political bias and not a racial one.[92] Thus, in the same way that *Mancari*'s preference would not apply to an unenrolled Indian, ICWA's placement preference does not extend beyond the tribal enrollment rolls either. Kennedy and the California courts seem to be especially concerned with Indian families that have no tribal or political connection; however, if you truly believe that tribes are sovereign political entities, like the United States, it does not matter that the family is not "involved" politically.[93] Simply by being a member of the nation or eligible for membership, they will come under the purview of the Act. This model of nationhood, which more similarly matches Western nationhood, is precisely what makes ICWA a strong piece of legislation. Thus, we can see that although Kennedy makes a strong argument that ICWA is based upon race, the reality is that it is a political statute that aims to prevent the breakup of Indian families and maintain strong tribal nations.

Arizona State Court Cases

Since the passage of ICWA in 1978, the Arizona state appellate courts have thirteen reported cases dealing with the Act. Early cases focused on the technical requirements outlined in ICWA, such as definitions, when notice to the tribe was required, and when the state courts have jurisdiction to hear a case, which is dependent upon the domicile of the child.[94] More recent cases have focused on the determination of who has jurisdiction to hear a case where jurisdiction is concurrent, which often occurs in reference to a tribe's request for transfer of jurisdiction.[95] While jurisdiction has been a common element in both early ICWA cases and current ICWA cases, the types of issues have changed. In early cases, the jurisdictional question revolved around whether a state court could hear a case involving a child domiciled on the reservation, for which ICWA provides exclusive tribal jurisdiction.[96] Current jurisdictional cases are dealing more with children domiciled off the reservation, where the state has concurrent jurisdiction, but must transfer the case to tribal court if requested, unless good cause to deviate exists.

EARLY ARIZONA STATE COURT CASES

Early Arizona state court cases focused largely on definitional and procedural issues. For example, the first Arizona case dealing with ICWA was *In Re Appeal in Pima County Juvenile Action No. S-903*.[97] In that case, a fifteen-year old Indian mother gave birth to her child in Nevada and executed a voluntary relinquishment of her parental rights to the Nevada Catholic Welfare Bureau, Inc., who made arrangements with the Catholic Social Service of Tucson to place the child with an adoptive family. Six months after the original voluntary relinquishment, the mother asked for the child back; however, the new adoptive family was unwilling to relinquish the child, causing the ensuing case. The mother's tribe intervened and requested transfer of jurisdiction.

The Arizona trial court held that the child was domiciled in Arizona because the mother had relinquished her parental rights and the child had resided in Arizona continuously for six months while the mother had no contact with the child. The court held that although the child was eligible for enrollment in the Assiniboine tribe in Montana, the best interests of the child were to remain with his adoptive parents. Thus, the trial court found, first, that it had concurrent jurisdiction, and second, that good cause existed not to transfer the matter to tribal court. In addition, the trial court found that the mother had abandoned the child. For that reason, the court ordered a termination of her parental rights.[98]

The mother appealed, and the appellate court rested its decision on the definition of domicile. The court found that the mother was an unemancipated minor. Because she was unemancipated, they found that she was domiciled on the Fort Belknap reservation in Montana since that was the domicile of her father.[99] Since a child takes the domicile of its mother until a new one is lawfully acquired,[100] the child was deemed to be domiciled on the reservation and must be returned to the biological mother.[101]

Two years later, the court heard *In Re Appeal in Maricopa County Juvenile Action No. A-25525*, where a non-Indian mother gave birth to a child and suspected that the father was a Pima Indian, but he was not listed on the birth certificate.[102] The Catholic Social Service of Phoenix listed the father as "allegedly" Indian, but noted that because the father had not acknowledged paternity the child was not eligible for membership in an Indian tribe. The Pima Indian Community appealed the adoption on the grounds that the Catholic Social Service of Phoenix did not follow the correct procedure in the primary adoptive placement and no "good cause" was found to deviate from the placement preferences set out in ICWA. The appellate court held that until such time as a putative Indian father acknowledges or establishes paternity, the provisions of ICWA are not applicable.[103]

In fact, a later Arizona case, *Arizona Department of Economic Security v. Bernini*, held that suspicion of being an Indian child triggers the notice requirement only and not the substance of the Act.[104] In that case, the trial court applied ICWA based on the father alleging that he had Indian blood and ordered the child returned within one week. The appellate court held that even though the father alleged that the child was an Indian child, this merely invoked the Act's notice provision, which required the inquiry as to whether the child was a member or eligible for membership in an Indian tribe. The Act was, however, inapplicable pending a determination that the child was, in fact, Indian.[105] Thus, if there is some evidence of a child being Indian, the Department of Economic Security must notify the tribe however the remainder of ICWA will not be applied to that child until such time as it is verified that the child is in fact enrolled or eligible for enrollment in a federally recognized tribe. This ruling means that a child may be subject to two separate placements if they are in fact found to be Indian, potentially causing undue emotional upset.

Another issue surrounding placement was decided in 1987: the Arizona appellate court clarified the "good cause" exemption from the placement preferences set out in ICWA in *In Re Appeal in Coconino County Juvenile Action No. J-10175*.[106] In this case, a Navajo and a non-Indian woman had a child who was enrolled in the Navajo Nation.[107] After the child's parents split up the child lived with the mother and stepfather in an "Anglo-type home."[108] State authorities stepped in because of the stepfather's abusive behavior towards the child and the mother's unwillingness to prevent the abuse by the stepfather. The Arizona Department of Economic Security had prepared a case plan that called for the child to live with the father, but the natural mother's younger sisters accused him of molesting them and the plan was modified.[109]

The trial court found that ICWA did not apply because the Act was clearly designed to prevent culture shock. Because the child was raised in an Anglo home, this was "simply the other side of the culture shock coin." The court also found that it was in the best interests of the child to keep her in a situation that was most like what she was used to, namely an Anglo home. The court noted that the mother's home was not adequate because of the presence of the stepfather. Lastly, the court held that the father's home was not a fit placement because it was remote and totally foreign to the child. In addition, the court found that doubts existed about the father's character.[110]

The appellate court reversed. The court found that once it was determined that a child was an Indian child, "the judge must, in the absence of good cause to the contrary, follow the provisions of the Act." The child may not be placed in foster care unless the judge finds by clear and convincing evidence that parental custody is likely to result in serious physical or emotional harm.[111] The court went on to state that the trial court's attempts to establish good cause by noting the culture shock that might follow were insufficient. "When the Act is read as a whole, it is clear that Congress has made a very strong policy choice that Indian children, including those who have a non-Indian parent, belong in an Indian home."[112] The court reiterated that a judge may not order foster care unless the judge first determines by clear and convincing evidence that parental placement is likely to result in serious emotional or physical harm to the child, and if the judge so finds, the judge must follow the placement hierarchy dictated in ICWA.[113]

The early Arizona state court cases dealt largely with definitional and procedural issues. Such early cases clearly established that an Indian baby takes the domicile of the mother, which then may lead to a determination that the tribe has exclusive jurisdiction to hear the case. Another case established the definition of an "Indian child," which is the key factor in determining whether ICWA applies or not. Yet another dealt with the definition of "good cause" to modify placement preferences. Basically, these cases have defined the scope of the state court's discretion on matters dealing with Indian child welfare cases. Arizona state courts have struggled with ICWA and its modification of the standard child welfare protocol. However, by and large, Arizona has interpreted ICWA using the plain language of the Act, and has avoided judicial overreaching.

CURRENT ARIZONA STATE COURT CASES

A comparison of the early Arizona state court cases with the cases that are currently coming through the courts highlights a shift. Increasingly, the Arizona courts are ruling on issues concerning concurrent jurisdiction. To obtain decisions that are more in line with both ICWA and tribal interests, tribes should step up their education efforts so that state judges and attorneys know that tribal courts are fair and just mediums for ICWA decisions. However, there have been some consistencies, such as the reaffirmation that Arizona will not follow the Existing Indian Family exception.

In 2000, an Arizona state court reaffirmed the rejection of the Existing Indian Family exception,[114] a doctrine that began in Kansas holding that if an Indian child is not part of an "existing Indian family," ICWA does not apply.[115] This type of judicial activism has done much to damage the potential success of ICWA. Fortunately, many states join Arizona in not following this doctrine.[116]

Arizona first rejected the Existing Indian Family exception in *In re Appeal in Coconino County, Juvenile Action J-10175*.[117] As discussed earlier, in that case, a child was taken from her non-Indian mother and stepfather's home after the stepfather abused her. The lower court held that the Indian child did not have to be placed with the Navajo biological father because, although he was found to be an adequate parent, he was "neither a completely traditional Navajo nor a completely Anglicized individual," and therefore the child would suffer from culture shock, defeating the purpose of ICWA.[118] The appellate court reversed, finding that this was a "child custody proceeding" as defined by the Act, and that the child was enrolled in the Navajo Nation and was an "Indian child."[119] Thus, absent good cause to the contrary, ICWA must be followed.[120] The appellate court found that unless the trial judge could find by clear and convincing evidence that the parental placement would be likely to result in serious emotional or physical harm to the child, the child may not be placed in foster care when the Indian parent is willing to take the child.[121]

The Arizona courts reaffirmed this rejection more recently in *Michael J., Jr. v. Michael J., Sr.*, stating that the judicial exception frustrates the policy of protecting the tribe's interest in their children.[122] In that case, an Indian child was born to a non-Indian mother who tested positive for cocaine use at birth.[123] At the time of the child's birth, the father, an enrolled member of the Tohono O'odham Nation, was incarcerated.[124] The Department of Economic Security requested that a guardian *ad litem* ("GAL") be appointed for the child, and the Tohono O'odham Nation intervened, acknowledging the Nation's jurisdiction over the child's siblings.[125] The father then moved to transfer jurisdiction to the tribal court, and the GAL filed an appeal.[126]

The court noted that ICWA grants the tribe exclusive jurisdiction over Indian children who are domiciled on the reservation, and concurrent but presumptively tribal jurisdiction for actions involving Indian children not domiciled on the reservation.[127] The GAL is not a party permitted by statute to object to a transfer of jurisdiction to tribal court, but may present evidence of good cause not to transfer.[128] However, in this case, she failed to present any evidence that Tohono O'odham could not support the child's allegedly special medical needs.[129] Therefore, there was no good cause not to transfer jurisdiction to tribal court.

The GAL also contended that ICWA should not apply, because the Department of Economic Security did not remove the child from an "existing Indian family."[130] The appellate court then reaffirmed Arizona's rejection of the Existing Indian Family exception, giving five reasons. First, adopting an Existing Indian Family exception frustrates the policy of protecting the tribe's interest in its children. Second, the language of the Act does not list an Existing Indian Family exception, and if the language of the statute is plain and unambiguous, the court must follow the plain meaning. Third, Congress rejected an earlier version of ICWA that included the Existing Indian Family exception.[131] Fourth, the Supreme Court has undermined the imposition of an Existing Indian Family exception, stressing that ICWA reflects Congress's concern with the tribe's interest in Indian children, and that Indian children have a corresponding interest in maintaining a relationship with the tribe, even if the parents do not share that interest.[132] Fifth, the Arizona appellate court had implicitly rejected the Existing Indian Family exception before in *In Re Appeal in Coconino County, Juvenile Action J-10175*.[133] The rejection of the Existing Indian Family exception has probably spared the Arizona appellate courts from having to hear many ICWA cases, because the issue of whether a child comes from an existing Indian family is highly fact-intensive, very controversial, and subject to individual interpretations, which makes it an issue ripe for appeals.

The issue of the Existing Indian Family exception is so pervasive that the International Indian Treaty Council (IITC),[134] a nongovernmental organization (NGO) with special consultative status with the United Nations, filed with the UN Commission on Human Rights a written statement outlining how the use of the Existing Indian Family exception was undermining ICWA.[135] The IITC cites the Existing Indian Family exception as "an example of continuing interference with parents, families and tribal members."[136] By allowing judges to determine whether the parents of a child appear to be "real" Indians and therefore fall under ICWA as an "Indian family" in need of protection amounts to the United States having allowed a judicially created[137] exception to circumvent the application and intent of the Act.[138]

Several years earlier, in 1994, the United States submitted its Initial Report of States to the UN Human Rights Committee. In this report, the United States stated that ICWA was passed in 1978 to "promote the placement of Indian children in foster and adoptive homes reflective of their unique cultural environment and heritage." Not only does the report state that the Act vests initial authority for Indian child placement with tribal courts and provides for full faith and credit to tribal court decisions, but it claims that because of the passage of the Act, there has been an increase in child welfare personnel who are familiar with tribal customs and values. Lastly, the report notes that ICWA authorized the federal government to provide grants to tribes and tribal organizations to establish family preservation programs; however, the report conveniently fails to mention that in over twenty-five years, no such grants have been authorized.[139]

The United States also failed to include in its report to the UN Human Rights Committee any information regarding the judicially created Existing Indian Family exception, and it would be nonsensical to assume that the U.S. State Department did not know of its existence. Thus, it appears that the official position of the United States has been to ignore the problem in the hopes that it will go away or resolve itself—a response all too familiar to Indian people. However, the danger is that this problem will only get worse, and with some state courts unwilling to relinquish control over Indian children to tribal courts, and federal courts' lack of jurisdiction over family matters, it appears that if a solution is to come, it must come from Congress.[140]

Another issue of great concern in Arizona has been that of transfer to tribal court for cases involving concurrent jurisdiction. In *In Re Appeal in Maricopa County*

Juvenile Action No. JS-8287, the court held that ICWA's good-cause exception to transfer to tribal court allowed the state court to apply a modified version of *forum non conveniens*.[141] In this case, a child was born to a Santo Domingo Pueblo woman living in Phoenix. The mother had a serious drinking problem and left her child with a friend, who evidently tried unsuccessfully to sell the child for $25 while the mother was incarcerated. The Santo Domingo Pueblo in New Mexico was notified concerning the termination proceeding against the mother and intervened shortly thereafter, but did not petition for transfer of the matter to their tribal court at that time. The Arizona Department of Economic Security's plan originally provided for rehabilitation and then for severance of parental rights, and sought adoption.[142]

Two years later, after it became clear that rehabilitation was unsuccessful, the Santo Domingo Pueblo filed a petition to transfer the proceedings to tribal court.[143] The Arizona appellate court noted that although there was concurrent jurisdiction with a preference for tribal jurisdiction, that preference could be overcome by a showing of good cause.[144] The court went on to state that because the Act does not define "good cause," a state court has discretion as to whether to transfer a matter to tribal court or retain jurisdiction.[145] Thus, the appellate court found that a modified version of *forum non conveniens* could apply to the decision of whether or not to retain jurisdiction over ICWA proceeding.[146] The court found that witnesses located in Phoenix would be unduly troubled with the time and expense required to travel to the Pueblo.

Furthermore, the Arizona court was unsatisfied with the Pueblo's delay in requesting transfer. The Pueblo maintained that it did not petition for transfer earlier because the original plan provided for rehabilitation and eventual reunion with the child. As noted before, this is a common strategy for tribes that do not have an abundance of resources; such tribes do not seek transfer unless they disagree with how the state court is handling the situation. This dispute could arguably have been avoided if the state and the tribal representatives better understood each other's situation. However, the court still found that the tribe had unreasonably delayed its petition for transfer after an adoptive family had been found.[147]

Finally, in *Rachelle S. v. Arizona Department of Economic Security*, the court dealt with the issue of whether an expert witness was required to have experience with Indian communities in order to qualify under ICWA.[148] Here, the parents appealed, arguing for an interpretation of ICWA that required that an expert in Indian children testify in order for a child to be placed in foster care. The court, however, did not agree, stating that the determination of the likelihood of future harm frequently involves predicting future behavior, which is influenced to a large degree by culture, but the Act does not limit a qualified expert to someone with expertise with Indian children or culture.[149] "Special knowledge of Indian life is not necessary where a professional person has substantial education and experience and testifies on matters not implicating cultural bias."[150] Thus, an expert with knowledge of Indian cultures is only necessary where cultural values, beliefs, and mores are involved. If an expert in child abuse were to testify on purely physical signs of abuse, no cultural expertise would be necessary in that situation. The court, therefore, held that the baby was correctly determined to be dependent because family members showed a lack of motivation to protect the baby and make changes that would prevent future abuse.[151] While this holding does not appear to invoke any type of cultural bias, one worries that if only one expert is needed and that expert testifies as to physical injuries, then no expert will be available to testify that it is culturally appropriate for multiple family members to help raise one child.

By comparing these current cases to the earlier cases, we can clearly see a shift in the focus of the litigation. There have been some consistencies, such as the rejection of the Existing Indian Family exception. However, there is also an increasing focus on issues surrounding the transfer of jurisdiction from state court to tribal courts. One case held that a modified version of *forum non conveniens* was applicable to good cause not to transfer the case.[152] Given the history of Indian mobility, this may create a problem for many tribes that are not located in the same state as the child placement proceedings.[153]

The doctrine of *forum non conveniens* is also problematic in light of the government-endorsed influx of Indians into urban areas in the twentieth century. During the 1950s, the United States government instituted a plan called the Relocation Act,[154] intended to help Indian families by providing funding to establish "job training centers" in various urban centers.[155] The government provided incentives for Indian people to move from the reservation to these urban centers, where they would be aided in obtaining a job and housing. In return, they had to sign an agreement stating that they would not return to the reservation to live.[156] Because of this program and high rates of unemployment on the reservation, many Indians decided to move, and the urban Indian population grew substantially. By 1975, the Indian population in urban areas was larger than the Indian population living on the reservations.[157] Similar problems like the lack of employment on or near many reservations have driven even more Indian people to relocate to urban environments since the repeal of the Relocation Act. According to the 2000 Census, there are currently approximately 2,680,355 urban Indians across the United States.[158] As a consequence, there are many Indian people from many tribes scattered across the United States, and it will be difficult to honor the rights that tribes have in these proceedings if this modified doctrine of *forum non conveniens* gains strength.

Then we saw a case regarding what types of cultural qualifications an expert witness needed when testifying on whether a child will likely be physically or emotionally harmed if they stay with their parents.[159] That case determined that if the expert's testimony concerns cultural mores, then the expert must be an expert in Indian culture, but if the expert's testimony is not influenced by cultural mores, the person need not be an expert in Indian culture as well.[160]

This shift indicates several things. First, the Arizona courts have dealt with the definitional issues that plagued them during the first ten years after the Act was passed. Second, tribes and tribal members have become more sophisticated in their arguments, leading to more intricate and novel questions in state court proceedings, such as the issue on qualifications of the expert witness. Third, tribal attorneys are willing to petition for transfer to tribal courts, if necessary. This analysis leads to the ultimate recommendation that tribes should continue their efforts at strengthening their institutions, especially their tribal courts, to allow for the transfer of more cases. The stronger (more independent and knowledgeable) the tribal courts become and the more financial support that is funneled in their direction, the more capable they will be to secure the safety and welfare of their people.

South Dakota State Court Cases

South Dakota has had a somewhat different evolution of ICWA jurisprudence. Perhaps most strikingly, South Dakota has nearly four times as many ICWA cases reaching the appellate court than Arizona. Thus the speed at which the courts deal with ICWA questions has necessarily been much quicker. The South Dakota courts dealt with many issues soon after the passage of ICWA. Then, between 1991 and 2001 there was a lull in the case law. However, in more recent years, the courts have begun to revisit the same issues that were decided in the first phase. Sometimes these revisitations result in a change in the law, other times they result in clarifications, and quite often they result in upholding the original interpretation. One large exception surrounds the question of notice. Although the state court judges have revisited this issue throughout the years since the passage of ICWA, they have been unwilling to overturn the concept of "substantial compliance," and consequentially repeatedly return to this issue. Overall, however, it is encouraging that the state court judges are refamiliarizing themselves with ICWA and that they are usually willing, when they feel it is necessary, to make changes.

SOUTH DAKOTA STATE CASES

Besides settling the definition of domicile, one of the first important cases coming out of the South Dakota Supreme Court tackled the issue of what constitutes an expert witness.[161] In *In re J.L.H and P.L.L.H.*, the court held that the practical experience of a witness can be used in conjunction with educational experience to qualify the witness as an expert.[162] Recall that ICWA requires the testimony of an expert that continued custody of the child by the parent will likely result in serious emotional or physical damage before any termination of parental rights can be ordered. Thus, unless the witness qualifies as an "expert," the termination ordered in this case would be invalid.[163]

In order to determine whether the witness qualified as an expert, the appellate court looked to South Dakota laws that "permit qualification as an expert to be based on knowledge, skill, experience, training or education."[164] The court then cited a South Dakota decision holding that "the admissibility of a claimed expert's opinion is within the discretion of the trial court.... The trial court's ruling will be disturbed only in case of a clear abuse of discretion."[165] This standard gives great deference to the trial judge to determine what constitutes an expert, making it difficult to challenge the qualifications of a witness as determined by the trial judge. Here, not only did the trial court use state standards in determining what an expert is, but they also used state law standards to overturn that determination. Although ICWA does not define "qualified expert witness," the BIA did promulgate guidelines in 1979 to help state courts determine the minimum standards of a "qualified expert witness."[166] This case makes no mention of these guidelines and instead institutes a standards based state law. Arguably, using such state law-based standards is contrary to one goal of ICWA, which was to provide a nationwide minimum standard for the removal of Indian children from their homes.

This issue of expert witness qualification was revisited by the Supreme Court of South Dakota in 2005 in *In re M.H., L.U.H., W.H., Jr., L.S.H., and T.H.*[167] The court held that to fulfill the requirement that a termination of parental rights be accompanied by "evidence beyond a reasonable doubt, including testimony of qualified expert witnesses, that continued custody of the child by the parent is likely to result in serious emotional or physical damage," only one witness was required, despite the fact that the statute uses the plural, "expert witnesses."[168] However, unlike the prior decision, which relied solely on state-law standards of what constituted an "expert" witness, this case incorporated the BIA Guidelines to "help inform the court as to when the witness offered as an ICWA expert has the requisite special knowledge, skill, experience or training to assist the trial court."[169]

The court found that the purpose of requiring an expert witness was to diminish the risk of cultural bias.[170] Therefore, the absence of a properly qualified expert witness necessitates an invalidation of the termination of parental rights. Using case law from other jurisdictions, the court stated that "experts should possess more than simply substantial education and experience in the area of their specialty. Rather, they should have expertise in, and substantial knowledge of, Native American families and their child-rearing practices."[171] The court, thus, held that an expert witness must have knowledge of the specific tribe's child-rearing practices. It was no longer acceptable to have general experience and knowledge in Native American cultures and child-rearing practices. This holding was reaffirmed in *In re O.S.*, later that same year.[172] Contrast this decision with the Arizona decision of 1998, which does not require an expert witness to have any experience with Indian culture if the issue can be determined without reference to culture.[173]

Perhaps the most disappointing case to come out of the South Dakota Supreme Court is that of *In re S.Z. and C.Z.*[174] In this case, parents' parental rights were terminated in September 1980 and in January of the following year; the parents petitioned the court to set aside the termination, alleging that ICWA had been violated because the notice that the Rosebud Sioux Tribe received did not comply with the requirements found in ICWA. Section 1912(a) requires that in an involuntary proceeding, notice must be sent to the Indian child's tribe by registered mail with return receipt requested, indicating the nature of the pending proceeding and notifying the tribe of their right to intervention. The section goes on to state that no foster care placement or termination of parental rights proceedings shall be held until at least ten days after receipt of notice by the parent(s) and the tribe.[175]

Notice to the tribe was sent on June 27, 1979, while the parents' first court appearance was on May 25, 1979. Thus, the tribe did not receive notice in a timely manner. The court, however, held that the notice "requirement was substantially complied with in the case at hand." The court found that the delay did not prejudice the tribe, and the fact that the tribe did not intervene was indicative of the tribe not availing itself of the opportunity to intervene. The court also noted that although the notice did not explicitly state that the tribe had the right to intervene, the "general tenor of the documents" and the novelty of the Act excused the omission.[176] In essence, the court gave leniency to the state for failing to provide proper notice because the Act was newly enacted, but opted not to extend leniency to the tribe for not intervening for that same reason. Essentially the court held that the state had substantially complied with the notice provision housed in ICWA. However, actual notice is not a synonym for registered mail, return receipt requested, and to hold so is to gut the notice provision of the Act. Furthermore, nowhere in ICWA does it provide for substantial compliance with the notice procedure, nor does it say that actual notice can substitute for notice via registered mail with return receipt requested. Congress set out a specific-notice method in ICWA that state courts should be required to follow.

Justice Wollman provided a strong dissent in this case, where he stated that "although a rule of substantial compliance may suffice to carry out the notice provisions of statutes governing mundane matters of property law ... more is required when the interests at stake are as important as those protected by ICWA."[177] He notes that ICWA was enacted by Congress to establish "minimum Federal standards for the removal of Indian children from their families."[178] He goes on to state that the right to intervene is "virtually meaningless unless notice of the proceedings is prompt."[179] Lastly, Justice Wollman remarks that this case does not fall into line with prior ICWA cases where the Supreme Court of South Dakota has required compliance with the Act.[180]

In early 1988, a brief glimmer of hope emerged in the case of *In re N.A.H. and K.A.H.*[181] The Supreme Court of South Dakota reviewed an appeal by an Indian mother of the termination of her parental rights. The mother argued that the state failed to prove its case beyond a reasonable doubt, as required by ICWA. The court, however, held that because the notice provided to the tribe did not inform the tribe of its right to intervene and was not sent by registered mail with return receipt requested, as required by ICWA, the state court did not have proper jurisdiction to order the termination of parental rights. The court noted that ICWA was primarily a jurisdictional statute, and the court must examine jurisdictional questions whether presented by the parties or not. Thus, "at a minimum, notice must conform to the standards found in 25 U.S.C. § 1912(a). Better practice would be to follow the Bureau of Indian Affairs guidelines."[182]

Many years after its first appearance, in *In re D.M, R.M. III, and T.B.C.*, the Supreme Court of South Dakota reaffirmed the substantial compliance doctrine.[183] The court notes, for the first time, that section 1912(a) is ambiguous as to whether notice via registered mail, return receipt requested, is necessary only at commencement of the proceedings or prior to every proceeding. The court decides, without providing reasoning, that such notice was not necessary prior to every hearing. Therefore, the state's sending of notice of a later hearing by facsimile substantially complied with ICWA.[184]

However, the court does not halt its analysis here, but goes on to state that the "State's failure to ensure that the Tribe received timely, official notice of the dispositional hearing in this case was negligent at best."[185] To most, this would seem to indicate that the state did not substantially comply with the notice requirements of ICWA. The court, nonetheless, determines that the tribe received actual notice, based upon the testimony of the social worker that she informed the tribe's ICWA specialist of the hearing, and the parents' statement that the children's attorney sent a letter notifying the tribe of the proceedings.[186] It should be noted that both evidences of notice are suspect. The department of social services (DSS) worker's job could depend upon her giving notice, and the children's attorney is not the party required to provide notice.

The court ends by chiding the tribe for having waited eleven months before moving to transfer the case to tribal court, and held that good cause existed to deny transfer due to the advanced stage of the proceedings.[187] Justice Konenkamp concurred and added that the reason the tribe waited to request transfer was largely due to the limited resources of tribes and tribal courts to handle all such ICWA cases. Because numerous cases on this exact issue have already come before the Supreme Court,

Konenkamp urges the use of creative solutions to this problem, such as creating a statewide coordinator for ICWA.[188]

Lastly, and somewhat prophetically, Konenkamp notes that the use of abuse of discretion in good cause not to transfer cases makes little sense, given that the burden is imposed upon those who oppose an ICWA transfer. "If the presumption is in favor of tribal jurisdiction then mere discretion to override an ICWA transfer is unacceptable." Instead, the "clear and convincing evidence" standard must be used to determine if good cause not to transfer exists. For support, Konenkamp uses numerous other state court decisions, dealing with ICWA instead of the Supreme Court's normal procedure of finding quasi-analogous state law.[189]

In 2005, Justice Konenkamp's dissent was transformed into the majority opinion in *In re T.I. and T.I.*[190] In this case, one Indian son was enrolled in the Yankton Sioux Tribe and the other was eligible for enrollment in the Yankton Sioux Tribe. Both sons were also eligible for enrollment in the Sisseton-Wahpeton Sioux Tribe.[191] Both tribes were provided notice and requested transfer. The Yankton Sioux Tribe withdrew its request for transfer in order to permit the case to be transferred to Sisseton-Wahpeton. The court noted that section 1903(5) of ICWA and the *Guidelines for State Courts: Indian Child Custody Proceedings* indicate that although an Indian child may be eligible for enrollment in more than one tribe, only one tribe can adjudicate the case.[192] The court refused to address Yankton Sioux's request for transfer because they voluntarily withdrew the request in order for the case to be transferred to Sisseton-Wahpeton.[193]

The court then addressed the issue of whether good cause existed to deny transfer to the Sisseton-Wahpeton Tribal Court. The court overruled its previous use of the standard of abuse of discretion. Instead, the court opted to use "the standard most consistent with the Act . . . clear and convincing evidence of good cause for a state court to refuse to transfer to tribal court." Using this standard, the court determined that good cause existed because the only court that has jurisdiction over both children is the state court, since the older son was already enrolled at Yankton and could not be enrolled at Sisseton-Wahpeton Oyate. Given ICWA expert's testimony that the children should be kept together, the trial court was deemed correct in declining to transfer the case to Sisseton-Wahpeton. Thus, although the Supreme Court did uphold the trial court's ruling, they also implemented a higher standard for denying transfer to tribal courts, which will likely result in more cases being adjudicated in the proper setting . . . tribal court.[194]

Justice Wollman, who dissented in *In re S.Z. and C.Z.*,[195] identified a key problem with some of South Dakota's interpretations of ICWA: the court's tendency to move away from the minimum standards set out in ICWA.[196] In *In re P.B.*, the court continually points to state-law cases with little similarity to ICWA cases. The court states that parents have a fundamental-liberty interest in the care of their child, but this interest is not absolute. This statement is supported by three South Dakota child welfare cases that do not involve Indian children or ICWA.[197] The court goes on to state that the "best interest of the child is the paramount consideration in determining whether to terminate parental rights." The judge cites a South Dakota code as well as two South Dakota cases, and again both cases do not involve Indian children or ICWA.[198] Finally, the decision adopts the least restrictive alternative test, which requires that the trial court must apply the least restrictive alternative, but not attempt every conceivable form of assistance.[199] Again, the use of this test is supported by a slurry of South Dakota cases.[200]

There are two overarching problems with using state-law child welfare principles independent of ICWA. The first is that this defeats one purpose of ICWA, which was to create a national standard. ICWA was enacted so that there would be uniformity in how Indian children were treated by courts across the nation. By using state standards, which vary greatly, this purpose is defeated. The second problem is that ICWA does not provide for many of these standards. Nowhere in ICWA does it state that the trial court must apply the least restrictive alternative. In fact, a close reading of ICWA should point to a stricter requirement for Indian children, such as one that requires that more alternatives be attempted to reunite Indian children with their parents since the burden of proof required to terminate parental rights is heavier. Likewise, ICWA does not state that only the best interest of the child is considered. ICWA provides a legislative rule that the best interest of the child is served by remaining with the tribe. Thus, both the tribe's and the child's interests must be used for a determination of whether parental rights should be terminated.

As time goes on, the South Dakota state courts have seemed to rely less and less on purely state court decisions. This may be because there is now a deeper understanding of ICWA issues and the uniqueness of the dual purpose of protecting Indian children while simultaneously protecting Indian tribes. It may also be due to the development of a body of case law from South Dakota regarding ICWA. South Dakota, like many states, may have an aversion to adopting case law from other jurisdictions; however, the fact remains that another similarly situated jurisdiction's case law on ICWA is more likely to be on point than a South Dakota case that deals with a different statute.

One large issue present nationwide but adjudicated by South Dakota courts is that of active efforts versus reasonable efforts. Section 1912(d) of ICWA states that any party seeking foster care placement or termination of parental rights to an Indian child must show that "active efforts" have been made to provide remedial services designed to prevent the breakup of the Indian family, and that these efforts have proved unsuccessful. The Adoption and Safe Families Act (ASFA) requires that the state make "reasonable efforts" to rehabilitate the family before terminating parental rights. These two standards have created much confusion in state courts. Many state courts use the terms interchangeably, but then this begs the question, "Why didn't Congress simply use the same phrase?"

In re E.M, A.M., and J.M., the DSS provided few services to the mother because they interpreted her behavior as uncooperative.[201] Later it was determined that the mother suffered from a learning disability; however, the DSS and the court went forward with the termination. The court stated that the DSS is not required to exhaust all possible services, and that the least restrictive alternative when viewed from the child's point of view necessitated the termination of parental rights, since the mother was unlikely to be able to acquire the parenting skills necessary to care for the children. Thus, even though the DSS terminated its efforts after only six weeks, these weeks of services miraculously rose to the level of active efforts.[202]

The dissent in this case remarks that the DSS "acknowledged that it did not take active efforts to help this young Indian mother (given her limitations)." Justice Henderson continues that when the DSS learned of the mother's learning disability, they should have stopped the dispositional hearing, based upon the newly discovered facts, and helped the mother by providing her with a parenting plan that was geared towards her abilities.[203] This case left a deeper discussion of the ASFA's effect on ICWA for a later date.

Over ten years later, the Supreme Court of South Dakota ruled that the ASFA did not relieve the DSS of *any* duty that it held under ICWA to provide active efforts to reunite an Indian family. The ASFA is an amendment to Title IV-B and Title IV-E of the Social Security Act.[204] Title IV-E is the primary basis for payment of foster care subsidies for Indian children; however, in order to be eligible, these children must be placed by a state court or a tribal court that has a cooperative agreement with the state. Tribes operating Title IV-E programs are subject to state-law definitions on "aggravating circumstances" that will negate the need to provide "reasonable efforts" of reunification. Allowing tribes to receive these funds directly, instead of having to receive them from the state and under the state's conditions, would facilitate the receipt of more money (due to decreased administrative costs) and would also enable them to determine for themselves how to best use the funding within their existing cultural framework. An amendment to the ASFA that would allow direct tribal funding, but ensure that tribes are not required to modify their modus operandi, would greatly increase efficiency by alleviating some of the tension between state and tribal standards.

In *In re J.S.B., Jr.*, the court reasoned that ICWA was the more specific statute, and thus controlled.[205] In addition, ICWA provides no exception to the requirement of active efforts to prevent the breakup of an Indian family. On the other hand, the ASFA recognizes that under certain circumstances, reasonable efforts may be unnecessary. Lastly, the court noted that statutes pertaining to Indians "must be construed in favor of the Indians, with ambiguous provisions interpreted to their benefit."[206] Thus, "While the presence of 'aggravated circumstances' may eliminate the need to provide 'reasonable efforts' under SDCL 26–8A-21, it does not remove DSS's requirement to provide 'active efforts' for reunification under ICWA."[207]

South Dakota has also extended ICWA to a relationship that, at first glance, ICWA seems not to consider. In *In re N.S.*, the Supreme Court of South Dakota held that ICWA applied to the termination of a Caucasian mother's parental rights to an Indian child.[208] The court acknowledged that despite the fact that the purpose of the Act was to maintain an Indian family, it is incorrect to "assess ... ICWA's applicability to a particular case, . . . focus[ing] *only* upon the interests of the existing Indian family" (emphasis original).[209] Thus, the Existing Indian Family theory, which has been used to justify the nonapplication of ICWA to some Indian children, should not be used to limit the applicability of the Act to Indian mothers.

The court in this case focuses on the Indian status of the child and not the Indian status of the parent. Congress stated two purposes for enacting ICWA. The first was to protect Indian children, and the second was to protect Indian families. The Act creates a presumption that it is in the best interests of an Indian child to remain with its Indian family. It is doubtful that by setting a higher standard for the termination of a non-Indian parent's rights to an Indian child either purpose will be achieved.[210] This expands the scope of ICWA to cover non-Indian parents and Indian parents, and may be an overextension of the congressional intent; however, a strict reading of the Act allows for this outcome.

In a final example, the Supreme Court of South Dakota decided a case dealing with the transfer of jurisdiction to tribal court. In *In re J.L*, the court upheld the trial-court decision to transfer jurisdiction to tribal court.[211] The court noted that ICWA provides for concurrent, but presumptively tribal court jurisdiction for Indian children domiciled off the reservation. In this case, the mother, who was residing off the reservation, contacted Catholic Family Services to place J.L. for adoption in March 2001. He was placed with an appropriate family. Two months later, she decided against the adoption and requested the return of her son. The very day that she was due to pick up her child, the department of social services received information that J.L.'s sister had been placed in the care of an aunt, where she was abused. Thus, the mother's care was questioned, and DSS took emergency custody of J.L.[212] The mother then returned to Standing Rock Reservation.

Following a period of sporadic contact, likely due to the physical distance between the mother and the child, both the Standing Rock Sioux Tribe and the foster parents were granted intervention in the case. The tribe moved for transfer to tribal court, and the foster parents objected, arguing *forum non conveniens*. They insist that the federal guidelines for interpreting ICWA provide that good cause to deny transfer exists when "evidence necessary to decide the case cannot be adequately presented to the tribal court without undue hardship to witnesses and parties."[213]

The South Dakota Supreme Court agreed, but noted that while all evidence of the neglect allegations were off the reservation, the evidence of J.L.'s current living situation was on the Standing Rock Reservation, since the mother had later been granted custody. The court stated that situs of evidence was inconclusive, because one side or the other would be inconvenienced and face hardship in the proceedings. Thus, the court found, contrary to the circuit court's conclusion, that *forum non conveniens* is, at best, a neutral factor in evaluating whether good cause exists to deny transfer. The court went on to state that because ICWA provides for presumptively tribal jurisdiction, a neutral factor does not rise to the level needed to provide a basis for denying a tribe's petition for transfer to tribal court.[214]

The court further analyzed the tribe's petition to transfer jurisdiction to tribal court. They noted that although the best interest of the child is a valid consideration in determining the issue of good cause not to transfer, the fact that a substitute parent might provide the child with as good or better care than the mother is not appropriate for this evaluation.[215] Next, the court noted that the child has been in the care of his mother for over nine months without any further allegations of neglect, and that the allegations of abuse of J.L.'s sister by her aunt, which started the entire neglect process on J.L., simply were not true. Finally, the court added a bit of practical advice by pointing out that even if they were to maintain jurisdiction and move towards termination of parental rights, the DSS would still be required to provide active efforts to prevent the breakup of the family, which would further add to the instability of J.L.[216]

This case provides an unfortunate example of the heartbreak that can occur for all parties involved when a child is removed from her Indian parents too quickly. It further provides an example of a state court making what likely felt like a tough decision to relinquish jurisdiction to tribal court for adjudication. Removing a case to tribal court does not necessarily mean that the Indian child will be returned to the parents. Tribal courts, like state courts, have the best interests of the children in mind when rendering their decisions. This state court's decision merely provided the tribal court with an opportunity to hear the case and make a proper decision in accordance with their laws and customs. In addition, tribal courts arguably have more latitude to implement creative custody solutions so that ties are not broken between those people that have been influential in the child's life. For example, a tribal court could allow the foster parents to have visitation rights if the court felt that it was in the child's best interest. The fact that a state court recognizes and respects tribal court's jurisdiction enough to release jurisdiction shows a certain level of maturity in the relationship between the tribal and state entities that can only be seen as a step in the right direction for Indian children's welfare.

South Dakota courts have been slowly reevaluating prior ICWA decisions in recent years. In many cases, such as those dealing with qualifying an expert witness, the South Dakota Supreme Court has modified its prior rulings to align better with ICWA. However, the court has not altered its "substantial compliance" doctrine for notice to the tribe. This has become such a problem that in 2004, the governor of South Dakota established the Governor's Commission on the Indian Child Welfare Act.[217] The commission made several recommendations dealing with the notice problem in South Dakota.[218] The following year, the South Dakota legislature passed a statute detailing the information required when providing notice to tribes of proceedings involving an Indian child.[219] This provides a perfect example of how educating state actors can help achieve tribal goals in implementing the Indian Child Welfare Act.

Tribal Court Cases

As mentioned earlier, ICWA provides for exclusive tribal jurisdiction over Indian children domiciled on the reservation, and concurrent but presumptive tribal court jurisdiction over Indian children domiciled off-reservation.[220] Thus, any discussion of the implementation of ICWA is incomplete without looking at tribal courts. Tribal courts often do not follow ICWA, but utilize their own tribal juvenile codes for the disposition of the child welfare case.[221] However, without a comparison of state court dispositions to tribal court dispositions, we cannot see the full spectrum of Indian child-welfare action outcomes.

Modern tribal courts were created following the Indian Reorganization Act of 1934.[222] This act allowed tribes to draft a constitution, establish a governmental system, and create a judicial system. After many years of assimilation and hardship, tribes were in a poor position to return to their traditional judicial systems, and thus the new tribal court system was designed similar to the BIA model.[223] These newly created courts were designed to operate under and enforce the new tribal codes.[224] The majority of cases heard in tribal courts are misdemeanors, family disputes, and minor civil matters.[225] In addition, many tribal courts operate under a system of restitution instead of retribution,[226] meaning that defendants often plead guilty and accept responsibility for their actions, with the result that disputes are resolved in a more mutually beneficial manner.[227] Unlike state courts, which are all-or-nothing models, many tribal courts attempt to heal the parties in the action.[228] These differences make nonmembers uneasy about appearing in front of tribal court because they do not know what to expect.

Many tribes have realized the importance of tribal courts in promoting tribal economic development. According to the Harvard Project on American Indian Economic Development, having a strong and independent tribal court is one of the keys to being economically successful.[229] An independent tribal court will support the separation of powers and will encourage outside businesses and entrepreneurs to develop on the reservation, because they can be assured that their investment will be safe and treated fairly by the tribal court.[230] Another key factor, according to the Harvard Project, is that tribes must use culturally appropriate methods, or what they term a "cultural fit," which leads to a view of legitimacy among tribal members.[231] Thus, a strong and independent tribal court should utilize traditional philosophies that the people will understand, but will also treat outsiders fairly. Lastly, a strong tribal court is one of the ultimate expressions of tribal sovereignty. Tribes have taken the responsibility of expressing their sovereignty through protecting their members by taking over institutions instead of relying on federal and state actors.

The next section of this paper focuses on tribes—specifically the Navajo, Cheyenne River Sioux, and Rosebud Sioux case law, and the Pascua Yaqui and White Mountain Apache statutory law. The Navajo Nation's courts are unique and considered by many to be one of the most effective among Native nations. The Peacemaker Courts of the Navajo Nation are an excellent example of a judiciary built on the traditions of conflict resolution. These courts utilize the traditional dispute-resolution methods used by the Navajo people for hundreds of years and recently revitalized through the adoption of Peacemaker Courts in 1982.[232] In these courts, an elder who is knowledgeable about traditional culture will hear the dispute and will counsel the people as to what the appropriate resolution is that will bring harmony and closure.[233]

The importance of family to Indian people runs deep. Tribal members depend upon their families for survival. Traditionally, the family and kinship ties that bind people also set out obligations and responsibilities that provided a safety net for any family members that were experiencing difficult times.[234] While the types of obligations may have changed, these kinship and familial relations have survived. For example, when a Navajo clan member knocks at your house door looking for a place to stay, you are obligated to provide that for him regardless of how well you know the individual or how long it has been since you have talked.[235] Today, these obligations still provide a method for clan members to travel from place to place in a cost-efficient manner. Knowledge of who one is and their place in the society is based on that person's family and relatives.

The importance of and view of family relations also influences how tribal courts implement ICWA. Many tribal courts have held in varying degrees that ICWA does not directly apply to them.[236] For example, the Pascua Yaqui Tribal Council has enacted its own placement guidelines, which not only the tribal court but also the state court must use.[237] Thus, while the Pascua Yaqui Tribe supports ICWA with its alternative placement regime,[238] once a case is transferred to tribal court, they will apply their own laws to the case. In addition, the Chitimacha Indian Tribal Court of Appeals held that "The I.C.W.A. does not apply to proceedings in tribal court, notwithstanding the failure of the act to specifically say so."[239] Yet another tribal court stated that although "no party forwarded the proposition that the Indian Child Welfare Act does not govern Tribal Court... ICWA is, at least, instructive."[240] Thus, this court was reluctant to simply follow ICWA, and instead opted to use ICWA as persuasive evidence and thereby not be bound by the Act. These types of tribal courts often utilize traditional beliefs concerning family and adoption in addition to modern laws. This difference in the interpretation of whether to apply ICWA, as well as the acknowledged difference in the view of family, gives rise to different reasonings in ICWA cases that come out of tribal courts as compared to state courts.

Before proceeding to the tribal court cases, it should be noted that many non-Indian litigants are apprehensive about bringing or transferring a case to a tribal court because they fear being treated discriminatorily; however, in practice these fears are largely unfounded. For example, in *In re Halloway*, the Window Rock District Court held that it was in a Navajo child's best interest to remain with the non-Indian foster family because of the bonding that had already occurred, but required that the child return to the Navajo reservation during the summer months to maintain the connection with her family and clan.[241] As Judge McKay, an Arizona judge, explained about one high-profile case, "The result reached by the Navajo Court ... is more flexible and resolves more problems than I was accustomed to seeing in my many years of practice in adoption work, in the courts of Arizona, and in child custody matters."[242] Here again we see the importance of a strong, independent tribal judiciary not only to quash the fears of outside litigants, but also to develop the many avenues open to tribal courts that may not be open to state courts.

The Navajo Nation Supreme Court considers the Navajo Nation's tribal codes to be the foremost law of the land.[243] The Navajo Nation courts are charged with interpreting these codes.[244] When the codes are unclear, the courts follow a choice of law, starting with the utilization of Navajo common law or traditional law, to interpret these codes.[245] Thus, the Navajo Nation has developed a system that incorporates their traditional culture into modern laws. This system folds the Old Ways into a modern legal environment, creating a system that the majority of the Navajo Nation membership will be able to understand and make their own.[246] Inevitably, this means that the legal system has legitimacy in the eyes of the membership.

Because of the unique blend of Navajo common law with the Navajo Nation's codes, the Navajo Nation does not utilize ICWA provisions in placement of Navajo children residing on the reservation in foster care or adoptive homes. The Navajo Nation Supreme Court has handed down only one decision that specifically addresses ICWA.[247] They have, however, handed down five other decisions that dealt with child welfare in general. In these later cases, ICWA would not have been applied had the issue arisen in state court.[248]

The one ICWA case that the Navajo Nation Supreme Court did hear set out the traditional law under which ICWA cases should be handled. In *In Re J.J.S.*,[249] a mother seriously neglected her child, and her parental rights were terminated. Upon termination, the mother expressed her desire that her child be adopted by Mr. and Mrs. Chee, her cousin. However, a petition for adoption by another non-Navajo couple was pending before the court. The court found that the Navajo Nation had original jurisdiction over all cases involving the domestic relation of Indians, such as divorce or adoption matters, and thus had jurisdiction to hear the case.[250] According to Navajo law, if there is an applicable custom of the tribe not prohibited by federal laws, then the court may apply those customs as well as any ordinances of the Navajo Tribe.[251] The court, thus, decided that it would only apply federal laws, such as ICWA, in the absence of a Navajo custom. Fortunately, a Navajo custom concerning adoption existed.

The Navajo conception of adoption is quite different from the American concept, which envisions adoption in terms of duties. In the American concept of child rearing, the natural parents have duties towards their children, and when those duties are breached, social services may take children away and give them to more worthy parents. Navajos, on the other hand, believe that familial relationships are ruled by mutual expectations, rather than obligations. "Desirable actions on the part of others are hoped for and even expected, but they are not required or demanded."[252] Therefore, the court stated that the Navajo view of the relationship of children to parents is not a simple parent-child relationship, but a pattern of expectation and desirable action surrounding children.[253] Furthermore, according to Navajo common law,[254] children are supposed to be taken care of, not just by their parents, but also by their clan members.[255]

The court stressed that Navajo adoption is also not necessarily permanent. "Adoption is merely a case of taking the children into the home for a limited time, or permanently, by extending family or parental agreement."[256] Navajo law is therefore concerned with the relationship of the child to a group, which shares the expectation that its members will take care of each other's children. Navajo common law deemphasizes the termination of parental rights.[257] Navajo adoption is thus informal and based upon community expectations.

The court noted that the Navajo tribal council is presumed to have these Navajo common law beliefs in mind when they enact statutes.[258] The tribal council has enacted laws that state that family ties should be preserved and strengthened whenever possible. The Navajo adoption policy states that the Navajo Nation favors formal adoption when the parents are dead, or when the children have been regularly and continuously neglected or abandoned.[259] The statute goes on to state that the Nation neither favors nor disfavors adoption of Navajo children by parents who are not members, and will consider each case individually.[260] Ultimately, the court held that in this case, an extended clan member (Ms. Chee, a maternal cousin) had stepped forth to assume her responsibility to care for the child, and she should be awarded custody instead of the nonmember.[261]

A couple of other Navajo Nation Supreme Court cases warrant a short discussion, even though they are not ICWA cases, because they concerned custody disputes between divorced couples, which is explicitly exempted in ICWA.[262] In *In re T.M.*, custody of the appellant (T.M.) was awarded to the father because the mother failed to comply with prior court orders. The appellant intervened and requested to be returned to the mother's custody, cease forced visitation with the father, and that therapy be ordered for the father and mother. The court stated that there was a legal fiction that children were not able to speak for themselves. The appellant cited the UN Convention on the Rights of the Child to support his position that because the child is capable of forming his own views, that he has "the right to express those views freely in all matters affecting [him, and that] the views of the child be ... given due weight in accordance with the age and maturity of the child."[263]

The Navajo Nation Supreme Court noted that although the Navajo Nation is not a state party to the Convention, and neither is the United States, the views in article 12 are consistent with Navajo common law. Thus, the court held that under the proper situation, a child may intervene in an action between his or her parents if, after an examination of the child's best interests and whether those interests are adequately represented by existing parties, the trial court determines that intervention is necessary. In this particular case, however, the court determined that intervention was not necessary, but that a spokesperson should be appointed. A spokesperson differs from a guardian *ad litem* in that they are not required to do an independent review of the facts and make recommendations, but to merely make the child's wishes known. This remedy not only allows the child to be heard but also follows the Navajo belief that "'it's up to him,' meaning that the individual must be consulted before action affecting his interest can be taken."[264]

In *In re A.O.*,[265] the Navajo mother and Anglo father were involved in a protracted custody dispute in state court when the mother took the child and returned to the reservation, where she filed a Petition for Adjudication of a Dependent Child, claiming that the father had sexually abused the child.[266] The father filed a Motion to Dismiss because of lack of jurisdiction, and the trial court granted the motion.[267] The Navajo Nation Supreme Court ultimately held that regardless of the proceedings in other jurisdictions, the Navajo Nation Children's Court had a duty to decide its jurisdiction and list findings of fact, which it did not do.[268] Thus, the court remanded the case back to the trial level for findings of fact.[269] The interesting part of this case is the reasoning that the court used for its holding. The ruling was justified in light of the Navajo Nation's recognized interest in its children, as stated in ICWA that "there is no resource that is more vital to the continued existence and integrity of Indian

Tribes than their children."[270] Thus, the court used ICWA's purpose as a justification for the creation of its own ruling based upon Navajo laws

The low number of would-be ICWA cases that have reached the Navajo Nation Supreme Court is surprising. Several possibilities exist, including that these cases are generally not appealed. However, it is difficult to imagine a more emotion-filled topic than those involving children and adoption. Another possibility is that because state courts seem to be withholding the transfer of ICWA cases, the difficult cases may never reach the Navajo Nation Supreme Court. While that may be true, I believe that a stronger theory is that the Navajo Nation places more of an emphasis on family preservation. Thus, families that are experiencing difficulties while living on the reservation are met with a culturally appropriate system designed to utilize the strengths that already exist in the family, and build up from there to cover the weaknesses. If I am correct in believing that these troubled families receive care that is better geared towards Navajo culture and therefore a positive outcome, then these ICWA-type cases would not see as much court action—partly because the families are more frequently preserved, and partly because if there is an out-of-home placement, it is with extended family and the natural parents do not disagree.

Although tribal custom is not used to the same degree that we see in the Navajo cases, custom does factor into tribal court decisions in South Dakota as well. In *Miner v. Banley*, the Cheyenne River Sioux Tribal Court of Appeals held that in evaluating the best interest of the child, the children's court must evaluate the needs of the minor for stability and the "physical, emotional, and cultural appropriateness of the placement."[271] Cultural factors include the ability of the placement family to familiarize the child with Lakota customs, traditions, and practices, and the Lakota tradition of returning the child to biological parents upon request. The case was ultimately decided on the grounds that an ex parte communication between the social worker and judge prevented one party from receiving a fair hearing, because they could not respond to the accusations. The court ruled that in evaluating the best interests of the child, the court cannot unduly hinder the rights of the parties to be heard.

An unusual issue of whose version of tribal custom to accept was litigated in *Barrera v. Poorman*.[272] This case came out of the Rosebud Sioux Tribal Court of Appeals in 1987. Here, the natural mother and Poorman were cousins and, according to Lakota custom, members of the same extended family. The mother gave Poorman custody of the child; however, the father, Barrera, petitioned for a change of custody to legitimate his claim to his child. The court held that it was the "universal right of a natural parent . . . to have custody of their own children absent a clear showing of gross misconduct or unfitness or some sound and compelling reason for denying it and that right is superior we find *even* in Lakota custom and belief." Although the court does not engage in a more detailed analysis of their interpretation that natural parents have superior rights over other Lakota extended-family members, they nevertheless were faced with two customs and unanimously agreed on the proper Lakota custom.

Unlike the previously discussed tribal courts, the Pascua Yaqui Tribal Court does not publish its decisions, making them nearly impossible to obtain. The Pascua Yaqui Tribal Council enacted the *Resolutions Adopting the Pascua Yaqui Tribe Child Welfare Policy Act* in 2002.[273] The recent date of the resolution suggests that while the tribal council was concerned about the issue of child welfare, they were only recently in the economic position to create and enforce tribal law on this topic. The resolution starts by stating that the preservation of Yaqui families is critical to the survival of the Pascua Yaqui Tribe, and ICWA recognizes the tribe's authority to enforce tribal law in state child welfare cases.[274]

In the Findings section of the act, it states that a survey of Yaqui families concluded that Yaqui members believe that children should be placed with extended family or other Yaqui families if their parents cannot properly care for them, and that Yaqui families do not believe that Yaqui children should be placed in state foster care.[275] The Findings go on to give a brief history of the necessity of this act. It states that at the time of the act, there were approximately sixty child dependency cases involving Yaqui children—approximately thirty in state court and thirty in tribal court.[276] The tribe acknowledged that they have not consistently exercised their sovereignty to transfer jurisdiction to tribal court, and in fact, only two cases had been transferred prior to 2002.[277]

Interestingly, the Pascua Yaqui Tribe Child Welfare Policy Act alters the placement preferences of ICWA. The following placement preferences are for both temporary and permanent placements, including foster care, permanent guardianship, and adoption. A Yaqui child shall be placed, in order of preference, with a local Yaqui extended family member, a local non-Yaqui extended family member, a local non-related Yaqui family, a local Indian family, a non-local Yaqui extended family member, a non-local Yaqui family, a non-local Indian family, and finally a non-local non-Indian family.[278] It is clear from these placement preferences that a placement close to the tribal community is of utmost importance to the tribe, as this would facilitate the continued incorporation of the child for tribal ceremonies.

The act goes on to set additional requirements if a Yaqui child is placed with a non-Yaqui family. These include that the child should have reasonable access to Yaqui family members; that if they wish to attend the tribe's cultural and religious ceremonies, the tribe's social services department must be notified so that appropriate arrangements can be made; that the child's name cannot be changed; that all correspondence from the tribe must be accepted; that the tribe must be kept informed of all address changes; that the tribe's social services department must be allowed to conduct reviews at least two times per year upon adequate advance notice from the tribe; that if the non-Yaqui family placement or parental rights are at risk, the tribe must be notified immediately.[279]

Similar to the Navajo common law disfavoring of termination of parental rights, the Pascua Yaqui Act prefers family reunification.[280] If reunification is not possible, the preference is placement in foster care or permanent guardianship with an extended family member, and only when absolutely necessary, termination of parental rights and adoption.[281] Lastly, the act establishes a Family Preservation Office in the Department of sSocial sServices.[282] This office will target at-risk families and develop a Child and Family Services Plan that reflects the tribe's preference for placing children with Yaqui families.[283] Having a centralized system in place to handle child welfare issues will increase efficiency and allow the tribe to focus on preservation.

Again, the fact that before the passage of the *Resolutions* the Pascua Yaqui Tribe had a department of social services but no separate family preservation office seems to support the theory that the tribe's slower evolution and ability to adequately take over these programs stems from a lack of resources. In support of this position, the act mentions that the family preservation office will aggressively obtain resources to support the office and its programs.[284] It also states that the tribe will negotiate a Title IV-E funds-sharing agreement with the State of Arizona.[285] Both provisions indicate that when creating this policy act, funding was a dominant issue in the minds of the tribal council.

Unlike both the Navajo Nation and the Pascua Yaqui Tribe, the White Mountain Apache have adopted ICWA in its entirety. In their juvenile code, the tribe reiterated that ICWA's purpose is to protect the best interests of the White Mountain Apache children and to promote the stability and security of the tribe.[286] The code recognizes that White Mountain Apache children would be "best served through the Tribal Judicial system which can implement as it always has, the Indian Child Welfare Act of 1978 and the rules and regulations promulgated by the Secretary of the Interior in Title 25 CFR parts 13 and 23 as well as the recommended guidelines for state court—Indian child custody proceedings."[287] It is unusual to see a tribe adopt fully ICWA, as a large number of tribes that have specifically addressed the issue feel that ICWA does not directly apply to them, although they do support it with respect to requirements placed upon the states.

The White Mountain Apache also have a "Termination and Restoration of Parental Rights" chapter in their juvenile code. This section does not set out a standard of proof required for termination of parental rights. Recall that ICWA requires that there be clear and convincing evidence that continued custody of the child by the parent is likely to result in serious emotional or physical damage to the child, and that termination of parental rights requires evidence beyond a reasonable doubt.[288] The White Mountain code allows the juvenile court to terminate parental rights if the "Court finds that the parents are: (1) unfit and incompetent to care and provide for such child and no alternatives are feasible ...; (2) habitually engages in conduct detrimental to the health, safety or welfare of the child; (3) wilfully [sic] refuse to care or provide for the child when able to do so; (4) are unable to care and provide for the child by reason of physical or mental incapacity; or (5) have abandoned the child."[289]

The White Mountain Apache code is also unusual in that termination of parental rights does not seem to be disfavored. There is no explicit statement that termination is disfavored, as in the Navajo Nation and Pascua Yaqui legislation, and there is little pomp and circumstance to the termination of parental rights. However, the code does state that whether "a child is delinquent or in need of supervision shall not be grounds for termination of parental rights."[290] Interestingly, the code provides that all terminations of parental rights are interlocutory in nature, and are thus subject to review within one year.[291] Furthermore, they may be immediately appealed by the parents.[292]

In addition, within six months, the parents may petition the court for "revocation of its termination order and restoration of parental rights on the grounds that a substantial change of circumstances has occurred which requires such revocation and restoration in the best interest of the child."[293] Thus, even though the code appears to take a rather hard stance on termination of parental rights, the fact that it is interlocutory and that parental rights can be restored seems to support the underlying message that the tribe does not wish to terminate parental rights unless absolutely necessary.

Reminiscent of White Mountain's full adoption of ICWA, the Northern Plains Intertribal Court of Appeals adopted the view that tribal courts were required to utilize the standards set out in ICWA for termination of parental rights. In *In re DeCoteau, Jr.*, a father's parental rights were terminated by the tribal court after he was imprisoned for severely beating his wife as the child watched. The child was an infant at the time, and by the time the case reached the appellate court, the child was two-and-a half-years old and had little bonding with the father. Not only did the appellate court require that the tribal court use the "beyond a reasonable doubt" standard, but it also endorsed the use of an expert witness to provide proof that continued custody would likely result in harm to the child.

A short, but strongly worded dissent by Judge Godtland stated that the "majority misplaces its reliance on the Indian Child Welfare Act.... The Act reflects congressional intent and federal policy to defer to tribal authority on matters concerning the custody of tribal children. Except for peripheral sections, ICWA does not apply to Indian children in tribal court."[294] This ruling is clearly an outlier in tribal jurisprudence.[295] Not only does it cramp the use of custom in decision making, but it also would be difficult to implement by many tribes due to budget constraints. As more ICWA decisions are made and reaffirmed on the reservation in tribal courts, more Indian children will obtain their family preservation services on-reservation. Many tribes are beginning to realize that the same cultural differences that sometimes prevent state courts from making the best decisions regarding their children also exist in the state social services system. Therefore, several tribes have begun to implement their own family preservation models, which draw upon their unique culture to help heal families.

Family Preservation Services

The use of tribal custom in tribal court decisions, along with creative family preservation services, goes a long way to further the goals encapsulated in ICWA. States, however, are still struggling with high numbers of Indian children in out-of-home placements. For example, in Minnesota, Indian children still make up 11 percent of out-of-home placements, although they only constitute just under 2 percent of the population.[296] The type of family preservation services and theories that are used by state social services and tribal social services plays a central role in the outcomes among Indian families in their service areas. The models used in family preservation programs can imprecisely, but helpfully, be categorized into two divergent theories.

The first model is geared toward "the provision of intensive brief services" to children in imminent danger of out-of-home placement, and the other is a family-support model emphasizing programs that provide a "range of continuously available primary prevention (FPS [family preservation services]) to all families" in perceived need of support.[297] Western family preservation services emphasize intense, short-term, multi-agency crisis intervention to stabilize the family.[298] These types of models can be characterized as dysfunction-based family preservation, which slowly began in the mid-twentieth century when social work turned towards individualist explanations of family and social dynamics.[299] Under this model, families were labeled as "inadequate" and lacking in certain characteristics and skills.[300] Some scholars have condemned this, saying that "such labeling puts into motion an adversarial relationship whereby the child welfare system views the best interest of Indian children as separate from parent and extended family relationships."[301] Once a child is removed from his/her home, "a determination of the child's best interest is based upon predicting which parents, biological or psychological [adopted/foster], will best serve the child."[302]

In contrast, the second family support model, which encompasses long-term continuous primary prevention, is a better fit for tribal cultures. This model can be termed "strength-based family preservation," and includes wraparound and multisystems approaches. The goal of strength-based social work is to facilitate a process of capacity-building within families.[303] These models emphasize empowerment from sources such as internal family supports, informal community assets, or formal services. Family members are not passive subjects or clients, but participants in the decision-making process regarding their treatment plans. The multisystems approach emphasizes family strengths by "recasting the cause of family issues from individual and family pathology to existence of constraints." This is in contrast to traditional deficit-based family preservation, which seeks to identify constraints, remove them, and allow the family to learn proper parenting. "Wraparound" is one multisystems, strength-based approach that focuses on individual needs and makes active linkages to the community. This model has received much acclaim from tribal scholars because it mirrors traditional tribal practice.[304]

There are several differences between the two models that make the later, strength-based wraparound model better suited for tribal cultures. First, as mentioned above, the wraparound model allows family members to be involved in the process of creating a family preservation plan.[305] Second, this model highlights what a family is doing right, and provides services to help the family change actions that are not positive for the family.[306] This change in perspective can be empowering, as families will feel that their situation is not hopeless and are able to progress towards a better family environment. Third, the wraparound model often involves smaller caseloads and emphasizes the social worker going to the family instead of requiring the family to find transportation, which is a huge problem on many reservations.[307] Fourth, this model allows the child to participate in decision making, which empowers the child and demonstrates that the child is invested in making the process work.[308] Fifth, this model extends the mainstream "nuclear" family to include extended family, kin and clan relations, community, and tribe.[309] Sixth, this model emphasizes using community members in the provision of family preservation services to instill trust in the families.[310] The belief that there are no failures is a principal feature in Fort Berthold family preservation policy, which is an excellent case study. The close connection of tribal communities allows one worker to state, "These are our relatives; we don't give up on our relatives."[311]

Forth Berthold Reservation's tribally run family preservation program exemplifies the strength-based traits. The program serves the Arikara, Hidatsa, and Mandan tribes of North Dakota.[312] Fundamental changes occurred in family services on the Fort Berthold Reservation in the early 1990s, when they developed and implemented their own programs using their own staff. The centerpiece of the Fort Berthold family preservation program is called "Sacred Child Project." This project uses wraparound theory, but reshapes it to fit tribal customs and reinforce extended-family systems already in place. The child picks a team of four to ten people, with the requirement that the majority must be some type of relative. The family discusses with the social worker what the plan should encompass, but it is ultimately the child's decision what to focus on. The child is allowed to pick three "life domains," which include spiritual, family, living situation, financial, educational and vocational, social and recreational, behavioral and emotional, psychological, health, legal, cultural, and safety.[313] By giving the child the self-determination to make their own choices, the children feel invested in the family preservation service, and they are an integral part in ensuring that the family does not break up.

Although several tribes across the country, like Fort Berthold, have implemented these powerful programs, many tribes have only implemented parts of these theories. Many tribal family preservation programs are still modeled after the mainstream deficit-based models. This is not to say that mainstream programs have not made some strides. These programs attempt to train their social workers to be more sensitive to cultural differences.[314] However, as Deborah Painte, director of the Sacred Child Project, said, "It's not how you integrate culture into services but how you integrate services into culture.'[315] Norma Martinez from Pasqua Yaqui also stated, "The tribes that have really been successful are those that have a broad vision—it's hard but it's worth it. When you try new things, it raises eyebrows. Social services had to take risks."[316]

Arizona tribes have implemented some of these theories to varying degrees. Some tribes have incorporated wraparound theories but still maintain vestiges of the mainstream deficit-based system, while others have incrementally overhauled their family preservation programs. For example, the Pascua Yaqui Tribe operates their own social services program, which has found that tribal members are resistant to intensive in-home services.[317] Thus, the tribe utilizes an extended and less invasive service plan in order to ensure that families stay with the program. In addition, Pascua Yaqui Social Services relies heavily upon informal support such as extended family members, elders, and especially religious leaders. However, the tribe still utilizes the same procedures as the state for determining which families are at risk,[318] and mirrors services provided by the state, such as psycho-education, family therapy, and one-on-one therapy.[319] Again, this is not to say that these services are not helpful, but merely to point out that these services are copied from the state service plan and may not be as culturally relevant as some more traditional methods. Tribes would be well served to implement some of the theories of strength-based multisystems wraparound services.

One tribe that has reevaluated and renovated their family preservation program is the Navajo Nation. Just over four years ago, Ronald Phillips designed the "K'e Project" for the Office of Promoting Safe and Stable Families, which provides more culturally appropriate family preservation techniques.[320] This program uses Navajo philosophies such as *k'e* and *hozho* to teach proper Dine parenting techniques. *K'e* is based upon respect and one's universal relationship with everyone and everything around them.[321] "*K'e* incorporates many values that bind [an] individual to family, clan, Navajos in general, and all people."[322] *Hozho* is also associated with kinship and relations, meaning that "there is a place for everything in this universe and there is harmony when everything is in its place, working well with everything else."[323]

Phillips reiterated the Pascua Yaqui observation, saying that Dine families usually take more time to open up to social workers, so the intensive Band-Aid style of family preservation that the state utilizes simply does not work with traditional Navajos. He stated that it usually takes at least one to two months to gain a rapport with his clients. His program focuses on high-risk families, such as ones that already have one child removed. Phillips also mentioned the importance of having community members as social workers, especially for the more traditional Navajos, who speak the Dine language instead of using jargon.[324]

The K'e Project teaches that there are two types of parenting techniques: 1) the Monster Way and 2) the Blessing Way. The Monster Way teaches children not to be lazy, by using an assertive voice when communicating with the child. Traditionally, children would run towards the east each morning to signify respect for the Monster Way. The Monster Way also teaches that the best time to talk to children and tell them moral teachings is in the morning when they are not quite awake yet, because this is when their brains are the most receptive to learning and guidance. In contrast, the Blessing Way is kind and caring. It is a passive method of parenting and allows the children to come into their own knowledge by experience. Phillips states that the counseling and teachings that he provides should allow a parent to know when the appropriate time is to do each one.[325]

Phillips teaches families to strive to live in *hozho* or "the perfect state."[326] He teaches them that there are four sacred mountains, four sacred colors, and four sacred cardinal directions.[327] Each of these have specific meanings and should be prayed to and lived by. As a brief example, the East represents the standards of life; the South represents how you make your living (thus, your work tools should be kept in the south of your house); the West represents your social competence, kinship, social skills, and storytelling; the North represents respect for nature, food, and animals.[328]

Lastly, the Navajo program teaches about the use of spiritual methods to help stabilize the family. Many clients believe that ceremonies cost a prohibitive amount of money, but the reality is that there are numerous ceremonies that the family can do on their own, or that do not require as much capital as the larger, more elaborate ceremonies.[329] For example, instead of hosting a Blessing Way ceremony, which is a grand event, the family could simply have a medicine man do a private blessing.[330] An even more frugal approach would be to do a family blessing with hot ashes, a cedar ceremony, a smoke ceremony, or even a talking circle.[331] These are all alternatives that families can take advantage of in order to achieve *hozho*.

Conclusion

States differ in their evolution of ICWA jurisprudence, but some generalizations can be made regarding important issues in ICWA implementation. Arizona has struggled through the aspects of ICWA that deal with exclusive tribal jurisdiction, and is now focusing on the more nebulous concurrent jurisdiction provisions. South Dakota, on the other hand, has been reexamining many earlier decisions. The issues of utilizing a modified version of *forum non conveniens* in order to justify good cause not to transfer is playing an increasingly more important role in ICWA jurisprudence of both Arizona and South Dakota. South Dakota has struggled with what constitutes the minimum requirements of notice to the tribe, which should be a simple provision in ICWA. Arizona, on the other hand, has developed a rather lax definition of what constitutes an expert witness, especially compared to South Dakota. Furthermore, Arizona has not yet dealt with the effect that the ASFA will have on ICWA. Given the importance of this issue, the courts will likely have to grapple with it soon. Happily, many of the problems that arise can be eased through increased communication between state social services and tribes.

As tribes and the state begin to build long-term relationships, the level of mutual understanding should be increased. For example, the state will begin to understand what types of information they must provide in order to obtain quick and accurate enrollment information. Tribes have an important role in ensuring that ICWA is properly implemented in state courts. Not only must the tribe monitor cases involving Indian children currently in state court, but they should take a proactive role in educating state social workers, politicians, lawyers, and judges about their culture and ICWA. Tribes should be willing to work with states to help incorporate cultural elements into state-run family preservation programs. Although states will not be able to duplicate the tribal programs, they can learn to be more culturally sensitive, and therefore help alleviate some of the individual tensions that occur when state social workers interact with tribal members.

In general, tribes should continue to focus their efforts on family preservation programs and on obtaining proper Indian out-of-home placements for Indian children who must be removed from their home. Because of the close-knit communities present on many reservations, once a child is placed out-of-home, usually with either a relative or other tribal member, the parents are often allowed to maintain a relationship with the children while they focus on their family preservation plan. Again, many tribes follow the Navajo belief that although you can legally terminate parental rights, you cannot terminate clan or kinship rights because those ties never break.

It has been nearly thirty years since ICWA was enacted. As noted, although much improvement has been made, especially in certain states, there is still more that can be done. Arizona has been working with tribes and has implemented an ICWA workgroup that meets regularly. This workgroup allows interested parties to discuss problems and solutions to tribal and state relationships in implementing ICWA. Similarly, in 2004 the South Dakota legislature established the Governor's

Commission on ICWA, charging them to study ICWA compliance in South Dakota. Innovative programs such as these allow seemingly divergent interests to see that their interests are more aligned than they may initially believe. ICWA is one of the most interesting aspects of Indian law because nearly all parties involved, whether it be state social workers, tribal social workers, state attorneys and judges, tribal attorneys and judges, Indian parents, Indian extended families, or Indian children, are benevolently motivated. They all have the best interests of the child at heart. They just approach the problem from a different cultural perspective, and often without fully understanding the other side.

NOTES

The author would like to thank Professors Barbara Atwood, Robert Williams, Nancy Parezo, and Jay Stauss for their time, effort, and encouragement in this endeavor.

1. Rose is a pseudonym.
2. 25 U.S.C. § 1901 et seq. (2000).
3. Lorie M. Graham, *"The Past Never Vanishes": A Contextual Critique of the Existing Indian Family Doctrine*, 23 AM. INDIAN L. REV. 1, 53–54 (1998). *See also* H.R. 1448 Hearing to Amend ICWA before the Committee on Indian Affairs, 103rd Cong., 2nd Sess. (1995) (Statement of Terry Cross, director of the National Indian Child Welfare Association, recounting story of a Navajo woman and her children), *reprinted at* 1995 WL 283199.
4. According to a House Report, the high rate of out-of-home placements of Indian children was often a product of state child welfare agents' lack of understanding of American Indian culture and child-rearing practices. The report concluded that in only 1 percent of cases were Indian children taken from their homes for physical abuse; thus the rest of the cases stemmed from neglect, which in reality was perceived neglect due to cultural differences in child rearing. H.R. Rep. No. 1386, 95th Cong., 2d Sess. 10 (1978).
5. H.R. Rep. No. 1386, 95th Cong., 2d Sess. 10 (1978).
6. Indian Child Welfare Program Hearings before the Subcomm. on Indian Affairs, U.S. Senate, 93rd Cong., 2d Sess. 15 (Apr. 8, 1974), reprinted in [1978] U.S. Code Cong. & Ad. News 7530, 7531 (Statement of William Byler, executive director of the AAIA).
7. *Id.*
8. 93rd Cong., 2d Sess. 1, 3 (1974).
9. *Id.*
10. 25 U.S.C. § 1901 et seq. (2000).
11. U.S. Gen. Acct. Off., *Indian Child Welfare Act: Existing Information on Implementation Issues Could be Used to Target Guidance and Assistance to States*, Rep. No. GAO-05-290 (April 2005), *available at* http://www.nicwa.org/policy/law/icwa/GAO_report.pdf#search='GAO%20ICWA'.

12. *Id.* at 2.
13. ICWA contains no provision for agency oversight. HHS does not have specific oversight authority with respect to ICWA, but it is responsible for ensuring that states provide meaningful information about ICWA compliance as part of Title IV-B reporting requirements. *Id.* at 58. HHS also has issued guidance to states on ICWA implementation; however HHS insists that they do not have the authority to hold states accountable for lack of implementation. *Id.* at appendix 3 at 79: Comments from the Department of Health and Human Services, dated March 21, 2005.
14. One of the largest problems with studying ICWA is that very little statistical data is available to form accurate conclusions about the effectiveness of ICWA implementation and formulate strategies for future action.
15. Interview with tribal attorney (Nov. 29, 2005) (interviewee requested not to be named in the footnote due to employment concerns).
16. Many people seem to believe that a tribal court cannot objectively decide what is in the best interests of the child. The reality is, however, that tribes can and do decide what is in the best interest of the child in an objective manner. For example, in *In re Adoption of Halloway*, 732 P.2d 962 (Utah 1986), the case was transferred from Utah court to the Navajo Nation court, where the Navajo Nation tribal court decided that although the child was Navajo, because of the bonding that had occurred over many years of living with the non-Indian family, it was in the Navajo child's best interest to remain with that family, but return to the Navajo reservation during the summer months. *In re Halloway*, WR-JV-CV-71-84 (Nav. Window Rock Dist. Ct., Nov. 10, 1987) (unpublished opinion on file with author).
17. U.S. Gen. Acct. Off., *Indian Child Welfare Act: Existing Information on Implementation Issues Could Be Used to Target Guidance and Assistance to States*, Rep. No. GAO-05-290 at 16–17 (April 2005), *available at* http://www.nicwa.org/policy/law/icwa/GAO_report.pdf#search= GAO%20ICWA.' *See also* Eddie F. Brown, Gordon E. Limb, Toni Chance, and Ric Munoz, *The Indian Child Welfare Act: An Examination of State Compliance in Arizona at 14* (December 2002), *available at* http://www.nicwa.org/resources/catalog/research/2002/01.ICWAAriz02.Rpt.pdf.
18. *Id.* at 16.
19. Interview with tribal attorney (Nov. 29, 2005) (interviewee requested not to be named in the footnote due to employment concerns).
20. John G. Red Horse, Cecilia Martinez, and Priscilla Day, *Family Preservation: A Case Study of Indian Tribal Practice* (December 2001), *available at* http://www.nicwa.org/resources/catalog/research/2001/01.Family%20Pres01.Rpt.pdf.
21. *Id.* at 17–22 (December 2001) *available at* http://www.nicwa.org/resources/catalog/research/2001/01.Family%20Pres01.Rpt.pdf. *See also* Scott W. Henggeler, *Multisystemic Therapy, Paradigm* (Winter 1999); Fred Wulczyn, *Family Reunification, Future of Children* (Winter 2004).
22. 25 U.S.C. § 1902 (1978); *See also* Roger A. Tellinghuisen, *The Indian Child Welfare Act of 1978: A Practical Guide with [Limited] Commentary*, 34 S.D. L. REV. 660 (1988–89).
23. 25 U.S.C. § 1901(3) (1978).
24. *See generally* 25 U.S.C. § 1902 (1978); *In re* Appeal in Pima County Juv. Action No. S-903, 130 Ariz.

202, 204, 635 P.2d 187, 189 (1981).
25. 25 U.S.C. § 1911(a) (2000) ("An Indian tribe shall have jurisdiction exclusive as to any State over any child custody proceeding involving an Indian child who resides or is domiciled within the reservation of such tribe, except where such jurisdiction is otherwise vested in the State by existing Federal law. Where an Indian child is a ward of a tribal court, the Indian tribe shall retain exclusive jurisdiction, notwithstanding the residence or domicile of the child.").
26. 25 U.S.C. § 1911(b) (2000) ("In any State court proceeding for the foster care placement of, or termination of parental rights to, an Indian child not domiciled or residing within the reservation of the Indian child's tribe, the court, in the absence of good cause to the contrary, shall transfer such proceeding to the jurisdiction of the tribe, absent objection by either parent, upon the petition of either parent or the Indian custodian or the Indian child's tribe: Provided, That such transfer shall be subject to declination by the tribal court of such tribe.").
27. *Id.* Included among the reasons that a tribe may decline transfer are that they do not have a tribal court or do not have enough funding to handle all of ICWA cases that come from urban areas.
28. *Id.*
29. 25 U.S.C. § 1911(c) (2000) ("In any State court proceeding ... the Indian child's tribe shall have a right to intervene at any point in the proceeding.").
30. 25 U.S.C. § 1911(d) (2000).
31. 25 U.S.C. § 1912(a) (2000).
32. 25 U.S.C. § 1912(d) (2000).
33. 25 U.S.C. § 1912(e) (2000).
34. 25 U.S.C. § 1912(f) (2000).
35. 25 U.S.C. § 1913(a) (2000).
36. 25 U.S.C. § 1913(b)-(c) (2000).
37. 25 U.S.C. § 1916(a) (2000).
38. 25 U.S.C. § 1914 (2000).
39. 25 U.S.C. § 1915(a) (2000).
40. 25 U.S.C. § 1915(b) (2000).
41. 25 U.S.C. § 1915(c) (2000). *See infra* note 274.
42. 25 U.S.C. § 1931-34 (2000).
43. RANDALL KENNEDY, INTERRACIAL INTIMACIES: SEX, MARRIAGE, IDENTITY, AND ADOPTION (Pantheon Books 2003) (providing an excellent historical analysis of American race relations from the rape and sexual exploitation of black women by white men to our sad history of racial classifications and laws banning interracial marriages and adoptions).
44. *Id.* at 416. When a case is brought to court, a judge normally rules based on prior precedent or decisions that the same court has handed down on the issue before. When a case is decided on a case-by-case basis, it means that the judge will look at each case on its own without looking to precedent.
45. *Id.* at 485.

46. *Id.* at 486.
47. *Id.*
48. Randall Kennedy, *supra* note 43, at 488–99.
49. *Id.* at 490–92.
50. *Id.* at 492.
51. *Id.* at 491–92.
52. *Id.* at 497.
53. *Id.*
54. *Id.* at 497–99.
55. *Id.* at 497.
56. *Id.* at 498 (citing B. J. JONES, THE INDIAN CHILD WELFARE ACT HANDBOOK 111 (American Bar Association 1995)).
57. *Id.* at 499.
58. *Id.* at 500.
59. *Id. See also* Carol Locust, *Split Feathers…Adult American Indians Who Were Placed in Non-Indian Families as Children*, 44 ONTARIO ASSOCIATION OF CHILDREN'S AID SOCIETIES (3) (2000) (tracking twenty Indian adults who were adopted by non-Indian families, but susceptible to many of the same criticisms as Dr. Westermeyer's study).
60. *Id.* at 501–02 (citing Dr. Joseph Westermeyer, *The Apple Syndrome in Minnesota A Complication of Racial-Ethnic Discontinuity*, 10 JOURNAL OF OPERATIONAL PSYCHIATRY 134 (1979)).
61. Joint Hearing by the Senate Select Committee on Indian Affairs and the House Committee on Interracial and Insular Affairs, Indian Child Welfare, 93d Cong., 2d Sess. (April 8–9, 1974).
62. S. 3777, 94th Cong, 2d. Sess. (1976).
63. S. 1214, 95th Cong., 1st Sess. (April 1, 1977).
64. H.R. 12533, 95th Cong., 2d. Sess. (1978).
65. President Carter signed ICWA on November 8, 1978.
66. The Convention on Protection of Children and Co-operation in respect of Intercountry Adoption (The Hague Convention), 32 I.L.M. 1134 (May 29, 1993); Intercountry Adoption Act, 42 U.S.C. §§ 14901–954 (2004). The Hague Convention built upon the Convention on the Rights of the Child, 1577 U.N.T.S. 3, 28 I.L.M. 1448 (Nov. 20, 1989), *available at* http://www.unhchr.ch/html/menu3/b/k2crc.htm (accessed Apr. 10, 2006). Interestingly, the United States is one of very few countries that has not ratified this convention; however, several bills have been introduced urging ratification. Although "a treaty has been sometimes said to have force of law only if ratified," courts often use nonratified treaties as aids in statutory construction. *Beharry v. Reno*, 183 F. Supp. 2D 584, 593 (E.D.N Y. 2002), rev'd. on other grounds, *Beharry v. Ashcroft*, 329 F.3d 51 (2d Cir. 2003).
67. Randall Kennedy, *supra* 43, at 497–99.
68. 41 Cal. App.4th 1483, 1512, 49 Cal. Rptr.2d 507 (1996). In *In re Bridget R.*, the California appellate court wrote a lengthy analysis justifying the existence of the Existing Indian Family exception on the grounds that without such an exception, the Act would be unconstitutional. The court

held that without the exception, ICWA's "application runs afoul of the Constitution in three ways: (1) it impermissibly intrudes upon a power ordinarily reserved to the states [which violates the 10th Amendment of the Constitution], (2) it improperly interferes with Indian children's fundamental due-process rights respecting family relationships; and (3) on the sole basis of race, it deprives them of equal opportunities to be adopted that are available to non-Indian children." The court applied a strict scrutiny test, which requires that ICWA serve a compelling governmental interest, be narrowly tailored, and be the least restrictive means of serving that compelling governmental interest. While the court conceded that there was a compelling state interest in protecting tribal stability, it held that ICWA's purpose of preserving Indian culture would not be served by applying it to children who did not have a significant relationship with an Indian community. *See infra* note 115.

69. Randall Kennedy, supra note 43, at 511.
70. *Id.* at 506.
71. *Id.* at 507–08.
72. *Id.* at 508.
73. *Id.*
74. Randall Kennedy, supra note 43, at 509–11.
75. *Id.* at 506; *See also* Carole Goldberg, *Descent into Race*, 49 UCLA L. REV. 1373, 1387 (2002).
76. *Id.*
77. *Id.* at 513.
78. *Id.* at 513, 518.
79. *Id.* at 513.
80. *Id.* at 35.
81. *Id.* at 488, 504–11; *See also* Barbara Atwood, *Fighting over Indian Children: The Uses and Abuses of Jurisdictional Ambiguity*, 36 UCLA L. REV. 1051 (1989) (discussing the complicated jurisdictional issues that arise from ICWA).
82. *Id.* at 513–16; *See also* Christine Metteer, *Hard Cases Making Bad Law: The Need for Revision of the Indian Child Welfare Act*, 38 SANTA CLARA L. REV. 419, 444–59 (1998).
83. *Id.* at 514.
84. *Id.* at 504–11.
85. *See generally* Christine Metteer, *Pigs in Heaven: A Parable of Native American Adoption under the Indian Child Welfare Act*, 28 ARIZ. ST. L. J. 589, 608 (1996) (discussing the difficulties arising from courts ignoring the Act definition of Indian and creating their own determination of Indianness).
86. Randall Kennedy, *supra* note 43, at 516.
87. Margaret F. Brinig, *The Child's Best Interests: A Neglected Perspective on Interracial Intimacies*, 117 HARV. L. REV. 2129 (2004).
88. *Id.* at 2148.
89. Nicole L. Sault, *Many Mothers, Many Fathers: The Meaning of Parenting around the World*, available at http://www.scu.edu/ethics/publications/other/lawreview/manymothers.html (accessed Apr. 20, 2006).

90. *Morton v. Mancari*, 417 U.S. 535 (1974).
91. Randall Kennedy, *supra* note 43, at 518.
92. 25 U.S.C. § 1903 (2006).
93. Consider how many U.S. citizens would be excluded if political affiliation were required.
94. *In re* Appeal in Pima County Juv. Action S-903, 130 Ariz. 202, 635 P.2d 187 (1981) (holding that the domicile of an Indian child is that of the mother); *Goclanney v. Desrochers*, 135 Ariz. 240, 660 P.2d 491 (1983) (holding that the domicile of a child is that of the mother); *In re* Appeal in Maricopa County Juv. Action No. A-25525, 136 Ariz. 528, 667 P.2d 228 (1983) (holding that Indianness must be established before any part of ICWA is applied, including notice to the tribe); *In re* Appeal in Maricopa County Juv. Action No. JS-7359, 159 Ariz. 232, 766 P.2d 105 (1989) (holding that you must perfect enrollment before ICWA applies).
95. *In re* Appeal in Maricopa County Juv. Action No. JS-8287, 171 Ariz. 104, 828 P.2d 1245 (1991) (holding that an out-of-state tribal court transfer can be denied because of *forum non conveniens*); *In re* Appeal in Maricopa County, Juv. Action No. JD-6982, 186 Ariz. 354, 922 P.2d 319 (1996) (holding that parental veto over transfer to tribal court is absolute); *Rachelle S. v. Arizona Dept. of Econ. Sec.*, 191 Ariz. 518, 958 P.2d 459 (1998) (holding that an expert witness does not need to be experienced on Indian culture if the culture is not relevant to their testimony); *Michael J., Jr. v. Michael J., Sr.*, 198 Ariz. 154, 7 P.3d 960 (2000) (affirming the rejection of the Existing Indian Family exception in Arizona courts).
96. 25 U.S.C. § 1911(a) (2006).
97. 130 Ariz. 202, 635 P.2d 187 (1981).
98. *Id.* at 204–05, 635 P.2d at 189–90.
99. *Id.* at 206, 635 P.2d at 191 (citing *Garay Uppen v. Super. Ct. of Pima County*, 116 Ariz. 81, 567 P.2d 1210 (app. 1977)).
100. *Id.* at 206, 635 P.2d at 191 (citing *Application of Morse*, 7 Utah 2d 312, 324 P.2d 773 (1958)). It should be noted, however, that this case was issued before *Mississippi Band of Choctaw Indians v. Holyfield*, which more or less resolved the dispute on bonding of an adoptive parent with an adoptive child by stating that "whatever feelings we might have as to where the twins should live, however, it is not for us to decide that question.... Had the mandate of ICWA been followed in 1986, of course, much potential anguish might have been avoided, and in any case the law cannot be applied so as automatically to 'reward those who obtain custody, whether lawfully or otherwise, and maintain it during any ensuing (and protracted) litigation.'" Although in *Holyfield*, the issue was whether the tribe had exclusive jurisdiction to hear the case and not the good cause exception of §1915, *Holyfield*'s language is widely known and is, at the very least, persuasive evidence of the Supreme Court's opinion on the import of foster parent bonding in the statute. 490 U.S. 30 (1989).
101. 130 Ariz. 202, 208, 635 P.2d 187, 193 (1981) (noting that appellant was entitled to the return of her child, and any potential emotional trauma to the child if the contemplated adoption is aborted was engendered by the conduct of the adoptive parents not adhering to the mandates of the Act).

102. *In re* Appeal in Maricopa County Juv. Action No. A-25525, 136 Ariz. 528, 530, 667 P.2d 228, 230 (1983).
103. *Id.* at 532–33, 667 P.2d at 232–33. The court went on to scold the Pima Indian community for unjustifiably waiting over a year to bring this claim. This recurring theme of courts annoyed at tribes for waiting to bring action in court can be seen as a background issue in many of the cases coming out of the Arizona and South Dakota courts.
104. 202 Ariz. 562, 48 P.3d 512 (2002).
105. *Id.* at 564–66, 48 P.3d 514–16.
106. 153 Ariz. 346, 736 P.2d 829 (1987).
107. *Id.* at 347, 736 P.2d 830.
108. *Id.*
109. *Id.* at 347–48, 736 P.2d at 830–31.
110. *Id.* at 348, 736 P.2d at 831.
111. *Id.* (citing 25 U.S.C. § 1912(e) (2000)).
112. *Id.*
113. *Id.* at 350, 736 P.2d at 833.
114. The Existing Indian Family doctrine holds that a child must come from an Indian family that lives on the reservation, have a deep connection with his or her tribe, or practice traditional culture to be an Indian child to whom ICWA applies. This doctrine has received heavy criticism as being an overt, judicially created exception that is contrary to the clear intention of ICWA; however, a detailed discussion of the history and its ramifications of the Existing Indian Family exception is beyond the scope of this paper. *See* Lorie M. Graham, *"The Past Never Vanishes": A Contextual Critique of the Existing Indian Family Doctrine*, 23 AM. INDIAN L. REV. 1 (1998); Barbara Ann Atwood, *Flashpoints under the Indian Child Welfare Act: Toward a New Understanding of State Court Resistance*, 51 EMORY L.J. 587 (2002); Charmel L. Cross, *The Existing Indian Family Exception: Is It Appropriate to Use a Judicially Created Exception to Render the Indian Child Welfare Act of 1978 Inapplicable?*, 26 CAP. U. L. REV. 847 (1997).
115. *In re Adoption of Baby Boy L*, 231 Kan. 199, 643 P.2d 168 (1982). The Kansas Supreme Court stated that "the overriding concern of Congress . . . was the maintenance of the family and tribal relationships existing in Indian homes and to set minimum standards for the removal of Indian children from their existing Indian environment. It was not to dictate that an illegitimate infant who has never been a member of an Indian home or culture, and probably never would be, should be removed from its primary cultural heritage and placed in an Indian environment over the express objections of its non-Indian mother."
116. States that have rejected the exception either by case law or by statute include Arizona, Alaska, Idaho, Iowa, Michigan, Montana, New Jersey, New York, North Dakota, Oklahoma, Oregon, South Dakota, Utah, and Washington. States that have applied the exception include Alabama, Indiana, Kansas, Kentucky, Louisiana, Missouri, and Tennessee. It should be noted that several states that have a large number of Indian children, especially in urban environments, have embraced this doctrine, such as California, Washington, and Oklahoma. *See In re Baby Boy C. v.*

State and Tribal Jurisprudence | 211

Tohono O'odham Nation, 27 A.D.3d 34, 805 N.Y.S.2d 313, 323 fn. 2 (2005).
117. 153 Ariz. 346, 736 P.2d 829 (1987).
118. *Id.* at 347, 736 P.2d 829, 830.
119. *Id.* at 349, 736 P.2d 829, 832.
120. *Id.* (citing 25 U.S.C. § 1915 (2000)).
121. *Id.* at 350, 736 P.2d 829, 833.
122. 198 Ariz. 154, 7 P.3d 960 (2000).
123. *Id.* at 155, 7 P.3d at 961.
124. *Id.*
125. *Id.*
126. *Id.* at 156, 7 P.3d 962.
127. *Id.*
128. *Id.* at 159, 7 P.3d 965.
129. *Id.*
130. *Id.* at 157–58, 7 P.3d 963–64.
131. The earlier version of the bill would have required "significant contacts" with a tribe before tribal court jurisdiction of an Indian child not living on the reservation would be considered. *See* Indian Child Welfare Act, S. 1214, 95th Cong. § 102(c) (1977) (citing S. Rpt. 95-597 at 4 (1977)).
132. 490 U.S. 30 (1989)
133. *Id.*
134. Pursuant to article 71 of the United Nations Charter, NGOs may apply for special consultative status, which means that they hold special competence in, and are concerned specifically with, only a few of the fields of activity covered by the Economic and Social Council (ECOSOC). Consultative Status with ECCSOC, http://www.un.org/esa/coordination/ngo/about.htm (accessed Apr. 16, 2006); United Nations Charter ch. 10, art. 71 (June 6, 1945), *available at* http://www.un.org/aboutun/charter/; Statement by International Indian Treaty Council Submitted to Commission on Human Rights, E/CN.4/1999/NGO/77 (March 5, 1999).
135. Statement by International Indian Treaty Council Submitted to Commission on Human Rights, E/CN.4/1999/NGO/77 at 3 (March 5, 1999).
136. The American legal system is designed so that the legislative body (Congress) creates the law, and the judicial body (courts) interprets those laws. Judges should not add to the law or read into the law anything that is not already there. If there is ambiguity in a particular law, a judge may look to the legislative history that goes along with the law when it was working its way through Congress or if there is a sufficient amount of ambiguity a judge may find the law void for vagueness.
137. Statement by International Indian Treaty Council Submitted to Commission on Human Rights, E/CN.4/1999/NGO/77 at 5–6 (March 5, 1999).
138. Initial Report of States by the United States to the UN Human Rights Committee, CCPR/C/81/Add. 4 at 849 (August 24, 1994).
139. 171 Ariz. 104, 828 P.2d 1245 (1992). *Forum non conveniens* is a doctrine that allows litigants to

change the venue or the location of a case based on the fact that the first venue is sufficiently not convenient so as to create a hardship on the parties involved.

140. Ultimately the author agrees with Kennedy that judicial activism in ICWA was invited by the law. If the goal is to get rid of the Existing Indian Family exception, then tribes must appeal to Congress, as it is likely that the U.S. Supreme Court will shy away from this issue. However, whether advocating for an amendment is strategically wise at this juncture is not considered by this paper.
141. *Id.* at 105–06, 828 P.2d at 1246–47.
142. *Id.* at 106, 828 P.2d at 1247.
143. *Id.* at 107, 828 P.2d at 1248 (citing *In re Robert T.*, 200 Cal. App. 3d 657, 668, 246 Cal. Rptr. 168, 175 (1988)).
144. *Id.* at 107, 828 P.2d at 1248 (citing Russel Barsh, *The Indian Child Welfare Act of 1978: A Critical Analysis*, 31 HASTINGS L.J. 1287, 1317–18 (1980)).
145. *Id.* at 107–08, 828 P.2d at 1248–49.
146. *Id.* at 108–09, 828 P.2d at 1249–50.
147. 186 Ariz. 354, 922 P.3d 319 (1996). *See supra* note 102.
148. 186 Ariz. 354, 922 P.3d 319 (1996).
149. *Id.* at 520–21, 958 P.2d at 4601–62 (citing Juv. Action No. JS-8287, Ariz. 104, 111, 828 P.2d 1245, 1252 (1991)) (citing *In re N.L.*, 754 P.2d 863, 867 (Okla. 1988)). Contrast this holding with the holding in *In re M.H., L.U.H., W.H., Jr., L.S.H., and T.H.* that an expert under ICWA "should have expertise in, and substantial knowledge of, Native American families and their child rearing practices." 691 N.W.2d 622, 2005 SD 4 (2005). *See infra* note 169.
150. *Id.* at 521, 958 P.2d at 462.
151. *In re* Appeal in Maricopa County Juv. Action No. JS-8287, 171 Ariz. 104, 828 P.2d 1245 (1992).
152. *Id.*
153. Pub. L. No. 84-959, 70 Stat. 986 (1956). *See also The Relocation Act Hearing* before the Committee on Indian Affairs 89th Cong. 302 (1966) (state. of Commr. Nash); *The Relocation Act Hearing* before the Committee on Indian Affairs 85th Cong., 293 (1958) (state. of Dep. Commr. Greenwood).
154. Ward Churchill and Glenn T. Morris, *Key Indian Laws and Cases*, in THE STATE OF NATIVE AMERICA: GENOCIDE, COLONIZATION, AND RESISTANCE (M. Annette Jaimes, ed., South End Press 1992).
155. *Id.*
156. Timeline of American Indian Relations with the Federal Government: 1787–1956 *available at* http://www.humboldt.edu/~g01/kellogg/PDF/part2hdot1.pdf#search='Relocation%20Act%20 indians%201956. *See also* Ward Churchill and Glenn T. Morris, *Key Indian Laws and Cases*, in THE STATE OF NATIVE AMERICA: GENOCIDE, COLONIZATION, AND RESISTANCE (M. Annette Jaimes ed., South End Press 1992).
157. *Available at* http://www.factfinder.census.gov (Database: Census 2000 Summary File 2 (SF-2) 100-Percent Data with Query: All urban areas/American Indian and Alaska Native alone or in combination with one or more other races).

158. *In re* Appeal in Maricopa County, Juv. Action No. JD-6982, 186 Ariz. 354, 922 P.2d 319 (1996).
159. *Id.*
160. 291 N.W.2d 278 (S.D. 1980).
161. *In re Guardianship of D.L.L. and C.L.L.*, 291 N.W.2d 278 (1980) (holding that reservation domicile was not lost by any alleged abandonment by the parent).
162. *Id.*
163. *Id.* (citing South Dakota Codified Laws 19-15-2 (2000)).
164. *Id.* (citing *Buckley v. Fredericks*, 291 N.W.2d 770, 771 (S.D. 1980)).
165. Guidelines for State Courts, 44 Fed. Reg. 67584 (Nov. 26, 1979).
166. 691 N.W.2d 622, 2005 SD 4 (2005).
167. *Id.* (citing 25 U.S.C. § 1912 (2006)).
168. *Id.* (citing *Matter of K.A.B.E. and K.B.E.*, 325 N.W.2d 840, 843–44 (S.D. 1982)).
169. *Id.* (citing *In re L.N.W.*, 457 N.W.2d 17, 18 (Iowa App. 1990)).
170. *Id.* (citing *Matter of K.H. and K.L.E.*, 981 P.2d 1190, 1193, 294 Mont. 466, 469 (1999)).
171. 701 N.W.2d 421 2005 SD 86 (2005).
172. *Rachell S. v. Arizona Department of Economic Security*, 191 Ariz. 518, 958 P.2d 459 (1998) (holding that "special knowledge of Indian life is not necessary where a professional person has substantial education and experience and testifies on matters not implicating cultural bias").
173. 325 N.W.2d 53 (1982).
174. *Id.* at 54.
175. *Id.* at 54–55.
176. *Id.* at 56 (Wollman, dissenting).
177. *Id.* at 57 (Wollman, dissenting).
178. *Id.* (citing R. Bash, *The Indian Child Welfare Act of 1978: A Critical Analysis*, 31 HASTINGS L.J. 1287, 1314 (1980)).
179. *Id.*
180. 418 N.W.2d 310 (1988).
181. *Id.* at 311.
182. 422 N.W.2d 597 (1988).
183. *Id.* at 774.
184. *Id.*
185. *Id.*
186. *Id.*
187. *Id.* at 774–75 (Konenkamp, dissenting).
188. *Id.* at 775 (Konenkamp, dissenting).
189. 707 N.W.2d 826, 2005 SD 125 (2005).
190. *Id.* at 826–33.
191. Sisseton-Wahpeton Sioux Tribe has since changed its name to Sisseton-Wahpeton Oyate. Many tribes across the nation are changing their names to more accurately reflect their linguistic and sociocultural heritage.

192. *Id.* at 835.
193. *Id.* at 834.
194. 325 N.W.2d 53, 56 (1982) (Wollman, dissenting) (stating that "although a rule of substantial compliance may suffice to carry out notice provisions governing mundane matters of property law . . . more is required when the interests at stake are as important as those protected by ICWA").
195. 371 N.W.2d 366 (1985).
196. *Id.* at 372.
197. *People in Interest of S.L.H.*, 342 N.W.2d 672 (S.D. 1983); *In re N.J.W.*, 273 N.W.2d 134 (S.D. 1978); *In re K.D.E.*, 87 S.D. 501, 210 N.W.2d 907 (1973).
198. *Id.* at 373. *People in Interest of S.L.H.*, 342 N.W.2d 672 (S.D. 1983); *In re M.S.M.*, 320 N.W.2d 795 (S.D. 1982).
199. 466 N.W.2d 168 (1991).
200. *Matter of D.H.*, 354 N.W.2d 185, 191 (S.D. 1984); *In re J.S.N.*, 361 N.W.2d 371 (S.D. 1985); *In re A.L.P.*, 368 N.W.2d 617 (S.D. 1985); *People in Interest of C.L.*, 356 N.W.2d 476 (1984).
201. *Id.* at 169–75.
202. *Id.* at 176–77 (Henderson, dissenting).
203. 670 N.W.2d 76, 2003 SD 113 (2003).
204. 42 U.S.C. 620 et seq. and 42 U.S.C. 670 et seq., respectively. If a tribe operates a Title IV-B program, it is facilitated through a direct grant from the Department of Health and Human Services (DHHS). However, if a tribe operates a Title IV-E program, it is often through a welfare agreement with state and/or counties. 42 U.S.C. 671(a)(15) as amended by section 101 of ASFA.
205. *Id.* at 619.
206. *Id.*
207. 474 N.W.2d 96 (1991).
208. *Id.* at 100 (citing *Matter of Adoption of Baade*, 462 N.W.2d 485 (SD 1990)).
209. This ruling will no doubt be beneficial to the child by providing stability in the home life; however, it is less clear that this is the type of relationship that Congress intended to protect.
210. 686 N.W.2d 647, 2004 SD 96 (2004).
211. *Id.* at 788–89.
212. *Id.* at 789.
213. *Id.* at 791.
214. *Id.*
215. *Id.* at 792.
216. Justin B. Richland and Sarah Deer, *Introduction to Tribal Legal Studies*, ch. 25: INTRODUCTION TO PEACEMAKING, 323–31 (Tribal Law and Policy Institute 1994).
217. State of South Dakota Office of the Governor, Indian Child Welfare Act Commission Report: Volume I, Narrative & Recommendations (2004). 2004 SD ALS 2 (2005).
218. *Id.* at recommendation 5, 7.
219. S.D. Codified Laws § 26-7A-15.1 (2005).

220. *See* notes 25–30 and accompanying text.
221. *See* notes 236–294 and accompanying text.
222. Indian Reorganization Act, 25 U.S.C. § 461 et seq. (2000).
223. VINE DELORIA, JR. AND CLIFFORD M. LYTLE, AMERICAN INDIANS, AMERICAN JUSTICE 116 (University of Texas Press 1983).
224. *Id.*
225. *Id.* at 117–18.
226. *Id.* at 162.
227. *Id.* at 118.
228. James W. Zion and Robert Yazzie, *Indigenous Law in North America in the Wake of Conquest*, 20 B.C. INTL. & COMP. L. REV. 55, 75–83 (1997). *See also* James W. Zion, *Monster Slayer and Born for Water: The Intersection of Restorative and Indigenous Justice*, 2 CONTEMPORARY JUSTICE REVIEW 359 (1999).
229. Stephen Cornell and Joseph P. Kalt, *Where's the Glue? Institutional Bases of American Indian Economic Development*, Harvard Project on American Indian Economic Development, 38–39 (1991), *available at* http://www.ksg.harvard.edu/hpaied/docs/PRS91-1.pdf. *See also* Andrea Skari, *The Tribal Judiciary: A Primer for Policy Development, A Report to the Following Tribes: Pascua Yaqui, Gila River, Hopi, Navajo, White Mountain Apache, San Carlos Apache, and Tohono O'odham*, Harvard Project on American Indian Economic Development (1989), *available at* http://www.ksg.harvard.edu/hpaied/docs/PRS89-6.pdf.
230. *Id.*
231. Stephen Cornell and Joseph Kalt, *Reloading the Dice: Improving the Chances for Economic Development on American Indian Reservations, What Can Tribes Do?: Strategies and Institutions in American Indian Economic Development*, 9 (UCLA 1992), *available at* http://www.ksg.harvard.edu/hpaied/docs/reloading%20the%20dice.pdf. State. of Prof. Joseph P. Kalt before the Sen. Comm. on Indian Affairs, 102nd Cong. (Sept. 17, 1996); State. of Prof. Stephen Cornell before the Standing Comm. on Aboriginal Affairs and Northern Development, Canadian House of Commons (June 6, 2000).
232. *See* Philmer Bluehouse and James W. Zion, *Hozhooji Naat'aanii: The Navajo Justice and Harmony Ceremony*, 10 MEDIATION QUARTERLY (4) (1993).
233. Jerrold E. Levy, *Community Organization of Western Navajo*, 64 AMERICAN ANTHROPOLOGIST (4): 781–801 (1962); Herbert Landar, *Fluctuation of Form in Navaho Kinship Terminology*, 64 AMERICAN ANTHROPOLOGIST (6): 985–1000 (1962). *See also* A. A. Goldenweiser, *The Social Organization of Indians of North America*, 27 JOURNAL OF AMERICAN FOLKLORE (106): 411–36 (1914); Justin B. Richland and Sarah Deer, *Introduction to Tribal Legal Studies*. ch. 14: TRIBAL KINSHIP, TRIBAL CULTURE, AND LAW (Tribal Law and Policy Institute 2004).
234. Personal Communication with Philmer Bluehouse (Dec. 5, 2005). *See also The Honorable Robert Yazzie, "Life Comes From It": Navajo Justice Concepts*, 24 N.M. L. REV. 175 (1994).
235. *In re J.D.M.*, No. JV-99-0001 (2000), *available at* http://www.tribalresourcecenter.org/opinions/opfolder/2000.NACH.0000001.htm; *In Re B.A.*, No. Confidential (Grand Ronde 2001), *available*

at http://www.tribalresourcecenter.org/opinions/opfolder/2001.NAGR.0000001.htm.
236. 25 U.S.C. § 1915 (2000); Pascua Yaqui Tribe Res. No. C04-06-02 (2002) (providing an example of a tribe that altered the placement preferences set out in ICWA). The option for a tribe to provide an alternative-placement standard is provided for in ICWA, but ICWA is silent on whether the tribal court must also adhere to these alternative-placement preferences, or whether only state courts must use these alternative-placement preferences.
237. Pascua Yaqui has chosen to supplant ICWA placement preferences with their own placement preferences, which state courts must follow. However, the Resolution on ICWA also states that TPR and adoption are not preferred, and the states are not formally bound by these preferences of the tribe. Arizona, however, has been willing to follow these preferences in most cases.
238. *In re J.D.M.*, No. JV-99-0001 (2000), *available at* http://www.tribalresourcecenter.org/opinions/opfolder/2000.NACH.0000001.htm.
239. *In re B.A.*, No. Confidential (Grand Ronde 2001), *available at* http://www.tribalresourcecenter.org/opinions/opfolder/2001.NAGR.0000001.htm.
240. S.H., Report of U.S. Commission on Civil Rights, 102nd Cong. 9 (1991).
241. *In re Halloway*, WR-JV-CV-71-84 (Nav. Window Rock Dist. Ct., Nov. 10, 1987) (unpublished opinion on file with author).
242. *In re Documenting the Marriage of Slim*, 3 Nav. R. 218 (1982) (holding that although there may be a traditional divorce mechanism that could be considered Navajo common law, the Navajo Tribal Council has enacted a statute that states that no person married by tribal custom can claim to be divorced and remarry until the Courts of the Navajo Nation issue a certificate of divorce and the statute overrides the Navajo custom). Res. No. CN-69-02 (November 13, 2002) ("Amending Title 1 of the Navajo Nation Code to Recognize the Fundamental Laws of the Dine").
243. Res. Nos. CN-69-02 (November 13, 2002) ("Amending Title 1 of the Navajo Nation Code to Recognize the Fundamental Laws of the Dine") and CO-72-03 (October 24, 2003) (amending Title VII of the Code) (mandating that Navajo courts interpret statutes consistent with Navajo common law and when statute is ambiguous interpret using Navajo common law, but when unambiguous using the plain language of the statute).
244. *Dawes v. Yazzie*, 5 Nav. R. 161, 165 (1987) (holding that judicial notice is appropriate in matters of custom and tradition of facts "every damn fool knows").
245. J. W. Zion, *The Navajo Peacemaker Court: Deference to the Old and Accommodation to the New*, 11 AM. INDIAN L. REV. 89 (1984). *See also* James W. Zion, *Monster Slayer and Born for Water: The Intersection of Restorative and Indigenous Justice*, 2 CONTEMPORARY JUSTICE REVIEW 359 (1999).
246. *In re J.J.S.*, 4 Nav. R. 192 (1983).
247. *In re Adoption of S.C.M.*, 4 Nav. R. 167 (1983); *Navajo Nation v. O'Hare*, No. SR-AN-248-86 (1987); *In re A.O.*, No. SR-AN-246-86 (1987); *Navajo Nation v. Hunter*, No. SC-CR-07-95 (1996); *Nelson v. Pfizer, Inc.*, No. SC-CV-01-02 (2003).
248. *In re J.J.S.*, 4 Nav. R. 192 (1983).
249. *Id.* at 193 (citing 7 N.T.C. § 204 (1985) (Res. No. CD-94-85 (Dec. 4, 1985)).
250. *Id.* at 193–94.

251. *Id.* at 194 (citing GARY WITHERSPOON, NAVAJO KINSHIP AND MARRIAGE 94–95 (University of Chicago Press 1975)).
252. *Id.* at 194 (citing Nav. Ct. Solicitor Op., 83-10 (1983)).
253. Navajo courts pronounced a preference for the term "Navajo common law" rather than "custom" because it is not widely understood that customs of the Navajo are actually laws. Thus, the English term more accurately reflects custom as law. *In re Estate of Apachee*, 4 Nav. R. 178, 180–81 (1983), *available at* http://www.tribalresourcecenter.org/opinions/opfolder/1983.NANN.0000070.htm.
254. *Id.* at 194.
255. *Id.* at 195 (citing Nav. Ct. Solicitor Op., 83-10 (1983)).
256. *Id.*
257. *Id.* at 195 (citing *In Re Estate of Apachee*, 4 Nav. R. 178 (1983)).
258. *Id.* at 196 (citing 9 N.T.C. § 615(a) (1960)); (Res. No. CN-64-60 (Nov. 18, 1960)).
259. *Id.* at 196 (citing 9 N.T.C. § 615(b) (1960)); (Res. No. CN-64-60 (Nov. 18, 1960)).
260. *Id.* at 196.
261. 25 U.S.C. § 1903(1) (2000).
262. 5 Nav. R. 121 (1987).
263. No. SC-CV-58-98 (2001) at 14 (citing UN Convention on the Rights of the Child, UN General Assembly Resolution No. 44/25, art. 12 (November 20, 1989)).
264. *Id.* at 25.
265. *Id.*
266. *Id.* at 122.
267. *Id.*
268. *Id.* at 123.
269. *Id.* at 123–24.
270. State courts have withheld transfer of ICWA cases to tribal courts because the tribe requested the transfer too late in the proceedings. The Navajo Nation also only has one attorney working on ICWA cases, which may reduce the ability of the tribe to effectively bring cases back to the reservation for trial.
271. 22 I.L.R. 6044, 6045 (Chy. R. Sx Ct. App., 1995).
272. 16 I.L.R. 6001 (1987).
273. *Id.*
274. *Id.* at § 1(e).
275. *Id.* at §1 (f).
276. *Id.* at § 1(g).
277. *Id.* at § 29(a)(i).
278. *Id.* at § 2(a)(ii).
279. *Id.* at § 2(b)(i).
280. *Id.* at § 2(b)(ii)-(iii).
281. *Id.* at § 3(b).

282. *Id.*
283. *Id.*
284. *Id.* at § 2(g).
285. White Mountain Apache Juvenile Code § 10.1, *available at* http://wmat.us/Legal/juvenile.html (accessed Apr. 12, 2006).
286. White Mountain Apache Juvenile Code § 10.2, *available at* http://wmat.us/Legal/juvenile.html (accessed Apr. 12, 2006).
287. 25 U.S.C. § 1901–02 (2000).
288. White Mountain Apache Juvenile Code § 8.3, *available at* http://wmat.us/Legal/juvenile.html (accessed Apr. 12, 2006).
289. White Mountain Apache Juvenile Code § 8.2, *available at* http://wmat.us/Legal/juvenile.html (accessed Apr. 12, 2006).
290. White Mountain Apache Juvenile Code § 8.5, *available at* http://wmat.us/Legal/juvenile.html (accessed Apr. 12, 2006).
291. White Mountain Apache Juvenile Code § 8.5, *available at* http://wmat.us/Legal/juvenile.html (accessed Apr. 12, 2006).
292. White Mountain Apache Juvenile Code § 8.7, *available at* http://wmat.us/Legal/juvenile.html (accessed Apr. 12, 2006).
293. Minnesota Dept. of Human Servs., *Children in Out-of-Home Care: A 1998 Minnesota Report by Race and Heritage*, Bull. No. 98-68-8, § 3 (May 25, 2000).
294. *In re DeCoteau, Jr.*, 17 I.L.R. 6081, 6083 (N. Plns. Intertr. Ct. App. 1990) (Godtland dissent) (citing 4 McCahey, Kaufam and Draut, Child Custody & Visitation Law and Practice § 29.03[4][a] (1989); 44 Fed. Reg. 67585).
295. The author was unable to verify whether this precedent is still good law or if it has since been overruled by the Northern Plains Tribal Appellate Court. As mentioned earlier, tribal courts are not always consistent about publishing case law, and therefore, it is not always clear what the current status of tribal law is, especially to an outside researcher. This paper attempts to breach this barrier, but tribal communities are still the best sources for legal commentary.
296. John G. Red Horse, Cecilia Martinez, Priscilla Day, Don Day, John Poupart, and Dawn Scharnberg, *Family Preservation: Concepts in American Indian Communities at 20* (December 2000) *available at* http://www.nicwa.org/resources/catalog/research/2000/01.FamilyPreservation.pdf.
297. *Id.* at 23.
298. John G. Red Horse, Cecilia Martinez, and Priscilla Day, *Family Preservation: A Case Study of Indian Tribal Practice at 17* (December 2001), available at http://www.nicwa.org/resources/catalog/research/2001/01.Family%20Pres01.Rpt.pdf.
299. *Id.*
300. *Id.*
301. *Id.* at 19.
302. *Id.* at 20. *See* personal communication with Ronald Phillips, Navajo Social Service Family Preservation Office (Dec. 1, 2005).

303. *Id.* at 20–22. John G. Red Horse, Cecilia Martinez, and Priscilla Day, *Family Preservation: A Case Study of Indian Tribal Practice at 53*; Center for Effective Collaboration and Practice, Institute for Research, *Promising Practices in Wraparound Programs for Children with Serious Emotional Disturbances and Their Families*, in 4 SYSTEMS OF CARE: PROMISING PRACTICES WITH CHILDREN'S MENTAL HEALTH (B. J. Burns and F. R. Goldman, eds., National Mental Health Information Center 1998); Native American Training Institute, *Wraparound in Indian Country: The Ways of the People Are Who We Are* (undated).

304. John G. Red Horse, Cecilia Martinez, and Priscilla Day, *Family Preservation: A Case Study of Indian Tribal Practice at 36*.

305. *Id.* at 20.

306. *Id.* at 50.

307. John G. Red Horse, Cecilia Martinez, and Priscilla Day, *Family Preservation: A Case Study of Indian Tribal Practice at 53*.

308. *Id.* at 45.

309. *Id.* at 37. In addition, once the tribe took over family preservation services, there was a marked increase in self-referrals, indicating that the community accepted the programs as legitimate.

310. *Id.*

311. *See generally* John G. Red Horse, Cecilia Martinez, and Priscilla Day, *Family Preservation: A Case Study of Indian Tribal Practice*.

312. *Id.* at 36–37. Interestingly, nearly all of the children chose spiritual and/or cultural as one of their life domains, seemingly indicating that these are areas that the younger generation feel the community, as a whole, needs to work on.

313. John G. Red Horse, Cecilia Martinez, Priscilla Day, Don Day, John Poupart, and Dawn Scharnberg, *Family Preservation: Concepts in American Indian Communities at 28*.

314. John G. Red Horse, Cecilia Martinez, and Priscilla Day, *Family Preservation: A Case Study of Indian Tribal Practice at 5.* (citing Native American Training Institute, *Wraparound in Indian Country: The Ways of the People Are Who We Are* (undated)).

315. *Id.* at 47.

316. Interview with Norma C. Martinez, MSW, Pascua Yaqui Social Services (Nov. 28, 2005).

317. This means that there is no extra vigilance on the part of social services to find the earliest signs of at-risk families, or to concentrate on preventative measures before any signs develop. They often rely on referrals from the states and from Pascua Yaqui Tribe Behavioral Health Department.

318. *Id.*

319. Interview with Ronald Phillips, Navajo Nation Promoting Safe and Stable Families Project (Dec. 14, 2005).

320. "Dine" is a term that Navajos use to refer to themselves and their culture.

321. *Id.*

322. *Id.*

323. Interview with Ronald Phillips, Navajo Nation Promoting Safe and Stable Families Project (Dec.

14, 2005).
324. Id.
325. A hogan is a traditional Navajo house. There are two types of hogans: the female hogan, which has six or eight sides and serves as the family home, and the male hogan, which is smaller and shaped like a pyramid. The male hogan is used for private gathering and ceremonies. SCOTT TYBONY, THE HOGAN: THE TRADITIONAL NAVAJO HOME (Southwest Parks and Monuments Association, 1998).
326. Interview with Ronald Phillips, Navajo Nation Promoting Safe and Stable Families Project (Dec. 14, 2005).
327. Id.
328. Id.
329. The Blessing Way ceremony is used to bless the one sung over to provide them luck and health. It is often done for expectant mothers, but is not limited to such an occasion. LELAND C. WYMAN AND BERARD HAILE, BLESSINGWAY (University of Arizona Press 1970).
330. Id.
331. 42 U.S.C. §§ 678, 673b, 679b (2006). *See* David Simmons and Jack Trope, *P.L. 105-89 Adoption and Safe Families Act of 1997: Issues for Tribes and States Serving Indian Children* (Nov. 1999), *available at* http://www.nicwa.org/policy/law/adoption_safe/asfa-issues.pdf.

Holding Back the Tide

The Existing Indian Family Doctrine and Its Continued Denial of the Right to Culture for Indigenous Children

Aliza G. Organick

His adopted parents had never told him what kind of Indian he was. They did not know. They never told him anything at all about his natural parents, other than his birth mother's age, which was fourteen. John only knew that he was Indian in the most generic sense. Black hair, brown skin and eyes, high cheekbones, the prominent nose. Tall and muscular, he looked like some cinematic warrior and constantly intimidated people with his presence. When asked by white people, he said he was Sioux, because that was what they wanted him to be. When asked by Indian people, he said he was Navajo, because that was what he wanted to be.

—Sherman Alexie, *Indian Killer*

While a long time in coming, the tide has turned when it comes to recognizing the self-determination rights of indigenous people across the world. The most dramatic example of this trend is the recent passage of the United Nations Declaration on the Rights of Indigenous Peoples (the Declaration).[1] The passage of the Declaration is the culmination of over twenty years of work, and while not legally binding, it is a reflection of the world community's commitment to the protection of indigenous peoples' rights.[2] Disappointingly, four UN member nations with significant indigenous populations did not vote for passage of the Declaration—Canada, Australia, New Zealand, and the United States.[3]

United States Indian policies have historically swung back and forth between assimilation and self-determination.[4] The failure, however, of the United States to endorse the Declaration is in keeping with its long-standing tradition of implementing policies that are detrimental to the well-being of Indian people. This paper explores how one court-created doctrine, the Existing Indian Family exception (EIFE), continues to perpetuate this resistance to the notion of self-determination for Native American peoples, and thus operates outside of emerging international norms. In practice, the EIFE circumvents the intended application of the Indian Child Welfare Act (ICWA). This is despite the fact that the plain language of ICWA makes no provision for an exception of its application.[5]

Over the past two decades, the rights of indigenous peoples have been addressed in key international instruments.[6] These instruments have sought to provide increased recognition and protection for the rights of indigenous peoples. Despite this worldwide movement, the United States has fallen behind the world community in its failure to recognize these rights. This rejection of a developing international consensus is underscored when state courts apply the EIFE. Although the EIFE is only applied in a small number of states, it continues to deny Indian children the right to a cultural identity, thereby undermining international norms.

The recognition of the right of identity for indigenous children is an extension of the recognition by the world community that indigenous peoples have the right to both their collective and individual identities as indigenous peoples.[7] When ICWA was enacted in 1978, there was also recognition of the importance of an Indian child's right to his or her tribal identity by the federal government.[8] The EIFE undermines these principles. While applied in only a minority of states, the continued application of the EIFE erodes the rights of indigenous children and their tribes.

The first section of this article discusses the development of the rights of indigenous people in international human-rights law. It reviews important international human-rights conventions that have contributed to the growing explicit recognition of key rights for indigenous people, and in particular, for indigenous children. The second section of the article provides a specific focus on the vulnerability of indigenous children, and the emerging international recognition that these children need special protection. The third section explores the history of United States federal policy toward Indian children, culminating in the passage of ICWA. It also discusses how the EIFE is inconsistent with the spirit and letter of ICWA and is a reflection of the unwillingness of states to accept the goals of the Act and to embrace its pluralistic intent.

The Development of Indigenous Peoples Rights in International Human Rights Law

This section provides an overview of the provision for the rights of indigenous people in international human-rights law. It discusses human-rights law development in general and, in particular, the development of international recognition of indigenous people's rights under international law. It then focuses on the rights that are recognized as critical for protecting the human rights of indigenous children worldwide.

The development of the modern human-rights movement began shortly after the Second World War.[9] However, the international community did not begin to explicitly address issues concerning indigenous peoples and cultures until 1957, when the International Labor Organization (ILO) established Convention 107.[10] ILO Convention 107 identified indigenous peoples and groups as being in need of special protection.[11] The goal of ILO Convention 107 was to promote the economic welfare of indigenous people and to encourage assimilation and integration into the broader societies in which indigenous people lived.[12]

Nevertheless, because ILO Convention 107 focused primarily on the assimilation of indigenous peoples rather than the promotion of their right to self-determination, it was eventually rejected and replaced by the ILO in 1989.[13] The ILO readdressed the needs of indigenous peoples a second time and adopted the ILO Convention on Indigenous and Tribal Peoples No. 169.[14] ILO 169 represented a fundamental shift in the way the international community considered the needs of indigenous peoples worldwide.[15] In particular, ILO 169 specifically recognized that indigenous peoples should have control over their own institutions, their own economic development, and the right to maintain their cultural identities "within the framework of the States in which they live."[16] ILO 169 is considered particularly important because it officially articulated the international community's recognition of the right of indigenous people to the protection of their culture.[17] These provisions can be found throughout this convention.[18] With the drafting of ILO 169, the organization explicitly affirmed that indigenous peoples are unique, and that their culture and identity are threatened throughout the world.[19] Despite the improvements in the language and intent that was adopted in ILO 169, there was a continued push by indigenous peoples themselves to develop a more comprehensive document that would more fully express all of their unique and varied needs and aspirations.[20] Indigenous peoples around the world continued to struggle for recognition of their right to identity and ways of life, and in 1985, the Working Group on Indigenous Populations (the Working Group) was established in order to give voice to their concerns.[21] In 1985, the Working Group began drafting a Declaration on the Rights of Indigenous Peoples.[22] This draft was completed in 1993, and the UN Commission on Human Rights began working on its draft of the document in 1995.[23] Dozens of indigenous organizations and groups participated in the drafting process[24]—a process that would take twenty-two years to come to fruition. The Draft Declaration on the Rights of Indigenous Peoples was, when it was completed, the most "comprehensive statement of the rights of Indigenous peoples" ever created.[25]

On September 13, 2007, after twenty-two years of effort on the part of over two hundred indigenous groups worldwide, the United Nations General Assembly adopted the Declaration on the Rights of Indigenous Peoples (the Declaration).[26] Although nonbinding on states, the Declaration outlines the rights of the world's indigenous people and outlaws discrimination against them.[27] The Declaration was approved by 143 member states and is important because it articulates the individual and collective rights of all of the world's indigenous people, "as well as their rights to culture, identity, and language. . . ."[28] The adoption of the Declaration is seen as the current high-water mark for international recognition of indigenous peoples' rights.

UN Declaration on the Rights of Indigenous Peoples

A number of articles in the Declaration describe the rights of indigenous children specifically. In particular, article 7.2 provides that "Indigenous peoples have the collective right to live in freedom, peace and security as distinct peoples and shall not be subjugated to any act of genocide or other act of violence, including forcibly removing children of the group to another group."[29] Additionally, article 8.2(d) requires states to provide mechanisms for both the prevention of and the redress of "[a]ny form of forced assimilation or integration."[30] Article 14 outlines the right of indigenous children to an education without discrimination, and in particular that indigenous children have the right "to an education in their own culture and provided in their own language."[31] Although the Declaration does not contain any new human-rights provisions, it does provide a new framework for states to recognize the rights that have continually been denied to the world's indigenous peoples.[32]

Protecting the Rights of the Child in International Law

The development of the international community's recognition of children's rights and indigenous peoples' rights were occurring simultaneously.[33] The focus on children's rights at the international level resulted in the United Nations Convention on the Rights of the Child (CRC).[34] The CRC contains fifty-four articles and two optional protocols.[35] It has been ratified by 191 countries, and only the United States and Somalia have yet to ratify it.[36] In drafting the CRC, the working group relied on the principles articulated in the Universal Declaration of Human Rights, the International Covenant on Civil and Political Rights, and the International Covenant on Economic, Social and Cultural Rights.[37] The nearly universal acceptance of the CRC is considered to exemplify a world standard that crosses political, economic, social, and cultural distinctions worldwide.[38]

The preamble of the CRC acknowledges in no uncertain terms that "childhood is entitled to special care and assistance."[39] It further states that the family is the fundamental social unit.[40] The convention itself, comprised of three parts, contains numerous references to ensuring and respecting the rights of each child, and states that those rights should be respected without discrimination of any kind.[41] Additionally, article 8 specifically refers to the child's right to "preserve his or her identity."[42] In addition, the CRC provides that if a child is illegally deprived of his or her identity, the state should provide assistance and protection with a goal to "re-establish his or her identity."[43] With respect to the state's responsibility for the child's education, the convention is clear that the state must respect the child's "cultural identity, language and values."[44] The CRC also provides that in states where there exist "ethnic, religious or linguistic minorities or persons of indigenous origin," the child "shall not be denied the right, in community with other members of his or her group, to enjoy his or her own culture...."[45]

Protecting the Cultural Rights and Identity of the Indigenous Child

In 2003, the Committee on the Rights of the Child (the Committee) held a Day of General Discussion on the Rights of Indigenous Children.[46] The day of discussion was held in response to the UN Permanent Forum on Indigenous Issues (the Forum).[47] The Forum urged the Committee on the Rights of the Child to promote "greater awareness of the rights of indigenous children."[48] This was in view of recommendations made at the first two sessions on the rights of indigenous children.[49] The Discussion Day on the Rights of Indigenous Children included two working groups specifically convened to address the issues of nondiscrimination and cultural diversity.[50] The working group on nondiscrimination addressed racism, xenophobia, and discrimination in access to services.[51] The second working group addressed the issue of cultural diversity in general, and specifically the right to identity and the right to education.[52]

The Discussion Day on the Rights of Indigenous Children led to a set of recommendations.[53] These recommendations focused attention on the fact that articles 30, 17 (d) and 29.1 (c) and (d) of the CRC are the only provisions in international law that explicitly recognize the rights of indigenous children.[54] The recommendations further underscored the need to recognize that indigenous children are disproportionately affected by an array of issues—including institutionalization, urbanization, armed conflict, and child labor, among others—but that state policies and programs do not adequately address their needs.[55]

The committee subsequently made a number of recommendations[56] and strongly recalled that states have obligations to promote and to protect the human rights of all indigenous children pursuant to articles 2 and 30 of the CRC.[57] In addition, the recommendations specifically recalled the Right to Identity articulated in articles 7 and 8 of the CRC, as well as recommending that all state parties take measures to "ensure that indigenous children enjoy their own culture and can use their own language...."[58] The recommendations also called for full implementation of articles

7 and 8, as well as addressing issues of family environment.[59] In particular, the committee recommended that states safeguard the integrity of indigenous families not only by assisting these families with child-rearing responsibilities, but also by reevaluating state foster care and adoption processes.[60] The committee went on to remind states that even where it might be in the best interest of the child to remove him or her from the family, that placement in an institution be a "last resort" and subject to periodic review.[61] Furthermore, the committee reminded states to ensure that the child's religious, cultural, ethnic, and linguistic background be safeguarded pursuant to article 20.3 of the CRC.[62]

In 2004, a year after the Committee on the Rights of the Child made their recommendations, the UNICEF Innocenti Research Center (the Center) produced *Digest No. 11: Ensuring the Rights of the Indigenous Child*.[63] The Center's report reiterated the CRC's position that indigenous children were one of the most marginalized and vulnerable groups in the world, and that the world's indigenous communities were living under enormous cultural and social stress.[64] The Center's report recognized that families, elders, and community leaders play a crucial role in helping their children understand their cultural identity and values, and that indigenous children have a special heritage "from which we can all benefit."[65]

The report defined four distinct initiatives as "key areas for the realization of Indigenous children's rights."[66] These initiatives focus on standards of health and nutrition, education, protection and support of the child's rights, and the child's participation in decision making processes.[67] While each initiative is given equal weight, it is important to note that the report's education initiative underscored that it was not enough to merely provide an education to indigenous children.[68] The report made it clear that it was also important that the education provided must account for indigenous languages and cultural contexts.[69]

U.S. Indian Policy and the Federal Government's Intervention in the Lives of Indian Children

The United States federal government has had a long history of intervening in the lives of Indian children in an attempt to undermine their right to cultural heritage and identity. In 1819, Congress enacted the Civilization Fund Act (CFA) in an attempt to provide education to Indian children and Indian tribes.[70] The CFA gave federal funds to religious institutions and to other private agencies in order to create education programs for Indian children in an effort to "civilize the Indian."[71] The federal policy underlying these programs was to separate, by force if necessary, Indian children from their tribes and their culture.[72] For the better part of the nineteenth century and well into the twentieth century, federal funds supported the creation of religious mission schools and boarding schools in order to effect this policy.[73]

While the federal government maintained its assimilationist Indian education programs in one form or another into the 1970s, there was a shift away from the education programs that had historically been delegated to largely religious institutions since the 1800s.⁷⁴ The policy shift was to move Indian children away from reservation schools and into boarding schools, which were often far from their aboriginal homelands.⁷⁵ The policy underlying the move from the reservation schools to boarding schools emerged from the general consensus by the federal government that as long as Indian children remained with their tribe, these children had an opportunity to learn the culture of their people and would, therefore, never fully assimilate.⁷⁶

The often horrific means used to accomplish the forced assimilation of Indian children are well documented. These means included severe corporal punishment for a variety of acts deemed offensive and that were seen to endanger the policy objectives of the government, such as when children spoke their native language.⁷⁷ Other methods were also used that were designed to be traumatic and wrenching, such as stripping Indian children of their traditional clothing, cutting their hair, and "disinfecting" them by using alcohol or kerosene.⁷⁸

Although there was some movement away from the most egregious acts perpetrated against Indian children following the Meriam Report in 1928 (the Report),⁷⁹ the assault on the cultural identity of Indian children continued to occur through the 1960s and 1970s, well over forty years after the Report was published.⁸⁰ Despite this, the Report was nevertheless important, particularly because it noted that "The Indian Service has not appreciated the fundamental importance of family life and community activities in the social and economic development of a people. The tendency has been rather toward weakening Indian family life and community activities than toward strengthening them."⁸¹

In 1969, the United States Senate Subcommittee on Indian Education (SSIE) issued another report on Indian boarding schools and found that not much had changed in these schools in the years since the Meriam Report was published.⁸² The SSIE report described not only continuing deplorable physical conditions in these schools, but also that the policy of cultural genocide remained essentially unchanged.⁸³ The SSIE reported that Indian children were still being taken away from their culture and enrolled in institutions that were focused on "making him a non-Indian."⁸⁴

The Indian Child Welfare Act

While the era of the Indian boarding school experiment was waning prior to the enactment of ICWA, another type of removal was occurring. Due to federal policy and state court intervention, many Indian children were now being removed as a direct result of adoption and foster care placement away from Indian homes. Between 1958 and 1967, the Bureau of Indian Affairs provided funding for the Indian Adoption Project (the Project).[85] The Project was administered by the Child Welfare League of America (the League), and during its administration of the program, the League placed nearly four hundred Indian children in non-Indian homes.[86] The outplacing of Indian children during this particular period is noteworthy because it occurred when "matching" in adoption cases was the dominant adoption practice.[87] After the Project terminated in 1967, other programs were devised to take its place.[88] The Adoption Resource Exchange of North America (ARENA) followed in 1968 and focused on placing children who had previously been deemed "difficult to place" in adoptive homes.[89] ARENA's practice of outplacing Indian children in non-Indian homes continued into the early 1970s.[90]

It was because of this long history of displacement of Indian children that Congress passed ICWA in 1978.[91] Prior to its passage, studies showed that as many as 25–35 percent of all Indian children were placed in some sort of out-of-home care, and that as many as 85 percent of those were being placed in non-Indian homes.[92] ICWA was enacted in direct response to what Congress recognized as an alarming number of Indian children who were being removed from Indian homes either through adoption proceedings or foster care placement.[93] Through the enactment of ICWA, Congress acknowledged that not only were tribes losing their most precious and vital resource, their children,[94] but also that these children were being deprived of and losing their cultural identity.[95] To staunch the flow of removal of Indian children from Indian homes and away from the tribes, ICWA set minimum state standards for the removal of Indian children.[96] Congress established that state courts must first determine whether a child in a state custody proceeding is an Indian child,[97] and once it has been determined that the child is an Indian child, that all of the provisions of ICWA apply.

Existing Indian Family Exception

It did not take long for these important provisions of ICWA to be undermined by state courts. In 1982, the State of Kansas decided the adoption case *In re Baby Boy L (BBL)*.[98] The issue in *BBL* was whether ICWA applied in an adoption proceeding involving an infant who was 5/16th Kiowa and born illegitimately to an Indian father and a non-Indian mother.[99] The mother consented to the adoption of the child, but the father, who was 5/8th blood Kiowa Indian and an enrolled member of the Kiowa Tribe, was in custody in state prison at the time of the proceedings and did not consent.[100] The Kiowa tribe petitioned to transfer the jurisdiction to the Court of Indian Offenses at Anadarko, Oklahoma, but the state court denied the transfer of jurisdiction.[101] The mother expressly stated that if ICWA did apply, she would take back the child and raise him herself.[102] The court found that ICWA did not apply in this case, because ICWA was enacted to preserve Indian families, and because this child was never a part of an Indian family relationship.[103] The court found that Congress never intended that the Act apply to these types of factual situations where there is no Indian family to preserve.[104] The court called ICWA a "complex federal legislation" and described it as "confusing."[105] In addition, the court also found that the legislation was not enacted "to dictate that an illegitimate infant who has never been a member of an Indian home or culture, and probably never would be, should be removed from its primary cultural heritage and placed in an Indian environment over the express objections of its non-Indian mother."[106] As a result of *BBL*, the Existing Indian Family exception (EIFE) to ICWA was born.

Other states followed the reasoning in the *BBL* decision when determining whether ICWA applies. While the EIFE is followed in a minority of states,[107] it nevertheless remains a troubling holdover of the pre-ICWA era, when state courts divested tribes of Indian children and divested Indian children of their right to an Indian identity and culture as explicitly protected in ICWA.

What remains so troubling about the EIFE is that it allows these courts to define whether a particular child is an Indian. This clearly takes that determination out of the hands of tribes. In addition, it allows these courts to decide whether and to what degree a particular parent is Indian enough, and whether and to what degree an Indian family is Indian enough for ICWA to apply. This not only runs afoul of congressional intent in enacting this legislation, but it also allows for these courts to make decisions that clearly only the tribes themselves are allowed to make. There are a number of states that now explicitly reject the EIFE, and this is an important step.[108] Nevertheless, in those states where the EIFE is alive and well, Indian children remain at risk of losing their cultural and tribal identity. The effect of the EIFE when used by state courts is that it denies indigenous children and indigenous people the important human rights that have been explicitly recognized at the international level. On a national level, the EIFE subverts congressional recognition of the important interests of tribes in the cultural upbringing of their children and, therefore, also subverts the rights of these children to their culture and heritage.

Conclusion

The international community has focused its attention on the rights of the world's indigenous peoples increasingly over the last twenty years. Establishing the rights of indigenous children has followed, and is an important component of, this effort. This work aims to ensure that the culture, language, and traditions of indigenous peoples are handed down to subsequent generations, and to promote not merely the survival of the world's indigenous cultures, but also to ensure that they flourish and grow. This is, and should remain, the most important aspiration of the world community. The EIFE not only runs contrary to existing international human-rights law but is also out of step with the policy that the federal government advocated through the enactment of ICWA itself.

NOTES

Special acknowledgment and thanks to my research assistant, Grace Talley, for her tireless support; to Matthew Fletcher and Wenona Singel and the Indigenous Law and Policy Center, Michigan State University College of Law; and to the law faculty of Washburn University for providing an opportunity to discuss the work with them early in its development. Special thanks to Sarah Sargent and to David Bury for their unending support. Thank you, Mom and Dad for absolutely everything else.

1. United Nations Declaration on the Rights of Indigenous Peoples, U.N. Doc. A/61/L.67 (Adopted September 13, 2007) [hereinafter Declaration].
2. *Id.*
3. *Id.*
4. *See* ROBERT W. VENABLES, AMERICAN HISTORY: FIVE CENTURIES OF CONFLICT AND COEXISTENCE, VOL. II CONFRONTATION, ADAPTATION & ASSIMILATION, 1783–PRESENT 263–64 (Clear Light Publishing 2004).
5. Indian Child Welfare Act, 25 U.S.C.A. 1901–1963 (1988).
6. *See* S. JAMES ANAYA, INDIGENOUS PEOPLES IN INTERNATIONAL LAW 49–79 (Oxford University Press 2004)(1996) [hereinafter Anaya] (discussing the development of the modern human-rights era and emergent customary law).
7. *See generally* Declaration, *supra* note 1.
8. 25 U.S.C.A. 1901(3) (1988).
9. *See* Anaya, *supra* note 6, at 54. ILO Convention No. 107 specifically addresses the Protection and Integration of Indigenous and Other Tribal and Semi-Tribal Populations in Independent Countries. It was adopted by the International Labor Conference in 1957 and came into force two years later. It was ratified by twenty-seven countries.
10. *Id.*
11. *Id.*
12. *Id.*
13. *Id.* at 58.
14. *Id.*
15. *Id.*
16. General Conference of the International Labour Organization, Convention Concerning Indigenous and Tribal Peoples in Independent Countries (Convention 169), Adopted June 27, 1989, 28 I.L.M. 1382 (entered into force September 5, 1991), *reprinted in* S. JAMES ANAYA, INDIGENOUS PEOPLES

IN INTERNATIONAL LAW (Oxford University Press 2004)(1996). Convention No. 169 states in the fifth preambular paragraph that "Recognizing the aspirations of these peoples to exercise control over their own institutions, ways of life and economic development and to maintain and develop their identities, languages, and religions, within the framework of the States in which they live . . . ."

17. *See generally* Anaya, *supra* note 9.
18. *Id.*
19. *Id.*
20. *Id.*
21. U.N. Permanent Forum on Indigenous Issues, History-UNPFII, United Nations Forum on Indigenous Issues, *available at* http://www.un.org/esa/socdev/unpfii/en/history.html (last visited October 6, 2007).
22. *Id.*
23. *Id.*
24. *Id.*
25. *Id.*
26. *See generally* Declaration, *supra* note 1.
27. *Id.*
28. doCip-Indigenous Peoples Global Consultation on the Declaration, United Nations Adopts the Declaration on Rights of Indigenous Peoples, September 13, 2007, *available at* http://www.docip.org/adopteden/htm (last visited September 26, 2007).
29. *See* Declaration, *supra* note 1, at art. 7.2.
30. *Id.* at art. 8.2(d).
31. *Id.* at art. 14.3. In addition to those articles cited here, the Declaration also specifically mentions children in articles 1, 21, and 22.
32. Statement of Les Malezar, Chairman, Global Indigenous Caucus, Statement at the Global Indigenous Caucus (September 13, 2007).
33. ILO 169 was adopted in 1989, and the CRC was adopted for signature, ratification, and accession by General Assembly 44/25 of November 20, 1989. The CRC entered into force on September 2, 1990.
34. United Nations Convention on the Rights of the Child, 1577 U.N.T.S., enacted September 2, 1990 [hereinafter UN CRC]. The CRC is one of six core human-rights treaties that established what is widely considered the human-rights framework. Other treaties are the International Covenant on Civil and Political Rights; the International Convention on Economic, Social and Cultural Rights; the Convention against Torture and other Cruel and Inhuman or Degrading Treatment or Punishment; the International Convention on the Elimination of All forms of Racial Discrimination; and the Convention on the Elimination of All Forms of Discrimination against Women.
35. *Id.*
36. *See* U.S. State Department Fact Sheet, *The Optional Protocol to the United Nations Convention on*

the Rights of the Child on the Sale of Children, Child Prostitution, and Child Pornography, December 24, 2002, *available at* http://www.state.gov/r/pa/prs/ps/2002/16216.htm (last visited October 6, 2007). While the United States has not ratified the convention, it has signed it and has indicated its support. In addition, the United States is a State Party to the Optional Protocol.
37. *See* UN CRC, *supra* note 34.
38. Sonia Harris-Short, *Listening to 'The Other': The Convention on the Rights of the Child*, MELB. J. OF INT'L L. (2001), *available at* http://beta.austlii.edu.au/journals/MelbJIL/200L/13.html (last visited April 23, 2007). UN CRC, *supra* note 34.
39. *Id.*
40. *Id.*
41. *Id.* Part 1 is the preamble, part 2 contains the substantive text in articles 1–45, and part 3 contains the ratification provisions.
42. *Id.* at art. 8(1).
43. *Id.* at art. 8(2). In addition, article 9 further provides that if it has been determined that it is in the best interest of the child to be separated from his or her family, the removal is subject to the appropriate judicial review.
44. *Id.* at art. 29(1)(d).
45. *Id.* at art. 30.
46. United Nations Committee on the Rights of the Child, Recommendations, 34th Session, September 15–October 3, 2003, *available at* http://www.treatycouncil.org/section 21188.htm [hereinafter UN CRC Recommendations].
47. *Id.* at 1.
48. *Id.*
49. *Id.*
50. Programme of the Discussion Day on the Rights of Indigenous Children, September 19, 2003, Palais Wilson, Geneva, *available at* http://www.unhchr.ch/html/menu2/6/crc/doc/days/programme_enpdf (last visited September 27, 2007).
51. *Id.* This working group also addressed issues relating to juvenile justice.
52. *Id.*
53. *See* UN CRC Recommendations, *supra* note 46.
54. *Id.*
55. *Id.*
56. *See generally* UN CRC Recommendations, *supra* note 46.
57. *Id.* at 1–2.
58. *Id.* at 3 (stating the need to take measures to ensure the "indigenous children enjoy their own ... language").
59. *Id.* at 3–4 (encouraging states to safeguard and support indigenous families by assisting them in child-rearing responsibilities).
60. *Id.*
61. *Id.*

62. *Id.* at 4. CRC article 20.3 states: "... opportunities in a manner conducive to the child's achieving the fullest possible social integration and the individual development, including his or her cultural and spiritual development."
63. UNICEF INNOCENTI RESEARCH, THE INNOCENTI DIGEST No. 11: *Ensuring the Rights of Indigenous Children* (2004). The digest has been described as UNICEF's commitment to the cause of indigenous children, and grounded in the principles and language of the CRC.
64. *Id.*
65. *Id.* at 1.
66. *Id.* at 14.
67. *Id.*
68. *Id.* at 15.
69. *Id.*
70. The Civilization Fund Act, 3 Stat. 516–17 (1819). The Civilization Fund Act was in effect from 1819–1873 and established a partnership between a variety of Christian denominations and the federal government. The federal government provided a portion of the costs of running these institutions, and the remainder of the costs were paid by the private organization and, in some cases, by the tribes themselves.
71. TERRY L. CROSS, CULTURAL SKILLS IN INDIAN CHILD WELFARE: A GUIDE FOR THE NON-INDIAN 5 (NICWA 2004) [hereinafter Cross].
72. *Id.*
73. *Id.*
74. Andrea A. Curio, *Civil Claims for Uncivilized Acts: Filing Suit against the Government for American Indian Boarding School Abuses*, 4 HASTINGS RACE & POVERTY L.J. 45, 54 (2006) [hereinafter Curio].
75. *Id.* at 55.
76. *Id.*
77. *Id.* at 59–60.
78. *Id.*
79. INSTITUTE FOR GOVERNMENT RESEARCH, THE PROBLEM OF INDIAN ADMINISTRATION (L. Meriam ed., 1928) [hereinafter Meriam Report].
80. Curio, *supra* note 74, at 70.
81. James E. Officer, *Informal Power Structures within Indian Communities*, 3 J. OF AM. INDIAN EDUC. 6 (1963) (quoting the Meriam Report).
82. *See* Curio, *supra* note 74, at 70.
83. *Id.*
84. *Id.*
85. *See generally* Ellen Herman, The Adoption History Project, *available at* http://darkwing.uoregon.edu/~ADOPTION/ (last visited September 26, 2007).
86. Cross, *supra* note 71, at 6.
87. *Id.* at 5–6. Race matching was the process that adoption agencies used to try and place a child

with a family that most closely duplicated his or her natural biological environment.
88. *See generally* The Adoption History Project, *supra* note 85.
89. *Id.*
90. *Id.*
91. *See* Cross, *supra* note 71, at 6–7.
92. *Id.*
93. Lorie M. Graham, *"The Past Never Vanishes": A Contextual Critique of the Existing Indian Family Doctrine*, 23 AM. INDIAN L. REV. 1, 24 (1999) [hereinafter Graham].
94. *Mississippi Band of Choctaw Indians v. Holyfield*, 490 U.S. 30, 32 (1989) (quoting Mr. Calvin Isaac, tribal chief of the Mississippi Band of Choctaw Indians and representative of the National Tribal Chairmen's Association, saying: "Culturally, the chances of Indian survival are significantly reduced if our children, the only real means for the transmission of the tribal heritage, are to be raised in non-Indian homes and denied exposure to the ways of their People.").
95. *See generally* Graham, *supra* note 93.
96. *See* 25 U.S.C.A. 1911(b) (requiring that any state have "good cause to the contrary" before removing the proceedings from the jurisdiction of the tribe).
97. *See generally* 25 U.S.C.A. 1911 (describing exclusive jurisdiction of the tribal courts and the circumstances under which tribal courts can intervene in state court proceedings).
98. *In Re Baby Boy L.*, 643 P.2d 168 (Kan. 1982). On March 27, 2009, the Kansas Supreme Court explicitly overruled the existing Indian Family Exception in Kansas. , 204 P.3d. 543 (Kan. Mar. 27, 2009).
99. *Id.* at 172.
100. *Id.*
101. *Id.* at 173.
102. *Id.* at 177.
103. *Id.* at 178.
104. *Id.* at 175.
105. *Id.* at 174.
106. *Id.* at 175.
107. *In Re Baby Boy C*, 805 N.Y.S2d 313 (NY 2005). The EIFE is followed in Alabama, Indiana, Louisiana, Missouri, and Tennessee. Currently, California state court districts are divided on whether the EIFE should apply.
108. *Id.* at 318. Fourteen states explicitly reject the EIFE, either by adopting legislation that codifies the rejection or in case law. These states include Alaska, Arizona, Idaho, Illinois, Iowa, Michigan, Montana, New Jersey, North Dakota, Oklahoma, Oregon, South Dakota, Utah, and Washington.

A Decade of Lessons Learned

Advocacy, Education, and Practice

Le Anne E. Silvey

The Indian Child Welfare Act of 1978 (ICWA), P.L. 95-608, was enacted due to the alarmingly high rate and often unwarranted removal of American Indian children from their families of origin. As a federal statute, ICWA supersedes state laws that govern the removal and placement of children in child protective proceedings. The legislative history behind the enactment of P.L. 95-608 describes the need for the rights and protection of American Indian children, their families, and the federally recognized tribes of which the children are members or eligible for membership.[1]

Prior to the passage of ICWA, American Indian children were being removed at a rate five times higher than the rate for children of any other group in the United States. According to S. S. Harjo, "from 1969 to 1974, 25% to 35% of Indian children were separated from their families and placed in foster care, with adoptive families, or in institutions."[2] The legislative history notes that the most prominent reasons for removal of American Indian children from their families of origin were poverty and alcoholism. In fact, of the Indian children removed between 1969 and 1974, approximately 85 percent of the children in foster care were in non-Indian homes.[3] This, in effect, proved deleterious not only for the children and their families, but also for the federally recognized tribes with which the children were affiliated, by depleting the tribes' membership and ultimate authority over its members. Many American Indian activists, scholars, and tribal communities referred to these removal rates as another form of genocidal practice and attempts at forced assimilation, not unlike the policies of the federal government towards American Indians for decades.[4]

In this chapter, I will draw on a decade of practice in Indian Child Welfare Act cases in the State of Michigan. Inherent in the lessons I learned is the steadfast need for ongoing advocacy, education, and training for human service professionals, lawyers, prosecuting attorneys, and judges in order to ensure the rights and protections of American Indian children, families, communities, and tribes afforded by P.L. 95-608. Despite thirty-one years of existence, the need still exists today for advocacy, education, and indigenous-centered practice to ensure that the minimum federal guidelines established in P.L. 95-608 are acknowledged, adhered to, and enforced.

Background

The Michigan Indian Child Welfare Agency (MICWA) is a tribally controlled and governed child placing agency for tribes in the state of Michigan. It began in 1978 through a research and development grant from the Administration for Children, Youth and Families. As the child placing agency for American Indian children of Michigan's tribal communities, it is headquartered in Sault Ste. Marie, Michigan, with satellite offices throughout the state. In 1984, I began my employment with MICWA as an MSW clinical supervisor in the Lansing office, with responsibilities for supervising ICWA staff, foster care, adoption, and tribal affiliation identification services for all of downstate Michigan.[5] In this capacity, I regularly interacted with tribal courts, state courts, Michigan Department of Social Services staff, and members of the American Indian community throughout the state. In 1988, I became the executive director of MICWA and was responsible for statewide operations, including contract negotiations with the State of Michigan and testifying as an expert witness in ICWA proceedings in both tribal and state courts in nearly all eighty-three counties of the state.

By the late 1980s, the Michigan Department of Social Services (now known as the Department of Human Services) established a Native American Task Force, which focused on system changes in hopes of improving the quality and effectiveness of social services delivery to low-income Native Americans in Michigan. I was appointed to serve on this task force, along with approximately twenty other members, indigenous and non-indigenous alike, representing state social services government staff, child placing agencies, tribes, and tribal communities. Chief among the task force's concerns were advocacy, education, training, and effective practice in implementing the Indian Child Welfare Act of 1978 for American Indian children, families, communities, and tribes in the State of Michigan. The task force met for two years and decided that a Native American Implementation Team was needed to oversee the implementation of twenty-seven recommendations the task force had established. In 1990, the DSS Native American Task Force Implementation Team was established and consisted of fifteen members, many of whom were members of the Native American Task Force established in 1988, including myself. Although the DSS Native American Task Force Implementation Team was in effect for two years, in 1990 a report on the implementation of the twenty-seven recommendations of the Native American Task Force was officially released.[6]

At the time of its release, the report discussed six major findings of the task force:

1. As a group, Native Americans remain the poorest of the poor of any group in the state.
2. Fifty percent of the Native American population was under the age of 18, making a focus on youth critical.
3. Disturbing trends in the delivery of social services showed an increase in out-of-home placements, in reports of sexual abuse involving children, and in protective services cases based on neglect due to alcohol abuse problems.
4. The unique political and legal status of Indian tribes was often misunderstood or ignored by not only the Department of Social Services but state government in general.
5. Programs and services which empowered tribes, Native communities or individuals had been and continued to be successful and had resulted in reduction of long-term reliance on public assistance.
6. Cultural ways, when taken into consideration in the development and delivery of social services, were continually proving to serve as strengths in the Native American community upon which efforts should be built.[7]

Based on these findings, the Native American Task Force recommendations centered on rebuilding or changing a system that would:

- Recognize and support diversity among all people, including Native Americans, as a way to improve the quality of life for all Michigan citizens.
- Invest in the future by enhancing the opportunities and circumstances which influence Native American children and youth.
- Empower Native American people to define and create their own future by promoting economic, social, and cultural self-sufficiency.
- Focus and maximize increasingly scarce resources.
- Involve partnerships that support and catalyze innovative and creative solutions to community development and, in turn,
- Continually evolve to meet the changing needs of a community of people.[8]

It should be noted that the Native American Task Force and Implementation Team members devoted four years to this undertaking. Unlike past Native American task force reports that "sat on a shelf collecting dust," members did not want their efforts to go unnoticed, with very little in the way of positive action having taken place. As a result, the report was officially released to draw attention to the ongoing need for advocacy, education, and indigenous-centered practice required to ensure the rights and protections afforded under ICWA, as well as to promote empowerment and a better quality of life for Native people in the state.

Advocacy and Education

As an American Indian social worker, scholar, and activist, it is my firm belief that advocacy and education go hand in hand. In my years of ICWA practice, I found that the overriding majority of the tasks I had were to advocate and educate on matters involving the legislative history and tenets of P.L. 95-608—the unique sovereign and legal standing of federally recognized tribes and their relationship with the State of Michigan; cultural beliefs, values, and practices of Michigan's indigenous tribes; and culturally relevant or indigenous-centered practice in carrying out the mandates of both ICWA and the social services manual policy for child protection proceedings. It was not uncommon to find child welfare professionals, attorneys, prosecuting attorneys, and judges who were unaware that the Indian Child Welfare Act of 1978 even existed, and for those who were aware that the federal statute existed, it was not uncommon to find that these human service and legal professionals lacked any semblance of knowledge or factual information about ICWA. Several attorneys informed me that they had no education or training about the Indian Child Welfare Act of 1978 in law school, let alone in any professional conferences they had attended since graduating from law school, no matter the sponsor. In addition, the Michigan Department of Social Services had no form of required training for its child welfare personnel on ICWA, and its social services manual policy outlining procedures for child protective services cases was far from being in compliance with the minimum federal guidelines established by law when dealing with Indian child welfare custody proceedings. Consequently, advocacy and education took center stage in my practice, as well as served as a focal point for the Native American Task Force and Implementation Team members during our years of service.

As a forefront to practice, advocating for and educating about Indian child welfare took on renewed meaning and urgency. It was not unusual to encounter questions and common refrains in the field from human service and legal professionals such as: "Why is there a special law for American Indian children and not for Blacks or Hispanics? What if the child has other ethnic identification besides being Indian, what happens to that part of a child's identity? How come the child's tribe isn't involved in the custody proceedings or isn't 'interested enough' to appear in court?" These are just a few examples of the many questions I encountered in the field, often by those with genuine interest and concern for American Indian children, although others asked with a noticeable tone of sarcasm and disbelief.

In light of my encounters in the field, some may wonder where one begins in the quest to advocate and educate others about the Indian Child Welfare Act of 1978. My response and advice was and is quite simple—begin at the beginning. Take the time to explain the legislative history leading up to the passage of P.L. 95-608, being careful to cite how American Indian children were being removed from their families of origin, often unjustifiably and at alarmingly high rates compared to children of any other group in the United States. The high rates of removal caused family disruption, oftentimes permanently; the breakdown of culture; and the loss of tribal membership and ultimately the supreme rights of tribes to exercise authority over their members. Not only were there high rates of removal, but history has shown that the overwhelming majority of children were placed in non-Native homes, which further served to decimate American Indian families, communities, tribes, and the transmission of cultural beliefs, values, and practices for generations.[9]

While investing effort in educating about the legislative history and passage of P.L. 95-608, it is equally important that education is focused on the unique sovereign and legal relationship that federally recognized tribes have with state governments. Predicated upon longstanding treaties between the federal government and American Indian tribes, this unique relationship has often been characterized as one wherein the federal government acts as a guardian or trust for tribes, much in the same vein as the relationship the state has with its ward.[10] Federally recognized tribes, such as the present thirteen indigenous tribes in the state of Michigan, have the right to govern themselves as sovereign nations. The relationship is one of government to government, with the federally recognized tribes granted full faith and credit as sovereign nations to govern themselves in the same way a state has to govern itself. In this manner, federally recognized tribes have the ultimate authority over such matters as their land, resources, implementation of services on and off the reservation, tribal membership criteria, and tribal members—including their children. The federal ICWA statute further supports tribes by setting minimum guidelines for ensuring the rights and protections of Indian children who are in danger of being removed from their families of origin. The statute is intended to preserve the integrity and authority of federal tribes by ensuring the rights and protections of their children, families, communities, culture, and ultimately their future.

Practice

The role of advocacy and education are central in the practice of Indian child welfare. Together, these interrelated and interconnected components are critical for all who engage in Indian child welfare practice, as every ICWA case demands equal investment in advocacy, education, and practice to ensure utmost compliance with P.L. 95-608. My experience in ten years of focused practice in Indian child welfare taught me that you must be prepared to engage in all three components at any point in time, as the welfare of Indian children, families, communities, and tribes are at stake. After all, there is no greater resource than our children, and they deserve our strongest advocacy, education, and practice efforts.

Child welfare professionals on the front lines need to make certain that they are knowledgeable about and diligently adhere to the minimum federal guidelines established with passage of ICWA. Upon initial contact, child protective services workers must make inquiry as to whether the family has any American Indian ancestry. This inquiry should be made without fail and is the first step in determining whether an Indian child welfare case is initiated and federal mandates are evident. Child welfare workers need to gather as much family-history information as possible relevant to Indian ancestry in order to determine if federal tribal affiliation is known via formal enrollment or eligibility for enrollment. If the family verifies federal tribal affiliation, membership, or eligibility for enrollment, the child welfare worker must then comply with both the social services manual policy and ICWA provisions throughout the child custody proceedings. This includes notifying the appropriate county juvenile court personnel, and triggering the departmental and juvenile court paperwork to notify the identified federal tribe that an Indian child welfare proceeding involves a member or potential member of the tribe. In the event tribal affiliation is known but the particular federal Indian tribe is not known, the child welfare worker follows department procedure for submitting a tribal affiliation identification request to MICWA. MICWA is contracted by the state to process tribal affiliation identification requests with tribes in Michigan as well as throughout the United States, if not directly with specific tribes then through the Bureau of Indian Affairs (BIA) field offices. In all cases, child welfare workers need to proceed according to the guidelines set forth in P.L. 95-608 for Indian child welfare cases pending formal notification from MICWA, the BIA, or the relevant federal tribe that the child is a member of, is eligible for membership in, or has no record of affiliation with.

During the years that the Native American Task Force and Implementation Team convened, members worked diligently to produce an updated social services manual policy that was in compliance with provisions of the Indian Child Welfare Act. The policy revisions included specific procedures I have described above, as well as revisions in department child welfare forms in child protective services, foster care, and adoption units. Revisions in child welfare forms included, but were not limited to, proper coding of an Indian child, a checklist of questions to ask about tribal affiliation identification for the child and parents, and the location of the tribe.

One of the more controversial issues I encountered during my years of Indian child welfare practice revolved around the issue of self-identification and who is an Indian. While many county social services staff worked cooperatively and in a timely fashion with MICWA on matters involving Indian child welfare cases, there were a few counties that fought complying with service manual policy and ICWA guidelines at every turn. For example, one county office had frontline staff who advocated for Indian children and wanted to cooperate in all steps of the process, but whose county director was vehemently against ICWA provisions. This particular county director believed that if his staff did not identify Indian children at the front end of a child custody proceeding, then by all rights the county did not have any Indian children in need of care, and thus there was no need to adhere to ICWA mandates. In actuality, this county had many Indian children in care, and once it came to MICWA's attention, MICWA fought on all fronts to ensure that Indian children and their families were afforded their due rights and protections under ICWA. Fighting this county director on behalf of Indian children was no simple matter. It got to the point where I had to file a Civil Rights complaint against the county as well as notify the director of the state department of social services, as required by MICWA's contract, that MICWA was going to file a lawsuit against the county for failure to comply with the federal statute and the state's own social services manual policy and procedures governing Indian child welfare cases. It was only after the state director intervened that action was taken to release Indian children from the county's authority, and then only a few of the children were turned over to MICWA for care. The county director saw to it that many of the Indian children were adopted out to non-Indian homes or were prematurely returned to their families of origin to avoid complying with state policy and federal law.

In the example highlighted above, the county director operated in a paternalistic fashion and firmly believed that he knew what was best for Indian children. He was consumed by his own biases and prejudice against American Indians generally, and American Indian children in his jurisdiction specifically. This paternalism translated into what I refer to as a "father knows best" mentality, wherein he firmly believed that Indian children were better off if they were placed in white, middle-class, religious families. Further, unless you had "pedigree papers" to prove you were an American Indian, he didn't believe any individual who self-identified as Indian.[11] While this example is extreme in my experience as an Indian child welfare practitioner, it is not unlike experiences I have heard about from other indigenous practitioners, tribes, and family members.

Conversely, I also had the experience of being pleasantly surprised by a judge in a large county where many Canadian Indians resided. This particular judge was well aware of ICWA and the fact that it did not cover Canadian Indian children. However, this juvenile court judge could be counted on to follow the spirit of the federal law in cases where Canadian Indian children were involved. These Canadian children were afforded many of the same rights and protections of ICWA, particularly as it related to notifying the tribe about an Indian child welfare proceeding and inviting a representative to attend hearings, as well as placement of the Canadian Indian child according to the placement provisions outlined in P.L. 95-608. There was a true spirit of cooperation and a genuine concern for the welfare of Indian children and their families in this judge's courtroom, no matter if they were of American or Canadian Indian descent.

Conclusions

The practice of Indian child welfare is steeped in advocacy and education, which I liken to a constant circular motion involving interrelated and interconnected components of advocacy, education, and practice. In my decade of focused Indian child welfare practice, I had many challenging, and equally rewarding, experiences. As well, I learned many lessons about advocacy, education, and practice by, for, and on behalf of indigenous children, families, communities, and tribes in Michigan. It has been thirty-one years since passage of the Indian Child Welfare Act of 1978. While many strides have been made along the way in the practice of Indian child welfare in the State of Michigan, we have many more yet to make.

Between 1988 and 1992, members of the Native American Task Force and Native American Implementation Team met to identify needs of the Native American population in the State of Michigan, as well as to identify system changes that, upon implementation, we believed would improve the quality and effectiveness of social services delivery to this citizenry. Out of this effort, twenty-seven recommendations were identified, and the Implementation Team was established to help make and oversee the changes in the system. While I have attempted to discuss some of the needs and changes that have been made in the Indian child welfare system, many of the original recommendations are still awaiting action. In fact, at the recent MSU College of Law The Indian Child Welfare Act at 30: Facing the Future conference, I was told that the twenty-seven recommendations I helped to make in the Native American Task Force Report of 1990 were all "still on the books," and the state was considering forming another task force to essentially do what previous members had already done.[12] Interestingly enough, the Empowering Native People report specifically stated that "the purpose of this report is to demonstrate to concerned individuals that this report has not 'been sitting on the shelf in the bureaucracy' but rather that *efforts to implement the recommendations have occurred and will continue.*"[13]

Finally, a critical lesson I have learned throughout all my experience and in the years since I worked with MICWA can be summed up as follows: You can write all the policies and procedures in the world, but without sanctions against performance, people do what they want. When the Indian Child Welfare Act of 1978 was enacted as P.L. 95-608, Congress did not appropriate funding, provide sanctions for noncompliance, or mandate an oversight committee or authority to ensure compliance with ICWA provisions. Professionals who knowingly violate tenets of ICWA and state social services manual policy and procedures lack integrity and ethics. The discussion of the county director whose paternalism equated to a belief that he knew what was best for Indian children is a concrete example of a human services professional who lacked integrity and ethics. Until we are able to prove one day that ICWA is no longer needed, there remains a critical need for advocacy, education, and ethical practice in Indian child welfare custody cases. As Chief Dan George aptly stated:

> What do we want? We want first of all to be respected and to feel we are people of worth; we want an equal opportunity to succeed in life. When you meet my children, respect each one for what he is: a child and your brother.
>
> Let no one forget it: we are a people with special rights guaranteed to us by promises and treaties. We do not beg for these rights nor do we thank you for them because, God help us, the price we paid was exorbitant. We paid for them with our culture, our land, our dignity and our self-respect. We have paid and paid and paid, until many of our people have become down-trodden, poverty-stricken and conquered.
>
> I know in your heart that you wish you could help. I wonder if there is much you can do, yet I know . . . there is a lot you can do.[14]

NOTES

1. J. A. MYERS, ED., THEY ARE YOUNG ONCE BUT INDIAN FOREVER (American Indian Lawyer Training Program 1981).
2. S. S. Harjo, *The American Indian Experience*, in FAMILY ETHNICITY: STRENGTH IN DIVERSITY 69 (H. McAdoo, ed., 2d ed., Sage 1999).
3. *Id.*, 63–71.
4. See, e.g., W. Byler, *The Destruction of American Indian Families*, in THE DESTRUCTION OF AMERICAN INDIAN FAMILIES 1–11 (S. Unger, ed., Association on American Indian Affairs 1977); C. T. Goodluck, *Necessary Social Work Roles and Knowledge with Native Americans: Indian Child Welfare Act*, in FAMILY ETHNICITY: STRENGTH IN DIVERSITY 293–300 (H. McAdoo, ed., 2d ed., Sage 1999); J. A. MYERS, ED., THEY ARE YOUNG ONCE BUT INDIAN FOREVER (American Indian Lawyer Training Program 1981); J. B. RICHLAND AND S. DEER 1 INTRODUCTION TO TRIBAL LEGAL STUDIES (Altamira Press 2004); L. E. Silvey, *Firstborn American Indian Daughters: Struggles to Reclaim Cultural and Self-Identity*, in FAMILY ETHNICITY: STRENGTH IN DIVERSITY 71–104 (H. McAdoo, ed., 2d ed., Sage 1999).
5. By downstate Michigan, I am referring to the entire lower peninsula of Michigan.
6. V. JOHNSON AND S. EVANS, EMPOWERING NATIVE PEOPLE (Michigan Department of Social Services 1990).
7. *Id.* at 2.

8. *Id.* at 2–3.
9. Byler, *The Destruction of American Indian Families*, in Meyers, *supra* note 1.
10. D. L. Fixico, Termination and Relocation: Federal Indian Policy, 1945–1960 (University of New Mexico Press 1986); Meyers, *supra* note 1.
11. I use the term "pedigree papers" to refer to formal tribal-enrollment identification papers.
12. Personal communication with Paul Cloutier, DHS Director of Native American Affairs, during *The Indian Child Welfare Act at 30: Facing the Future* conference on March 16, 2007, in East Lansing, Michigan. Paul informed me that the very same twenty-seven recommendations we made in 1990 were "still on the books," and that DHS was looking to assemble another task force to review the system again.
13. Johnson and Evans, *supra* note 6.
14. Chief Dan George, cited in Valorie Johnson and Sylvia Evans, Empowering Native People 1 (Michigan Department of Social Services 1990).

Where Have All the Children Gone? When Will They Ever Learn?

Maylinn Smith

> Culturally, the chances of Indian survival are significantly reduced if our children, the only real means for the transmission of tribal heritage, are raised in non-Indian homes and denied exposure to the ways of their people.
> —Chief Calvin Isaac of the Mississippi Band of Choctaw

Every tribe is one generation away from cultural and political extinction. Without a critical mass[1] of children, meaningful tribal acculturation cannot occur. Gone are the tribal languages.[2] Gone is the knowledge regarding the protection and use of medicinal native plants.[3] Gone are ceremonies for welcoming a child into this world.[4] Gone are the rituals connected to puberty, rites of passage, and physical and psychological healing.[5] Gone are the rich oral histories and indigenous knowledge reflecting hundreds upon hundreds of years of existence on tribal homelands within the area now known as North America.[6] Gone is the understanding of what it means culturally, politically, and ethically to be a member of an Indian tribe.[7] Gone is the understanding that being Indian is good.[8] Gone are the core characteristics that make Indian tribes "distinct, independent political communities"[9] with recognized retained sovereign powers.[10] Gone are the songs and ceremonies for sending spirits on their journey.[11]

In response to European contact, tribes and tribal people repeatedly expressed concerns over federal policies and practices[12] that facilitated and perpetuated cultural genocide.[13] Historically, tribal voices were ignored by the federal government when developing federal Indian policy and laws.[14] Protecting and preserving tribal culture has been a constant struggle for tribes. After surviving two centuries of federal policies designed to annihilate Indian culture and assimilate Indians into non-Indian society,[15] tribes and Indian child welfare organizations[16] finally developed a specific legislative package to halt the disproportionate removal of Indian children from their families.[17] As one of the few pieces of federal legislation requested by tribes, the Indian Child Welfare Act (ICWA)[18] does something for the benefit of tribes, as opposed to detrimental federal legislation imposed on tribes.

This article looks at the various aspects of representing parents and Indian custodians in involuntary ICWA proceedings. Part 1 briefly looks at the legislative history behind ICWA. Part 2 reviews historical and cultural factors that create both barriers and opportunities for working effectively with Indian families involved in state child custody proceedings. Part 3 discusses both the general requirements of the Act and the unique provisions that demand extra attentiveness when representing parental or Indian custodial interests. Part 4 considers deficiencies within the existing Act and makes recommendations for improving and enforcing the Act. Appendix A is a checklist that may assist practitioners when representing parents, or the Indian custodian, in an involuntary ICWA proceeding.

Part 1

All I want is right and justice.

—Red Cloud

The civil rights activities in the sixties and seventies sparked a change of focus in federal Indian policy. Congressional legislation began enhancing tribal self-governance,[19] tribal cultural preservation,[20] tribal economic and resource development,[21] and tribal education,[22] demonstrating a significant policy shift away from previous practices designed to eliminate the "Indian problem."[23] Along with federal policies supporting tribal self-determination and self-governance, Congress specifically recognized the impact state actions had on assimilating and annihilating the cultures of tribal people.[24] To remedy the devastating effect state child welfare practices had on Indian families, Congress conducted hearings over a four year period[25] and ultimately enacted ICWA in 1978.[26]

As the congressional findings recognized, "an alarmingly high percentage of Indian families [were] broken up by the removal, often unwarranted, of their children from them by nontribal public and private agencies and that an alarmingly high percentage of such children [were] placed in non-Indian foster and adoptive homes and institutions."[27] By establishing "minimum Federal standards for removal of Indian children"[28] and a procedural framework for handling state child custody matters involving Indian children, Congress anticipated a significant reduction in the number of Indian children found in state foster care systems.[29]

Nearly three decades later the statistics still show disproportionate representation of Indian children in the foster care system.[30] Overrepresentation of Indian children in child welfare systems is problematic from both a legal and social perspective.[31] Does this overrepresentation reflect a greater degree of abuse among Indian families than in the general population?[32] Are the children primarily being removed due to perceived neglect or poverty issues?[33] Or, does the disproportionate removal of Indian children indicate a continued lack of cultural awareness by state workers, judges, and attorneys? These questions cannot easily be answered due the lack of detailed data collection, particularly in several states with large Indian populations.[34] What the available information does reflect is that ICWA has not alleviated the disproportionate removal of Indian children from their families.[35]

Although helpful, evidently legislation alone cannot eliminate the overrepresentation of Indian children in state social service systems. Further exacerbating the problems of compliance is the indifference, ignorance, or arrogance[36] often exhibited by representatives of state and federal child welfare systems regarding tribal cultural preservation principles. Being able to successfully advocate for compliance with ICWA becomes critical when these attitudes factor into state decisions. Moving away from a Eurocentric view of family and societal norms, and towards meaningful application of tribal cultural values, will require a broader awareness of tribal cultures and a greater understanding of tribal histories.[37] Until this type of awareness is uniformly achieved among the various players in dependency and neglect matters, promoting and protecting parental and Indian custodial tribal interests, as well as the best interest of the Indian child, will continually be a challenge for the attorney representing the parent or Indian custodian.

Prior to passage of ICWA, surveys indicated that approximately 25–35 percent of all Indian children were separated from their families due to state actions.[38] Based on the survey results factors contributing to "the destruction of Indian family and community life"[39] were the federal boarding school and dormitory programs, state standards for defining mistreatment, and "ignorance of Indian cultural values and social norms."[40] Congress also found problematic the state court reliance on the testimony of social workers. These social workers "often lack[ed] the training and insights necessary to measure the emotional risk"[41] to an Indian child. This lack of cultural sensitivity by social workers was further exacerbated by state judges having no knowledge of tribal customs and traditions, and applying a Eurocentric standard of what constitutes abuse and neglect.[42] As Congress noted, state administrative and judicial bodies contributed to the "often unwarranted"[43] removal of Indian children from their families by failing "to take into account the special problems and circumstances of Indian families and the legitimate interest of the Indian tribe in preserving and protecting the Indian family as the wellspring of its own future."[44] The legislative history of ICWA raises the lack of cultural understanding, the lack of legal representation, the economic incentives associated with federally subsidized foster care programs, and the general social conditions often found within Indian communities as key factors in the disproportionate number of Indian children being placed in non-Indian foster homes.[45]

Despite its findings, Congress elected to not remove Indian child custody proceedings from the jurisdiction of state courts,[46] but instead imposed "certain procedural burdens upon state courts in order to protect the substantive rights of Indian children, Indian parents, and Indian Tribes in state court proceedings for child custody."[47] ICWA establishes a procedural framework for state custody proceedings involving an Indian child. ICWA, however, does not supply the vast historical and cultural knowledge necessary for eliminating the various biases impacting the breakup of Indian families. Nor can this legislation provide the requisite advocacy skills needed for working effectively with Indian families.

Part 2

> Natives and nonnatives tell two very different versions of history. These stories chronicle the clash of two worldviews.[48]

Federal legislation can be a powerful tool in changing societal practices. However, without sufficient knowledge of all applicable tribal, state, and federal laws; respect and understanding for tribal historical events; and an appreciation for the social dynamics of working with Indian families, the ability to adequately represent the parties in an ICWA proceeding may be seriously compromised.

In a perfect world, cultural sensitivity would be taught and modeled in the home, the schools, the workplace, and at all social events. Cultural preservation would automatically occur without any special efforts, and children would never be removed from their families absent verifiable, nonsubjective evidence of physical or emotional harm. Unfortunately, these socialization principles are not present in most communities, and subjectivity filters into state decision-making actions. Until a greater level of cultural sensitivity is uniformly achieved, ICWA cases will require more than minimal advocacy endeavors. Advocating for compliance with ICWA will require cultural awareness, active efforts, and the ability to educate the social workers, attorneys, and judges on the purpose and intent of ICWA.[49]

Awareness efforts include not only instilling an appreciation for factors contributing to the present situation, but also an understanding of how past and future conditions can impact the present situation. Historically, tribal people have not been dealt with in a good way.[50] Federal policy has created trauma, grief, and a lingering distrust among Indian families towards the U.S. government and child welfare systems.[51] Forced removal from, or diminishment of, tribal homelands;[52] broken agreements;[53] the decline in Indian population due to federal expansion, extermination, and assimilation policies;[54] the placement of Indian children in boarding schools;[55] the continuous erosion of tribal sovereignty;[56] and the termination of federally recognized tribes[57] are a few of the historical events contributing to the pervasive distrust by tribal people towards federal and state agencies.

Distrust of state and federal governmental authorities in the area of social service programs is further magnified when the communication methods, parenting styles, and core values of those authorities differ significantly from those found in tribal communities. Depending on the level of acculturation among the parties involved in any ICWA matter, this conflict between cultures can create additional stress, anxiety, and frustration during the resolution process.[58]

Traditional Indian values and Eurocentric values do not always mirror each other. Since value considerations influence methods utilized when resolving disputes, understanding these differences can help minimize needless conflict. A comprehensive comparative values chart is included in *Understanding Native American Culture: Insights for Recovery Professionals*.[59] The topics included in the chart 'are actually a mixture of values, behaviors, attitudes and life styles."[60] Underestimating the impact these values have in an ICWA case frequently derails efforts to prevent the breakup of an Indian family or to reunify an Indian family.[61]

Certain conflicts routinely surface in ICWA cases, reflecting cultural differences. Tribal concepts relating to cooperation, the importance of community or extended family, patience, generosity, avoidance of direct criticism, modesty, respect for age, indirect communication, and orientation towards the present often create reunification obstacles for Indian families. Any clash in cultural values usually works against the Indian family due to the control exercised by state social workers in dependency and neglect proceedings.

Cooperative structures emphasize maintaining or restoring harmony within the designated group.[62] The focus is less on process and more on desired outcomes when dealing with conflict. Resolution relies heavily on consensus building. In contrast, competitive or adversarial systems rely on hierarchy and authority vested in the few, encourage opposition among the various players, and create a winner/loser scenario.[63] Utilizing a cooperative model in ICWA cases can create a vastly different outcome from the results achieved in an adversarial model. Cooperation requires different advocacy skills than those commonly employed in state-handled ICWA cases.

The importance of extended family should not be ignored in ICWA cases.[64] Including extended family in ICWA process can be challenging, but the ability to appreciate and effectively utilize extended family[65] can drastically improve reunification efforts. Resolution of the perceived parenting problems often can be achieved with less resistance when key players within the extended family have meaningful input into the legal process.[66] In contrast, when extended family feels ignored, or feels actively excluded from participating in state proceedings, additional barriers will likely emerge, hindering resolution of the matter in a timely fashion or in accordance with ICWA requirements.[67]

Good listening skills, patience, respect, and cooperative resolution principles are essential for diminishing cultural barriers[68] and helping to ensure that the best interests of Indian children are achieved in ICWA cases. Communication frequently occurs on several levels with Indian clients: directly, indirectly, and culturally.[69] In order to communicate appropriately with a client, familiarity with all three aspects may be required. In addition, the advocate may need to act as a cultural translator between the client and other parties to the action in order to ensure that the needs of the client are being met.[70] This is particularly true when the client primarily adheres to traditional practices.

Indirect communication styles found in tribal communities can profoundly impact the final outcome in ICWA matters. Indirect communication encompasses all types of interactions between the state and the Indian family. The manner in which an Indian client responds to a question,[71] a client's comfort level with direct eye contact,[72] how requests for assistance are made,[73] whether the Indian client detects any disconnect between the words being said and the body language being observed,[74] and differences in how information is processed[75] are all elements of indirect communication. Frequently, problems arise when what the state says causes some misunderstanding, or offends a key player in ICWA process because of the manner in which a statement is made. Cooperation usually decreases and resistance increases when the indirect elements of communication give a different message from what is being communicated directly to the client or extended family.

Another common philosophical difference between Indians and Euro-Americans is the stronger orientation toward the present, as opposed to the future, and less emphasis on material possession among Indian peoples. Accumulating surplus wealth, in the broadest sense, for individual use, and developing long-term plans can be contrary to traditional values within tribal communities.[76] These cultural differences can create significant challenges in reunification efforts due to the value placed on individuality, self-sufficiency, the "puritan work ethic," and planning for the future by many state social workers.[77]

Barriers created through cultural biases are intensified by assumptions based on stereotypes. Ask someone to, "Draw a picture of an Indian outside of their home doing something." What that picture looks like can reveal a multitude of stereotypes and misconceptions.[78] Common stereotypes regarding Indian people, tribal systems, and living conditions within Indian Country produce obstacles to effectively resolving

ICWA cases. Although the Bureau of Indian Affairs (BIA) Guidelines attempt to minimize the impact of bias and stereotypes in ICWA matters,[79] it is hard to eliminate all the effects of state attitudes where Indian people are involved.[80]

Ultimately, education will be the most effective tool for changing the approaches used in ICWA cases. Education that discusses not only the history of the United States from the Indian perspective, but also tribal customs, traditions, values, spirituality, contemporary tribal communities, and the effects of raising Indian children outside their own cultural system should all be part of this educational process.[81] Ideally, this type of education would occur at all levels and throughout all age groups of society in order to facilitate a permanent shift in thinking patterns.

Until this paradigm shift occurs, judges, attorneys, social workers, service and treatment providers, and foster families all need to understand and appreciate tribal cultures when dealing with Indian families. This understanding will be much easier to achieve when Indian perspectives and issues are integrated into the mainstream, general-education system of the United States, thereby debunking myths, stereotypes, and biases pertaining to Indian people.[82] Certainly, compliance with ICWA would be simpler without cultural myths and misunderstandings factoring into the decision-making process.

Part 3

> Let us put our minds together, and see what life we will make for our children.
> —Tatanka Lotanka (Sitting Bull)

ICWA is not a complex piece of legislation. The requirements of ICWA are not ambiguous. The goals of ICWA are not unreasonable. Yet after more than thirty years, Indian children are still disproportionately removed from their families by states,[83] basic compliance with ICWA remains problematic,[84] and cultural bias still influences the decision making process.[85] These conditions make effective advocacy on behalf of parents or Indian custodians essential for halting the exodus of Indian children from their families and ensuring that the best interests of Indian children are attained.[86]

Determining ICWA's applicability requires only two factors: a state custody proceeding and an Indian child.[87] State custody proceedings are statutorily defined.[88] Additional inquiry may be necessary in certain circumstances to evaluate whether the matter falls within the scope of ICWA. For example, juvenile proceedings normally are excluded from the application of ICWA.[89] An exception to this rule is when the delinquency proceedings involve a status offense, and the child is not being returned to the parents or Indian custodian due to perceived inadequacies in the care or supervision of that Indian child. In this type of situation, ICWA applies.[90]

The term "Indian child" is also statutorily defined.[91] The key element in this determination is the issue of membership.[92] ICWA requires that the child be a member of a federally recognized tribe.[93] Tribes with only state recognition, however, may still be able to utilize ICWA,[94] unless prohibited by state laws, since states are free to provide greater protections than ICWA requires.[95] If a child is enrolled in a federally recognized tribe, proof of tribal enrollment satisfies this element. "Enrollment is the common evidentiary means of establishing Indian status, but it is not the only means nor is it necessarily determinative."[96]

The BIA Guidelines promulgated in connection with ICWA deal with how membership is established when a state does not know if the child is enrolled in a federally recognized tribe, or is even Indian.[97] Tribal pronouncements regarding membership are conclusive and will override any BIA findings regarding membership.[98] State courts are not qualified to determine tribal membership and should be challenged if they attempt to make this type of determination.[99]

Verification of membership should be made by contacting every tribe[100] in which the child possibly could be a member, as well as contacting the BIA office for the area in which the child is potentially a tribal member.[101] Effective advocacy may also require additional investigative activities if there is any reason[102] to believe a child involved in a state custody proceeding might be a tribal member or the child of a tribal member. Establishing Indian status often requires repeated contact with tribal entities in order to get meaningful input from the tribe. Both patience and perseverance are usually needed to get tribal participation in ICWA matters. The attorney for the parent or Indian custodian should undertake this verification if the state does not actively investigate the Indian-status issue.

In those few states employing some type of "Existing Indian Family" doctrine,[103] it is critical that information regarding membership, tribal connections, and the importance of protecting tribal culture be introduced into the state court record in order to ensure compliance with ICWA and preserve the issue for appeal. Tribal involvement is particularly important when a state employs some version of the Existing Indian Family doctrine, and the child's parents or Indian custodian wish to utilize the provisions of ICWA. When a tribe is actively involved in the ICWA process, it is difficult for states to find there is no tribal connection and no existing Indian family.

Once a case has ICWA status, several procedural steps must occur. Notice requirements are explicit, mandatory, and time sensitive.[104] In addition to the parents or Indian custodian receiving notice, the Indian child's tribe must receive notice of the proceedings in order for the state action to be valid. ICWA status also triggers appointment-of-counsel requirements,[105] jurisdictional determinations,[106] evaluation of whether the initial removal of the Indian child complies with the statutory requirements,[107] specific placement requirements,[108] and "[f]ull faith and credit to public acts, records, and judicial proceedings of Indian tribes."[109] Failure to comply with the statutory requirements can jeopardize the validity of ICWA proceedings.[110]

Jurisdictional determinations require special attention in ICWA cases. If the child is a ward of a tribal court or is domiciled within a tribe's recognized jurisdiction, the appropriate tribal court has exclusive jurisdiction.[111] When the tribal court has exclusive jurisdiction, the parents or Indian custodian must file a motion to transfer jurisdiction and dismiss the state proceedings to resolve the state action.[112]

In situations where there is concurrent jurisdiction between the tribal and state courts,[113] the parents or Indian custodian must decide whether they wish to request that the matter be transferred to the tribal court; which tribal court should have jurisdiction, if more than one tribal court could assume jurisdiction;[114] whether they will support any request by a tribe to transfer jurisdiction; or whether they will object to the transfer of jurisdiction.[115] Jurisdiction should be resolved at the earliest allowed point in the proceedings—after the tribe, parents, or Indian custodian have received notice of the proceedings.[116] Tribal delays in responding to the notice complicate any transfer requests to the tribal court.[117]

Transfer does not automatically occur when a parent or Indian custodian requests that the tribal court handle the matter. Tribal courts may decline the assumption of jurisdiction from the state,[118] and in some circumstances there may be no tribal forum available to take jurisdiction.[119] Frequently the state opposes transferring the custody proceedings on alleged "good cause" grounds.[120] Due to the discretionary nature of the "good cause" concept, cultural biases are often embedded in the reasons for a state court denying a request to transfer jurisdiction. Compliance with the BIA Guidelines[121] assists in curbing the impacts of state biases in transfer matters, but the ability to propose creative solutions[122] to perceived "good cause" arguments can further support transfer efforts by the parents or Indian custodian.

The burden of showing that good cause exists to not transfer the proceedings always rests with the party opposing the transfer.[123] In theory, that sounds good. In practice, the factors impacting this determination may revolve around the perceived capabilities of the tribal court and tribal service programs. Convincing the state court that the matter should transfer often feels like a best-interest determination. This "best interest" standard is contrary to the requirements of ICWA and should be challenged.[124] Good cause should be narrowly construed and limited to the factors in the BIA Guidelines.[125]

When an ICWA case remains in state court, a thorough review[126] and assessment of the initial removal should occur to ensure compliance with the statutory requirements[127] and standards of ICWA.[128] Of particular concern are the "active efforts"[129] requirements "designed to prevent the breakup of the Indian family."[130] Except in emergency situations, the state must provide remedial and rehabilitative services to the Indian family prior to removal. If these services have not been provided, the removal may be improper, and the proceedings should be stayed to determine whether the initial removal complied with ICWA.[131]

In addition to meeting the "active efforts" requirement, the state must show by "clear and convincing evidence, including the testimony of qualified expert witnesses, that the continued custody of the child by the parent or Indian custodian is likely to result in serious emotional or physical damage to the child."[132] Due to this heightened standard, the attorney should exercise caution prior to consenting to any state request for temporary legal custody.[133]

Expert witnesses are required at two points in ICWA proceedings: prior to removing a child from an Indian family,[134] and at the point when the state moves to terminate parental interests.[135] This requirement places a special burden on the state and should be closely scrutinized to ensure that the person testifying is, in fact, qualified. The BIA Guidelines provide a list of characteristics a person qualified to testify in an ICWA matter should possess.[136] A key characteristic of an expert witness is having knowledge about tribal customs and child-rearing practices within the Indian child's tribe.[137] In addition to being qualified, the expert witness must testify to specific conditions that would likely result in serious physical or emotional damage to the Indian child.[138] Challenging the expert witness, both on qualifications and the sufficiency of the testimony provided, is particularly critical when the state is attempting to avoid the placement preference of ICWA.

Reunification plans require close inspection. The plan should clearly state what is expected of the client, along with what assistance, both directly and indirectly,[139] the state will provide to ensure reunification of the family. Locating culturally appropriate services and resources for the purpose of alleviating the concerns leading to removal of the Indian child from the home is a component of the active efforts a state must make in ICWA matters.[140] The state's criteria for evaluating compliance should be clearly stated and should reflect objective standards. The time frames proposed should reflect realistic goals given the nature and availability of needed services.[141] Frequently the state tries to impose requirements set forth in the Adoption and Safe Families Act (ASFA)[142] in reunification plans. Where the principles of both statutes can be successfully integrated, both acts can be utilized. If the statutes conflict, ICWA trumps, since specific legislation trumps general legislation.[143]

Placement remains an area where noncompliance with ICWA routinely occurs.[144] States generally contend that the lack of appropriate extended family and licensed Indian foster homes prevents placement in accordance with ICWA,[145] or a tribal act establishing different placement preferences.[146] This position not only ignores the "diligent search"[147] requirements of the Act, but also ignores the limited grounds for avoiding compliance based on "good cause."[148] Tenacity is required when the state attempts to use this best interest principle to ignore ICWA placement preferences.[149]

Best interest of an Indian child is not the same as for a non-Indian child. Best interest is the standard commonly used in any custody proceeding, but courts have found "it is an improper test to use in ICWA cases because ICWA expresses the presumption that it is in an Indian child's best interest to be placed in accordance with the statutory preferences."[150]

Obtaining compliance with ICWA placement preferences is much easier when extended family has come forward requesting that they be considered as a placement option. Under ICWA, the state is required to place the Indian children in accordance with the placement preferences.[151] The parents or Indian custodian can assist in these efforts by providing names and contact information about appropriate placement options to the attorney. Getting extended family to come forward for consideration as a placement option may require persistence and good indirect communication skill's.[152] If the state does not make a diligent search for extended family, the attorney for the parent or Indian custodian should assist in locating suitable placement options for the Indian child. The more placement options the state has, the greater the chances for compliance with ICWA.

It is common for Indian families to believe "that once a child goes into foster care, he or she never returns home."[153] This perception helps explain the hesitation by extended family to have a child placed with them by the state. The extended family may fear that the extended family member's child will never be placed back with the parent or Indian custodian, or that their own children will be removed if the state is allowed access to their home. States often view this reluctance as evidence that extended family is unwilling to be considered as a placement option. This is often not the case. In situations where immediate reunification is not feasible, the attorney for the parent or Indian custodian can help facilitate placement of the Indian child with extended family by establishing a level of trust with the extended family, and by emphasizing the need for assistance in restoring the family.

So long as the state supports reunification in an ICWA proceeding, the parent or Indian custodian and state normally have the same goals. Allowing direct contact between the client and the social worker may be acceptable, and most issues can probably be resolved by carefully worded stipulations. If at some point in the proceedings the state shifts towards involuntarily terminating parental rights or custody, the nature of the ICWA proceeding needs to transform into an adversarial format to protect the client's interests. At this point, client contact with the social worker should only occur with counsel present, and communications should be reduced to writing whenever possible.

Even when reunification is not feasible, remedies other than termination of parental rights can be utilized in ICWA cases. Long-term or permanent guardianships can be established to ensure permanency and protect the Indian child from physical or emotional harm. Guardianships have the advantage of not requiring termination of parental rights, and they frequently utilize extended family. This remedy is preferable in many tribal communities since it is consistent with child-rearing practices historically used by tribes.[154]

Another option under ICWA is "consent to adoptive placement."[155] The advantage to this method of placement is that consent "may be withdrawn for any reason at any time prior to the entry of a final decree of termination or adoption."[156] A parent or Indian custodian can select who should adopt the Indian child. Parental rights do not have to be terminated prior to commencing the consent-to-adoption proceedings. This process protects a parent's request to terminate parental rights but still have input into selecting where the child will be placed. In this scenario, parental rights terminate virtually simultaneously with the finalization of the adoption. This process allows for the withdrawal of consent up until the moment the adoption is finalized.

Generally, adoption proceedings cannot commence until parental rights have been terminated. Once parental rights are terminated, the state may not support an adoption consistent with a parent's wishes, leaving the parents with no simple remedy for ensuring that their desires for adoptive placement are considered.[157] Consent to adoption proceedings avoids this type of situation and is consistent with the open-adoption concept common within Indian Country.[158]

If the state insists on involuntarily terminating parental rights or custody, it has the burden of showing beyond a reasonable doubt that allowing the child to remain in the custody of the parent or Indian custodian would likely cause serious emotional or physical harm to the child.[159] Like any initial removal from the Indian family, this action requires testimony from a qualified expert witness.[160] Given the level of proof required to terminate parental rights in ICWA cases, effective cross-examination and independent expert witnesses[161] can often cast sufficient doubt to thwart a state's attempt to terminate parental rights involuntarily, particularly if less severe options such as guardianship can be utilized.

The final areas deserving mention are motions to invalidate an action for violation of ICWA,[162] writs, and federal remedies. A parent or Indian custodian "may petition any court of competent jurisdiction to invalidate"[163] a state action that does not comply with key sections of ICWA. The parent may also withdraw any consent "obtained through fraud or duress"[164] within two years of a finalized adoption. In addition to invalidating the proceedings, noncompliance with ICWA may be grounds for writs of mandamus or prohibition when state courts fail to follow the statutory requirements. Once there is documented noncompliance with ICWA, a federal cause of action against the state can be initiated.[165] As the above remedies reflect, ensuring compliance with ICWA is rarely simple. Absent amendments to ICWA addressing compliance issues, effective advocacy still remains the primary tool for protecting tribal cultures from extinction due to state child custody practices.

Part 4

> Change is inevitable, and change is important. Sometimes you get that uncomfortable feeling that you can't change anything.
>
> —Joe David, Haida Nation

Although numerous attempts have been made to modify ICWA,[166] it has never been substantively amended. This track record indicates that changing ICWA is difficult. However, two modifications that could improve compliance with ICWA are the inclusion of incentives and sanctions. The Adoption and Safe Families Act utilizes an incentive program. ASFA has been in effect for a decade. Unlike with ICWA, ASFA reports do not indicate widespread concerns regarding noncompliance issues.[167] Technical and financial assistance is routinely given to states to improve rates of compliance with AFSA. The financial and technical assistance provided in the ASFA could be duplicated by ICWA.[168]

States could receive federal awards for transferring jurisdiction to tribal courts, for making active efforts to prevent the breakup of the Indian family, for following the placement preferences of ICWA, and for utilizing permanency methods that do not require termination of parental rights. Since the incentives program appears to have positive impact on ASFA, it could be equally effective in ICWA matters.

Along with incentives, sanctions should be an option. Currently, states not complying with ICWA face little fear of repercussions. ICWA proceedings may be invalidated[169] or a federal action initiated,[170] but these remedies only occur after the damage has already been done to the Indian child and the Indian family. Neither of these actions significantly inconvenience the state entities, who either actively or passively avoid compliance with ICWA. Absent some type of consequence, meaningful change rarely occurs. Perhaps the possibility of financial sanctions would motivate greater compliance with ICWA and reduce the impact of cultural bias in many ICWA cases.

Both of these modifications would address the continuing problems with compliance that have plagued ICWA since its enactment. Like many federal acts with good intent, enforcement has proven problematic. Significantly increasing available resources to meet the statutory mandates could only improve compliance.

Conclusion

> We need to find a way for all of us to walk in two worlds at once, to be part of the world culture without sacrificing the cultural heritage of our own families and traditions.
>
> —Jack Weatherford, *Savages and Civilization—Who Will Survive?*

Advocacy is more than simply adequately representing a client. Advocacy is about educating both yourself and others about tribal history, applicable laws, and the characteristics that make tribes distinct and unique political entities with rights of self-governance. In ICWA matters, vigorous advocacy can help halt, if not reverse, the cultural genocide of Indian peoples. Overcoming the effects of ignorance, arrogance, and indifference requires cultural awareness, compassion, and passion. Utilizing these advocacy concepts is appropriate when a tribe's most valuable resources are at stake: its children and future.

NOTES

In memory of Paul Raftery, who went the extra mile, often on his bike, for his ICWA client; and Chief Judge Louise Burke, who taught me the importance of appreciating tribal customs and traditions when children were involved. A special thanks to Mistee Rides at the Door for her research, to Stacey Gordon for her exceptional research and editing skills and to J.N.R. for working at being a healthy parent in order to get her children back via the Indian Child Welfare Act.

1. In *Grutter v. Bollinger*, 539 U.S. 306, 335–36 (2003), the Supreme Court recognized the "critical mass" concept for purposes of promoting diversity in higher education.
2. Charles Wilkinson discusses the effects of losing tribal languages. In many tribes, only the middle-aged and elders are now fluent speakers. In the United States there are only thirty-six tribes with more than 1,000 fluent speakers. CHARLES WILKINSON, BLOOD STRUGGLE: THE RISE OF MODERN INDIAN NATIONS 358–67 (W.W. Norton 2005). Language preservation is important given the oral nature of tribal histories. Darrell Kipp explained tribal members' support for the Blackfeet immersion program this way: For the "[s]ame reason you don't burn down your libraries we keep our language. Our language is our library. . . . For example, in Blackfeet, there is no gender, so the world can be suddenly seen in a different fashion." *Id.* at 363.
3. DAVID HURST THOMAS, JAY MILLER, RICHARD WHITE, PETER NABOKOV & PHILIP J. DELORIA, THE NATIVE AMERICANS: AN ILLUSTRATED HISTORY 39–40 (Betty and Ian Ballantine, eds., Turner Publishing 1993).
4. JOSEPHA SHERMAN, INDIAN TRIBES OF NORTH AMERICA 11, 74, 86, 92, 124, 128 (Portland House 1990).
5. *Id.* at 11, 29, 74, 86, 128. *See generally* Tarrell A. A. Portman, Michael T. Garrett, *Native American Healing Traditions*, 53 INTL. J. DISABILITY, DEV. AND EDUC. 453–69 (2006).
6. Charlotte Goodluck and Angela A. A. Willeto, *Native American Kids 2000: Indian Child Well-Being Indicators* 17–20, *available at* http://nicwa.org/resources/catalog/research.
7. In *Morton v. Mancari*, 417 U.S. 535, 554 (1974), the Supreme Court recognized Indian preference applied not because the person was a member of a racial group, but rather because the individual

was a member of a federally recognized tribe, making this a political classification rather than a racial one.

8. During the comment period after the Second Plenary Session on Emerging Issues, Frederick Lomayesva, associate judge for the Hopi Tribe Appellate Court told of an ICWA case in which he had been recently involved. Paternity had not been established. The presumed father was Indian. The other attorneys and the judge were non-Indian. Justice Lomayesva relayed their discussion about whether it would be better for the child if he were found to not be Indian. (Indian Law Clinics and Externship Symposium, Albuquerque, New Mexico, June 23, 2007) (Author's notes from Symposium).

9. *Worcester v. Georgia*, 31 U.S. 515, 559 (1832).

10. *Cohen's Handbook of Federal Indian Law*, §§ 4.01–4.03 (Nell Jessup Newton et. al., eds., 2005 ed., Lexis).

11. Sherman, *supra* note 4, at 11, 36, 86.

12. In 1819, the federal government enacted policies designed to assimilate the Indian population into American society and eradicate any values, customs, and traditions associated with being Indian. *Civilization Fund Act*, Ch. 85, 3 Stat. 516–17 (1819).

13. *See Proclamation of Sovereign Tribal Nations Supporting President Clinton's Policy on Genocide*, Michael J. Anderson, *Facing the Future in the New Millennium*, reprinted in ROBERT ODWAI PORTER, SOVEREIGNTY, COLONIALISM AND THE INDIGENOUS NATIONS: A READER 49, 50 (Carolina Academic Press 2005). PETER NABOKOV, NATIVE AMERICAN TESTIMONY: A CHRONICLE OF INDIAN-WHITE RELATIONS FROM PROPHECY TO THE PRESENT, 1292–2000, at 90–116 (rev. ed., Penguin Books 1999). *See* Statement of Senator Abourezk at Hearings before the Subcommittee on Indian Affairs of the Committee on Interior and Insular Affairs, *Indian Child Welfare Program*, 93rd Cong., 2d Sess., 1, 3 (1974).

14. Nabokov, *supra* note 13, at 117–69.

15. Kevin Gover, *Remarks at the Ceremony Acknowledging the 175th Anniversary of the BIA* (September 8, 2000), *available* at http://www.tribal-institute.org/lists/kevir_gover.htm. *See generally* John W. Ragdale, Jr., *The Movement to Assimilate the American Indians: A Jurisprudential Study*, 57 UMKC L. REV. 399 (1989).

16. Both the Association of American Indian Affairs (AAIA) and the Devil's Lake Sioux Tribe, nka Spirit Lake Tribe, were instrumental in the initial efforts to get legislation introduced addressing the problems surrounding removal of Indian children from their families. Marc Mannes, *Factors and Events Leading to the Passage of the Indian Child Welfare Act*, 74 CHILD WELFARE 264–82 (1995).

17. Wilkinson, *supra* note 2, at 258–59. Bert Hirsch, an attorney with the AAIA, became aware of problems in North Dakota in 1967. This led to national efforts involving tribal leaders and Indian organizations to get this issue addressed in Congress. Although Charles Wilkinson indicates that legislation was introduced in 1972, the legislative history reflects that nothing was introduced in Congress until 1974. 93rd Cong., 2d Sess., 1 (1974).

18. 25 U.S.C. §§ 1901–63 (2000).
19. Indian Self-Determination Act, 25 U.S.C. §§ 450–450e-3 (2000).
20. *E.g.*, American Indian Religious Freedom Act, 42 U.S.C. § 1996 (2000); Native Graves Protection and Repatriation Act, 25 U.S.C. §§ 3001–13 (2000); and Native American Language Act, 25 U.S.C. §§ 2901–06 (2000).
21. *E.g.*, National Indian Forest Resources Management Act, 25 U.S.C. §§ 3101–20 (2000); Development of Tribal Mineral Resources Act, 25 U.S.C. §§ 2101–08 (2000); Indian Energy Resources Act, 25 U.S.C. §§ 3501–06 (2000); American Indian Agricultural Resource Management Act, 25 U.S.C. §§ 3701–46 (2000); and Native American Business Development, Trade Promotion and Tourism Act, 25 U.S.C. §§ 4301–07 (2000).
22. *E.g.*, Tribally-Controlled School Grants Act, 25 U.S.C. §§ 2501–11 (2000); Indian Education Act, 25 U.S.C. §§ 2601–06 (1988) (repealed 1994); Tribally-Controlled College or University Assistance Act, 25 U.S.C. §§ 1801–52 (2000); Indian Higher Education Programs, 25 U.S.C. §§ 3301–71 (2000); and Standards for Basic Education of Indian Children in BIA Schools, 25 U.S.C. § 2001 (2000).
23. Several pieces of federal legislation have purportedly been the solution to the Indian problem. Many of these "solutions" involved education in some form. *See* Raymond Cross, *American Indian Education: The Terror of History and the Nation's Debt to the Indian Peoples*, 21 UARLR L. REV. 941, 952–53 (1999).
24. Prior to 1978, approximately 25 percent of Indian children were removed from their homes, and 85 percent of these children were living in non-Indian homes. Eddie F. Brown, Gordon E. Limb, Ric Munoz & Chey A. Clifford, *Title IV-B Child and Family Service Plans: An Evaluation of Specific Measures Taken by State to Comply with the Indian Child Welfare Act* 9 (2001), *available at* http://nicwa.org/resources/catalog/research.
25. Senator James Abourezk of South Dakota first introduced legislation in 1974 to address concerns about the removal of Indian children from their families. Mannes, *supra* note 16, at 264.
26. 25 U.S.C. §§ 1901–63 (2000).
27. *Id.* at § 1901(4).
28. *Id.* at § 1902.
29. H.R. Rep. 95-1386 (1978), reprinted in 1978 U.S.C.C.A.N. 7530, 7532.
30. National foster care statistics showed that American Indians/Alaska Natives (AI/AN) made up 2 percent of the children in the foster care system in 2004, although this group represents only about 1 percent in the general population. National Data Analysis System, *CWLA Fact Sheet and Relevant Research*, *available at* http://ndas.cwla.org/research_info/specialtopic1a.asp [hereinafter CWLA Fact Sheet].
31. The National Incidence Studies of Child Abuse and Neglect conducted in 1980, 1986, and 1993 by the federal government found that children of color are not abused at higher rates than white children. National Incidence Studies, *Third National Incidence Study of Child Abuse and Neglect*, *available at* http://www.healthieryou.com/cabuse.html [hereinafter NASCAN].
32. The 2005 statistics for children reflect that 7.3 percent of maltreated AI/AN children are victims of physical abuse, and 4.1 percent of AI/AN are victims of sexual abuse. Administration for

Children and Families, *Race of Victims by Maltreatment Type, 2005, available at* http://www.acf.hhs.gov/programs/cb/stats_research/index.htm [hereinafter Maltreatment Type Report 2005].

33. *Id.* The 2005 statistics for children reflect that 65.7 percent of maltreated AI/AN are victims of neglect.

34. Kathleen Earle, *Child Abuse and Neglect: An Examination of American Indian Data* 25–26 (2000), *available at* http://nicwa.org/resources/catalog/research; Terry Cross, Kathleen Fox, Jody Becker-Green, Jamie Smith, Angela Willeto, *Case Studies in Tribal Collection and Use,* 7–17 (2004), *available at* http://nicwa.org/policy/research.

35. A recent article from Oregon reports that "recent numbers from the state Department of Human Services show that 12.4 percent of the more than 16,000 Oregon children in foster care last year were Native American, while Native Americans account for 1.3 percent of the Oregon population 18 and younger." Michelle Cole, *Number of Minority Kids in Foster Care Draws Concern: Families—Black and Native American Children Are Vastly Overrepresented in Foster Homes, a Study Shows,* THE OREGONIAN ON-LINE (July 25, 2007). Similar statistics can be found in most states with large Indian populations. *See* statistics on AI/AN in the state foster care system *at* http://www.fostercaremonth.org/Newsroom/Facts/Pages/StateData.aspx.

36. Former Fort Peck tribal judge A. J. Stafne once stated that most problems relating to Indian law issues can be attributed to these three principles. A very similar view was recently expressed in a radio segment dealing with domestic violence against Indian women living within Indian Country. National Public Radio. *Rape Cases on Indian Lands Go Uninvestigated,* NAT. PUB. RADIO, July 25, 2007 (radio broadcast), *available at* http://www.npr.org.

37. Nabokov, *supra* note 13, at 69–72.

38. H.R. Rep. 95-1386.

39. *Id.*

40. *Id.* at 7532. Congress looked at the role extended family played in raising Indian children, and the more permissive parenting style utilized in Indian families. Congress also considered the cultural bias against Indian families regarding alcohol abuse and noted that removal of children rarely occurred when non-Indian parents were abusing alcohol.

41. *Id.*

42. *Id.* at 7533.

43. 25 U.S.C. § 1901(4).

44. Report, *supra* note 38, at 7541.

45. *Id.* at 7533–34.

46. *Id.* at 7536–41.

47. *Id.*

48. Charlotte Goodluck and Angela Willeto, *Native American Kids 2000: Indian Child Well-Being Indicators* 17 (2002), *available at* http://nicwa.org/resources/catalog/research.

49. Rachel Bennett, National Resource Center for Foster Care & Permanency Planning, *Information Packet: American Indian Children in Foster Care* 5 (2003), *available at* http://www.hunter.cuny.edu/socwork/nrcfcpp/downloads/american-indian-children-in-fc.pdf.

50. *See generally*, Helen Hunt Jackson, A Century of Dishonor (Harper & Brothers, 1881). Numerous documentaries address the United States federal Indian policy. *The Way West* (PBS Home Video 1994) (DVD) chronicles the impacts westward expansion by non-Indians had on Indian people and lands. *In the White Man's Image* (PBS Video 1992) (videotape) discusses federal Indian policies, including the boarding school efforts. A recent documentary produced by the Tanana Chiefs Conference in 2006 entitled *Tribal Nations—The Story of Federal Indian Law* provides an excellent general overview of the development of U.S. Indian law and policies.

51. Gover, *supra* note 15. Maria Yellow Horse Brave Heart, *Oyate Ptayela: Rebuilding the Lakota Nation through Addressing Historical Trauma among Lakota Parents*, reprinted in VOICES OF FIRST NATIONS PEOPLE: CONSIDERATIONS FOR HUMAN SERVICES 109-26 (H. Weaver, ed., The Haworth Press 1999).

52. DOCUMENTS OF UNITED STATES INDIAN POLICY, n. 42, 52–53 (Francis Paul Prucha, ed., University of Nebraska Press 1975). The Indian Removal Act of 1830 gave President Jackson the authority to give lands in the West to Indian tribes located in the east in exchange for giving up their homelands in any existing U.S. state or territory. This policy ignored the fact that the lands in the west were already occupied by tribal groups. There are approximately 55 million acres of tribal and individual trust Indian land within the United States. This is down 64 percent from the land base guaranteed by treaties of approximately 156 million acres in 1881. Indian Lands Tenure Foundation, *Frequently Asked Questions, available at* http://www.indianlandtenure.org/faqs/faqs.html.

53. Nabokov, *supra* note 13. "Although the drama of Indian-white warfare has always captured the popular imagination, Native Americans lost far more of their land and independence by the bloodless process of signing treaties than they ever did on the battlefield. Indeed, most of the violence between Indians and whites flared up because Native Americans were being deprived of the very land promised them in earlier treaties." *Id.* at 117.

54. *See* Douglas H. Ubelaker, *North American Indian Population Size, A.D. 1500 to 1985*, 77 AMERICAN JOURNAL OF PHYSICAL ANTHROPOLOGY 289–94 (2005). Estimates of North American Indian population size suggest that the indigenous population numbered about 1,894,350 around A.D. 1500, and 530,000 by 1900. *Id.* at 291. The 2000 population data shows 4,119,301 American Indian/Alaska Natives in the United States. *Available at* http://www.census.gov/compendia/statab/tables/07s0042.xls.

55. In 1880 there were 60 Indian boarding schools. By 1911 there were 156 Indian boarding schools. In 1983 there were 57 BIA-funded boarding schools. *Report on BIA Education: Excellence in Indian Education through the Effective Schools Process. Final Review Draft* 15–17 (1988), *available at* http://www.eric.ed.gov.

56. David Getches discusses the impact Supreme Court decisions have had on tribal sovereignty under Chief Justice Rehnquist. *Beyond Indian Law: The Rehnquist Court's Pursuit of States' Rights, Color-Blind Justice and Mainstream Values*, 86 MINN. L. REV. 267, 279–86 (2001).

57. During the 1950s, Congress terminated the federal relationship with more than one hundred tribes. *See* DAVID H. GETCHES, CHARLES F. WILKINSON & ROBERT A. WILLIAMS, JR., CASES

AND MATERIALS ON FEDERAL INDIAN LAW 11 (5th ed., West Publishing 2005)
58. *See generally* Charles Horejsi, Bonnie Heavy Runner Craig, and Joe Pablo, *Reactions by Native American Parents to Child Protection Agencies: Cultural and Community Factors* (1992). Originally published in 71 CHILD WELFARE 329 (July/August 1992), *available at* http://www1.dshs.wa.gov/ca/pubs/manuals_ICWAppA_6.asp.
59. DON COYHIS, UNDERSTANDING NATIVE AMERICAN CULTURE: INSIGHTS FOR RECOVERY PROFESSIONALS 61 (Coyhis Publishing 1999). The chart in this publication was prepared by Joann Sebastian Morris (Chippewa/Oneida).
60. *Id.* at 47.
61. *Id.* at 46.
62. Robert Yazzie, *"Life Comes From It": Navajo Justice Concepts*, 24 N.M. L. REV. 175, 180–87 (1994). Justice Yazzie uses the terms "vertical justice" and "horizontal justice" to explain the differing approaches to dispute resolution.
63. *Id.* at 177–78.
64. Horejsi et al., *supra* note 58, at 328.
65. Occasionally the extended family member with the most influence over the parents or Indian custodian may not be a biological relative, but instead be related in accordance with tribal traditions. Members of the extended family often bring their own issues into these proceedings; being able to recognize and minimize any negative impact on the client requires a solid understanding of family and cultural dynamics.
66. Coyhis, *supra* note 59, at 48–49.
67. Horejsi et al., *supra* note 58, at 338–40.
68. Coyhis, *supra* note 59, at 53.
69. How you say something is as important as what is said. Culturally explaining the matter in the form of a story may be more effective, or apologizing for possibly offending anyone by what might be said before discussing a topic may be appropriate. Knowing the cultural norms is very important and should be viewed as part of adequate representation.
70. At a recent family group conference meeting in an ICWA case, the grandfather of the Indian child repeatedly raised the issue that he had not gotten to see the child. The state kept telling him to call and request a visit. Finally I intervened and made a direct request for a visit on behalf of the grandfather at the meeting.
71. Coyhis, *supra* note 59, at 53–54. Indian people may not respond immediately to a question. Silence makes some people uncomfortable. The person then concludes that the Indian individual either does not understand the question, was not listening, or is being uncooperative. Frequently none of these conclusions would be correct. By jumping in to fill the silence, the person demonstrates a lack of respect for tribal culture and may impair the working relationship with the Indian client, simply by not recognizing the more passive communication style of many Indian people.
72. *Id.* at 55. Many tribal cultures do not value direct eye contact in the same manner as Euro-Americans. "Lowering the head or eyes means that respect is being shown for the other person. It doesn't mean the client is not listening." *Id.*

73. Clients may have literacy issues that adversely impact proceedings. English may be a second language, and reading may be difficult. A client had been working with the state for approximately a year before I began representing him. The state complained that he did not do what was required under the reunification plan. During our first visit, I discovered he could not read. The social worker had never read the reunification plan to this parent, nor had the social worker discovered that he could not read. Everything the state asked him to do, he did. If it was simply in the plan and they had not verbally asked him to complete it, it was not done.
74. Coyhis, *supra* note 59, at 56.
75. *Id.* at 51–53. Indian people often approach problems from a "right-brain" or nonlinear framework that may conflict with the step-by-step approach commonly used by state agencies, which creates additional communication challenges. Effective advocacy can require an ability to convert the Indian client's "story" into a sequentially formatted, direct proposal, and the state's timeline approach into a story.
76. *Id.* at 49–50.
77. Considering the viewpoints and needs of extended family can be contrary to the concepts of individuality. Several families living together may not reflect self-sufficiency, and working to meet current needs without planning for possible future needs is not favored.
78. Evelyn Stevens, an attorney at the Confederated Salish and Kootenai Tribes, tells a story about an ICWA hearing in California in which the judge asked if the extended family still lived in a teepee. In the movie *Smoke Signals*, one of the characters states that he doesn't drink. The sheriff responds by asking what type of Indian he is. Although statistics show alcohol usage is no greater in Indian communities than in the general population, the myth of the drunk Indian persists. *See* survey results, SAMHSA, Office of Applied Studies, National Survey on Drug use and Health, Table 2.62B, *available at* www.oas.samhsa.gov/nhsda/2k3tabs/Sect2peTabs55t069.pdf.
79. Bureau of Indian Affairs Guidelines for State Courts, Indian Child Custody Proceedings, 44 Fed. Reg. 67584 (November 26, 1979) § B.3(a) [hereinafter BIA Guidelines], *available at* http://www.nicwa.org/policy/regulations/icwa/ICWA_guidelines.pdf.
80. *See generally* Lorie M. Graham, *The Racial Discourse of Federal Indian Law*, 42 TULSA L. REV. 103 (2006).
81. Lou Matheson, *The Politics of the Indian Child Welfare Act*, 41 SOCIAL WORK 232–36 (1996).
82. Montana is the only state that specifically recognizes the importance of preserving Indian culture through education in its constitution. Mont. Const. Article X, Section 1(2)(1972).
83. CWLA Fact Sheet, *supra* note 30.
84. A report to the Montana legislature found widespread noncompliance with ICWA in several areas. Legislative Audit Division, State of Montana, *2002 Performance Audit: Child Protective Services* 59–81, *available at* http://leg.mt.gov/content/audit/download/02p-02.pdf. *See also* B. J. Jones, Jodi A. Gillette, Deborah Painte, Susan Paulson, *Indian Child Welfare Act: A Pilot Study of Compliance in North Dakota*, 40, 44, 48 (December 2000), *available at* http://nicwa.org/resources/catalog/research.

85. *See generally* Jeanne Louise Carriere, *Representing the Native American: Culture, Jurisdiction, and the Indian Child Welfare Act*, 79 IOWA L. REV. 585 (1994). A Minnesota task force found that sufficient evidence existed to believe that bias played a part in the overrepresentation of Indian children in the state foster care system. *Minnesota Supreme Court Task Force on Racial Bias in the Judicial System Final Report* 82 (May 1993), *available at* http://www.courts.state.mn.us/documents/0/Public/Court_Information_Office/Race_Bias_Report_Complete.pdf.
86. The checklist provided as an appendix to this article goes through the procedural requirement of ICWA and gives practice tips for representing parents or Indian custodians in a simplified format.
87. 25 U.S.C. § 1903.
88. *Id.* at § 1903(1).
89. *Id.* at § 1903(1).
90. BIA Guidelines, *supra* note 79 at § B.3(a).
91. 25 U.S.C. § 1903(4).
92. *Id.* at § 1903(4)(b).
93. Currently there are 561 federally recognized tribes. 72 FED. REG. 13648 (March 22, 2007).
94. *In re K.S.*, 317 Mont. 88, 75 P.3d 325 (2003). The Court found it was better to err on the side of applying ICWA when the children were members of the state-recognized Little Shell Band of Chippewa Indians—a tribe still awaiting federal recognition.
95. BIA Guidelines, *supra* note 79, at § A.2.
96. BIA Guidelines *supra* note 79, at § B.1 commentary, citing *United States v. Broncheau*, 597 F.2d 1260, 1263 (9th Cir. 1979). *See In re Junious M.*, 144 Cal. App. 3d 786, 792, 193 Cal. Rptr. 40, 43 (Calif. 1983); *In re Baby Boy Doe*, 849 P.2d 925, 931 (Idaho 1993); and *Matter of Adoption of Riffle*, 922 P.2d 510, 513 (Mont. 1996) [hereinafter Riffle II].
97. BIA Guidelines, *supra* note 79, at § B.1 (including commentary).
98. *Riffle II*, 922 P.2d at 513.
99. *In Re Riffle*, 902 P.2d 542, 545 (Mont. 1995) [hereinafter Riffle I].
100. BIA Guidelines, *supra* note 79, at § B.2 (including commentary).
101. A list of the area offices can be found at 25 C.F.R. § 23.11(2004).
102. BIA Guidelines, *supra* note 79, at § B.1(b) list several circumstances that can trigger an inquiry into whether the child is Indian.
103. Most states do not use the Existing Indian Family doctrine to determine applicability of ICWA. States currently applying this doctrine include Kentucky, Louisiana, and Missouri. *See Rye v. Weasel*, 934 S.W.2d 257 (Ky. 1996); *Hampton v. J.A.L.*, 658 SO.2d 331 (La. App. 1995); *In re Interest of S.A.M.*, 703 S.W.2d 603 (Mo. App. 1986)..
104. 25 U.S.C. § 1912(a).
105. *Id.* at § 1912(b).
106. *Id.* at § 1911.
107. *Id.* at §1912(d) and (e).
108. *Id.* at § 1915.

109. *Id.* at § 1911(d).
110. *Id.* at § 1914.
111. *Id.* at § 1911(a); *Mississippi Band of Choctaw Indians v. Holyfield*, 490 U.S. 30 (1989).
112. As a practical matter, the motion to transfer and any proposed order should reflect that the state proceedings do not terminate until the tribal court has officially accepted jurisdiction in order to avoid a situation where the Indian child is potentially not in anyone's legal custody during the transfer process between state and tribal courts.
113. 25 U.S.C. § 1911(b).
114. BIA Guidelines, *supra* note 79, at § B.2 and commentary.
115. 25 U.S.C. § 1911(b).
116. *Id.* at § 1912(a) sets forth the notice requirements and hearing time frames.
117. BIA Guidelines, *supra* note 79, at § C.2(b) and § C.3.
118. 25 U.S.C. § 1911(b).
119. BIA Guidelines, *supra* note 79, at § C.3(a).
120. 25 U.S.C. § 1911(b). *See In re D.M.*, 685 N.W.2d 768 (S.D. 2004); *In re M.E.M.*, 635 P.2d 1313 (Mont. 1981); and *In re Robert T.*, 246 Cal. Rptr. 168 (Calif. 1988).
121. BIA Guidelines, *supra* note 79, at § C.3(b) and commentary.
122. The tribal court may be willing to conduct hearings at the location where the majority of the parties are located, thereby alleviating any additional travel burden for witnesses. Arrangements can also be made to conduct hearings through a variety of technological options that allow for remote, interactive, audio, and visual communication. The state may be allowed to remain a party to the action to advocate for possible state interests.
123. BIA Guidelines, *supra* note 79, at § C.3d and commentary.
124. *Id.* at § C. 3 and commentary.
125. *Id.*
126. 25 U.S. C. § 1912(c) addresses access to reports and other documents.
127. *Id.* at § 1912(d); and BIA Guidelines, *supra* note 79, at § B.8.
128. *Id.* at § 1912(e), (f).
129. BIA Guidelines, *supra* note 79, at § D. 2 and commentary.
130. 25 U.S.C. § 1912(d).
131. BIA Guidelines, *supra* note 79, at § B.8 and commentary.
132. 25 U.S.C. § 1912(e). The BIA guidelines set forth the characteristics of a qualified expert witness in section D. 4b and its commentary.
133. In an ICWA case handled through the Indian Law Clinic, the parent was actively engaged in a rehabilitative program that extended beyond the six months of the temporary legal custody [TLC]. The state of Montana requested that the parent agree to an extension of the TLC. As part of the stipulation, the state included a statement that the state had made active efforts to prevent the breakup of the family. In this situation, the state had not assisted in finding or funding either the current or the previous treatment program for the parent. The parent ultimately agreed to continuation of the TLC so she could complete the treatment program. Although the final

language in the stipulation reflected that active efforts had been made, the section contested to whom these efforts could be attributed. This allowed the parent to continue with treatment, while still preserving an "active efforts" challenge in the event the state attempts to terminate parental rights.

134. 25 U.S.C. § 1912(e).
135. *Id.* at § 1912(f).
136. BIA Guidelines, *supra* note 79 at § D.4(b) and commentary. As a general rule, social workers are not going to meet the qualifications of an expert witness under ICWA. The BIA Guidelines indicate that the expert should have "extensive knowledge of prevailing social and cultural standards and childrearing practices with the Indian child's tribe." *Id.* at § D.4(b)(ii). A member of a plains tribe would probably not have the necessary knowledge to be an expert in a case involving a child from the Southwest or Pacific Northwest. Questioning the expert is important when the person is not a member of the Indian child's tribe. *See generally In re Matter of K.H. and K.L.E.*, 981 P.2d 1190 (Mont. 1999) (social worker not an expert); *People ex rel. M.H.*, 691 N.W.2d 622 (S.D. 2005) (attorney not expert); and *Oregon ex rel. State Office for Services to Children and Families v. Amador*, 30 P.3d 1223 (Or. App. 2001) (tribal member qualified to be a witness given background, training, and recognition by tribe).
137. BIA Guidelines, *supra* note 79.
138. BIA Guidelines, *supra* note 79 at § D.4(a) and commentary.
139. Indirect service can be as important as direct service. If a person does not have reliable transportation, access to phone service, adequate housing, or employment, compliance with a reunification plan is often jeopardized.
140. 25 U.S.C. § 1912(d).
141. The parent or Indian custodian is being set up to fail if a six-month time frame is utilized and the services required will not be available for three months and will require six months to complete.
142. Adoption and Safe Families Act, 42 U.S.C. § 1305 (2000).
143. David Simmons and Jack Thorpe, *P.L. 105–89 Adoption and Safe Families Act of 1997: Issues for Tribes and States Serving Indian Children* 10–16 (1999), *available at* http://www.nicwa.org/policy/law/adoption_safe/asfa-issues.pdf.
144. A study conducted in the Los Angeles area in 2000 found that 29 percent of the Indian children in foster care were placed with non-Indian families or in group homes. *See* Heidi Frith-Smith and Heather Singleton, *Urban American Indian Children in Los Angeles County: An Investigation of Available Data* 14 (prepared for the Los Angeles County American Indian Children's Council, June 2000), *available at* http://www.aisc.ucla.edu/rsrch/uaichildren.htm.
145. 25 U.S.C. § 1915.
146. *Id.* at § 1915(c).
147. BIA Guidelines, *supra* note 79, at § F.3a(iii) and commentary. At a minimum, diligent search requires that the state contact the tribal social services department, review all county and state listings for available Indian homes, and contact "nationally known Indian programs with

available placement resources." *Id.* at commentary.
148. *Id.* at § F.3 and commentary. The guidelines only list three grounds for avoiding placement in accordance with ICWA: the request of the parents, or child if old enough to provide input; the documented extraordinary physical or emotional needs of the child; and the unavailability of a family after a diligent search.
149. *In the Matter of C.H.*, 997 P.2d 776 (Mont. 2000), was a case in which Montana argued that the non-Indian foster family should adopt the Indian child, even though extended family, licensed as a foster family in another state, had expressed a willingness to take the child within six weeks of when the child was originally removed. The county attorney in this case was a board member for the foster care home run by the non-Indian foster family. He argued that the child had bonded with this family and had extraordinary needs, creating good cause to avoid the placement preferences. The lower court applied a balancing test between the foster family and the extended family and determined that it was in the best interest of the child to remain with the foster family. The Montana Supreme Court overturned this decision. The Court found that the best interest of an Indian child is met by complying with the placement preferences of ICWA, and that good cause to avoid the placement preferences occurs in a very narrow set of circumstances. Risk of possible future problems was "simply too nebulous and speculative a standard." *Id.* at 783. Emotional bonding could not be "considered an extraordinary emotional need." *Id.* at 784. This child was almost three months old when removed. The child turned three a week before going to live with her extended family and her younger sibling, who had been placed with this extended family during the course of these ICWA proceedings.
150. *Id.* at 784, citing *Riffle II*, 922 P.2d 510, 514–15 (Mont. 1996) and *In re Adoption of M.T.S.*, 489 N.W. 2d 285, 288 (Minn. App. 1992).
151. 25 U.S.C. § 1915. A member of the Indian child's extended family is given first preference in both foster care and adoptive placement situations.
152. Patty LaPlant, a member of the Blackfeet Tribe, recently suggested a process that could be used to identify potential placement opportunities with extended family. Members of the Indian child's extended family would be asked to identify at least five individuals or families that should be considered as a placement option. A comparison of the extended family lists would probably reveal three or four individuals that everyone agrees on for placement, without creating needless conflict or division among the extended family.
153. Horejsi et al., *supra* note 58, at 335.
154. *Id.* at 338.
155. 25 U.S.C. § 1913(b).
156. *Id.*
157. *In re C.H.*, 997 P.2d 776 (Mont. 2000) (parents "voluntarily" terminated their parental rights as part of a plea agreement in the criminal matter. This termination was partly influenced by their understanding that the child would be placed with extended family. Once the termination was finalized, the state advocated for adoption by the non-Indian foster family.).
158. *See* Lisa Jaeger, *Tribal Court Development: Alaska Tribes* (Tanana Chiefs Conference 2002),

available at http://thorpe.ou.edu/AKtribalct/chapter_five.htm#Adoptions.
159. 25 U.S.C. § 1912(f).
160. *Id.*
161. If the parent or Indian custodian does not have sufficient resources to retain an expert witness, a motion should be made to the court requesting funds. This expense should be allowed, given the fundamental rights involved and the similarity of this proceeding to a criminal matter.
162. 25 U.S.C. § 1914.
163. *Id.*
164. *Id.* at § 1913(d).
165. 25 U.S.C. § 1983 (2000). *See Native Village of Venetie v. Alaska*, 155 F. 3d 1150 (9th Cir. 1998).
166. Amendments to ICWA have consistently been proposed since its enactment. *E.g.*, since 1996 several bills have been introduced; 1996 [S. 1962, H.R. 3828, H.R. 2644 & H.R. 1448]; 1997 [S. 569 & H.R. 1082]; 1999 [S. 1213]; 2002 [H.R. 2644 & H.R. 4733]; and 2003 [H.R. 2750].
167. Wade Horn, Assistant Secretary for Children and Families, U.S. Dept. of Health and Human Services, testified before a House Committee on April 8, 2003, that timely achievement of permanency outcomes, especially adoption, for children in foster care was one of the weakest areas of state performance under the ASFA. (Testimony *available at* http://www.hhs.gov/asl/testify/t030408.html).
168. An eligible state can receive a bonus of $4,000 for each foster child adopted and $6,000 for each adoption of a child with special needs previously in foster care under the ASFA. *See* Child Welfare League's summary of the ASFA, *available at* http://www.cwla.org/advocacy/asfapl105-89summary.htm.
169 25 U.S.C. § 1914.
170. The Ninth Circuit Court has found violations of ICWA claims may be enforced through 42 U.S.C. § 1983 and attorney's fees awarded in accordance with 42 U.S.C. § 1988. *See* Village of Venetie v Alaska, 155 F. 3d 1150 (9th Cir 1998).

In Defense of ICWA

The Constitution, Public Policy, and Pragmatism

Carol L. Tebben

The Indian Child Welfare Act (ICWA or the Act) was passed by the United States Congress in 1978, largely as an acknowledgement of failed national and state policies concerning tribal nations and their children.[1] Congress found that

> An alarmingly high percentage of Indian families are broken up by the removal, often unwarranted, of their children from them by nontribal public and private agencies and that an alarmingly high percentage of such children are placed in non-Indian foster and adoptive homes and institutions . . . .[2]

The Act is a detailed statute that imposes exacting standards upon the state when tribal children are in need of adoptive or foster care placement.

ICWA is a congressional attempt to remedy past failures by the states "to recognize the essential tribal relations of Indian people and the cultural and social standards prevailing in Indian communities and families."[3] In the Act, Congress umpires tribal-state jurisdictional boundaries by placing federal limitations upon the state in child welfare cases that involve placement of tribal children. The Indian Child Welfare Act's modification of state child welfare authority can vary greatly, depending upon such considerations as where the child lives,[4] whether the tribe chooses to take jurisdiction, and other federal statutes affecting state jurisdiction.[5] Unless there is good cause to the contrary, the state is required to relinquish jurisdiction to the child's tribe;[6] the state's authority is also limited when good cause is established and the state retains jurisdiction of the case.

The stated purposes of the Act are "to protect the best interests of Indian children and to promote the stability and security of Indian tribes and Indian families...."[7] Although the Act does make demands upon states to protect the families, children, sovereignty, and cultural interests of tribes, there are adequate, even compelling, justifications for ICWA. The purposes of this discussion are to identify many of the reasons that justify both the passage of ICWA and state compliance with its mandates. Included are constitutional issues of trifederalism, equal protection, and due process; the public policy issues of tribal self-determination, government-to-government interaction, and protection of tribal nations; and the beneficial practical outcomes verifying the value of the Indian Child Welfare Act.

Trifederalism

A strong preference expressed by Congress in ICWA is that state child welfare cases involving tribal children be turned over to the sovereign authority of the child's tribal government. As evidenced in the Act, the United States is composed of three kinds of constitutionally recognized limited sovereigns, a fact that often gives rise to confusion over legal and political boundaries.[8] This American trifederalism involves a constant interaction among the national government, the states, and tribal nations over the appropriate allocation of sovereign authority. As sovereign nations, tribes have a significant status that commands respect for their decision making authority, jurisdictional boundaries, and right to protect tribal children.

Tribes were brought into the framework of American jurisprudence as sovereigns.[9] United States public policy recognizes the sovereign authority of tribal self-government not only in congressional legislation such as the Indian Child Welfare Act, but also in the Indian Reorganization Act, the Indian Self-Determination and Education Act, and the Indian Gaming Regulatory Act.[10] The Supreme Court has recognized sovereign tribal authority to determine membership, levy sales taxes, levy severance taxes, tax non-Indian leaseholds, resolve internal conflicts in tribal court, create immunity from lawsuit, prosecute an individual with no double jeopardy concerns as between the federal courts and tribal courts, and are not limited by either the Bill of Rights nor the Fourteenth Amendment.[11] In addition, tribal sovereignty has been recognized in state public policy by legislation,[12] and in state supreme court opinions.[13]

As is the case with national sovereignty and state sovereignty, tribal sovereign authority is limited, yet it does exist. The Supreme Court asserted in Chief Justice Marshall's *Worcester v. Georgia* decision that

> The very term "nation," so generally applied to [tribes], means "a people distinct from others." The constitution, by declaring treaties already made, as well as those to be made, to be the supreme law of the land, has adopted and sanctioned

the previous treaties with the Indian nations, and consequently, admits their rank among those powers who are capable of making treaties.[14]

This articulation by the Court that the Constitution admits, or recognizes, the rank of tribes as sovereigns capable of making treaties is further clarified by the statement in *Worcester* that tribes are "independent, political communities, retaining their original natural rights."[15] Treaties represent another example of the federal public policy recognition of tribes as sovereigns, and it is significant that some treaty rights still stand, such as off-reservation spear fishing in Wisconsin.

In *Cherokee Nation v. Georgia*, the Cherokee tribe attempted to bring their jurisdictional dispute with the state before the Supreme Court under the Court's original jurisdiction. The Court determined that the tribe was not a foreign nation—and therefore the suit did not qualify for its original jurisdiction—but rather that tribes are domestic nations within the United States.[16] Tribes are within the United States and they are nations. Even though the sovereign authority of tribal nations long predates the United States Constitution, the back-door creation of a trifederal framework began to occur unnoticed. Tribal nations holding their inherent right of self-government were included as "domestic nations" within the structure of American government. It has been through the Supreme Court's interpretation of the Constitution, particularly in reference to the states' lack of constitutional authority to regulate tribes, that sovereign tribal authority has been modestly recognized.

This inclusion has occurred over time. Since United States citizenship for all tribal citizens born within the United States did not take hold until 1924,[17] tribal nation status was recognized by the Supreme Court before tribal citizens became part of the people of the United States. That "nation" status, never revoked by the United States, still remains in effect. The Tenth Amendment indirectly recognizes the power of tribal governments by asserting that the people of the United States (and also the states themselves) retain reserved power not delegated to the United States government by the Constitution. The power of the people is expressed in the Tenth Amendment:

> The powers not delegated to the United States by the Constitution, nor prohibited by it to the States, are reserved to the States respectively, or to the people.[18]

As citizens of the United States, the states in which they reside, and the tribes to which they belong, the members of tribes have delegated some power to the federal government, reserved some power in their states, and reserved some power for their tribal governments. The Supreme Court made clear in *Winans* that the term "reservation," most often used to refer to tribal land retained after other land was taken, also applies to the reservation of rights retained by tribal nations when treaties were signed with the United States.[19] The inherent natural right of self-government is retained by *all* United States citizens, and tribal citizens were uniquely encompassed within the United States with that right intact, though not always respected. This quiet reality comes to light in ICWA, an explicit attempt by Congress to protect the inherent sovereign authority of tribal nations to govern their children, and to protect tribal governments from the inappropriate encroachment of state power in the placement of tribal children.[20]

Since the children of each tribe are tricitizens, three sovereigns claim responsibility for their care. These claims of responsibility can give rise to jurisdictional misunderstandings over which kind of court or which kind of child welfare agency has authority. The issue is again complicated because funding that has been allocated for the care of children often must go from the national government, through the state (and county), to the tribe. Tribal-state interaction under the federal mandates of ICWA occurs within the trifederal framework of American government—a framework that recognizes the sovereign status of tribes.[21] It is a combination of this "political status, as well as the biased treatment of Indian children and families under public and private child welfare systems, that is the basis for the Indian Child Welfare Act."[22]

Historical Context of ICWA

The maltreatment of the peoples of our First Nations, from the imposition of European colonization through the adoption and foster care policies of the 1960s, serves as a backdrop for the passage of ICWA. Anti-tribal federal policies have included, for example, removal from tribal homelands,[23] allotment of tribal lands,[24] military force,[25] treaty breaking,[26] relocation,[27] and termination.[28] From colonial times, Native peoples were viewed as culturally inferior to European immigrants. In settling a disputed land claim, John Marshall reasoned for the Supreme Court that tribal nations did not possess an absolute title to their land, because they were "a people over whom the superior genius of Europe might claim an ascendancy."[29] This decision was grounded in the jurisprudence of discovery and conquest, a legal philosophy that has informed relations between the government of the United States and tribal nations for centuries.

ICWA is a rejoinder to the longstanding and concerted legal effort that had been effectuated in the United States to influence the children of tribal nations to abandon their tribal heritage. The commissioner of Indian Affairs reported to Congress in 1867 that the only effective way to solve the so-called "Indian problem" of the time was to "separate the Indian children completely from their tribes."[30] During the boarding school approach to this assimilation and forced acculturation policy, tribal children were taken from their families to attend live-in schools for months, sometimes years at a time.[31] Native language was prohibited, non-Indian dress was required, Native ceremonies were punished, harsh penalties were commonplace, and family visits were generally forbidden. The boarding school era of federal Indian policy had a devastating effect upon the cohesiveness of tribal families, and lasted approximately from the 1880s to the late 1950s.[32]

In the state of Wisconsin, one elder of the Menominee Nation reflected upon his boarding school experience in the 1950s. He explained that he was not allowed to see his family during the entire school year, except at Christmas, even though he could see his home from the boarding school window.[33] One of the purposes of boarding schools was to separate tribal children from the influence of their families. This was done in order to permanently change the tribal values, attitudes, and traditions that were so often misunderstood and undervalued by non-tribal members.

As many of the abuses of boarding schools were coming to light, federal policy began to shift to another strategy of separating tribal children from their families. The Bureau of Indian Affairs, an agency that claimed to protect and assist tribal nations, "contracted with the Child Welfare League of America to operate a clearinghouse for the interstate adoption of Indian children by non-Indian families."[34] The Indian Adoption Project was significant not only because it placed hundreds of tribal children in non-Indian homes, but more importantly because it served as a model to the states, which placed "thousands more Native children for adoption in white homes following the project's example."[35] During this era, the loss of tribal children due to adoption was significant, meriting official apologies from both the Bureau of Indian Affairs and the Child Welfare League.[36]

Wisconsin was one of several states in which the practice of removing tribal children from the influence of their respective tribal nations led Congress to pass ICWA. During the congressional hearings preceding passage, it was asserted that in Wisconsin "[by] a per capita rate Indian children were removed from their homes and placed in adoptive homes or foster care 15.6 times more often than non-Indian children . . . ."[37] This comparison was considered to be a minimum, since private adoptions were not included in the calculation of this rate. The magnitude of loss may also be expressed in another way, by considering the national percentage of tribal children who were taken from their tribes for adoption, foster care, and institutional placements. Approximately 25 percent, and possibly up to 35 percent, of tribal children were removed from tribes for placement.[38] About 85 percent of those taken from the tribes were placed in non-Indian homes or institutions.[39]

One tribal judge in Wisconsin expressed the importance of ICWA from his perspective with the insight that

> As I have the opportunity to travel across the United States, I often engage in conversations with tribal elders from various tribes. All too often I hear their accounts of "boarding schools"; their tales of separation from family and

community, not just for short periods of time, but for most of their "development" years. All too often, as children, their stories reflect being removed from their homes and raised by strangers in communities and cities far away. It has often been said that an Indian's idea of home is not a house, but a community that supports and embraces the Indian identity and values. These stories tell of the, intentional or unintentional, stripping of these identities and values, leaving the children to eventually return to their Indian "home" lacking the knowledge of who they are as a people, and with a value system that conflicts with those at "home."

Even today, I hear stories from children of these elders, struggling with the experiences of their parents; a gap between true identity and an identity cluttered with urban, non-Indian values. Although it is understood Indians live in a dual society, the assimilation policies continue to affect Indian people today.

One experience that has remained with me for a number of years was a conversation with a Zia Pueblo elder, who asked me if I spoke my language. In response to his question, I explained that my people were Christianized early in our contact with the Europeans and our language was lost. His reply was, "that's too bad because your laws are locked in your language. Once a child learns the language, it knows the rules." This impacted me on the importance of Indian children remaining in contact with their culture, their people, and their "home." This concept was reinforced while riding an elevator up to the tenth floor of a hotel. On the elevator was a young Indian woman with a small child. As I entered the elevator I reached to push 10 on the panel when this small child reached up to push the button. I asked her if she could count to 10 and she did, in a language I didn't understand. Her mother smiled with pride and said "Navajo." It was then that I realized the importance of ICWA. This young child was learning how to be Navajo first, learning the rules of her people. This could not happen if this child were to be separated from her identity through some sort of legal mechanism that ignored the values and traditions of her people. To prevent Indian children from having to re-identify with their people, it is best for them to first learn the culture and values of their people, and then to step into living in the dual society that exists today. This is why the Indian Child Welfare Act is so important from this tribal judge's perspective.[40]

In Chicago, a man who was eligible for tribal membership was taken at the age of three from his working mother, years before the passage of ICWA. He spent several years in foster homes, and was eventually adopted by a non-Indian family. He did not discover his Ho-Chunk tribal identity until a member of his tribe in Wisconsin was able to track him down when he was twenty-nine years old. In his explicit support for ICWA's protection of the connection of tribal children to their heritage, he describes the experiences of his childhood as "identity theft."[41] Passage of ICWA was a congressional response to this often repeated kind of story, and to the pleas from tribal nations for Congress to intercede in the wholesale loss of tribal children.

ICWA as a Violation of Equal Protection?

Indian Child Welfare Act provisions to protect the relationship of tribal children to their heritage have been argued by some to be racial discrimination in conflict with the constitutional guarantees of equal protection.[42] When the state for good cause retains jurisdiction to place tribal children, certain ICWA preferences must be met. In state adoption placements, unless there is good cause to the contrary, the Act requires that placements be culturally appropriate under the following preferences:

- a member of the child's extended family;
- other members of the Indian child's tribe; or
- other Indian families.[43]

In foster care placements, unless there is good cause to the contrary, the Act requires that placements be culturally appropriate under the following preferences:

- a member of the Indian child's extended family;
- a foster home licensed, approved, or specified by the Indian child's tribe;
- an Indian foster home licensed or approved by an authorized non-Indian authority;
- an institution for children approved by an Indian tribe or operated by an Indian organization that has a program suitable to meet the Indian child's need.[44]

The preference in ICWA for state relinquishment of jurisdiction to the tribes for placement of tribal children has also been challenged.

If a government action is challenged as being racially discriminatory, the government is held to a standard of strict scrutiny. Under strict scrutiny, the government cannot discriminate unless it has a compelling reason to do so, and the law in question is necessary to achieve that compelling governmental interest. In another context, the Court has determined that the affirmative action preferences in school admittance do not violate the Constitution when race is not the sole determinant of preference and there is compelling justification for its continuance.[45]

The Supreme Court addressed the issue of whether or not a custody decision could be based upon a racial preference in *Palmore v. Sidoti*.[46] In that case, the child's biological father was seeking modification of a previous divorce settlement in which the mother was granted custody of their daughter. The daughter and her parents were Caucasian. Later, the mother married a man of African descent. The father's argument in *Palmore* was that his daughter would be harmed if raised by a family in which her stepfather was African American. The state trial court had decided that the child should be removed from the custody of her mother because the child would suffer from the effects of racial discrimination. The reasoning for this decision was made clear with the assertion that

> This Court feels that despite the strides that have been made in bettering relations between the races in this country, it is inevitable that [the child] will, if allowed to remain in her present situation and attain school age and thus more vulnerable to peer pressures, suffer from the social stigmatization that is sure to come.[47]

In its analysis of the trial court's reasoning, the Supreme Court recognized the central question in the *Palmore* case to be "whether the reality of private biases and the possible injury they might inflict are permissible considerations" for the Florida court's custody decision.[48] The Court determined that these were not permissible considerations, adding that "the Constitution cannot control such prejudices but neither can it tolerate them."[49] It is also significant that the Supreme Court concluded in *Palmore* that the trial court "was entirely candid and made no effort to place its holding on any ground other than race."[50] Thus the Court rejected the position that custody should be removed from the mother based upon a preference that Caucasian children should be raised by Caucasian parents to prevent a child from suffering racial discrimination. It was determined in *Palmore* that the state had no compelling reason to remove a child from the custody of her mother solely on the basis of the potential for racial discrimination; therefore the custody placement was considered to be constitutionally prohibited.

Critics of the Indian Child Welfare Act have sometimes emphasized comparable statements about the effects of racial discrimination made at pre-ICWA hearings as an indication that the Act lacked appropriate justification. It was in fact argued in defense of the creation of ICWA that tribal children placed in non-Indian homes tended to suffer from the effects of racial discrimination because of such placements. Testifying before Congress, one social psychiatrist testified that tribal children who were raised in non-Indian homes had difficulty coping with white society. He explained that

> They were raised with a white cultural and social identity. They are raised in a white home. They attended predominantly white schools, and in almost all cases, attended a church that was predominantly white.... Then during adolescence, they found that society was not to grant them the white identity that they had.... For example, a universal experience was that when they began to date white

children, the parents of the white youngsters were against this.... The other experience was derogatory name calling in relation to their racial identity.[51]

One tribal leader put it another way, as he lamented that

> I think that the cruelest trick that the white man has ever done to Indian children is to take them into adoption courts, erase all of their records and send them off to some nebulous family that has a value system that is A-1 in the state of Nebraska and that child reaches 16 or 17, [and] he is a little brown child residing in a white community.... [T]hey effectively make him a non-person and I think ... they destroy him.[52]

There may be some similarity in the recognition, both in *Palmore v. Sidoti* and in the ICWA hearings, that children caught between two racial identities can experience discrimination and difficulty. Although the protection of tribal children from possible racial discrimination in non-Indian homes was mentioned in congressional hearings prior to the passage of ICWA, the stated purposes for the legislation did not include this concern. Unlike *Palmore v. Sidoti*, several compelling federal interests do exist, other than the effects of racial discrimination, to vindicate ICWA preferences.

One justification for the passage of ICWA and its preferences is protection of the best interests of tribal children.[53] Best interests of a child can include many factors, and for a tribal child, heritage is one of those factors. An Arizona state court concluded that ICWA "is based on the fundamental assumption that it is in the Indian child's best interest that its relationship to the tribe be protected."[54] The Supreme Court of the United States quoted this statement approvingly in *Mississippi Band of Choctaw v. Holyfield* when it stated, "the conclusion seems justified."[55] The 1977 Senate Report indicated that the placement of a tribal child in a non-Indian home was "depriving the child of his or her tribal and cultural heritage."[56] The 1978 House Report stressed that ICWA "seeks to protect the rights of the Indian child as an Indian ...."[57] The Indian Child Welfare Act indicates clearly that the policy motivation for its passage was "to protect Indian children from arbitrary removal from their families and tribal affiliations."[58] This strengthens the argument that with the passage of ICWA, Congress has recognized a tribal child's heritage, so often under state and national attack in the past, to be a compelling governmental interest.

Congress was careful to explain that the very existence of tribal nations was one of the compelling justifications for the passage of ICWA, by stating that there is "no resource more vital to the continued existence and integrity of Indian tribes than their children...."[59] ICWA's congressional statement of policy includes the purpose of promoting "the stability and security of Indian tribes...."[60] A member of Congress expressed his concern about the necessity for ICWA passage by declaring that

Indian tribes and Indian people are being drained of their children and, as a result, their future as a tribe and a people is being placed in jeopardy.[61]

In addition to protecting tribal children for the purpose of preserving the tribe's existence, it is also compelling that inherent tribal sovereign authority be honored. When the United States Supreme Court explained that tribes are "independent, political communities, retaining their original natural rights,"[62] in the context of being "domestic nations,"[63] it gave explicit recognition to the reality and importance of sovereign tribal authority. Tribal authority is protected in ICWA with the requirement for tribal notification, the right of the tribe to intervene, and the transfer of jurisdiction from state to tribal court. The Indian Child Welfare Act has been a critical instrument for protecting the interests of a child's tribal heritage, preventing a tribe's loss of children, and honoring tribal sovereign authority. When government preferences are racial in character, there must be compelling purposes for such preferences. In addition, the law must be necessary to achieve these purposes. Congress provided ample evidence that threats to tribal sovereignty over child welfare, and the loss of tribal children by state placement practices, would continue without passage of ICWA. The kinds of protection created by the Act have been necessary to achieve its many purposes.

These compelling interests are offered to demonstrate that special treatment for tribal child welfare issues is appropriate. Compelling interests would justify a racial preference in ICWA. The preferences in ICWA, however, are not racial in character. In *Morton v. Mancari*, the Supreme Court was asked to determine whether or not Bureau of Indian Affairs hiring preferences for Indians violated the Fifth Amendment Due Process Clause as racial discrimination.[64] The Court declared that they were not a constitutional violation, based upon the reasoning that

> The preference is not directed towards a "racial" group consisting of 'Indians"; instead it applies only to members of "federally recognized" tribes. This operates to exclude many individuals who are racially to be classified as "Indians." In this sense, the preference is political rather than racial in nature.[65]

In order to qualify for Bureau of Indian Affairs hiring preferences at the time of *Morton v. Mancari*, a person had to be of one-fourth or more degree Indian blood and have membership in a federally recognized tribal nation.[66] In other words the *Mancari* decision designated tribal members as a political rather than a racial classification, even though blood quantum was at that time a factor in qualifying for the preference. As the *Mancari* decision explained, one reason for this result was the fact that some people who also had the same blood quantum did not qualify as tribal members.

The ICWA definition of Indian child contains no reference to blood quantum. "Indian child" is defined in the Act as

Any unmarried person who is under eighteen and is either
(a) a member of an Indian tribe or
(b) is eligible for membership in an Indian tribe and is the biological child of a member of an Indian tribe.[67]

Common sense tells us that referring to a person as a tribal member usually does have some racial component. However, the category of tribal membership, which is determined by the tribe alone,[68] is not singularly a racial one. An Indian child, or more accurately a tribal child, often has ancestry that does not come completely through the tribe.

If the child is not a tribal member, but eligible to be so, there is an additional requirement that a biological parent be a tribal member. Again, it is possible that the parent of the child eligible for tribal membership might in a given case be a tribal member but have only partial tribal ancestry. Thus, this ICWA classification that a biological parent be a tribal member is more political than racial as well. In a similar way, tribal membership is relevant in ICWA cases to define an Indian parent, custodian, or family as "any person who is a member of an Indian tribe . . . ."[69]

The Supreme Court in *Mancari* has placed significance upon the political nature of tribal-member status, rather than simply defining it as a racial category. The placement provisions in ICWA are largely political because they are based upon tribal membership.

Consultation and Collaboration

To ensure the effectiveness of the Indian Child Welfare Act in accomplishing the intentions of Congress, a state's child welfare system from the top down must have effective interaction with the tribal governments located within the state. The State of Wisconsin is discussed here to demonstrate the value of tribal-state interaction encouraged by ICWA. In a four-year study of Wisconsin compliance with the Act, the state was found to be actively engaged in remedying past deficiencies in state-tribal consultation and collaboration.[70]

Wisconsin's child welfare system is administered by its counties and supervised by the state's Department of Children and Families (DCF).[71] The U.S. Department of Health and Human Services required Wisconsin to assess its child welfare system in 2003 to determine if the state was in compliance with federal child welfare regulations, including ICWA. This process resulted in the state's *Statewide Assessment*.[72] In another document, the *Federal Review*, the state offered summaries of the federal government's evaluation of Wisconsin's child welfare system, including ICWA compliance.[73] The federal review process has not only evaluated Wisconsin compliance, but apparently has also had a positive effect upon that compliance.

The state has implemented an ongoing process of state consultation and collaboration with tribal nations to make appropriate tribal-state relationships more effective at serving tribal children under the mandates of ICWA than in the past. In 2003, Division of Child and Family Services (DCFS) staff began efforts to meet with tribal child welfare personnel on a bimonthly basis.[74] These meetings are held at times in Madison and at times on one of the reservations. In the past, final written child welfare documents would be created by the state, then submitted to the tribes for approval after the fact. Tribal child welfare directors are now involved in the creation of state plans for performance enhancement, as well as the state's five-year child welfare plans. This collaboration is meaningful, as tribes take advantage of the opportunity to voice concerns, and as the state responds effectively to address these concerns.

At the February 2005 meeting, representatives of the DCFS conducted a training session for tribal child welfare directors on access to, and the use of, a new electronic system of tracking children in Wisconsin who have been identified as needing service or placement. This online system, known as eWiSACWIS, offers electronic communication, better access to child welfare forms and policy, templates for better identification of tribal children, opportunities to determine a child's placement status and needs for intervention, and access by both state and tribal child welfare workers to critical information on tribal children. The collaboration on this technology alone has the potential to have an enormous impact on the improvement of services to tribal children, and to enable tribes to have greater and more effective involvement with their children throughout the child welfare process. The tribes retain the choice to access and use the system or not.

One ongoing effort at state-tribal consultation has been the joint implementation of an annual conference of state and tribal child welfare personnel to discuss issues of concern and to share professional experiences. This ICWA conference was begun in 1993 and has involved both state and tribal presenters.

The (former) Division of Child and Family Services worked with a limited budget and a very limited number of personnel to oversee child welfare throughout the state.[75] The state has added an "Indian child welfare specialist position to work on compliance issues and provide technical assistance to counties and tribes."[76] This position was discussed at DCFS–tribal meetings in which tribal child welfare personnel advocated the hiring of either a tribal person in Wisconsin who was well-versed on ICWA, or a non-tribal person who was well-versed on ICWA and familiar with the tribal nations in Wisconsin. The voices of tribal child welfare directors were incorporated into the selection process, including participation in conference-call interviews.

Wisconsin's Department of Children and Families also has an ongoing collaborative program known as "161 Agreements" between counties and tribal nations as part of the process of state compliance with ICWA.[77] The 161 Agreements between counties and tribes originally "were designed to identify the responsibilities of each agency in terms of the funding of placements of children ordered by tribal courts,"[78] yet that purpose has been expanded to create more comprehensive tribe-county cooperative relationships.

These voluntary agreements can also include provisions for treatment services to tribal children and their families, independent living, child protective service investigations, and the development and implementation of case plans. Tribes and counties can set up a meeting schedule by agreement, coordinate county-tribal efforts to identify tribal children in need of protective services, and agree upon appropriate contact information for better ongoing communication. The agreements typically require the tribe to provide notice to the county of child placement or removal from placement, and often require the creation of a tribal case plan and case review for the county. This is true even if the case is entirely handled, and placement occurs, on the reservation. The federal funding that flows to the state, then to the counties is intended to benefit all children in the county, including reservation children.[79]

Funding still remains the central provision in 161 Agreements. When tribes have exclusive jurisdiction over children on the reservation, when there is concurrent tribal-county jurisdiction over the reservation, and when cases have been transferred from state to tribal court, these agreements can be helpful to smooth the process of placement, to facilitate funding, and to contribute to the achievement of better quality placement experiences for tribal children.

For tribal nations who have chosen not to exercise their exclusive child welfare jurisdiction on the reservation, and therefore have concurrent jurisdiction with the state over reservation minors, 161 Agreements can be of benefit to the county-tribe sharing of responsibility for tribal children. One example is that county child welfare personnel can be available to assist in an investigation by a tribal child welfare specialist for a child in need of protective services.[80] If the child welfare case must be adjudicated for placement, it can then go to tribal court or county court.[81] Cases that have more expenses involved tend to go to county court.[82] If the tribe lacks criminal jurisdiction over the parents' actions, that issue could go to the county. Parents may then be prosecuted in county court, even if the tribal court deals with the child placement issue. Under circumstances such as these, when tribe and county work in tandem to serve the needs of tribal children, the complex tangle of interaction ostensibly could make it difficult to ascertain whether the state or the tribe is taking jurisdiction over the tribal child. In Wisconsin, both tribe and county in fact often significantly share in the work. As tribal resources and availability of tribal child welfare staff increase, tribes tend to take over more responsibility from the county for child welfare services.

Tribe-county relationships present a dynamic and varied picture throughout the state. When the state does relinquish jurisdiction to the tribe, or when the tribe directly handles a case from the beginning, 161 Agreements can facilitate the process of providing permanence for tribal children. This was pointed out by the *Federal Review* in its statement that

> Division staff have been meeting for over a year with representatives of the Indian Child Welfare agencies operated by each of Wisconsin's 11 tribes. There are philosophical and cultural issues associated with the concept of permanence that vary among tribes. It is critical that procedures for protecting and providing for permanence for Indian children and assuring the rights of tribes to raise their children are safeguarded through 161 Agreements and other policies that are uniform across the state.[83]

The Social Security Act provides funding for tribal (and state) placements of children. Presently this funding must go from the federal government through the state to the county and then to the tribe.[84] In Wisconsin, about one-half of the cost of child welfare services are paid by the state (partially with such federal funding), and the other half of the cost is borne by the counties (and the tribes). Each county child welfare agency is overseen by a county board of supervisors that must approve spending and county policy for the delivery of child welfare services. By involving counties in the distribution of federal monies to tribes for child placement, tribes can be put at a disadvantage. Counties, already strapped for adequate funding for their own placement needs, can sometimes find it difficult to part with money for tribal placements. The county and tribe have the flexibility to accommodate the needs of tribal children and to meet federal requirements by working together. If a situation does arise that the tribe is not adequately staffed to handle, the county can supply staffing or take jurisdiction of the placement in order to assist the tribe.[85]

Continuing efforts at making the collaboration process with tribes meaningful are reflected in an official policy statement from the Wisconsin Department formerly known as Health and Human Services. Recognizing the trifederal structure of American government, its statement asserts that

> The various states have a unique legal relationship with sovereign American Indian Tribal governments, as affirmed and described in federal law. This relationship is set forth in the Constitution of the United States, treaties, statutes, laws and court decisions. Wisconsin Executive Order #39, issued February 2004, affirms the government-to-government relationship between the State of Wisconsin and American Indian Tribal governments located within the State of Wisconsin.
>
> Government-to-government relations involve respectful and cooperative communication and dealings that are designed to achieve a consensus, to

the extent possible, before a decision is made or an action is taken, and to implement programs in a collaborative manner. The Wisconsin Department of Health and Family Services (DHFS) is committed to such government-to-government relations with the federally recognized Tribal governments in Wisconsin. The State will employ its best efforts to achieve positive outcomes from its consultation and collaboration. The intent of this policy is to improve the planning and delivery of health and human services to Tribal governments, Tribal communities, and Tribal people by developing principles and a process for consultation on human services policies in Wisconsin. It is for this purpose that this policy has been developed....

Each of the federally recognized sovereign Tribes in the State of Wisconsin is recognized by the State for its unique status and its right to existence, self-government, and self-determination. The Department of Health and Family Services respects the fundamental principles that establish and maintain the relationship between Tribes and the DHFS and accord Tribal governments the same respect accorded to other governments.[86]

As collaboration and consultation continue, tribal concerns are being identified and joint planning occurs. A major result of state-tribal meetings has been a collaborative request to the Wisconsin legislature for detailed and complete incorporation of ICWA into state child welfare legislation. At its core, ICWA contemplates an effective tribal-state government-to-government relationship, and that relationship, as it strengthens, reinforces the federal encouragement of such efforts by ICWA.

Since effective state ICWA compliance necessitates good training, the expense of this educational process is sometimes used to argue against ICWA implementation. The State of Wisconsin, for example, is changing from offering optional ICWA training to making ICWA training for state child welfare personnel mandatory. In addition, that training will be available to all counties, superseding the former policy of offering the training only in some counties where reservations are located.[87]

Tribal nations have teamed with the state to create Child Welfare Training Partnerships so that there can be ongoing efforts at educating county (and tribal) child welfare personnel on ICWA compliance. Some of the potential topics for further study are ICWA mandates, tribal codes and ordinances, notification, tribal membership determination,[88] foster care licensure, full faith and credit, and tribal cultural issues. The state plan that has emerged since the *Federal Review* recommendations to provide mandatory training will result in ICWA certification.

According to the DCFS Program Enhancement Plan, in the future "all training should include an Indian co-trainer."[89] The state's implementation of this plan to add a tribal co-trainer adds greater breadth and depth to the content of the training, particularly on tribal culture and tribal policies. Wisconsin is also creating a web-based

ICWA training program, and has requested technical assistance from the National Indian Child Welfare Association for further ICWA education. Those involved in child welfare training include child placement agencies, child protection services, family preservation and support services, guardians *ad litem*, prosecutors, and judges.

Implementation of ICWA involves not only the state child welfare system serving the needs of children, but also the state judicial system that lends authority to child placement. Both systems are required to follow ICWA mandates. Some training has been available for judges; however training options often are limited, short in duration, and lacking an emphasis on tribal culture. The Wisconsin Tribal Judges Association,[90] an organization composed of tribal judges from the eleven federally recognized tribes in the state, noticed roadblocks to adequate judicial training. A common assumption was made by the state that only the few judges who work near a reservation need ICWA training. In reality, since a significant percentage of tribal members live outside reservation boundaries, a tribal child can be in need of services anywhere within the state. Collaboration by the Wisconsin Tribal Judges Association, Wisconsin Judicare, and the University of Wisconsin-Parkside provided extensive ICWA training for state and tribal judges at the university[91] Since tribal judges sponsored the training and participated in its implementation, tribal cultural issues were greatly emphasized.

Although ICWA training potentially could be an expensive process, the willingness of tribal members, tribal attorneys, tribal judges, nonprofit aid organizations, and university faculty to participate in providing this training at no extra cost to the state makes arguments against ICWA education expenditures less convincing. In addition, both state child welfare workers and state judges are required to receive continuing education for their work, so there is good reason to include ICWA in the already existing efforts at training state personnel. These factors simply strengthen the other underlying validations for continued and better ICWA implementation.

The Capabilities of Tribal Governments

Tribal governments often have been underestimated. Tribes have always cared for their children, but ICWA has been a major catalyst in encouraging the growth of tribal institutions that are more relevant and recognizable to the states in order to prevent inappropriate state control. As ICWA has required states to relinquish jurisdiction to tribes, tribal courts and child welfare agencies have responded. Tribes have benefited from this increased workload as they gain more experience, expertise, and effectiveness in protecting tribal culture and heritage, communicating with the state, and expanding tribal self-government.

Tribes have been underestimated in other ways. Non-tribal members have at times been reluctant to appear in tribal court for fear of being deprived of due process of law, a principle expected to be applied in state and federal courts.[92] Sovereign tribal governments and tribal courts, although not required by the Bill of Rights or by the Fourteenth Amendment to offer due process protections,[93] are so required by the Indian Civil Rights Act. Tribes do honor the principle of due process.[94]

One way this is evidenced is in the determination of competing interests in child welfare cases. A landmark interpretation of ICWA by the United States Supreme Court involved a case in which a tribal mother placed her twins for adoption immediately after birth with a non-Indian couple in a state adoption proceeding.[95] The mother's tribe challenged the adoption because the mother's domicile was on the reservation, and based upon the domicile of the mother, the tribe argued that it had exclusive jurisdiction to decide the case. The Supreme Court under ICWA agreed with the tribe about jurisdiction. It was then decided in tribal court that according to the best interests of the child doctrine, the twins should remain with their adoptive parents. The adoptive parents received due process of law.

In the case of *In re Adoption of Halloway*, a Utah couple had adopted a baby boy whose mother lived on the Navajo Reservation.[96] Years later, the adoptive parents were challenged by the Navajo mother, who wanted the boy returned. On appeal, the Utah Supreme Court decided according to the Indian Child Welfare Act that the state did not have jurisdiction over the case, but rather the Navajo tribal nation. The Navajo court found that the child, who was now ten years of age, should stay with his adoptive parents, and also that he should visit his biological mother.[97] Due process of law again was honored in tribal court. *Holyfield* and *Halloway* are two cases of many that illustrate the kind of care that tribal courts give to adoption and foster care placements. To tribal courts, tribal heritage is an important component of the best interests of a tribal child, but not the only interest or necessarily the most important one.

These cases also illustrate the central and foundational concern expressed in ICWA, that unless there is good cause to the contrary, tribal nations have the power to determine the care of tribal children.[98] This congressional recognition of who appropriately has the power to decide, based upon concerns for sovereign authority, cultural heritage, and tribal existence, are further justified by tribal due process and the concern shown in tribal courts for a child's best interests and the rights of all litigants.

Conclusion

The longstanding history of federal strategies to disrupt tribal cultures and traditions, particularly those targeting tribal children, was a foundational incentive for the Indian Child Welfare Act.[99] The troubling flow of children from their tribes because of past federal and state adoption and foster care policies directly accounts for the passage and strict requirements of ICWA to cut off this hemorrhaging.[100] Congressional concern for the unique trifederal status of tribes as nations within a nation underlies the rigorous jurisdictional requirements of ICWA to protect the children, families, and sovereignty of each tribe.

By passing ICWA, Congress has recognized that tribal heritage is a major consideration in the protection of the best interests of a tribal child, and that there is an inherent right of tribal families to remain together. Though tribal traditions and cultures may differ from those of non-Indians, they merit respect and protection. In tribal culture, when parents have difficulties and children are in need, family seems to have a larger context than it may have in a nontribal setting. Congress expressed in ICWA a willingness to protect this kind of tradition and heritage. There is a clear and express preference by Congress to place tribal children with their families, with tribal members, or with others who are defined by ICWA as Indian, and these preferences are not simply or necessarily racial in character. The passage of ICWA is critical to the protection of tribal culture and heritage.

As states comply with ICWA mandates to honor the sovereign authority of tribal governments to place their own children, tribal courts and child welfare agencies have the opportunity to grow in experience. Tribal governments also grow by helping states better comply with ICWA. This symbiotic improvement stands as a pragmatic justification for the mandates of ICWA.

It has become apparent through this process of investigation that many dedicated state and tribal officials are actively committed to the common concern of improving the lives of tribal children. Mark Mitchell, of the former Wisconsin Division of Child and Family Services, expressed the importance of tribal child welfare issues this way:

> Long ago I decided that my work in child welfare would be guided by the question "Would I feel comfortable if my children needed services from child welfare?" This is even more important when we're talking about Indian children, families, and tribes, because there is so much at stake. The wrong decisions and actions will continue to take their toll not just on the children and their families, but also on the future of the tribes. We can't afford to get this wrong.[101]

As tribal-state ICWA collaboration continues to help tribal children and their families, people get to know and respect one another. This in itself is endorsement for ICWA. The states and tribes will benefit greatly from more of this kind of positive interaction, as will the tribal children who are the reason for this ongoing effort, and who are singularly the greatest validation for the Indian Child Welfare Act.

NOTES

1. 25 U.S.C. § 1901 et seq. (1978).
2. *Supra* note 1, at § 1901 (4).
3. *Supra* note 1, at § 1901 (5).
4. 28 U.S.C. § 1360 (1953). Public Law 280 gives some states jurisdiction over reservation minors. In non–P.L. 280 states, tribes retain their exclusive jurisdiction over reservation children. In P.L. 280 states, states can have jurisdiction over tribal children both on and off the reservation. However, since tribes already possessed inherent jurisdiction over reservation minors, P.L. 280 created concurrent tribal-state jurisdiction in those states affected by the law. With the passage of ICWA, a process was created for tribes to reassert their inherent exclusive jurisdiction over reservation minors in P. L, 280 states, *supra* note 1, at § 1918 (a). A Ninth Circuit Court of Appeals decision underscores how critical it is for a tribe to follow the ICWA procedure in order for a court to recognize the tribe's jurisdiction over reservation minors as exclusive, *Doe v. Mann*, 415 F.3d 1038 (2005). In Wisconsin, tribes have relied on an assertion by a former state attorney general that tribes have exclusive jurisdiction over reservation minors, without complying with the ICWA resumption process.
5. For a discussion of the effect upon ICWA of the Adoption and Safe Families Act of 1997, which is an amendment to Title IV-B and Title IV-E of the Social Security Act, 42 U.S.C. § 620 et seq. and 42 U.S.C. § 670 et seq., see Carol Tebben, *A Family Lawyer's Guide to the Indian Child Welfare Act*, 20 AM. J. FAMILY LAW 117 (2006).
6. ICWA requirements only apply to U.S. federally recognized tribes; some states have voluntarily notified, allowed intervention by, transferred cases to, or placed tribal children with tribes located outside the United States.
7. *Supra* note 1, at § 1902.
8. Carol Tebben, *An American Trifederalism Based upon the Constitutional Status of Tribal Nations*, 5 U. PA. J. CONST. L. 318 (Winter 2003). Tribes are recognized in the Commerce Clause: "The Congress shall have power ... to regulate Commerce with foreign nations, among the several states, and with the Indian Tribes," U.S. CONST., art. I § 8.
9. *See Tebben, supra* note 8.
10. Indian Child Welfare Act, *supra* note 1; Indian Reorganization Act, 48 Stat. 787 (1934); Indian Self-Determination and Education Act, 88 Stat. 2203-17 (1975); Indian Gaming Regulatory Act, 102 Stat. 2467-88 (1988).
11. *Santa Clara Pueblo v. Martinez*, 436 U.S. 49 (1978) (tribal membership); *Washington v. Confederated Tribes of the Coleville Indian Reservation*, 447 U.S. 134 (1980) (levy sales tax); *Merrion v. Jicarilla Apache Tribe*, 455 U.S. 130 (1982) (levy severance tax); *Kerr-McGee Corp. v. Navajo Tribe of Indians*, 471 U.S. 195 (1985) (tax non-Indian leasehold); *Williams v. Lee*, 358 U.S. 217 (1959) (resolve internal conflict in tribal court); *Okla. Tax Comm'n v. Citizen Band Potawatomi Tribe of Okla.*, 498 U.S. 505 (1991) (tribal sovereign immunity from lawsuit); *U.S. v. Wheeler*, 435 U.S. 313 (1978) (tribal and federal suit against same individual for same crime does not violate double jeopardy based

upon separate sovereigns); *Talton v. Mayes*, 163 U.S. 376 (1896) (neither federal Bill of Rights nor Fourteenth Amendment limit tribal governments).

12. Wis. Stat. Ann. § 806.245 (West 1994), Wisconsin's tribal full faith and credit statute.
13. "[A]lthough the tribal court is located within the geographic boundaries of the state, it is not a Wisconsin court; it is the court of an independent sovereign." *Teague v. Bad River Band*, 612 N.W.2d 709, 717 (2000).
14. *Worcester v. Georgia*, 31 U.S. (6 Pet.) 515, 559 (1832). The United States created treaties with tribal nations up until 1871, when Congress prohibited the creation of any new treaties with tribes, and asserted that prior treaties with tribes should be honored; Act of Mar. 3, 1871, ch. 120, 15 Stat. 544 (1871).
15. *Id.*
16. *Cherokee Nation v. Georgia*, 30 U.S. 1 (1831).
17. Citizenship to Indians Act of 1924, ch. 233, 43 Stat. 253 (1924).
18. U.S. CONST., amend. X.
19. *United States v. Winans*, 198 U.S. 371, 381–82 (1905).
20. *Supra* note 1, at § 1901 (4), (5).
21. *Supra* note 8.
22. DAVID SIMMONS AND JACK TROPE, ISSUES FOR TRIBES AND STATES 5 (University of Southern Maine 1999).
23. Removal Act, 4 U.S. Stat. § 411 et seq. (1930). Whole tribes were taken from homelands and typically moved west.
24. General Allotment Act, 24 U.S. Stat. § 388 et seq. (1887). Tribal land was divided into farm-sized plots, and the "excess" sold to non-Indians.
25. DEE BROWN, BURY MY HEART AT WOUNDED KNEE: AN INDIAN HISTORY OF THE AMERICAN WEST (Holt, Rinehart & Winston 1970); ANGIE DEBO, AND STILL THE WATERS RUN: THE BETRAYAL OF THE FIVE CIVILIZED TRIBES (Princeton University Press 1973 (1940).
26. *Lone Wolf v. Hitchcock*, 187 U.S. 553 (1903), in which the Supreme Court recognized an authority in Congress to break treaties with tribal nations.
27. JOHN WUNDER, RETAINED BY THE PEOPLE: A HISTORY OF AMERICAN INDIANS AND THE BILL OF RIGHTS 105 (Oxford University Press 1994).
28. Concurrent Resolution, 108 U.S. Stat. § 132 (1953). The purpose of this legislation was to end the legal relationship between the federal government and tribal nations.
29. *Johnson v. M'Intosh*, 21 U.S. (8 Wheat.) 543 (1823).
30. National Indian Child Welfare Association testimony, Senate Com. on Indian Affairs and House Resources Com. (June 18, 1997).
31. Lila J. George, *Why the Need for the Indian Child Welfare Act*, 5 J. OF MULTICULTURAL SOCIAL WORK 165166–68 (1997).
32. *Id.* Large numbers of tribal children were also "placed out" to work on farms in the East and Midwest to learn about "the values of work and the benefits of civilization," *supra* note 31.
33. Wesley Martin, guest lecture, University of Wisconsin-Parkside (April 8, 2002).

34. *Supra* note 31, at 169.
35. *Id.* This federal project in the 1950s and 1960s placed approximately 395 tribal children.
36. Shay Bilchik, Executive Director, Child Welfare League, *Child Welfare League Apology*, National Indian Child Welfare Association 19th Annual Conference, Anchorage, Alaska (April 2001). Commissioner of Indian Affairs Kevin Gover apologized during the Clinton administration on behalf of the Bureau of Indian Affairs.
37. Hearing, U.S. Senate Select Com. on Indian Affairs, 95th Congress (August 4, 1977).
38. 1969 and 1974 studies by the Association on Indian Affairs, Hearings, Subcommittee on Indian Affairs, Senate Com. on Interior and Insular Affairs, 93d Cong., 2d Sess. (1974), at 15.
39. *Supra* note 31.
40. *Correspondence*, February 2005, Chief Judge David Raasch, Stockbridge-Munsee Band of Mohicans. Judge Raasch served as president of the Wisconsin Tribal Judges Association and travels extensively throughout the United States to teach about tribal-state relations.
41. John Dall, *Identity Theft*, 33 READER: CHICAGO'S FREE WEEKLY (Oct. 17, 2003).
42. Since no equal protection clause exists in the Constitution affecting the federal government, the Supreme Court created an equal protection component in the Due Process Clause of the Fifth Amendment to limit racial discrimination by the federal government. Since the Due Process Clause declares that a person cannot "be deprived of life, liberty, or property without due process of law," it was interpreted by the Court to include the liberty to be treated equally. U.S. CONST. amend. V.; *Bolling v. Sharpe*, 347 U.S. 497 (1954). State, county, and local governments are limited by the Equal Protection Clause of the Fourteenth Amendment from racially discriminatory actions. U.S. CONST. amend. XIV; *Brown v. Board of Education*, 347 U.S. 483 (1954).
43. *Supra* note 1, at § 1915 (a).
44. *Supra* note 1, at § 1915 (b) (i–iv). In addition, ICWA requires states to provide culturally appropriate services to Indian children and their families, unless there is good cause to the contrary, ICWA § 1915 (d).
45. *Regents of the University of California v. Bakke*, 438 U.S. 265 (1978); *Grutter v. Bollinger*, 539 U.S. 306 (2003), in each of which the compelling justification was a diverse student body.
46. *Palmore v. Sidoti*, 466 U.S. 429 (1984). The Equal Protection Clause of the Fourteenth Amendment was applied in this case, U.S. CONST. amend. XIV.
47. *Id.*
48. *Supra* note 46, at 433.
49. *Supra* note 46, at 432.
50. *Supra* note 46, at 432.
51. Statement of Dr. Joseph Westermyer, *Hearings before the Subcommittee on Indian Affairs of the Senate Committee on Interior and Insular Affairs*, 93d Cong., 2d Sess. at 3 (1974).
52. Senate Report on the Indian Child Welfare Act, No. 95-597 at 43 (1977).
53. *Supra* note 1, at § 1902.
54. *In re Appeal in Pima County Juvenile Action No. S-903*, 635 P.2d 187, 189, cited in *Mississippi Band of Choctaws v. Holyfield*, 490 U.S. 30 (1989).

55. *Id., Holyfield.*
56. *Supra* note 54, *Holyfield.*
57. H.R. Rep. No. 95-1386, at 23 (1978).
58. *Supra* note 1, at § 23.3.
59. *Supra* note 1, at § 1901 (3).
60. *Supra* note 1, at § 1902.
61. Representative Morris Udall, 124 Cong. Rec. 38102 (1978).
62. *Supra* note 14. The Wisconsin Supreme Court also gave recognition to a Wisconsin tribal nation as "an independent sovereign." *Teague v. Bad River Band*, 612 N.W.2d 709, 717 (2000).
63. *Supra* note 16.
64. *Morton v. Mancari*, 417 U.S. 535 (1974).
65. *Id., FN* 24.
66. *Supra* note 64.
67. *Supra* note 1, at § 1903 (4).
68. *Santa Clara Pueblo v. Martinez* 436 U.S. 49 (1978), in which the Supreme Court declared that a tribe has the sovereign authority to determine its own tribal membership.
69. *Supra* note 1, at § 1903 (3).
70. This information was gathered in a four-year study of Wisconsin compliance with the Indian Child Welfare Act through independent research, personal interviews, participation in ICWA training of judges and child welfare personnel, and attendance at state-tribal collaborative meetings.
71. The Department of Children and Families (DCF), created in 2008, was formerly the Division of Child and Family Services. Tribes have most child welfare interaction with the counties; counties derive their sovereign authority from the state. The terms "state" and "county" are sometimes used interchangeably.
72. Child and Family Services Review: Statewide Assessment, Division of Child and Family Services, Wisconsin Department of Health and Family Services, 1 Wilson Street, Madison, Wisconsin, 53708-8916 (June 17, 2003).
73. Child Welfare in Wisconsin: A Report on Wisconsin's Child and Family Services Federal Review, Wisconsin Department of Health and Family Services, Division of Child and Family Services, Feb. 2004. This state summary of the federal review reflects the evaluations in the review in a more understandable and concise format.
74. Program Enhancement Plan. Wisconsin Division of Child and Family Services, 2003.
75. There are seventy-two counties within the state, seventy-one of which have county child welfare agencies. In Menominee County, the boundaries of the county and the Menominee Reservation are the same, so the Menominee Nation operates the child welfare agency within that county. Menominee County does handle child placement funding, including funding for the tribe.
76. *Supra* note 74.
77. Wis. Stat. 161 (1983).
78. *Id.* Federal funding to aid in the costs of child placements is dispersed to the state, and then from

the state to the counties for specific allocation. Since tribal children are also county children, some of the money given to the county is applied to the costs of tribal placements.

79. Significant collaboration is occurring between the DCF and the tribes to modify existing Wisconsin child welfare legislation, including efforts to modify child welfare funding to the tribes.
80. These cases are known as "youth in need of care" cases on the Stockbridge-Munsee Band of Mohicans Reservation. *Correspondence*, Natalie Young, Mohican Child Welfare Director, Jan. 26, 2005.
81. This has happened on the Stockbridge-Munsee Band of Mohicans Reservation, *id.*
82. "One case can eat up the whole 161 account." *Phone Interview*, Steve Boulley, Tribal Prosecutor, Red Cliff Reservation, Jan. 26, 2005.
83. *Supra* note 73, at 36–37. See also *supra* note 5, "A Family Lawyer's Guide," for more discussion of permanence and ICWA.
84. Social Security Act, 42 U.S.C. § 670 et seq.
85. This has happened between Red Cliff and Bayfield County, *supra* note 82.
86. DHFS Policy on Consultation with Wisconsin's Indian Tribes, State of Wisconsin Department of Health and Family Services at 2 (2005).
87. *Supra* note 74.
88. With every child who becomes involved with the state child welfare system, it must be ascertained whether or not that child is a tribal member or eligible to be so.
89. *Supra* note 74.
90. Goals of the organization are to serve tribal members, strengthen tribal-state relations, and assist in the training of state and tribal personnel, including child welfare personnel and judges.
91. This training for state judges held in 2004 was sponsored by the Wisconsin Tribal Judges Association and qualified for judicial education credits at no cost. Training was provided by tribal judges and attorneys, Wisconsin Judicare attorneys, DCFS personnel, and university faculty.
92. Lynn Vincent, *Drawing Blood*, WORLD MAGAZINE, April 22, 2006.
93. *Supra* note 11, *Talton.*
94. Indian Civil Rights Act of 1968, 25 U.S.C. § 1302(8).
95. *Supra* note 54, *Holyfield.*
96. *In re Adoption of Halloway*, 732 P2d 962 (1986).
97. *Id.* This result was encouraged by the adoptive parents.
98. ICWA allows for states to retain jurisdiction if good cause is established, *supra* note 1, at § 1915 (a–b).
99. *Supra* notes 23–28.
100. *Supra* note 2. Children are referred to as the lifeblood of a tribe.
101. *Correspondence*, March 8, 2007.

Contributors

SUZANNE L. CROSS (Neshiink Kwe; Bird Woman), is an associate professor in Michigan State University's School of Social Work. She is a citizen of the Saginaw Chippewa Indian Tribe of Michigan, and she was a member of the CSWE Board of Directors 2005–2008, a CSWE Senior Scholar 2007–2008, and the Chair of the CSWE Native American Task Force 2008–2009. Her research areas include gerontology with a focus on American Indian elders, grandparents parenting on and off reservations, bereavement therapy relevant to historical grief, the Indian Child Welfare Act (ICWA), and Collaborations with local Tribal Nation communities. She has been a member of the Hartford Team with the goal of enhancing gerontology in the MSW Program, and is the primary investigator for the BEL grant, which was recently awarded. Dr. Cross has mentored several Tribal and non-Tribal students during her career, offering a unique cross-cultural approach to teaching and learning. Her latest publications are on the topics of kinship care and ICWA.

TERRY L. CROSS is an enrolled citizen of the Seneca Nation of Indians and is the developer, founder and Executive Director of the National Indian Child Welfare Association. He is the author of the *Heritage and Helping,* an eleven manual curriculum for tribal child welfare staff. He is also author of the *Positive Indian Parenting* curricula, as well as *Cross-Cultural Skills in Indian Child Welfare.* He co-authored "Toward a Culturally Competent System of Care" and "Reclaiming Customary Adoption." He has thirty two years of experience in child welfare, including ten years working directly with children and families. He served on the faculty of Portland State University School of Social Work.

ANGELIQUE G. DAY, MSW, is a policy and outreach associate for Michigan's Children, a statewide, private nonprofit legislative advocacy organization in Lansing, Michigan. She is also a doctoral student, studying in the interdisciplinary health science program at Western Michigan University, and a member of the Tribal State Partnership.

MATTHEW L. M. FLETCHER is an associate professor at Michigan State University College of Law and director of the Indigenous Law and Policy Center. He also sits as an appellate judge for the Pokagon Band of Potawatomi Indians, the Poarch Band of Creek Indians, and the Hoopa Valley Tribe, and is a consultant to the Seneca Nation of Indians Court of Appeals. Professor Fletcher is an enrolled citizen of the Grand Traverse Band of Ottawa and Chippewa Indians, located in Peshawbestown, Michigan.

Professor Fletcher recently published *American Indian Education: Counternarratives in Racism, Struggle, and the Law*. He has published articles with *Arizona Law Review, Harvard Journal on Legislation, Hastings Law Journal, Houston Law Review*, and *Tulane Law Review, and* he is currently co-authoring the sixth edition of *Cases on Federal Indian Law* with David Getches, Charles Wilkinson, and Robert Williams, and writing a book on the history of the Grand Traverse Band.

Professor Fletcher graduated from the University of Michigan in 1994 and the University of Michigan Law School in 1997. He has worked as a staff attorney for four Indian Tribes—the Pascua Yaqui Tribe, the Hoopa Valley Tribe, the Suquamish Tribe, and the Grand Traverse Band. He has litigated more than twenty tribal court cases. He is married to Wenona T. Singel and they have two sons, Owen and Emmett.

KATHRYN E. FORT is the staff attorney and adjunct professor for the Indigenous Law and Policy Center at Michigan State University College of Law. In her role with the Center, she teaches both clinical and doctrinal classes, researches and writes on behalf of clients, and manages administrative aspects. She was recently published in the *George Mason Law Review* and the *American Indian Law Review*. She researches and writes on land claims, the Indian Child Welfare Act, and legal history in federal Indian law. Ms. Fort received her J.D. magna cum laude from Michigan State University College of Law with the Certificate in Indigenous Law, and is licensed to practice law in Michigan. She received her B.A. magna cum laude in History (with honors) from Hollins University in Roanoke, Virginia.

LORIE M. GRAHAM is a professor of law at Suffolk University Law School in Boston Massachusetts, where she teaches courses on indigenous peoples' rights, property, and international human rights. She has served as legal consultant on a range of matters impacting indigenous nations in the United States, such as land claims, economic development, environmental protection, and jurisdictional disputes. Professor Graham serves on a number of committees, including the International Law Association Rights of Indigenous Peoples Committee and the Harvard University Native American Advisory Board. She is the former director of the Harvard University Native American Program and has been a visiting lecturer at Harvard Law School and University of Massachusetts–Amherst. Previously she practiced law at Kramer, Levin in New York City, and clerked for the Honorable Richard D. Simons of the New York Court of Appeals. Some of Professor Graham's most recent publications include Cog; *Reparations, Self-Determination, and the Seventh Generation*; *The Racial Discourse of Federal Indian Law*; *Intellectual Property and Indigenous Peoples Rights*; *Economic Development in Indian Country*; *Self-determination for Indigenous Peoples after Kosovo: Translating Self-Determination "Into Practice" and "Into Peace"*; and *"The Past Never Vanishes": A Contextual Critique of the Existing Indian Family Doctrine*.

MARY JO B. HUNTER is an enrolled citizen of the Ho-Chunk Nation, formerly known as the Wisconsin Winnebago Nation. She graduated from the University of Wisconsin with a journalism degree in 1978, and she obtained her law degree from the UCLA School of Law in 1982. She is a clinical professor of the Child Advocacy Clinic for Hamline University School of Law.

Professor Hunter was elected as the first chief justice of the Ho-Chunk Nation Supreme Court in July 1995. She was re-elected in 2002, and again in 2007, and she continues to preside over that court. Currently, she is serving as an associate justice for the Supreme Court of the Winnebago Tribe of Nebraska and chief justice for the Prairie Island Indian Community's Appellate Court. In the past, Justice Hunter has also served as an associate justice for the Turtle Mountain Band of Chippewa Tribal Appellate Court. Professor Hunter has also conducted workshops and training on the Indian Child Welfare Act and Cultural Issues of American Indians.

Presently she serves as a Guardian Ad Litem (GAL) for Indian children who are subject to the Indian Child Welfare Act and represents other GALs in cases involving ICWA. In addition, Professor Hunter teaches the Native American Law seminar course for Hamline University Law School.

Professor Hunter has served as the Chair of the St. Paul Indian Education Parent Committee and as a member of the State of Minnesota Indian Child Welfare Advisory Council as an Urban Representative for the Indian community in St. Paul. Currently, she serves on the board of directors for Southern Minnesota Regional Legal Services. She has two adult children and six grandchildren.

B. J. JONES is the director of the Tribal Judicial Training Institute at the University of North Dakota School of Law, where he also teaches several Indian law-related courses as an adjunct. He is the chief judge for the Sisseton–Wahpeton Oyate Tribal Court in South Dakota and the Prairie Island Indian Community Tribal Court in Minnesota. He also serves as the chief justice for the Turtle Mountain Tribal Court of Appeals and as an associate justice for the Flandreau-Santee Sioux Tribe and the Oglala Sioux Nation Supreme Court, as well as an associate judge for the Fort Berthold District Court, the Mille Lacs Band of Chippewa Tribal Court, and the Leech Lake Tribal Court. Previously he was the litigation director for Dakota Plains Legal Services. He has served on the North Dakota Supreme Court Committee on Tribal–State Court affairs and the ABA Committee on the Unmet Needs of Children.

ALLIE GREENLEAF MALDONADO (Little Traverse Bay Bands of Odawa Indians) serves as the Assistant General Counsel for her Tribe. She received her law degree from the University of Michigan Law School, where she earned a place as a Contributing Editor for the University of Michigan Law Review and graduated in the top third of her class. Allie also distinguished herself outside the classroom as the Chair of the University of Michigan Native American Law Students' Association (NALSA). Upon graduation she won the University of Michigan Jane L. Mixer Award for public service.

After graduation, Allie was selected through the highly competitive Honors Program at the Department of Justice to become a litigator in the Indian Resources Section of the Environment and Natural Resources Division. She is only the 15th enrolled tribal citizen to ever enter the DOJ through its prestigious Honors Program since its inception in the 1950s.

She worked for her Tribe indirectly as a lobbyist on Capital Hill through the law firm of Monteau & Peebles, LLP, in Washington, D.C., before returning home and accepting the position of Assistant General Counsel for the Little Traverse Bay Bands of Odawa Indians in September of 2002. She has found the most fulfilling work of her of life promoting and protecting the legal interests of her Tribe and working with its political leadership to shape its future for later generations.

LORINDA MALL is a regulatory analyst at the Bureau of Land Management, Department of Interior, where she drafts regulations affecting public lands, including certain tribal lands. Prior to her appointment, she practiced Indian law at a Washington, D.C., law firm. Her work there focused on federal recognition, fee-to-trust acquisitions, and environmental law. Ms. Mall serves on the boards of the Native American Bar Association–D.C. and the Pacific Islander Access Project. She is a graduate of the University of Arizona Rogers College of Law, where she is currently pursuing a SJD in Indigenous Peoples Law and Policy. Ms. Mall has also earned a MA in American Indian Studies from the University of Arizona and a BA in Anthropology from the University of California, Los Angeles. She is a citizen of the Cherokee Nation of Oklahoma.

ROBERT J. MILLER is a professor at Lewis & Clark Law School in Portland, Oregon, where he teaches Indian Law courses and Civil Procedure. He graduated from Lewis & Clark in 1991 and clerked for Judge Diarmuid O'Scannlain of the U.S. Court of Appeals for the Ninth Circuit. He has taught and practiced Indian law since 1993. He has also been a part-time tribal judge since 1995 and is now the chief justice of the Court of Appeals for the Grand Ronde Tribe. He has published numerous articles, editorials, and book chapters on Indian issues and has spoken at dozens of federal, state, and private conferences in more than thirty states, as well as in England, Canada, and Australia. In 2003 he was appointed by his tribe to the Circle of Tribal Advisors, which was part of the National Council of the Lewis & Clark Bicentennial. His book *Native America, Discovered and Conquered: Thomas Jefferson, Lewis and Clark, and Manifest Destiny* was published in 2006. Professor Miller is currently writing a book on Indian economic development. He was on the board of the National Indian Child Welfare Association from 1995 until 2004. Professor Miller is a citizen of the Eastern Shawnee Tribe of Oklahoma.

ALIZA G. ORGANICK is an associate professor of law at Washburn University School of Law. She earned her JD from the University of New Mexico in 1996 and her BUS from the University of New Mexico in 1992. She is a citizen of the Dine Nation and born to the Tsénijíkiní (Cliff Dwelling) Clan. Professor Organick is licensed to practice in New Mexico and Kansas and is admitted to practice in the Prairie Band Potawatomi Nation Tribal Court, the Kickapoo Nation of Kansas District Court, and the Iowa Nations Tribal Court. She teaches in the clinical program at Washburn University School of Law and teaches seminar courses on tribal court practice and law of indigenous peoples.

MICHAEL D. PETOSKEY has been a judge for various Michigan Indian tribes since 1986. He began his judicial career with the planning, implementation, and development of Grand Traverse Band of Ottawa and Chippewa Indians Tribal Court, while he was a staff attorney for Michigan Indian Legal Services. Judge Petoskey is a Grand Traverse Band citizen and licensed Michigan attorney. He was the chief judge for his tribe for more than sixteen years, until his retirement from the position.

Judge Petoskey's career interest has been working with newly reaffirmed tribes to plan, implement and develop their courts from just a dream. In 2006 he retired from the Little Traverse Bay Bands of Odawa Indians after nine years service as chief judge after starting the court there. However, Judge Petoskey continues his work career as chief judge for the Pokagon Band of Potawatomi Indians and chief judge for the Nottawaseppi Huron Band of Potawatomi Indians, where he continues with similar work in both communities.

Judge Petoskey is a retired chief justice of the Little River Band of Ottawa

Indians Court of Appeals, a position he held from 1999 to 2009, and in 2008 he completed a six-year stint as an associate justice of the Saginaw Chippewa Indian Tribe of Michigan Court of Appeals.

Judge Petoskey was appointed co-chair of the State Bar of Michigan Standing Committee on American Indian Law when it was established in 1994, and he remained in that position until he was term-limited out in 2001. Also, Judge Petoskey served on the Michigan Commission on Indian Affairs for seven years by appointment by former Governor James Blanchard. He is a former chairman of that body.

In 2000 the American Indian Law Section of the State Bar of Michigan honored Judge Petoskey and Michigan Supreme Court Justice Michael Cavanagh with the Section's annual "Tecumseh Peacekeeping Award" for their leadership in moving Michigan state courts and tribal courts away from conflict and toward cooperation.

Judge Petoskey received his undergraduate degree from Michigan State University in Economics in 1975 and his JD from the University of New Mexico in 1983. Judge Petoskey is a Vietnam veteran having served as an infantry medic.

EMILY C. PROCTOR, MSW, is the MSU Extension tribal educator for Children, Youth, Families and Communities. She is a citizen of the Little Traverse Bay Bands of Odawa Indians, Harbor Springs, Michigan. She is a member of the Council on Social Work Education—Native American Task Force for 2008–2009, and has worked as a child protective services worker for her tribal nation.

WENONA T. SINGEL is an assistant professor at the Law College of Michigan State University as well as the associate director of the Indigenous Law and Policy Center. Professor Singel is the chief justice of the appellate courts of the Little Traverse Bay Bands of Odawa Indians and the Grand Traverse Band of Ottawa and Chippewa Indians. She has served as a member of the Little Traverse Bay Bands' Economic Development Commission. She is of counsel to the law firm of Kanji & Katzen, PLLC, a firm with offices in Ann Arbor and Seattle that specializes in representing tribes in Indian law matters. Professor Singel graduated from Harvard University in 1995 and Harvard Law School in 1999. She has worked at Dickenson Wright PLLC, Kanji & Katzen PLLC and was an assistant professor at the University of North Dakota School of Law. She is admitted to practice in Michigan and the 6th Circuit Court of Appeals. Professor Singel is an enrolled citizen of the Little Traverse Bay Bands of Odawa Indians.

LE ANNE E. SILVEY, PhD, ACSW, LMSW, is a citizen of the Little Traverse Bay Bands of Odawa Indians from the Petoskey–Harbor Springs area of Michigan. Currently an associate professor, she has been on faculty at Michigan State University in the Department of Family and Child Ecology since fall of 1999. Dr. Silvey has a BS in social work, a Master's in social work, and she received her PhD in family studies with a cognate in sociology in 1997 from MSU. She is an affiliate faculty member with the American Indian Studies Program at MSU.

Prior to pursuing her PhD, Dr. Silvey was the executive director of the Michigan Indian Child Welfare Agency, a statewide child placing agency for the tribes in Michigan. She practiced in the field of Indian child welfare for more than nine years and was often an expert witness in Indian child welfare cases throughout the state. Other clinical experience consists of psychiatric social work, work with adolescent runaway youth, and work with developmentally disabled in group homes, sheltered workshops, respite care, and housing.

MAYLINN SMITH is an associate professor of law and director of the Indian Law Clinic at The University of Montana School of Law. She currently supervises and assists third year law students with their clinical work which includes drafting model tribal codes and working on projects promoting economic development within Indian country; representing individuals in tribal court on civil matters; representing tribes, Indian children or parents in Indian Child Welfare Act cases; addressing treaty rights issues and jurisdictional issues in federal, tribal or state court systems; and providing training on a variety of Indian law issues to tribal and non-Indian entities. In addition to her work in the Indian Law clinic, she has taught federal Indian law; advanced problems in federal Indian law; Indian child welfare; and criminal law and procedure in Indian country, tribal courts/tribal law, and federal courts. Her previous experiences include serving as chief judge of the Southern Ute Indian Tribe and as a tribal appellate judge, working in private practice and as legal counsel for the Salish & Kootenai Tribal Court.

CAROL L. TEBBEN is an associate professor emerita at the University of Wisconsin–Parkside, where she taught constitutional law and directed the legal studies program. Her teaching included such courses as civil liberties, government power, criminal law, environmental law, diversity law, and tribal nations. Tebben's published research has addressed the due process and equal protection rights of fathers, the equitable parent doctrine, executive privilege, federalism as a political question, tribal versus state sovereignty in Wisconsin courts, Indian Child Welfare Act policy, and trifederalism. Her graduate education includes J.D., University of Idaho School of Law; Ph.D. in government, Claremont Graduate University; and LL.M., University of Wisconsin Law School.